DRAWING WITH GREAT NEEDLES

< >

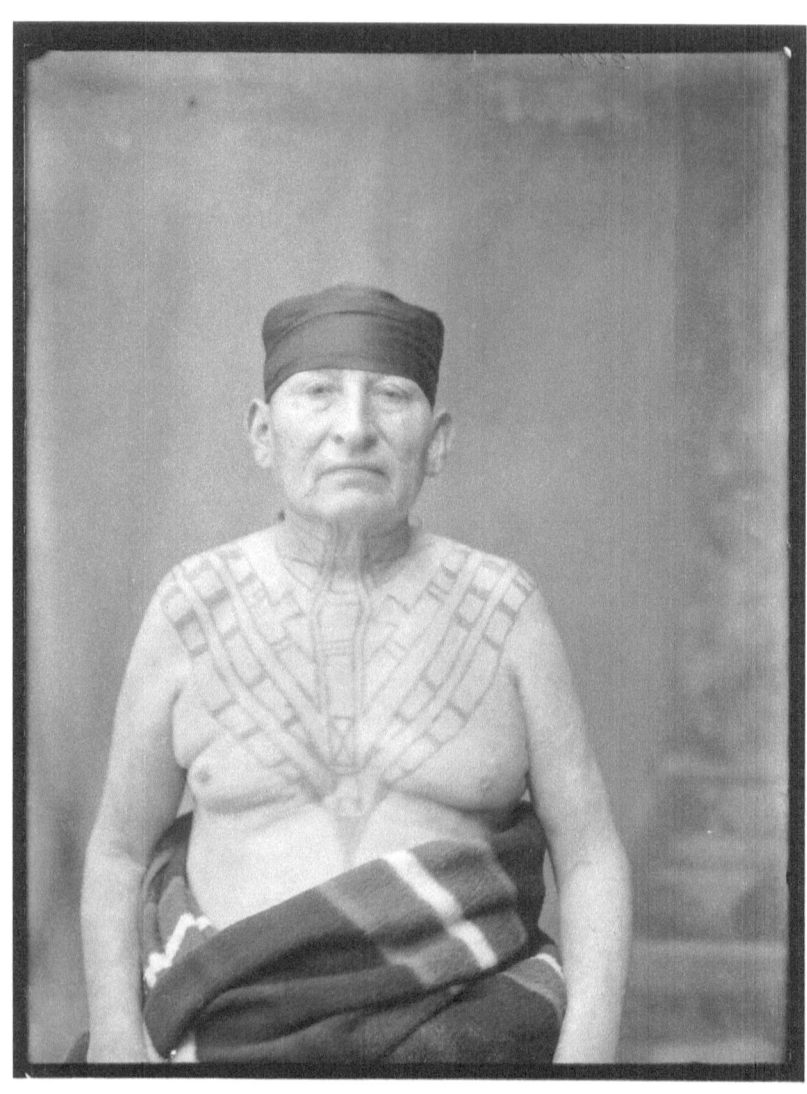

DRAWING WITH GREAT NEEDLES

Ancient Tattoo Traditions of North America

< >

EDITED BY AARON DETER-WOLF
AND CAROL DIAZ-GRANADOS

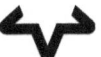

University of Texas Press, Austin

FRONTISPIECE: Tattooed Osage man. Photo Lot 89-8, Negative T13408, National Anthropological Archives, Smithsonian Institution, Suitland, Maryland.

Requests for permission to reproduce material from this work should be sent to:
Permissions
University of Texas Press
P.O. Box 7819
Austin, TX 78713-7819
http://utpress.utexas.edu/index.php/rp-form

♾ The paper used in this book meets the minimum requirements
of ANSI/NISO Z39.48-1992 (R1997) (Permanence of Paper).

LIBRARY OF CONGRESS CATALOGING-IN-PUBLICATION DATA

Drawing with great needles : ancient tattoo traditions of North
America / edited by Aaron Deter-Wolf and Carol Diaz-Granados.
    p.   cm.
Includes bibliographical references and index.
ISBN 978-0-292-74912-2 (cloth : alk. paper)
ISBN 978-1-4773-0211-8 (paperback)
1. Tattooing—North America—History. 2. Indian art—North
America. 3. Indians of North America—Social life and customs.
I. Deter-Wolf, Aaron, 1976–
    GT2346.N6D73 2013
    391.6'5—dc23   2013002835
            doi:10.7560/749122

< >

On m'a fait asseoir sur une peau de tygre; un Sauvage a brûlé de la
paille dont il a délayé la cendre dans de l'eau; il s'est servi de cette
composition très-simple pour dessiner le chevreuil; il a ensuite suivi
le dessein avec de grosses aiguilles, en piquant jusqu'au vis pour faire
sortir du sang; ce sang mêlé à la cendre de la paille forme une em-
preinte qui ne s'effacera jamais.

I was seated on a wildcat skin. An Indian burned some straw, the
ashes of which he mixed with water. He used this simple mixture to
draw the deer. He then traced the drawing with great needles, prick-
ing me until I bled. The blood mixed with the ashes of the straw
forms a mark which can never fade.

—JEAN BERNARD BOSSU,
Nouveaux Voyages aux Indes Occidentales, VOL. I (1768:122).

CONTENTS

ACKNOWLEDGMENTS

The editors would like to extend special thanks to Theresa J. May, assistant director and editor-in-chief of the University of Texas Press. Dr. F. Kent Reilly III provided guidance during the editing process and was essential in helping to facilitate the publication of this volume. The senior editor would also like to extend his gratitude to the James E. Walker Library and the Department of Sociology and Anthropology at Middle Tennessee State University, and to Tennessee State Archaeologist Michael C. Moore for his research support and encouragement.

INTRODUCTION

Carol Diaz-Granados and Aaron Deter-Wolf

People in the Punjaub who tattoo themselves believe that
at death the soul . . . will go to heaven blazoned with the
same tattoo patterns which adorned the body in life.

FRAZER (1911:30)

There is no single "place of origin" for the phenomenon of tattooing the human body. It is present on all continents and in most cultures. The very act of tattooing goes back over eight thousand years and possibly millennia earlier. But just what is it that makes the human species feel the need to use their body as a canvas? Why do people feel the need to place marks on their bodies? People in most cultures around the world use ink, scarring, or painting to place various designs on their skin that have significance for them, and often, too, importance for their culture or ethnic group.

The human body is the most personal canvas for self-expression and messaging. For thousands of years humans have been aware of the capacity of their bodies to bear permanent markings, and cultures have devised body modifications and rituals to define, classify, decorate, enhance, and sanctify themselves and others. On the other hand, tattoos have also been applied to penalize an individual believed to have perpetrated a wrongdoing or simply to mark that person as being lower in the ranks of society.

The best-known evidence of actual tattoos on ancient human skin dates to 3300 BC with the discovery of the Neolithic/Bronze Age "Iceman" (Ötzi) on the Italian-Austrian border in 1991. Numerous markings were found on his skin in places that would have been covered by clothing, and it is possible that the tattoos may have been executed to aid in the relief (magical or otherwise) of ailments such as arthritis. Although Ötzi is understandably famous, he is neither the only nor the oldest direct example of ancient tattooing. A Chinchorro mummy from Chile dated to 6000 BC exhibits a "mustache" tattoo on its upper lip, while still other instances of both decorative and potentially medicinal tattoos have been documented on ancient fleshed remains from Siberia, western China, Egypt, Greenland, Alaska, and throughout the Andes.

These are just several major examples of a practice that appears to have been as natural as any other cultural ritual—permanently marking the skin. There is a copious amount of information on the phenomenon of early peoples tattooing their skin and the possible significance of those markings. New information is being uncovered through archaeological excavations and discoveries of tattoo imagery on frescos, pottery, statues, and parietal pictographs.

For thousands of years prior to acculturation, Native American groups throughout the Eastern Woodlands and Great Plains used the physical act and visual language of tattooing to construct and reinforce the identity of individuals and their place within society and the cosmos. The tattooing process and associated ritual activity served as a rite of passage, as supplication, and as a demonstration of lineage. The composition and use of the tattoo toolkit was intimately related to group identity and origin narratives. Despite the cultural importance that tattooing held for its prehistoric and early historic Native American practitioners, there have been few previous scholarly examinations of the subject.

Until recently, the archaeological elusiveness of ancient tattooed human skin, combined with the modern cultural stigma (or religious bias) associated with body modification, has impeded our understanding of the practice. Until the final decades of the twentieth century, America and the Western world in general regarded tattooing as fringe or deviant behavior primarily associated with marginal and "primitive" groups. Consequently, the implications of ancient tattooing were not seriously considered, and tattooed symbols were not assigned the same cultural significance as imagery inscribed on media such as pottery, shell, copper, and stone.

The increased prevalence and acceptance of tattooing in Western society over the past several decades has combined with post-processual philosophy to spark new interest among archaeologists in the identification, documentation, and discussion of ancient body art and body modification. The research presented in this volume is part of ongoing efforts to understand the role that phenomena such as iconography, gender, and the physical body played in the cultural systems of ancient peoples throughout the world. This work is based on the symposium "Tattooing and Body Modification in the Prehistoric and Early Historic Southeast," held at the 2009 meeting of the Southeastern Archaeological Conference in Mobile, Alabama, organized and chaired by the senior editor of this volume, Aaron Deter-Wolf.

The book is comprised of eight chapters by researchers in the disciplines (or subdisciplines) of archaeology, anthropology, and art history. These scholars examine a wide variety of topics including historical background, ethnohistorical and ethnographic data, material evidence of tattooing in the archaeological record, ceramic motifs compared to tattoo designs, warrior tattoo pictography, tattoo tools, prehistoric iconography, tattoos and gender roles, and meaning that tattoos held for Dhegiha Sioux and other Native American groups.

In Chapter 1, Antoinette Wallace compiles ethnohistorical documentation and art historical evidence of Native American tattooing in the protohistoric and early historic Southeast. These accounts from European and Euro-American explorers, settlers, and artists provide an essential window into the extent and variety of indigenous tattoo traditions that existed prior to European contact. Evidence assembled in this chapter documents how these traditions persevered through the early twentieth century before finally succumbing to the widespread adoption of European dress and less permanent forms of body decoration.

Although tattooing occurred throughout the Eastern Woodlands and Great Plains prior to initial European contact, the antiquity of the practice and its archaeological footprint are poorly understood. Chapters 2 and 3 use artifact data, ethnohistorical and ethnographic accounts, and cross-cultural comparisons to examine ancient Native American tattooing and how the practice may appear in the archaeological record. Chapter 2, by Aaron Deter-Wolf, compiles archaeological and ethnohistorical identifications of indigenous tattooing technologies, including descriptions of both needles and pigments. The ethnohistorical accounts of tattoo implements are then compared with archaeological data from the region in an effort to recognize potential correlates and to suggest possible archaeological criteria for the identification of tattoo tools.

In Chapter 3, Benjamin Steere explores the possible function of Woodland period Swift Creek ceramic designs as patterns for tattooing. By marshaling cross-cultural data from tattooing societies in Africa, Brazil, Borneo, and Polynesia, Steere demonstrates a correspondence between motifs tattooed or marked on the human body and those applied to material culture. Steere also examines the archaeological record of the Middle Woodland to identify potential iconographic representations of tattooing and archaeological finds of tattoo implements.

Native American tattooing served a variety of functions prior to acculturation, including as a medicinal practice, a marker of group affiliation and social status, and the display of honors. Chapters 4 and 5, by noted tattoo anthropologist Lars Krutak, focus on historic Native American groups in the Northern Woodlands and Great Plains, examining both the scope and meaning of tattoo traditions in these regions through a variety of documentary and artistic sources. Among the Iroquois and their neighbors, tattooing signified military achievement and connection with a personal guardian spirit, or *manitou*. Chapter 4 examines warrior tattoo pictography from Iroquoia and the Northern Woodlands through the ethnographic record, early historic portraiture, and comparisons with late prehistoric Mississippian art. Krutak examines these sources to explore the forms and meanings of martial symbols inscribed on the bodies of Northern Woodlands warriors and on associated material culture, including personal war clubs.

Among historic Siouan groups of the Great Plains, tattoos served to reinforce and enhance personal status and to improve people's access to supernatural power. In Chapter 5, Krutak marshals published and unpublished ethnographic accounts and art historical evidence to explore the social honors and ideological implications of male and female tattooing among the Dhegiha and other Siouan speakers. He also examines how tattooing invoked and channeled spiritual energy through the origins, composition, and deployment of ancestral tattoo bundles.

Chapters 6 through 8 explore the significance of both the iconographic symbols and the physical act of tattooing for the Mississippian culture and their Siouan descendants. In Chapter 6, Kent Reilly discusses depictions of tattooed preternatural beings in early Mississippian period parietal art from Missouri and Wisconsin. Reilly shows that the patterns of body decoration on these "Other-Than-Human-Persons" comprise a shared set of motifs that also appear on ritual shell objects belonging to the Braden-style art of the middle Mississippi valley. For Braden artists and the initiated in Mississippian society, these motifs signaled the presence of nonhuman forces and linked ritual objects to specific otherworldly beings.

In Chapter 7, James Duncan examines the variety of functions tattoos held for Dhegihan speakers and their ancestors, including as a means to consecrate the sacred, empower the individual, and designate lineage. Duncan shows that motifs that appear as tattoos in the earliest examples of Braden-style art endure well into the historic period throughout the Great Plains and Eastern Woodlands. This correspondence of iconographic elements illustrates direct cultural transmission and suggests that interpreting the iconography of tattoos that appear in the Braden style may inform our understanding of Mississippian ideology as expressed in these motifs.

The volume concludes with a chapter by David Dye that further explores the connection between Mississippian religious beliefs and nineteenth-century Dhegihan philosophies by examining symbols that appear both in western Mississippian art and on the skin of historic Dhegihan speakers. According to Dye, tattooing among the western Mississippians reflected beliefs that life could be captured, controlled, and recycled in an unending cycle of death and rebirth. Ethnographic accounts of tattooing symbolism and rituals among the Osage, Omaha, and other Dhegihan groups show that women and men held equally significant yet opposing roles in the recycling of the life force through childbirth and warfare, respectively.

As you read through these chapters, you will find that the running theme is to derive cultural meaning from the tattoo iconography, the act of tattooing, or both. It is from this study of past cultural behaviors that we learn about the human past and in the case of this volume, the desire, the *need*, to decorate or consecrate one's body with permanent or semipermanent markings.

DRAWING WITH GREAT NEEDLES

< >

< 1 >

Native American Tattooing in the Protohistoric Southeast

Antoinette B. Wallace

//// /

The physical body is the link between the individual and the outside world and is the medium through which a person most directly projects him- or herself in a society. Therefore, the decision of an individual to augment the natural body through temporary or permanent decoration reveals precise information regarding that person's social role, whether actual or conceptualized. Body decoration also reflects information on the society the individual inhabits. Specific colors, patterns, ornamental items, and the manner and timing with which these materials are applied to the body are all part of a culturally defined communication code (Brain 1979; Ebin 1979). In this regard, body decoration reflects overall social, religious, and political systems, as well as an individual's place within these systems.

Early historical documents from the American Southeast reveal widespread traditions of body decoration among Native American groups. When Europeans first encountered the indigenous inhabitants of North America in the sixteenth and seventeenth centuries, they reported that the natives decorated their faces and bodies extensively with paint and tattooing. Throughout the eighteenth century, European and Euro-American traders, missionaries, and settlers reported on extensive body decoration practices among Native Americans they encountered. In the late nineteenth and early twentieth centuries ethnological studies were conducted with the few remaining members of the nations of the Southeast in an attempt to recover information on Indian culture and customs, including body decoration.

The forms of indigenous body decoration identified in these various accounts included face and body painting, greasing, scratching, and tattooing. Of these, only tattooing permanently altered the body and so was used to convey enduring information such as affirming an individual's place in the social order or denoting a permanent change in status. This chapter examines the historical and artistic evidence for Southeastern Indian tattooing between the sixteenth and early twentieth centuries, and is intended to provide a framework for subsequent chapters in which other authors examine the social context, figural art, and physical materials of the practice during both the prehistoric and historic period.

/ Research Design /

This summary of the documentary evidence for indigenous Native American tattooing is based on research conducted for my thesis on Southeastern Indian body decoration for Harvard University (Wallace 1993). A number of previous scholars have presented discussions of historic evidence for early American Indian body decoration and/or tattooing (e.g., Hudson 1976; Mallery 1893; Sinclair 1909; Swanton 1946). This chapter draws from these earlier sources, but was prepared with the goal of creating an exhaustive rather than selective compilation of evidence for indigenous tattooing in the American Southeast.

For purposes of this study, the Southeastern culture area is defined as an area bounded on the east by the Atlantic Ocean, on the south by the Gulf of Mexico, on the west by the dry country of Texas and the Plains, and on the north by the colder climate areas of the upper Mississippi and Ohio Rivers of the Midwest. Several groups on the periphery of the Southeastern culture area are included in this study because early chroniclers provided particularly useful or illustrative information or because significant prehistoric materials indicate cultural connections with the Southeast.

Because much of the information used in this research comes from ethnohistorical documents, a word of caution is needed. Historic journals, commentaries, reports, and even published histories frequently exhibit a biased view depending upon the nationality and profession of the observer. European and Euro-American observers sometimes embellished their commentaries, and missionaries were overly focused on certain aspects of indigenous life. Writers often copied from one another, intermingled information without citing references, and relied on a combination of hearsay, earlier accounts, and their own observations. Tribal affiliations were not always distinguished or were confused, and certain Indian groups received much attention and others very little.

It is also important to acknowledge the limits of historic vocabulary in regard to Native American tattooing, particularly in the earliest accounts of the practice. The term *tattoo* does not enter the European lexicon until the late eighteenth century following Captain Cook's voyages through the South Pacific (Jones 2000). Prior to that time, European chroniclers relied on a variety of descriptive terms to discuss the tattooing they observed in North America (Fleming 2000), including *pounce, prick* (French, *piqué*), *list, mark,* and *raze*. In certain instances chroniclers misunderstood the process entirely, and referred to tattooing using unrelated verbs such as *stamp, paint, burn,* and *embroider*. Although early accounts may contain misnomers for both tattoos and tattooing, the intent of the chroniclers can frequently be deciphered based on context, and modern editions of ethnohistorical sources often replace earlier terms with *tattoo* rather than providing literal translations.

Artists whose work is discussed in this chapter also exhibited biases in their visual reporting. In some instances, they painted or drew what they wanted or expected to see, while in other cases they borrowed from other artists, staged scenes after the fact using inappropriate models or templates, or painted from memory. It is also sometimes difficult, without the aid of a caption, for modern scholars to distinguish between historic depictions of tattoos and temporary body paint.

Perhaps the most problematic visual depictions of Southeastern Indian tattooing are those produced by the Flemish engraver Theodore de Bry. Although de Bry did not visit the New World himself, his late sixteenth-century reproductions (both actual and attributed) of works by Jacques Le Moyne de Morgues and John White provided the first images of Native Americans widely available to the European public (Lorant 1965). Scholars now generally acknowledge that de Bry "liberally embellished, restructured, and recrafted" (Harvey 2008:xix) the works on which his engravings were based. Recent critiques of de Bry's ethnohistorical credibility have pointed to his use of an idealized Mannerist style not duplicated in verifiable source material (Fleming 2000); anachronistic inclusions of European and South American tools, weapons, and clothes in illustrations of Southeastern peoples (Harvey 2008; Milanich 2005); and allegations of outright propaganda regarding his depictions of the Spanish (Gravatt 2007). It is clear at this point that the de Bry engravings should be regarded with healthy skepticism and not relied upon exclusively as depictions of Native American culture or as faithful reproductions of earlier artworks (Kuhlemann 2007). Nevertheless, these works were a formative source for European conceptions of Native Americans

(Gaudio 2008; Kuhlemann 2007). This chapter therefore selectively includes de Bry engravings, which are accompanied by textual evidence for tattooing.

This research is presented in the form of a historical narrative that begins with the first sighting of Native Americans by Columbus and concludes with ethnological studies of Southeastern Indians in the early twentieth century. European and Euro-American observations of tattooing in the Southeast are discussed, as are selected studies by ethnologists. Pictures accompanying these texts that clearly depict tattooing are also discussed.

/ Fifteenth and Sixteenth Centuries /

The first recorded European observation of American Indian body decoration was made by Christopher Columbus upon his arrival at the Island of San Salvador in the eastern Caribbean on October 13, 1492. Although Columbus records evidence of indigenous body painting during his initial encounters, it is not until his second voyage, in 1493, when a possible mention of tattooing appears. During that voyage, the Spanish physician Dr. Diego Alvarez Chanca wrote a letter to the Council of Seville in which he noted that inhabitants of an island in the Lesser Antilles "paint their heads with crosses and a hundred thousand different devices, each according to his fancy; which they do with sharpened reeds" (Chanca 1906:293). Although Chanca does not specify that the sharpened reeds were being used to puncture the skin, this account may represent the first European observation of tattooing in the Western Hemisphere.

Subsequent documentation from other Spanish chroniclers describe tattooing practices throughout Central America and the Caribbean (e.g., Fernández de Oviedo y Valdés 1851:204; Landa 1864:120). Those accounts fall outside the geography of the present study area, and interested readers are directed to the discussion of tattooing in the West Indies, Mexico, and Central America compiled by Sinclair (1909:362–368).

The islands of the Caribbean and the mainland of Mexico and Central America were colonized by the Spanish a full twenty-five years before the first concerted European attempts to settle the continental United States (excluding Norse settlement efforts during the eleventh century). However, coastal explorations of the eastern North American continent by Portuguese, English, French, and Spanish navigators and fisherman were taking place as early as 1497, and provide the earliest reports of body decoration on the North American continent.

The earliest ethnographic accounts of indigenous North American body decoration were recorded in October 1501 by Italian diplomats Alberto Cantino and Pietro Pasqualigo in letters relating to the second voyage of the Portuguese captain Gaspar Corte-Real. That expedition explored the east coast of North America including the area between Delaware and Nova Scotia, and returned to Lisbon carrying a number of captive native men. Cantino (1893:233–234) observed that these men "have their face marked with great signs," while Pasqualigo (1893b:235) wrote that the captive Native Americans were "marked on the face in several places, some with more, others with fewer lines." In a separate letter to his brothers, Pasqualigo (1893a:237) wrote of the captives that "their faces are marked in the fashion of the Indians, some with six, some with eight, some with no lines." Unfortunately it is not clear from the accounts if these facial markings constitute body paint or tattooing.

Initial contact with Indians of the southeastern United States was made by Spanish conquistadors searching the Florida Peninsula for native empires and riches similar to those found in Mexico and Peru. Spain made several unsuccessful attempts at settlement of the Southeast during the sixteenth century, including those by Juan Ponce de León, Pánfilo de Narváez, Hernando de Soto, Lucas Vazquez de Ayllon, and Tristán de Luna y Arellano. Other Spanish navigators (e.g., Pineda and Córdoba) touched the shores of east and west Florida, but did not attempt to establish settlements. Of the reports from these various efforts, only chroniclers of the de Soto expedition document indigenous tattooing in the Southeast.

Each of de Soto's four chroniclers describes unexpectedly encountering the Spaniard Juan Ortiz in Florida during June of 1539. Ortiz had sailed with the fleet delivering the Narváez expedition to Florida in 1527. He later returned to the Tampa Bay area to search for Narváez, but was captured by the Uzita. While in captivity he was tortured and suffered severe burns over one side of his body (Hudson 1997). Ortiz subsequently escaped to live among the Mocoso, who in 1539 dispatched him to greet the de Soto expedition.

Ortiz was tattooed during his time among the Mocoso, a fact that is recorded by several of the chroniclers. The Gentleman of Elvas records the first encounter with Ortiz as follows:

Ablate de Gallegos, on going into the level terrain two leagues from town, saw ten or eleven Indians, among whom was a Christian, naked and on that account burned by the sun. He had his arms tattooed[1] after the manner of the Indians, and in no wise did he differ from them. (Elvas 1993 [1557]:59)

Luys Hernández de Biedma is less specific regarding the manner of the marks, saying that Ortiz "was naked like them, with a bow and some arrows in his hand, his body decorated like an Indian" (Biedma 1993 [1841]:225). Garcilaso de la Vega was not present at the encounter; he relied on eye-witness accounts from three members of the expedition. Although he does not specifically mention that Ortiz was tattooed, Garcilaso de la Vega (1993 [1605]:104) does describe how the young man was tortured by his captors and the resulting scars. It is likely that Ortiz was adorned with a combination of scars, tattoos, and body paint.

De Soto's chroniclers recorded tattooing in only one other location along their journey. After crossing the Mississippi River, the expedition marched through Arkansas, where in 1541 they encountered and fought a pitched battle with the Tula, possibly a Caddoan-speaking group (Hudson 1997). Of the various chroniclers only Garcilaso de la Vega (1993 [1605]:413) describes the Tula as tattooed, noting that they "prick their faces with flint needles, especially the lips, inside and out, and color them black, thereby making themselves extremely and abominably ugly."

Spanish interests along the Florida coast were dealt their first serious challenge by another European power in 1562 when French admiral Gaspard de Coligny organized an expedition under Jean Ribaut to establish a French presence there. The initial settlement effort failed, but in 1564 Coligny sent a second Huguenot colony to Florida. This new expedition was commanded by Rene de Laudonnière and established Fort Caroline on the St. John's River near Jacksonville, Florida (McGrath 2000).

The Spanish king Phillip II dispatched a fleet under Pedro Menéndez de Avilés to clear the French from Florida. Menéndez captured Fort Caroline and massacred the French defenders. The few survivors included the carpenter Nicolas Le Challeux, Laudonnière, and the artist and cartographer Jacques Le Moyne de Morgues. Le Challeux's account of Fort Caroline mentions possible tattooing among the local Indian population only briefly, stating that "for ornament they have their skins inlaid[2] in a strange fashion" (Gaffarel 1875:461).

Laudonnière wrote an account of his participation in the aborted French expeditions entitled *L'Histoire Notable de la Florida*, which was published posthumously in 1586. After describing the use of berries and herbs to make paints and dyes, Laudonnière (2001 [1586]:9–11) states: "Most of [the men] ornament their bodies, arms, and thighs with handsome designs. The ornamentation is in permanent color because it is pricked into the skin." Laudonnière (2001 [1586]:77) also records that one chief among the Timucua used tattoos to mark his captives, who instead of being put to death were "[marked] on their left arm with a great sign or brand."[3]

Jacques Le Moyne de Morgues accompanied Laudonnière to the St. John's River as the expedition artist and cartographer. When Le Moyne fled the Spanish attack on Fort Caroline, he was forced to leave behind most or all of his paintings and records. He made his way to London, where he wrote an account of his experience and made a series of paintings from memory depicting the French colony and his experiences there (Harvey 2008; Lorant 1965). In 1587, one year after Laudonnière's account was published, the engraver Theodore de Bry visited Le Moyne in London and offered to purchase his memoir and images from Florida.

Although Le Moyne refused to sell his works, following his death a year later both the paintings and narrative came into de Bry's possession. In 1591, de Bry published the narrative and a series of engravings ostensibly based on Le Moyne's original paintings in the second volume of his *Grands Voyages*. Stephan Lorant republished the de Bry version of the narrative in English, along with the engravings, in 1946.

The Le Moyne narrative included in *Grands Voyages* does not include any mention of tattooing. However, thirteen of the forty-two de Bry engravings attributed to Le Moyne originals depict Florida chiefs and/or their wives as heavily tattooed with elaborate geometric designs. Other Native Americans depicted in the engravings are not shown with body decoration. No original versions of Le Moyne's paintings still exist (Harvey 2008), and given recent critiques of de Bry's efforts and a lack of original source material with which to compare the engravings, these images probably should not be regarded as literal representations of Timucua tattooing. Nevertheless, the de Bry images serve to illustrate an essential fact of tattooing among the Florida Indians. The entire corpus of de Bry engravings that depict Timucua tattoos are widely available in print and digital sources (e.g., Lorant 1965; Florida Center for Instructional Technology 2001), and so are not reproduced here.

Although tattooing appears in many of the engravings of Florida from the second volume of *Grands Voyages*, the practice is only described in a single image caption. The engraving entitled *The King and the Queen Take a Walk* (Figure 1.1) depicts the Timucua leader Saturiba and his "queen" surrounded by their attendants. Saturiba is tattooed with vertical lines down his face and parallel, petal-banded motifs across much of his body. His partner is marked across her limbs, torso, and forehead with a step-fret design, parallel lines across her lower face, and concentric petal motifs around her breasts. The caption for this illustration reads: "All these chiefs and their wives paint the

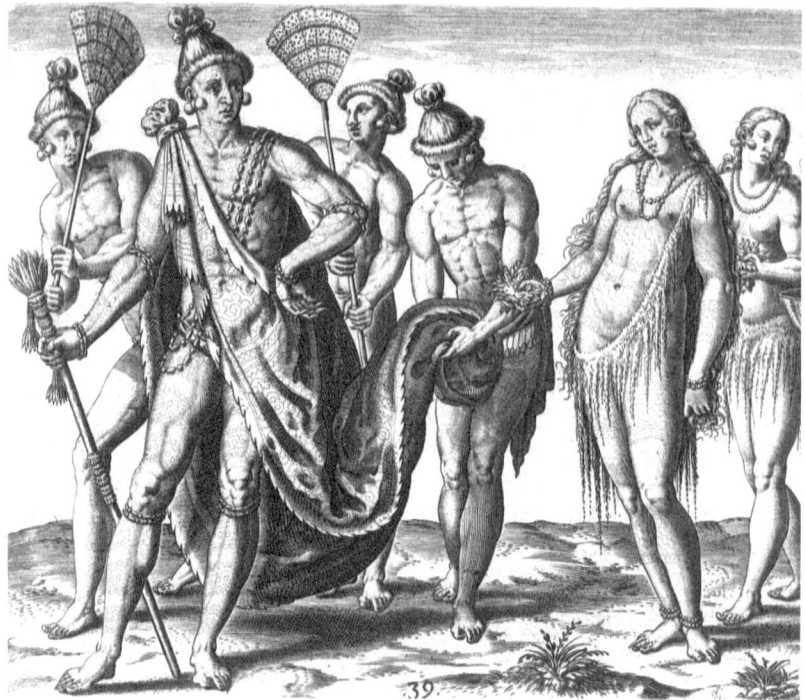

FIGURE 1.1. Detail of *The King and the Queen Take a Walk*. Engraving by Theodore de Bry, 1591. Image courtesy of the University of South Florida Libraries.

skin around their mouths blue and are tattooed[4] on the arms and thighs with a certain herb which leaves an indelible color. The process is so severe that it sometimes makes them sick for seven or eight days" (Lorant 1965:113). It is not clear if captions to this and the other engravings attributed to Le Moyne originals in *Grands Voyages* were authored by Le Moyne, or if they instead represent work by de Bry or another author.

One final source of information on the French colony in Florida is a narrative written by John Sparke, a sailor with Sir John Hawkins. Hawkins stopped at Fort Caroline on his return from a voyage to Africa and the West Indies in 1565. Of the Indians on Florida's east coast, Sparke says:

> They do not omit to paint their bodies also with curious knots, or antique work, as every man in his own fancy deviseth, which painting to make it continue the better, they use with a thorn to prick their flesh, and dent in the same, whereby the painting may have better hold. (Payne 1907:56)

The last sixteenth-century attempt at colonization of the southeastern United States was undertaken by the English. In 1584, Queen Elizabeth granted Sir Walter Raleigh exclusive rights to explore and settle in North America. Raleigh organized and sponsored three voyages to the Virginia and Carolina coasts between 1584 and 1587, culminating with the "Lost Colony" of John White.

Both White and Thomas Hariot were members of the second Roanoke mission, which sailed in 1585 under the command of Sir Richard Grenville. During the year that the expedition remained on Roanoke, Hariot and White conducted a survey of the area and created a series of documents regarding the natural resources and indigenous inhabitants. White made sketches and watercolor drawings depicting various indigenous people, plants, and animals from the mid-Atlantic region (Hulton 1984). Seventy-five of these watercolors, including examples by White himself and others made after his originals, now reside in the collection of the British Museum.

White's images of Native Americans have been widely reproduced, and recently were discussed and illustrated in color in the volume *A New World: England's First View of America*, by Kim Sloan (2007). Of the seventy-five watercolors in the British Museum, six individual portraits depict tattooed Native Americans. Two of these depict Timucua inhabitants of Florida, while the remaining four show Algonquian speakers who lived in towns near the English settlement at Roanoke.

John White did not himself visit Florida or directly encounter Timucua Indians. Instead, it has been proposed that his portraits of a Timucua chief and his wife (Figure 1.2) were copies of lost Le Moyne originals (Sloan 2007:133). White's depictions show the Florida inhabitants covered by tattoos on their arms, legs, chests, and shoulders. The man wears a vertical stripe of red face paint, while the woman is shown with a tattooed headband and a single vertical tattooed line running from her lower lip to her chin. Sloan (2007:134) notes that the tattoo patterns shown in White's watercolors do not correspond to any of those depicted in de Bry's adaptations of Le Moyne. The pattern is instead reminiscent of details from Elizabethan armor, suggesting that either Le Moyne or White adapted a familiar design to "fit missing details in their recollected views of the New World" (Sloan 2007:134).

None of the Algonquian men depicted in John White's portraits are tattooed, although the paintings include four depictions of tattooed women. The details of the marks that appear on the woman identified as the wife of a chief from Secotan have faded considerably on the original watercolor.

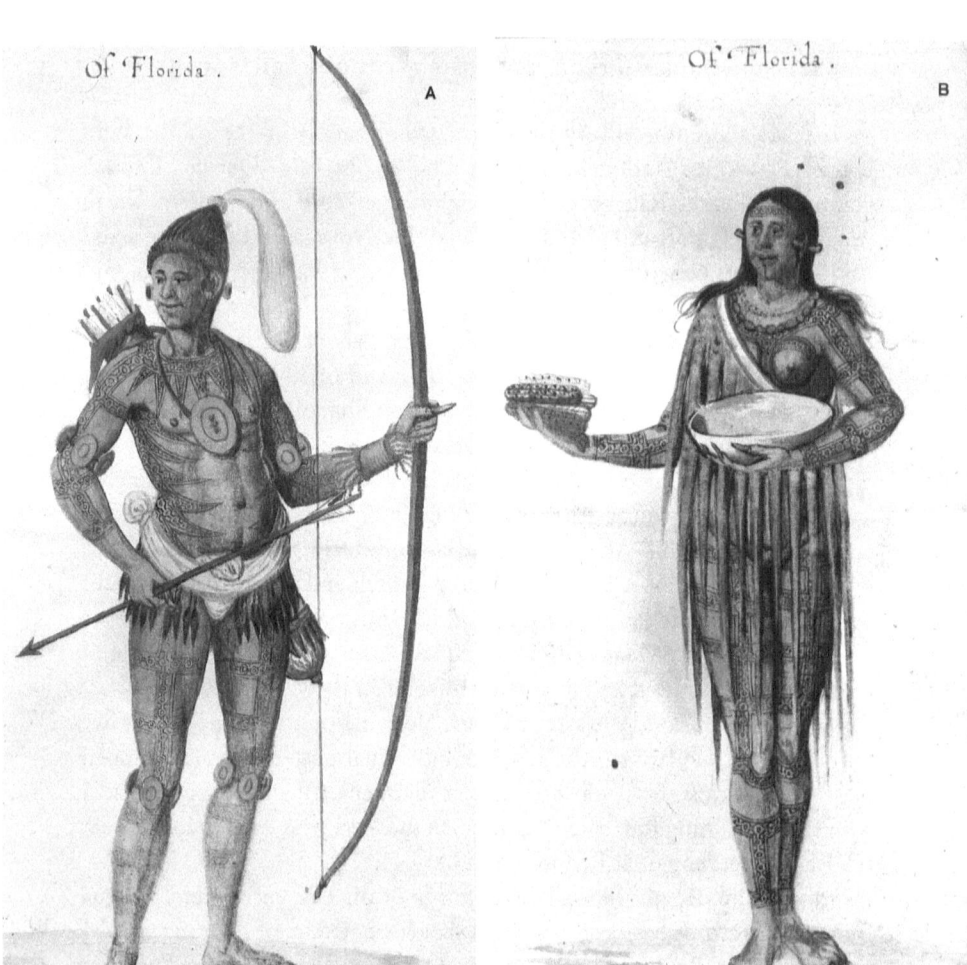

However, a copy of this image appears in the Sloane Album (Figure 1.3) and provides additional details regarding the woman's face and body designs. She is shown with geometric tattoos encircling her biceps, forearms, and calves, and a deep V-shape encircling her neck. Her face is marked with a descending "V" on the forehead, a sideways "V" beside her eye, parallel stepped lines on the cheek, and three vertical lines beneath her lower lip. These chin markings are highly reminiscent of historic period facial tattooing practiced

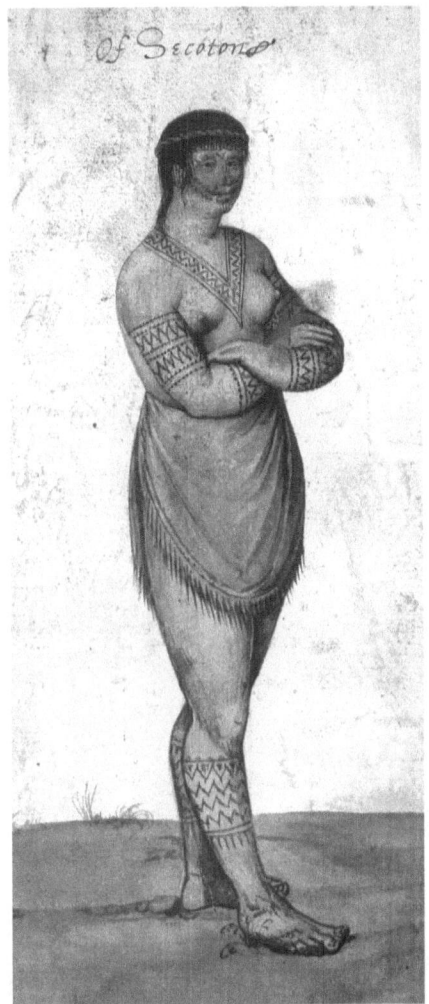

FIGURE 1.3. *Tattooed Algonquian Woman.* Detail of John White watercolor. © Trustees of the British Museum, registration number SL,5270.5.

by Native American women throughout North America (Krutak 2007; Mallery 1886, 1893; Sinclair 1909).

White's portrait of the wife of Chief Wingina (Figure 1.4) features designs encircling her calves, biceps, and wrists. She has V marks on her forehead and beside her eye, parallel dotted lines on her cheeks, and three vertical stripes on her chin. These same facial designs also appear on the wife of a chief from Pomeiooc (Figure 1.5A). This latter woman also has tattoos on

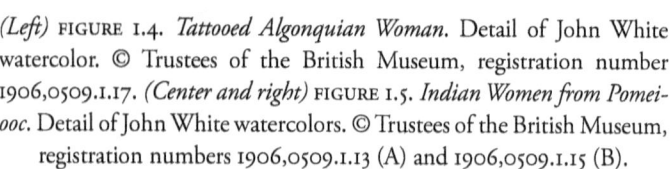

(Left) FIGURE 1.4. *Tattooed Algonquian Woman.* Detail of John White watercolor. © Trustees of the British Museum, registration number 1906,0509.1.17. *(Center and right)* FIGURE 1.5. *Indian Women from Pomeiooc.* Detail of John White watercolors. © Trustees of the British Museum, registration numbers 1906,0509.1.13 (A) and 1906,0509.1.15 (B).

her biceps, as well as a design encircling her neck that could be a tattoo or a necklace. Identical bicep designs are also shown on another woman from Pomeiooc (Figure 1.5B), whom White depicts carrying a young child.

After returning to England, Hariot prepared a report on his experience titled *A Briefe and True Report of the New Found Land of Virginia*. That document was published in Latin in 1588 and the following year was incorporated in Richard Hakluyt's book *The Principal Navigations, Voyages, Traffiques and*

Discoveries of the English Nation. Hakluyt's volume also included White's journal from the 1587 expedition to Roanoke. These works, and particularly the account by Hariot, provided the first report of conditions in North America widely available to Europeans.

In 1590 Theodor de Bry adapted White's original watercolors as engravings for a new edition of Hariot's account. Hariot prepared captions for the engravings, seven of which discuss tattooing. Beneath de Bry's version of the woman from Secotan, Hariot (2003 [1590]:42) writes, "Their foreheads, cheeks, chynne, armes and leggs are pownced. About their necks they wear a chaine, ether pricked or paynted." For the wife of Wingina (retitled *A Younge Gentill Woeman Daughter of Secota*), the caption states: "They pounce their foreheads, cheecks, armes and legs" (Hariot 2003 [1590]:44). Beneath the illustration of the woman and her daughter from Pomeiooc, Hariot (2003 [1590]:46) writes that the women of that town also "have their skinnes pownced." Finally, for the woman carrying the child (retitled *Their Manner of Careynge the Childern and a Tyere of the Cheiffe Ladyes of the Towne of Dasamonquepeuc*), the caption reads, "The woemen are attired, and pownced, in suche sorte as the woemen of Roanoac are, yet they weare noe worathes uppon their heads, nether have they their thighes painted with small pricks" (Hariot 2003 [1590]:48).

Beneath the portrait of a chief of Roanoke, Hariot (2003 [1590]:45) notes that high-status males were neither painted nor tattooed. This statement is contradictory to other images and captions in the de Bry version of Hariot's account. For example, the scene entitled *A Weroan or Great Lorde of Virginia* (Figure 1.6) depicts a standing male with lines and patterns on his calves, shoulders, chest, and stomach. The caption for that image reads: "They ether pownes, or paynt their forehead, cheeks, chynne, bodye, armes, and legs" (Hariot (2003 [1590]:41).

The de Bry engraving of the "great Lorde of Virginia" is based on a watercolor by John White that itself includes a caption describing the man's body decoration. Above the image, White writes that he has depicted "the manner of their attire and *painting* them selves when they goe to their general huntings, or at theire Solemne feasts" (Sloan 2007:121; emphasis added). It is clear from the original caption that the decorations John White showed on the man's body are intended to represent temporary, event-specific markings rather than permanent tattoos.

The de Bry edition of Hariot's account also includes an engraving titled *The Markes of Sundrye of the Chief Mene of Virginia* (Figure 1.7), which appears to be loosely based on the same John White original as the "great Lorde of

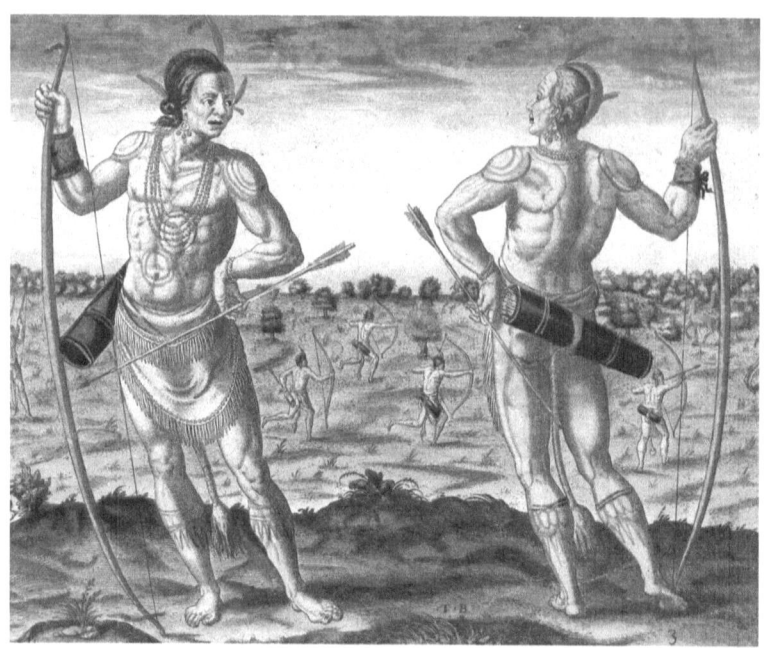

FIGURE 1.6. Detail of *A Weroan or Great Lorde of Virginia*. Engraving by Theodore de Bry, 1590. Image courtesy of the North Carolina Collection, University of North Carolina at Chapel Hill Library.

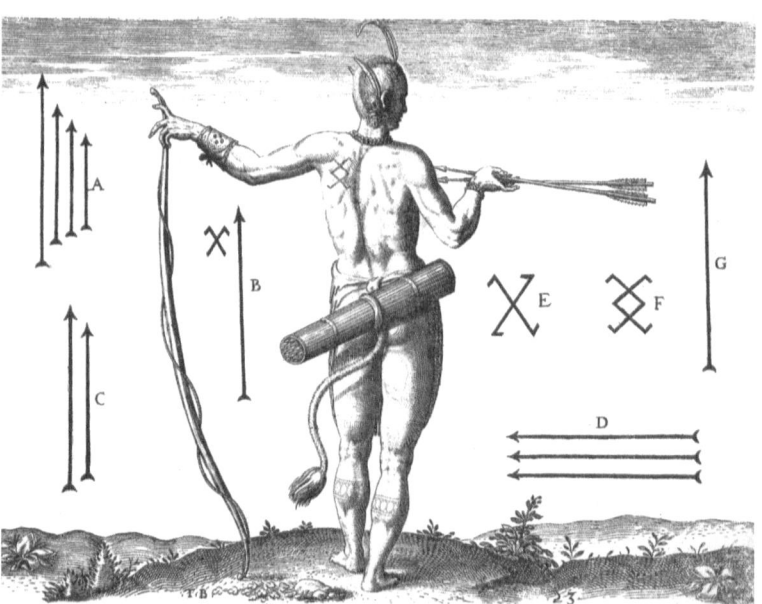

FIGURE 1.7. *The Markes of Sundrye of the Chief Mene of Virginia*. Engraving by Theodore de Bry, 1590.

Virginia." This image depicts a man with tattoos encircling his calves and an intersecting X pattern on his left shoulder blade. The background of the engraving includes seven patterns (A–G). In regard to these designs, the caption by Hariot states:

> The inhabitants of all the cuntrie for the most parte have marks rased on their backs, wherby yt may be knowen what Princes subiects they bee, or of what place they have their originall. For which cause we have set downe those marks in this figure, and have annexed the names of the places, that they might more easelye be discerned. Which industrie hath god indued them withal although they be verye sinple, and rude. And to confesse a truthe I cannot remember, that ever I saw a better or quietter people then they.
>
> The marks which I observed a monge them, are heere put downe in order folowinge.
>
> The marke which is expressed by A. belongeth to Wingino, the cheefe lorde of Roanoac.
>
> That which hath B. is the marke of Wingino his sisters husbande.
>
> Those which be noted with the letters, of C. and D. belonge unto diverse chefe lordes in Secotam.
>
> Those which have the letters E. F. G. are certaine cheefe men of Pomeiooc, and Aquascogoc. (Hariot 2003 (1590):66)

/ Seventeenth Century /

The English founded the Jamestown colony in 1607 on the James River in Virginia. Diaries from several of the earliest Jamestown colonists have survived and contain information about indigenous tattooing during the seventeenth century. Of the Indian women in general, colonist George Percy wrote:

> The women kinde in this Countrey doth pounce and race their bodies, legges, thighes, armes, and faces with a sharpe Iron, which makes a stampe in curious knots, and drawes the proportion of Fowles, Fish, or Beasts; then with paintings of sundry lively colours, they rub it into the stampe which will never be taken away, because it is dried into the flesh where it is sered. (Percy 2007 [1907]:931)

Jamestown colonists John Smith and William Strachey also systemati-
cally recorded their experiences in order to publish histories. Captain John
Smith was president of the council of the colony between 1608 and 1609;
William Strachey was secretary of the colony between 1610 and 1611. Smith
wrote three narratives on Virginia history between 1608 and 1624, each sup-
plementing his previous efforts with the addition of new material. The final
version of this narrative, entitled *The Generall Historie of Virginia, New England, and the Summer Isles*, includes an early ethnological study of the local
Algonquian Indians. Smith provides a detailed observation of Algonquian
tattooing, writing: "Their women, some have their legs, hands, breasts and
face cunningly imbrodered with divers workes, as beasts, serpents, artifi-
cially wrought into their flesh with blacke spots" (Smith 2007 [1624]:283).

Strachey's *The Historie of Travaile into Virginia Britannia* was first published in 1612 and provides a description of women's tattooing taken almost
verbatim from Smith's history, although with some additional information:

> The women have their armes, breasts, thighes, showlders and faces, cuningly
> imbrodered with divers workes, for pouncing and searing their skyns with a
> kind of Instrument heated in the fire, they figure therin flowers and fruits of
> sondry lively kyndes, as also Snakes, Serpents, Eftes, etc., and this they doe
> by dropping upon the seared flesh sondry Coulers, which, rub'd into the
> stampe, will never be taken awaye agayne, because yt will not only be dryed
> into the flesh, but grow therein. (Strachey 1612:1057)

During the last quarter of the seventeenth century European travelers,
explorers, and missionaries began to approach the Southeast from other directions. French explorers and missionaries from Quebec gradually extended
their explorations westward through the Great Lakes and down the Mississippi River. In 1673, Jacques Marquette and Louis Jolliet descended the
Mississippi as far as the mouth of the Arkansas. Marquette's journal records
body decoration on a party of Indians of the Huron-Iroquois family, possibly
Tuscarora, camped along the Mississippi near the St. Francis River. Marquette
writes that these individuals "tattoo[5] their bodies after the Hiroquois fashion," although he does not describe the specific markings (Marquette 1900
[1681]:149).

In 1687, René-Robert Cavelier, Sieur de La Salle, was returning overland
from Texas to Canada after an unsuccessful attempt to find the mouth of the
Mississippi by way of the Gulf of Mexico when he was murdered by several

of his own men. The remaining members of the La Salle expedition, including military officer Henri Joutel, continued on to the Mississippi River and eventually reached Canada. Joutel's journal of the expedition contains the best early description of the Caddoan-speaking tribes of Texas and Louisiana, and was first published in English in 1714.

Following La Salle's murder, the remaining Frenchmen arrived at a village of the Cenis (Hasinai), a tribe of the western band of Caddo. They remained at this site for about a month, and Joutel describes the tattooing practices of the group in some detail:

> The Indians are generally Handsom, but disfigure themselves by making Scores, or Streaks on their Faces, from the Top of the Forehead down the Nose to the Tip of the Chin; which is done by pricking the Skin with Needles, or other sharp Instruments, till it bleeds, whereon they strew fine Powder of Charcoal, and that sinks in and mixes with the Blood within the Skin. They also make after the same Manner, the Figures of living Creatures, of Leaves and Flowers on their Shoulders, Thighs, and other Parts of their Bodies, and Paint themselves, as has been said before, with Black or Red, and sometimes both together.
>
> The Women are generally well Shap'd, and would not be disagreeable, did they adhere to Nature; but they Disguise themselves as ridiculously as the Men, not only with the Streak they have like them down their Face, but by other Figures they make on it, at the corners of their Eyes, and on the other Parts of their Bodies; whereof they make more particular Show on their Bosom, and those who have the most, are reckoned the handsomest; tho' that pricking in that Part be extremely painful to them. (Joutel 1906 [1714]:143)[6]

While at this village Joutel encountered two French deserters from La Salle's earlier travels through the area. The Frenchmen had apparently received tattoos during their time with the Indians, as Joutel describes them having "so perfectly [injured] themselves to the Customs of the Natives, that they were become meer Savages. They were naked, their Faces and French Bodies with Figures wrought on them, like the rest" (Joutel 1906 [1714]:149).

Henri de Tonti, learning of the death of La Salle, set out from the Illinois country to find the remnants of the French expedition. In 1690, he encountered the Cadodacchos on the Red River and noted, "The men and women prick[7] their faces and whole bodies with marks they believe to be most beautiful. Such is the strangeness of the human mind, that what makes a deformity in one country is considered beautiful in another" (Tonti 1697:325).

Several members of the La Salle expedition were captured by Indian tribes, including the brothers Pierre and Jean-Baptiste Talon and several of their siblings. The brothers quickly became acculturated, adopting Indian dress and language, and receiving tattoos (Foster 1995). In 1690 a Spanish expedition under Father Damián Massanet and Alonso de León ransomed Pierre and Jean-Baptiste from the Hasinais and Karankawas, respectively. The brothers and their surviving siblings were sent to Mexico, and from there to Spain. In 1698 the Talon brothers were interrogated about their experiences along the Gulf Coast. The record of their interview describes the tattooing process as follows:

> The said Talons have already said something of their particular movements and how they fell into the power of the savages, who first tattooed[8] them on the face, the hands, the arms, and in several other places on their bodies as they do on themselves, with several bizarre black marks, which they make with charcoal of walnut wood, crushed and soaked in water. Then they insert this mixture between the flesh and the skin, making incisions with strong, sharp thorns, which cause them to suffer great pain. Thus, the dissolved carbon mixes with the blood and oozes from these incisions and forms indelible marks and characters on the skin. These marks still show, despite a hundred remedies that the Spaniards applied to try to erase them. (Bell 1987:238)

There are numerous other references to Native Americans tattooing both themselves and Europeans in the southeast portion of French Louisiana, as documented by scholars including Balvay (2008), Swanton (1942), and most recently Friedman Herlihy (2012). For example, the Frenchman Jean-Baptiste Le Moyne de Bienville explored the Red River in 1700 and reported that all of the Nakasa, a Caddo tribe, "have a circle pricked around the eyes and on the nose, and three lines on the chin" (Bienville 1880 [1700]:440). A year earlier, Pierre Le Moyne d'Iberville recorded that among the Bayogoulas some of the women "have their bodies pricked and are marked with black on their face and breast" (d'Iberville 1880:172). Early reports of tattooing in this area were also affirmed by Spanish missionaries who traveled through the region in the late seventeenth century and throughout the eighteenth century.

Only a single visual representation of Southeastern Indian body decoration exists from the seventeenth century. That image consists of an etching done in England by the Czech printmaker Wenceslaus Hollar. The etching is titled *Indian of Virginia, Male, Age 23, W. Hollar, Made from Life, 1645.* The individual is depicted with seven closely spaced horizontal parallel lines, presumably tattoos, running from temple to temple across his eyes and nose (Figure 1.8).

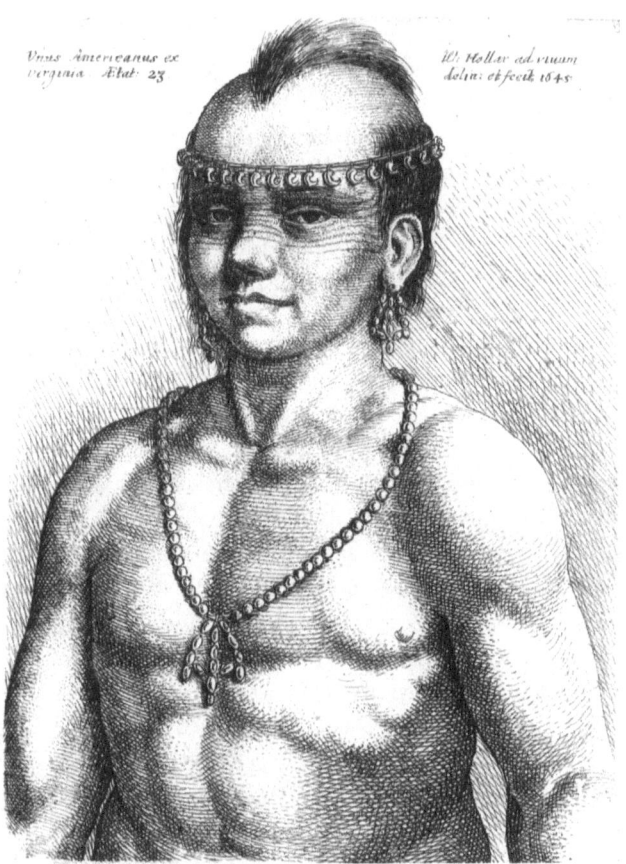

FIGURE 1.8. *Indian of Virginia Male, Age 23, Made from Life, 1645.* Etching by Wenceslaus Hollar, 1645.

/ Eighteenth Century /

In 1736, a German by the name of Philip Georg Friedrich von Reck escorted a group of Austrian and German Lutherans to Georgia, where they established a settlement under General James Oglethorpe. Von Reck traveled through the surrounding region with the express purpose of returning to Europe with sketches and records of the new land. Upon reaching Germany, von Reck prepared a narrative based on his travel diary in which he described the plants, animals, and Indians of Georgia, supplemented by fifty watercolor and pencil sketches of what he had seen. In his narrative, von Reck has the following to say about Yuchi tattooing:

> The men paint the face and chest, but the women only the arms and chest. The figures on the chest are pricked in with a needle or other pointed instrument, until they bleed, and in them they sprinkle fine powder or charcoal dust, which mixes in the blood, remains in the skin, and appears blue-black. Red and blue are their favorite colors for bedaubing themselves on festival days. But when they paint their faces black and red, it is an indication that they have done injury or want to do so. (Hvidt 1980:45–46)

Some of von Reck's close-up sketches and watercolors present detailed images of Yuchi tattooing. Today the folio of his drawings is in the collection of the Royal Library in Copenhagen and can be viewed online through that institution's web page (Det Kongelige Bibliotek 2011). Several of the von Reck images are discussed further by Lars Krutak in this volume.

Von Reck made three paintings and two sketches (both close-up studies of the paintings) that depict painted and tattooed Yuchi. In the painting entitled *Georgia Indians in Their Natural Habit* (Figure 1.9), von Reck depicts a paired man and woman. The man is not tattooed, whereas the woman is shown with a single row of arrows and two spool-shaped figures on her arm, and a curved line under her breasts. Von Reck's caption for this image reads, "The arrows and lines under the breast are burned" (Hvidt 1980:110–113). Throughout his captions, von Reck substitutes the word *burned* for *tattooed*. The same pattern of tattooed arrows and a sketch of the chest design also appear on a pencil sketch titled *An Indian Woman Weaving a Basket of Reed*.

Von Reck also painted a picture of Kipahalgwa, the "supreme commander of the Yuchi Indian nation" (Figure 1.10). His caption for that image reads, "The face is painted in this way with the Black signs on the temple, the breast and neck burned" (Hvidt 1980:114–115). Kipahalgwa's neck is covered with

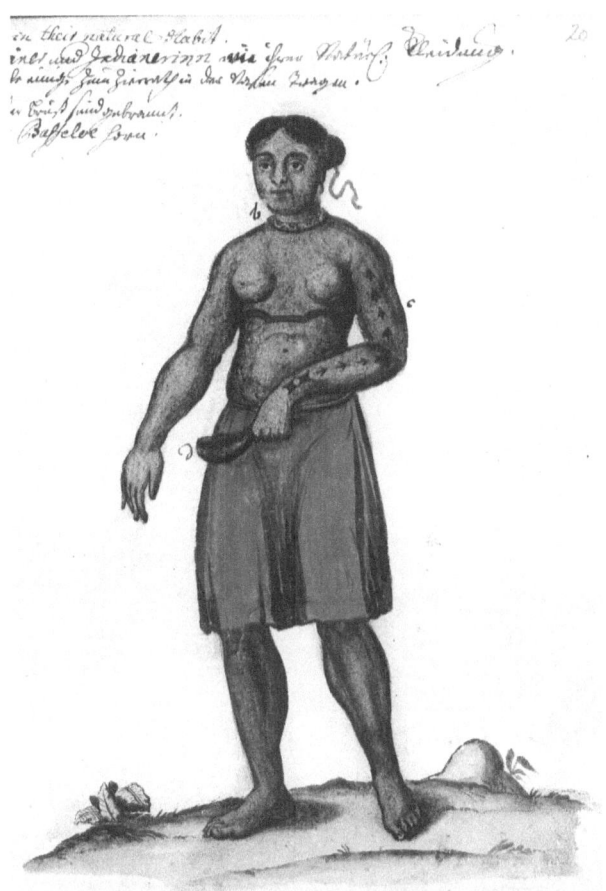

FIGURE 1.9. *The Georgia Indians in Their Natural Habitat.* Detail of watercolor by Philip Georg Friedrich von Reck, 1736. Image courtesy of the Royal Library of Denmark (Det Kongelige Bibliotek), Copenhagen: NKS 565 4°, 20r.

black, closely spaced horizontal lines. His face is painted black and red with a yellow zig-zag band across the forehead, and his chest is extensively tattooed with tapered vertical lines.

The last painting by von Reck that depicts Yuchi tattooing is entitled *The Indian King and Queen of the Yuchis, Senkaitschi* (Figure 1.11). The caption to that painting reads, "The signs on their face, neck and breast are burned." Although no tattooing is visible on the woman, Senkaitschi is elaborately tattooed with black lines on the chest and face, and a tattooed band with bird designs on his neck. The general design of his chest tattoo is identical

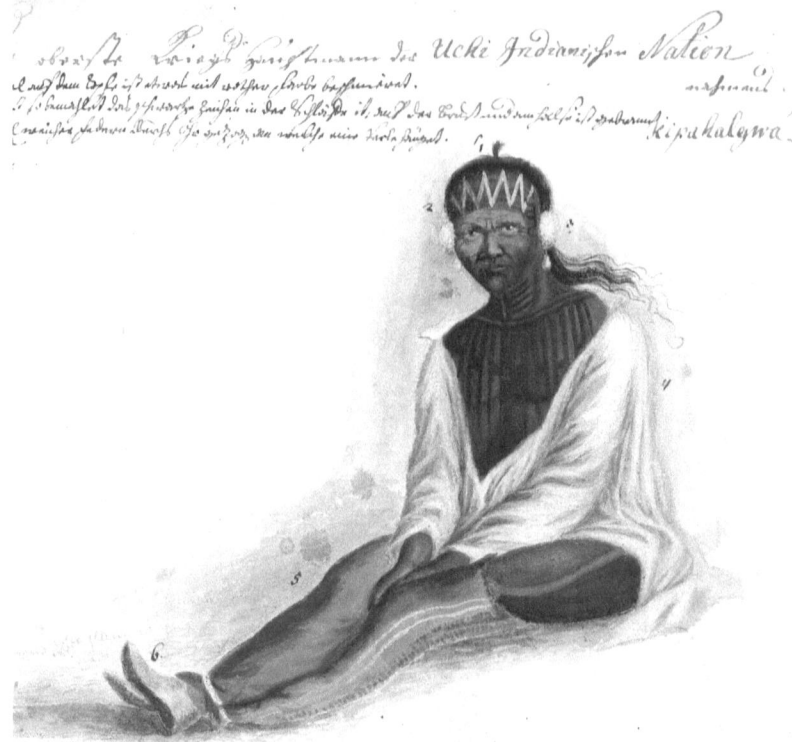

FIGURE 1.10. *The Supreme Commander of the Yuchi Indian Nation, Whose Name Is Kipahalgwa*. Detail of watercolor by Philip Georg Friedrich von Reck, 1736. Image courtesy of the Royal Library of Denmark (Det Kongelige Bibliotek), Copenhagen: NKS 565 4°, 16r.

to that of Kipahalgwa. Senkaitschi's face shows a wavy line tattooed on the forehead, horizontal lines on the cheeks, and verticals on the chin. These are especially visible in a pencil study for the portrait (see Figure 4.14). Hvidt (1980:120–121) suggests that the tattooed wavy line on the forehead would have served to mark the separation between the red color and the black color when war paint was applied.

The horizontal stripes and vertical V-shaped chest motifs present in von Reck's depictions of Senkaitschi and Kipahalgwa are remarkably similar to those on a portrait of the Yamacraw-Creek chief Tomochichi and his young nephew Tonahowi (Figure 1.12). Tomochichi traveled from the Savannah area to London in 1734 as part of a delegation led by James Oglethorpe, and during that visit had his portrait painted by William Verelst. Tomochichi also has a tattooed mark on his left cheek (Fundaburk 1958:112, plate 112; Viola 1976:11).

In 1761–1762, Lt. Henry Timberlake traveled as an emissary to several Overhill Cherokee towns in East Tennessee. In the account of his travels he briefly described tattooing, noting that "the Cherokees are of a middle

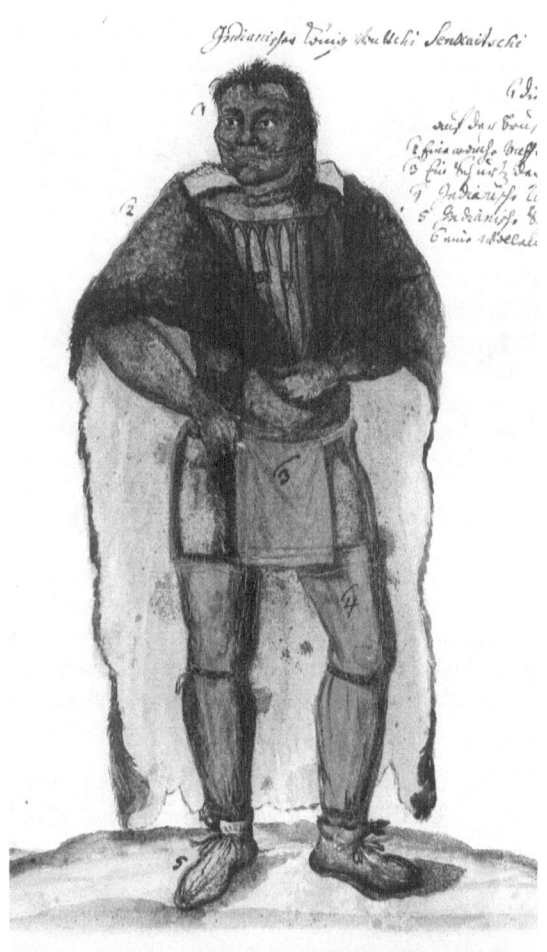

FIGURE I.II. *The Indian King and Queen of the Yuchis, Senkaitschi*. Detail of watercolor by Philip Georg Friedrich von Reck, 1736. Image courtesy of the Royal Library of Denmark (Det Kongelige Bibliotek), Copenhagen: NKS 565 4°, 27r.

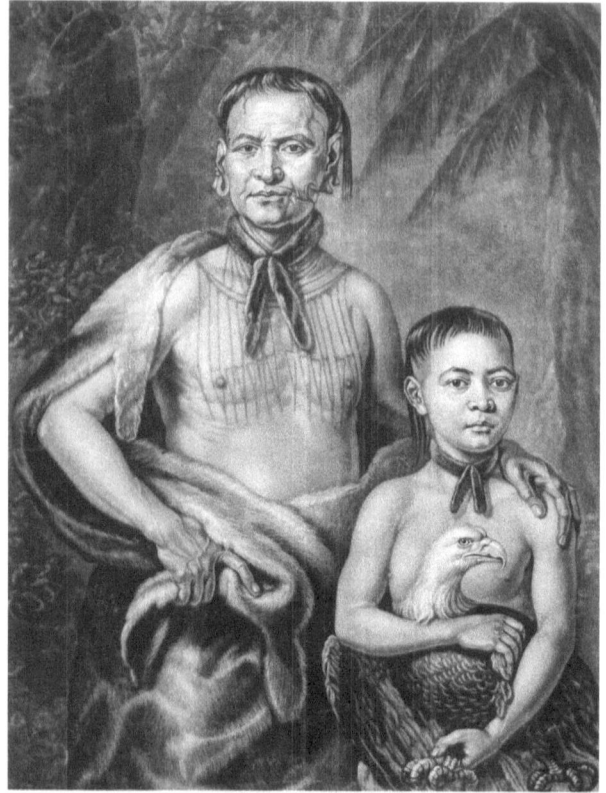

FIGURE 1.12. *Tomo Chachi Mico or King of Yamacraw, and Tooa-nahowi His Nephew, Son to the Mico of the Etchitas.* Mezzotint by John Faber the Younger (1739) based on a 1735 painting by William Verelst. Image courtesy of the Mabel Brady Garvan Collection at the Yale University Art Gallery.

stature, of an olive colour, tho' generally painted, and their skins stained with gun-powder, pricked into it in very pretty figures" (Timberlake 2007 [1765]:24). Timberlake returned from his trip accompanied by Ostenaco, chief of the Overhill town of Tomotley.

In 1762, Timberlake accompanied Ostenaco and two other Cherokees to London, where the delegation met King George III and sat for portraits by Sir Joshua Reynolds and Francis Parsons (Sturtevant 2007). In his portrait by Parsons, the Cherokee named Cunne Shote is depicted wearing European attire and exhibits a partially visible neck tattoo (Figure 1.13). That design consists of a circle on the throat flanked by parallel lines running beneath his collar.

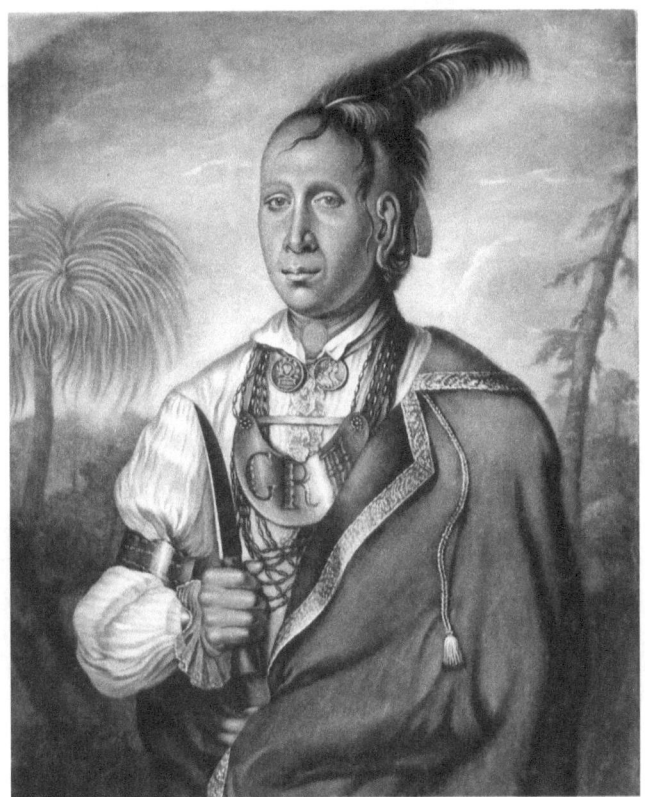

FIGURE 1.13. *Cunne Shote, the Indian Chief.* Mezzotint by James McArdell based on a ca. 1762 painting by Francis Parsons. Image courtesy of the Mabel Brady Garvan Collection at the Yale University Art Gallery.

A number of other illustrations of the members of the Cherokee delegation were generated as a result of the 1762 trip. One relatively well-known example of these works is a copper engraving by George Bickham that depicts individualized face and neck tattooing on Ostenaco and his associates (Figure 1.14), entitled *The Three Cherokees Came Over from the Head of the River Savanna to London, 1762.*

Works by Bickham and other engravers depict all three Cherokee men with elaborate facial tattooing. However, variations in the patterns between engravings and their absence from the Cunne Shote portrait by Parsons indicate that the images by Bickham and others were not made from life.

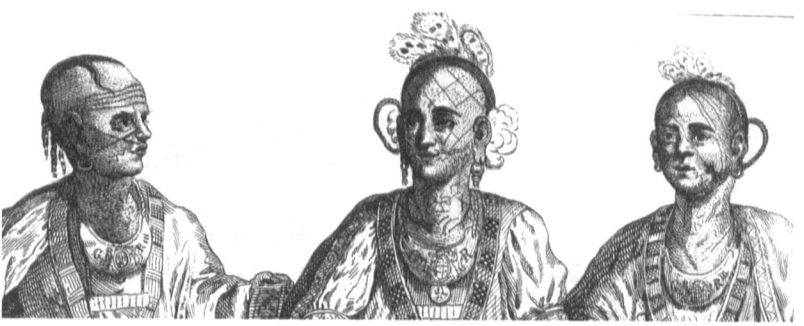

FIGURE 1.14. *The Three Cherokees Came Over from the Head of the River Savanna to London, 1762.* Detail of engraving by George Bickham.

Instead, it is likely that these works were based on John Verelst's depictions of four Iroquois who visited London in 1710, fifty years before (Krutak 2005). The body poses, the basic outlines of the clothing, and the face and neck markings in Bickham's work are very similar to those in the images by Verelst (see, e.g., Figure 4.7), although details regarding costume, background, and items held in the hand are different. Several of the Verelst paintings feature elaborate facial tattooing.

In 1735, James Adair immigrated to South Carolina and immediately became engaged in the Indian trade. Adair wrote a book about his experiences as a trader in and around the Appalachian Mountains and in northern Mississippi, which was published in 1775. Although Adair presented a series of arguments supporting the theory that the American Indians originated from the lost tribes of Israel, the book also contains important firsthand descriptions of body decoration for eighteenth-century Indians in the central Southeast. Of tattooing, Adair writes:

> Those captives who are pretty far advanced in life, as well as in war-gradations, always atone for the blood they spilt, by the tortures of fire. They readily know the latter, by the blue marks over their breasts and arms; they being as legible as our alphabetical characters are to us. Their ink is made of the soot of pitch-pine, which sticks to the inside of a greased earthen pot; then delineating the parts, like the ancient Picts of Britain, with their wild hieroglyphics, they break through the skin with gair-fish-teeth, and rub over them that dark composition, to register them among the brave; and the impression is lasting. I have been told by the Chikkasah,

that they formerly erased any false marks their warriors proudly and privately gave themselves—in order to engage them to give real proofs of their martial virtue, being surrounded by the French and their red allies; and they degraded them in a public manner, by stretching the marked parts, and rubbing them with the juice of green corn, which in a great degree took out the impression. (Adair 2005 [1775]:384)

A Dutchman by the name of Bernard Romans was sent to America as a civil engineer by the British government in 1755, and three years later was appointed chief deputy surveyor of the Southern District. Romans was trained in botany and cartography, and was also an artist and engraver. In 1775 he published *A Concise Natural History of East and West Florida*, in which he described the manners and customs of the Creek, Chickasaw, and Choctaw Indians.

Romans drew a picture of the upper bodies of two Choctaw women entitled *Characteristick Chactan Busts* (Romans 1999 [1775]:136) (Figure 1.15). The image presents two heavily tattooed women, one having horizontal and curvilinear parallel lines over neck, chest, and arms; the other zig-zag broad stripes in the same areas. Their faces may have some cheek and eye decoration but are very difficult to see in the drawing so this cannot be affirmed. Romans also drew another image of a male Indian bust (Romans

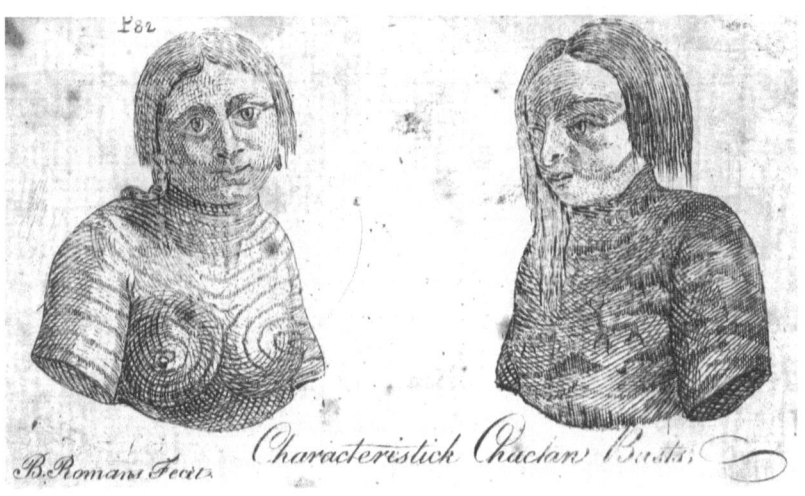

FIGURE 1.15. *Characteristick Chactan Busts.* Drawing by Bernard Romans (1999 [1775]:136).

1999 [1775]:122) that may show facial markings on the cheeks, although the style of drawing makes it difficult to distinguish.

Some of the best descriptions of tattooing in the eighteenth century are provided by naturalists who worked in the Southeast. The earliest is by Mark Catesby, an Englishman who traveled in Virginia from 1712 to 1719 and in South Carolina from 1722 to 1725. He writes:

> Their war captains and men of distinction have usually the portrait of a serpent, or other animal, on their naked bodies; this is done by puncture and a black powder conveyed under the skin. These figures are esteemed not only as ornamental, but serve to distinguish the warriors, making them more known and dreaded by their enemies. (Catesby 1747:9)

Between 1773 and 1777, the American-born naturalist and artist William Bartram traveled through the coastal Carolinas, east and west Florida, Georgia, Alabama, and the Cherokee country of the southern Appalachian Mountains. On the way, he had frequent encounters with the Indian inhabitants, which he recorded in detail and subsequently published in 1791. In discussing Native American dress, Bartram does not designate a specific tribe but writes:

> The head, neck and breast, are painted with vermilion, and some of the warriors have the skin of the breast, and muscular parts of the body, very curiously inscribed, or adorned, with hieroglyphick scrolls, flowers, figures of animals, stars, crescents, and the sun in the centre of the breast. This painting of the flesh, I understand, is performed in their youth, by picking the skin with a needle, until the blood starts, and rubbing in a blueish tinct, which is as permanent as their life. (Bartram 1996 [1791]:400)

Bartram also authored a work entitled *Observations on the Creek and Cherokee Indians*, which was first published by the American Ethnological Society in 1853. The description of Creek tattooing in that document is extremely detailed:

> But the most beautiful painting now to be found among the [Muscogee], is on the skin and bodies of their ancient chiefs and *micos*, which is of a bluish, lead, or indigo color. It is the breast, trunk, muscular or fleshy part of the arms and thighs, and sometimes almost every part of the surface of the body, that is thus beautifully depicted or written over with *hieroglyphics*: commonly the sun, moon, and planets occupy the breast; zones or belts, or

beautiful fanciful scrolls, wind round the trunk of the body, thighs, arms and legs, dividing the body into many fields or tablets, which are ornamented or filled up with innumerable figures, as representations of animals of the chase—a sketch of a landscape, representing an engagement or battle with the enemy, or some creature of the chase, —and a thousand other fancies. These paintings are admirably well executed, and seen to be inimitable. They are performed by exceedingly fine punctures, and seem like *mezzotinto*, or very ingenious impressions from the best educated engravings. They are no doubt hieroglyphics, or mystical writings or records of their tribes or families, or of memorable events. (Bartram 1996 [1853]:533–534)

In the eighteenth century, the French again become a source of significant information on Indian body decoration. French explorers, missionaries, settlers, and soldiers recorded information on the many tribes living along the lower Mississippi as well as the Creek tribes to the southeast, and the Siouan and Algonquian tribes to the north and west of the Mississippi River.

Jean-Bernard Bossu was a young French military officer who traveled up the Mississippi valley and through Alabama from New Orleans and Mobile between 1751 and 1762. Bossu's observations of the tribes he visited were recorded in letters to patrons in France. These letters were first published in 1768 as *Nouveaux Voyages aux Indes Occidentales*, and are a valuable resource on the Creek, Choctaw, Natchez, Arkansas, and Illinois nations. They also provide some very informative data on tattooing among those groups.

Bossu records an initiation of young men among the Alabama that involves scratching or tattooing. After the initiation is complete, the men have become warriors and earned the right to receive honor markings. Bossu 1962 [1768]:134) writes: "When they have done something outstanding in battle, they are tattooed."[9] Among the Choctaw, Bossu records the collection of scalp-tally tattoos, stating, "A warrior wears as a trophy the scalp of an enemy killed in battle. He commemorates the event by having a mark tattooed on his body" (Bossu 1962 [1768]:166). Moving west to the Natchez, Bossu relates that all Natchez chiefs were called "Suns" and all were related to the "Great Sun, their sovereign, who wore on his chest a picture of the sun from which he claimed descent" (Bossu 1962 [1768]:31).

Bossu himself received a tattoo during an adoption ceremony among the Quapaw, and describes the process as follows. This account provides one of the most thorough descriptions of an indigenous tattooing ceremony from the Southeast.

Before ending my letter, I should like to tell you about an event which will seem very strange to you, but which, in spite of its insignificance, could be very useful to me during my stay in America. The [Quapaw] have just adopted me. A deer was tattooed on my thigh as a sign that I have been made a warrior and a chief. I submitted to this painful operation with good grace. I sat on a wildcat skin while an Indian burned some straw. He put the ashes in water and used this simple mixture to draw the deer. He then traced the drawing with big needles, pricking me until I bled.[10] The blood mixed with the ashes of the straw formed a tattoo which can never be removed. After that I smoked a pipe and walked on white skins which were spread under my feet. They danced for me and shouted with joy. They then told me that if I traveled among the tribes allied to them, all I had to do to receive a warm welcome was to smoke a peace pipe and show my tattoo. They also said that I was their brother and that if I were killed they would avenge my death. (Bossu 1962 [1768]:65–66)

In another of his letters, Bossu again discusses tattooing at length. He remarks that a visiting Osage who had killed a very large and dangerous snake had an image of that creature tattooed on his body. He then goes on to note that only those who had performed great deeds could earn tattoos, and that considerable ire was directed at any who acquired the marks under false pretenses:

If one should take it into his head to have himself tattooed without hav-ing distinguished himself in battle, he would be disgraced and considered a coward, unworthy of the honor due to only those who risk their lives to defend their tribe . . . I knew an Indian who, although he had never done anything outstanding in defense of his tribe, decided to have himself tat-tooed with one of these marks of distinction in order to impress those who judge others by outward appearances. This show-off wanted to pass himself off as a valiant man so that he could marry one of the prettiest girls of the tribe, who was ambitious even though she was a savage. Just as the match was about to be concluded with the girl's relatives, the warriors, who were indignant upon seeing a coward display a symbol of military merit, called an assembly of war chiefs to deal with this bit of audacity. The council decided, in order to prevent such abuses which would remove the distinction between courageous men and cowards, that this false hero who unjustly decorated himself with the tattoo of a tomahawk, without ever having struck a blow in battle, would have the design torn off him, skin and all, and that the same would be done to others like him. (Bossu 1962 [1768]:95–96)

The tattooing Bossu witnessed was not limited to men or warriors. Instead, he notes that Indian women had themselves tattooed everywhere, even "on such delicate and sensitive parts of the body as the breasts. They bear the pain with the same courage as the men in order to please them and to appear more beautiful to them" (Bossu 1962 [1768]:97).

An anonymous source that concentrates on the Choctaw was written by a French officer in the middle of the eighteenth century. In discussing war customs, he notes:

Each family has its quarterings tattooed on the stomach and on the arms [of its warrior members]. They also put them on the handles of their war clubs, and when they wish to meet in the woods they make a mark on the trees, where they put their arms, by which the one who has made the mark is known, the trail he has taken, and where he has gone. (Swanton 1931:163)

Tattooing was practiced by almost every tribe in the lower Mississippi valley for which we have reports. There are several detailed eighteenth-century discussions of tattooing among the Natchez. One of the earliest of these accounts appears in an anonymous 1752 memoir titled *Memoire sur la Louisiane ou le Mississippi*, which records that prior to 1718,

the greater part [of the Natchez] have fantastic marks imprinted on the face, the arms, the legs, and the thighs; so far as the body is concerned, this is a right which belongs only to the warriors, and one must be noted on account of the death of some enemy in order to merit this distinction. They imprint on the stomachs of their heroes an infinity of black, red, and blue lines; which is not done without pain. They begin by tracing the design on the skin, then with the needle or a little bone well sharpened they prick until the blood comes, following the design, after which they rub the punctures with a powder of the color that the one who has himself marked demands. These colors having penetrated the skin and the flesh are never effaced. (Swanton 1911:56)

In 1715, French governor of Louisiana Antoine La Mothe Cadillac conducted a tour of the Illinois country during which he alienated and insulted a number of Native American groups, precipitating the First Natchez War

(Woods 1978). Louis Poncereau de Richebourg, who was captain of the company assigned to Bienville, prepared an official record of the events surrounding the first Natchez uprising. In that document he writes that Bienville asked the leaders of the Natchez to provide satisfaction for the death of four Frenchmen by delivering the heads of both the murderers and the chiefs who had given them their orders. Bienville was not content to receive their scalps, but instead wished to view their heads in order to confirm their identities based on the patterns of their facial tattoos (Richebourg 1851:245).

Jean-François Benjamin Dumont de Montigny lived in Louisiana for almost twenty years, and served at Fort Rosalie from 1726 to 1728. He returned to France in 1738 and fifteen years later published *Mémoires Historiques sur la Louisiane*. In that work, Dumont describes tattooing among the Natchez:

> But the greatest ornament of all these savages of both sexes consists in certain figures of suns, serpents, or other things, which they carry pictured on their bodies in the manner of the ancient Britons . . . The warriors, as well as the wives of the chiefs and the Honored men, have these figures pictured on the face, arms, shoulders, thighs, legs but principally on the belly and stomach. It is for them not only an ornament, but also a mark of honor and distinction, which is only acquired after many brave deeds, and here is how these pictures are made: First, in accordance with the color that is desired, a man makes either a black mixture of pine charcoal or, indeed of gunpowder dissolved in water, or a red of cinnabar or vermilion. After this five medium-sized sewing needles are taken, which are arranged on a little flat, smooth piece of wood and fastened to the same depth, so that one point does not extend out beyond the others. These needles are then soaked in the color and moved quickly, being applied lightly to the design, which had before been traced on the body, and the color insinuates itself between the skin, which afterward dries and falls into dust, but the figure imprinted on the flesh through these needle prickings, whether in red or black, is never effaced. It is carried to the tomb. (Dumont de Montigny 1753:139–140 [as translated by Swanton 1911:56–57])

Dumont also painted a number of watercolors of scenes in eighteenth-century Louisiana. Two of these pictures depict groups of male and female Indians. In the image of men, a single individual is shown as tattooed, with zig-zag lines on his legs, arms, and stomach, and a sun design on his chest (Figure 1.16A). He is shown holding a gun, and the caption beneath him

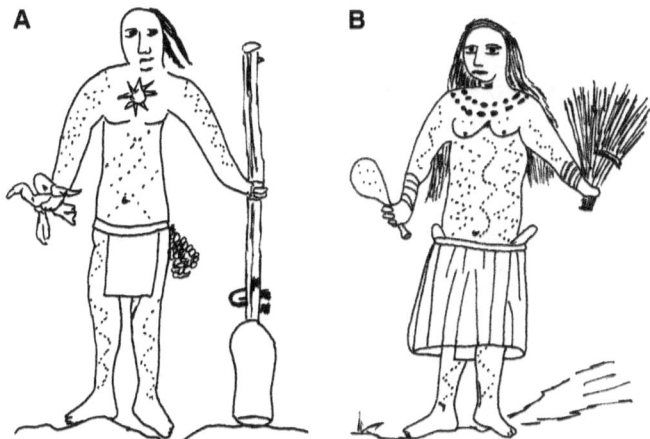

FIGURE 1.16. *Tattooed Native Americans from Louisiana.* Details of watercolors by Dumont de Montigny, 1747 (after Newberry Library Ayer Collection MS 257, plates 15 [A] and 17 [B]).

reads, "a tattooed savage [*sauvage piqué*] with his new weapon." The image of the tattooed woman shows her similarly marked, but without the sun design on her chest (Figure 1.16B).

Antoine Simon Le Page du Pratz was a Louisiana planter who lived in Natchez, Mississippi, from 1720 to 1728. His volume on the history of Louisiana was first published in French in 1758 and contains detailed information on the customs and ceremonies of the Natchez. About tattooing he reports:

> From their early youth the women get a streak pricked cross their nose; some of them have a streak pricked down the middle of their chin; others in different parts, especially the women of the nations who have the R in their language. I have seen some who were pricked all over the upper part of the body, not even excepting the breasts which are extremely sensible. (Le Page du Pratz 1947 [1758]:345)

About young men, Le Page du Pratz writes:

> They likewise have their nose pricked but no other part till they are warriors, and have performed some brave action, such as killing an enemy and bringing off his scalp. Those who have signalized themselves by some gallant exploit, cause a tomahawk to be pricked on their left shoulder, underneath

which is also pricked the hieroglyphic sign of the conquered nation. Whatever figure they intend to prick, is first traced on the skin with a bit of charcoal, and having fixed six needles in a piece of wood in two rows, in such a
manner that they only stick out about the tenth part of an inch, they prick
the skin all over the mark, and then rub charcoal dust over the part, which
enters the punctures, and leaves a mark that can never be effaced. This
pricking generally gives a fit of sickness to the patient who is obliged for
some time to live only on boiled maize. (Le Page du Pratz 1947 [1758]:346)

Records also exist for tattooing of other tribes in the Mississippi valley.
Father Jacques Gravier, a Jesuit missionary who traveled down the Mississippi in 1700, noted that the Houma women on the lower Mississippi "have
the face tattooed and the hair plaited like the Tounika and Natches" (Gravier 1900 [1861]:153). On the appearance of the Acolopissa and Natchitoches,
who had recently been relocated to Lake Pontchartrain, the carpenter André
Pénicaut noted in 1706:

The [Natchitoches] are handsomer and have better figures than the [Acolo-
pissa], because the [Acolopissas'] bodies, men's and women's, are all tattooed.
They prick almost their entire bodies with needles and rub the pricks with
willow ash crushed quite fine, which causes no inflammation of the punctures. The arms and faces of the [Acolopissa] women and girls are tattooed
in this way, which disfigures them hideously; but the [Natchitoches], men as
well as women and girls; make no use of such punctures, which they loath.
That is why they are so much better looking. (Pénicaut 1953 [1883]:110)

Pénicaut asserts that the Natchitoches do not tattoo, but Joutel (1906
[1714]) identified tattooing among various Caddoan-speaking tribes throughout Texas and northwest Louisiana.

Alexandre de Batz, who was an architect or engineer connected with
the French military, drew several pictures of the tribes that were visiting or
that lived in the vicinity of New Orleans in the 1730s. These images were
published by Bushnell in 1927 as part of the *Smithsonian Miscellaneous Collections*. One of the de Batz images, titled *Desseins de Sauvages de Plusieurs
Nations, N. Orleans 1735*, depicts Illinois, Fox, and Atakapa Indians camped
by the Mississippi River. Three of the Illinois men are shown carrying weapons and are extensively tattooed or painted (Figure 1.17). Elsewhere in the
picture, an Atakapa man has a vertical line down his forehead and nose, and
possibly a small facial tattoo over the left eye.

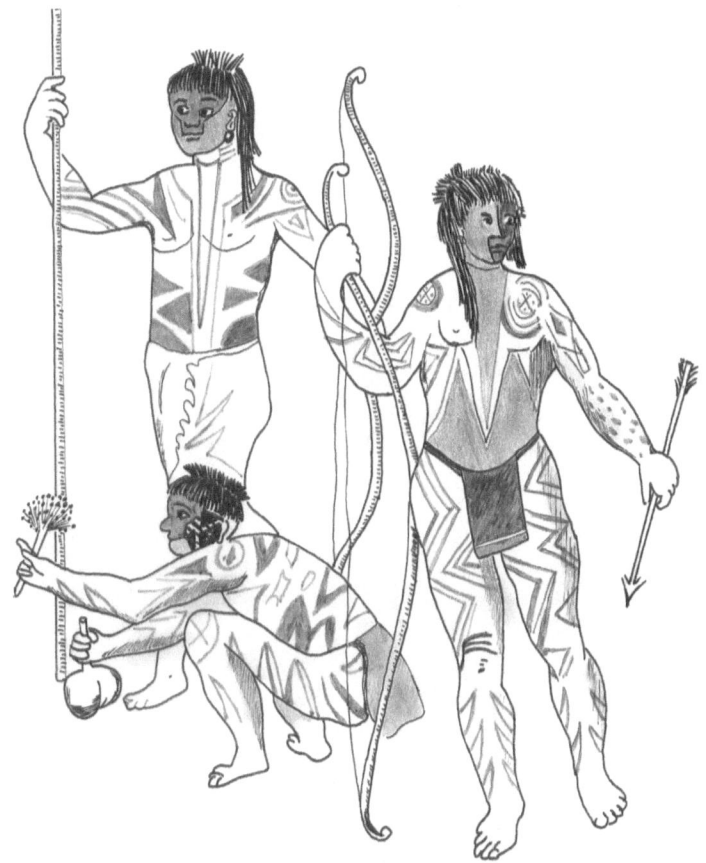

FIGURE 1.17. Detail of *Desseins de Sauvages de Plusieurs Nations, N. Orleans 1735* (after original by Alexandre de Batz, Peabody Museum number 41-72-10/20).

Another picture by de Batz, entitled *Sauvages Tchaktas Matachez en Guerriers qui Portent des Chevelures,* shows two warriors with face paint in red and black stripes, both holding poles with attached scalps. The man in the center of the image has a circle and parallel lines tattooed across his throat and a deep V-shape descending to his sternum (Figure 1.18). The upper portion of this design appears identical to the tattoo seen in the portrait of Cunne Shote (see Figure 1.13), while the V shape is reminiscent of the motif illustrated by von Reck and others (see Figures 4.7 and 4.17). A Natchez chief with a feather headdress and European shirt is seated in the background of the de Batz image. His face is painted red and black, and he appears to have a similar tattoo at his neck.

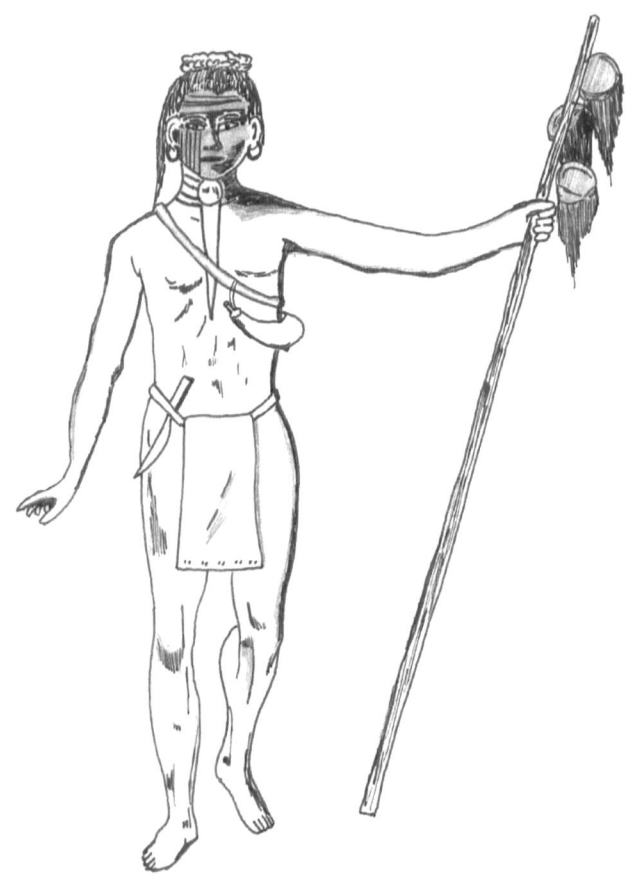

FIGURE 1.18. Detail of *Sauvages Tchaktas Matachez en Guerriers qui Portent des Chevelures* (after original by Alexandre de Batz, 1732, Peabody Museum number 41-72-10/19).

/ Nineteenth Century /

During the early nineteenth century, the new government of the United States debated the prospect of ridding itself of the "Indian problem" in the East by moving all remaining Indians to remote areas west of the Mississippi River. By the 1830s, Congress had decreed the removal of the Cherokee, Creek, Chickasaw, Choctaw, and Seminole to Indian territory in Arkansas and Oklahoma. Treaties to extinguish Indian claims in the Southeast with offers of lands west of the Mississippi were negotiated throughout the first three decades of the century. Although groups such as the Creeks and Seminoles decided to fight the U.S. government, eventually all but a few undefeated Seminole warriors in the Everglades of southern Florida and enclaves of Choctaw, Creek, and Cherokee were relocated.

Thomas McKenney, the head of the Bureau of Indian Affairs, commissioned a series of portraits of Southeastern Indian chiefs who were part of Indian delegations visiting Washington to negotiate treaties during the 1820s and 1830s. Most of these portraits were painted by Charles Bird King, copied by Henry Inman, and lithographed and published in "the Great Portfolio" by McKenney and James Hall (1836–1844). Between 1824 and 1826, King painted a Choctaw delegation from Mississippi, a Creek delegation from Fort Mitchell, Alabama, nine Seminoles, and several Cherokee and Yuchi chiefs. Half of King's Creek portraits show facial decoration consisting of either tattooing or painting (Figure 1.19). The Yuchi and Choctaw portraits have no facial decoration, and only one of the Seminole portraits appears to have face paint. None of the seven Cherokees are decorated.

In 1832 the Swiss artist Karl Bodmer traveled to America as illustrator on a scientific expedition to the upper Missouri country, organized by Maximilian, prince of Wied-Neuwied, Germany. Bodmer's work concentrated

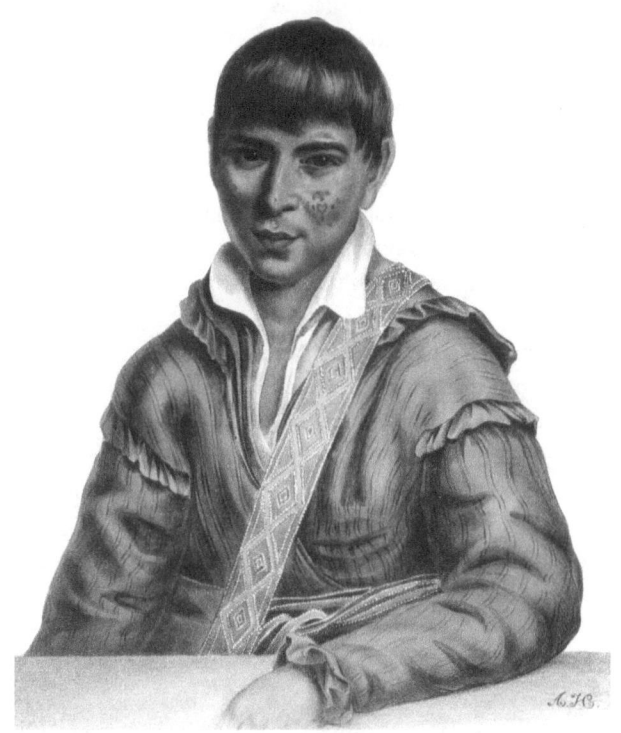

FIGURE 1.19. *Paddy Carr, Principal Interpreter for Creek Chiefs*. Painting by Charles Bird King, 1826.

on the Plains Indians and is unsurpassed in artistic and ethnographic quality. Bodmer also painted several pictures of Choctaw and Cherokee Indians during a January 1833 trip down the Mississippi to New Orleans. One of his watercolors depicting two Choctaw women and a baby in New Orleans clearly depicts facial tattooing. Both women have a number of lines from the corner of the mouth to the chin with the number of lines differing for each woman (Bodmer 1984:111).

Ethnohistorical data on Southeastern Indian body decoration reflects both dramatic and subtle changes beginning in the mid-nineteenth century. These shifts were both a result of the policies of forced removal and the consequence of ongoing acculturation. In the 1840s, Hitchcock noted that although many of the Creeks in Oklahoma refused to wear European-style clothing following forced removal, they did not retain the tradition of body painting: "They were not painted; the Creeks are dispensing with that custom except on special occasions" (Hitchcock 1930:144).

The decline in tattoo traditions during the mid-nineteenth century is reflected in the work of artists such as George Catlin and John Stanley. Although these artists tended to concentrate their attention on the tribes of the plains and Southwest rather than resettled Southeastern groups, both Catlin and Stanley also painted several portraits of Cherokee and Seminoles. Some of these images depict facial and/or body decoration among formerly Southeastern peoples, but none can be conclusively identified as tattooing.

In 1881–1882, the Swiss ethnographer and linguist Albert Gatschet studied the few Chitimacha remaining on Bayou Teche at Charenton, Louisiana, and wrote the following regarding their tattoos:

> The [Chitimacha] men . . . adorned themselves with much care and artistic taste, and tattooed their legs, arms, and faces in wavy punctured lines. . . . The warriors enjoyed a peculiar kind of distinction, as follows: Certain men especially appointed for the purpose, had to paint the knees of the warriors with pulverized charcoal, and this made to stick by scarifying the skin with the jaw of a small species of garfish until it began to bleed slightly, after which the coloring matter was rubbed on. This manipulation had to be repeated every year. (Gatschet 1882:153)

/ Twentieth Century /

By the onset of the twentieth century, documentary evidence of Southeastern Indian body decoration in general, and tattooing in particular, becomes extremely sparse. In the late 1930s Frank Speck completed an ethnological study of the Catawba still living in South Carolina, where he recorded that "neither memory or hearsay reveal knowledge of ceremonial dress or face painting" (Speck 1939:41). Less than a century before Speck sought to identify the remnants of Catawba ceremonialism, James Merrell reported that "a Catawba warrior was still feared far and wide, still cut his hair a certain way, and still tattooed his face to show his status" (Merrell 1979:57). The warriors identified by Merrell were likely among the last generations of Southeastern Indians to have their bodies permanently inscribed.

David Bushnell Jr. studied the few remaining Choctaw still living near Bayou Lacomb on the northern shore of Lake Pontchartrain between 1908 and 1909. Bushnell's discussion of Choctaw tattooing relied on informants who appear to be describing an extinct practice:

> Tattooing . . . was practiced by both men and women, but only to a very limited extent. An old woman who died a few years ago is said to have had lines of tattooing extending from the corners of her mouth across both cheeks to her ears. According to the writer's informants, no totemic devices were ever represented, and tattooing was done only as a means of ornamenting the face. In some cases the shoulders were tattooed, but no other part of the body. The method of tattooing practiced was as follows: A needle was used to puncture the skin and soot caused by a fire of yellow pine was rubbed over the surface. This was then wiped off and more soot rubbed in, to make certain that all the punctures were filled. The soot gave a bluish tinge to the dots. No other substance or color was ever employed. (Bushnell 1909:10)

The facial markings that Bushnell's informants describe are likely the tattoos known as "bridle" marks. In 1937, Choctaw judge Thomas W. Hunter remembered in an interview that "the majority of 'Six Town' Indians were known by the tattoo marks on their faces, also by the numerous ear-rings, necklaces and armlets they wore . . . The 'Six Town' Indians were sometimes called 'bridle' Indians because of the tattoo marks from the corner of the mouth to the ears" (Greene 1937:106). The eighteenth-century engraving by Bernard Romans shown in Figure 1.15 may also depict "bridle" tattoos.

/ *Conclusions* /

Traditions of tattooing among Native American groups from the southeastern United States that were recorded by the earliest European observers persisted over nearly four centuries of European and Euro-American influence before dwindling away in the late nineteenth and early twentieth centuries. The earliest data show that Native American tattooing served a variety of functions, including communicating affiliation and membership, and identifying an individual's place in the social order. The extent of tattooing on any individual was indicative of that person's ascribed status and/or achieved martial endeavors.

For most of the Indians of the Southeast, the loss of their original customs and rituals began in earnest during the mid-nineteenth century after the tribes were removed from their home lands and relocated to territories west of the Mississippi. Tattooing traditions documented among the various Southeastern groups between the sixteenth and eighteenth centuries appear to have been virtually abandoned by the late 1900s. Some ethnological studies from the late nineteenth and early twentieth centuries suggest a shift toward nonpermanent face painting to fulfill the symbolic role formerly held by tattooing. Both Speck (1907a, 1909) and Swanton (1928a, 1928b) report that during this time the formerly tattooed Yuchi, Creek, and Chickasaw used face painting to communicate membership in towns and societies. However, by the mid-twentieth century, most or all traditional Native American practices of decorating the face and body had been abandoned, or their meanings largely lost. Of the varied methods of Southeastern Indian body decoration, only the practice of scratching persisted through this period and is still practiced at some busks today.

Over the course of the late twentieth and early twenty-first centuries, and especially since the cultural movements of the 1960s and 1970s, Native Americans and indigenous peoples throughout the world have been seeking a renewed sense of identity. This search has corresponded to increased interest in languages, histories, traditions, and cultural identities that were lost, or nearly lost, over centuries of colonialism and oppression. One facet of this process has been the reappearance of traditional body ornamentation, and in particular of traditional tattooing themes and practices (see, e.g., Krutak 2010; Rainer 2004).

This review of the ethnohistorical and ethnological sources on Native American tattooing from the American Southeast presents data intended to support the work of other authors in this volume who seek to examine the social context, symbolic implications, and ancient remains of Native American tattooing traditions. This research also provides a historical background that can inform future anthropological, sociological, and art historical research into Native American body decoration. Finally, it provides a framework within which Native Americans and scholars can work together to reconstruct traditional tattooing practices, thereby contributing to the collective understanding and possible revival of this important form of Native American body decoration and communication.

/ Notes /

1. Modern translations of the Elvas narrative use the word *tattoo* in this passage; earlier English translations employ the terms *painted* (Elvas 1686 [1557]:25) and *razed* (Elvas 1850 [1557]:124).

2. In the original, *marqueté*.

3. A French version of the Laudonnière narrative published by Gaffarel (1875:63) reproduces this same passage, describing the captives as marked with "a large sign like a stamp, printed as if with a hot iron."

4. The second edition of the German text, from 1603, uses *stampfen* instead of *tattoo*.

5. French editions of Marquette's narrative use the verb *marquer*: "se marquent par le corps à la façon des hiroquois" (Marquette 1873 [1681]:75).

6. The 1998 edition of Joutel's narrative, edited by William C. Foster, presents a somewhat different version of this passage, in which no mention is made of the use of needles or the tattooed images:

> The women are quite well shaped in the bust, and their facial characteristics are rather handsome, but they disfigure themselves in different ways. Some make a stripe from the tops of their foreheads to their chins; others make a sort of triangle at the corners of their eyes, along with the marks they make on their breasts and shoulders. They also prick their lips, and once they are pricked, it is for the rest of their lives. I do not doubt that they are in pain when they do these things to themselves for the blood must gush in order for the coal to penetrate. (Joutel 1998 [1714]:219)

7. "Les hommes & les femmes sont *piquez* au visage . . ." (Tonti 1697:325; emphasis added).

8. An 1878 French edition of the Talon brothers' interrogation uses *marquèrent* (Margry 1878:610).

9. An earlier edition of Bossu's account, edited by John Reinhold Forster (Bossu 1771 [1768]:235), translates this same passage more literally as "they are marked with needles."

10. Alternately, "he then followed the drawing with great needles, pricking them deep into the flesh till the blood comes out" (Bossu 1771 [1768]:235).

< 2 >

Needle in a Haystack

Examining the Archaeological Evidence
for Prehistoric Tattooing

Aaron Deter-Wolf

/ / / /

European explorers and settlers who traveled throughout the Eastern Woodlands and Great Plains beginning in the sixteenth century left behind both textual and visual documentation of their journeys and of the people they encountered. The specific geographic areas and indigenous groups documented in the ethnohistorical record vary widely. However, one consistent aspect of these accounts is the description of permanent patterns and colors inscribed on the flesh of various Native American groups who interacted with the European chroniclers.

It is unlikely that the indigenous tattoo traditions documented throughout the Great Plains and Eastern Woodlands beginning in the sixteenth century were recent cultural innovations. However, after more than a century of scientific archaeology very little is known about the origins or material culture of prehistoric tattooing in the study area. The introduction of European metal needles as trade items quickly replaced indigenous technology and thereby permanently altered traditional tattooing practices. To date archaeologists have seldom attempted to identify the artifact remains of prehistoric Native American tattooing, and the actual antiquity of the practice both in the study area and in the continental United States remains unclear.

In this chapter I combine ethnohistorical sources and archaeological evidence to examine the material culture of prehistoric tattooing in the Great Plains and Eastern Woodlands. I begin with a discussion of the antiquity of tattooing in the region. Next, ethnohistorical and ethnographic sources are examined to identify descriptions of indigenous tattoo pigments and tools. That textual evidence is then compared to archaeological data from the region, including rare formal identifications of prehistoric tattoo needles, in an effort to recognize potential correlates. Finally, I discuss associations and context useful for identifying tattoo implements in the archaeological record.

/ *The Antiquity of Native American Tattooing* /

Archaeological evidence for the antiquity of tattooing has been recovered from several locations throughout the Western Hemisphere. The oldest direct evidence for tattooing anywhere in the world consists of human remains from the Chinchorro culture of South America, where a mummy with an upper lip tattoo has been dated to ca. 6000 BC (Allison 1996). Prehistoric tattoo traditions were widespread throughout South America, where tattooed mummies have also been recovered from the Chimu, Moche, and Tiwanaku cultures (Allison 1996; Krutak 2008b; Williams 2006). Tattooed remains from Saint Lawrence Island, Alaska, reveal that the tattooing was practiced in the Arctic by AD 380 (Zimmerman 1998).

At present there is no direct evidence in the form of ancient tattooed human remains to conclusively establish the antiquity of tattooing in subarctic North America. A number of desiccated, naturally preserved corpses were recovered from limestone caves in the Southeast during the nineteenth and early twentieth centuries, and although some of these remains have been discussed by modern scholars (e.g., Boedy et al. 2010; El-Najjar et al. 1998; Tankersley et al. 1994; Watson and Yarnell 1986), none have been carefully inspected for the presence of tattoos. It is unlikely that these markings were ignored (if present), but rather that darkening of the epidermis during the natural mummification obscured any tattoos from view.

Most of the naturally preserved human remains from the region are no longer extant. The single surviving curated example may be the "Rock Creek Mummy" from McCreary County, Kentucky, which is housed at the William S. Webb Museum of Anthropology at the University of Kentucky in Lexington. Unfortunately the Webb Museum and the United States Forest Service have both rejected proposals to conduct nondestructive, near-infrared digital examinations for tattooing on the McCreary County remains, and at best there will be limited future opportunities to establish direct proof of the antiquity of North American tattoo traditions.

There is sufficient, albeit indirect, evidence within the corpus of prehistoric iconography to suggest tattooing was practiced in the Eastern Woodlands and Great Plains by at least the first century AD. Lines and patterns inscribed on human figural representations in ancient art of the region had been tentatively identified as tattoos by the late nineteenth century

(Buckland 1888; Holmes 1883; Thruston 1890) (Figure 2.1), and the practice is now regularly mentioned in discussions of both Mississippian and Woodland art and iconography (e.g., Brown 2007a, 2007b; Diaz-Granados 2004; Giles 2010; Duncan 2011; Reilly and Garber 2011; Swartz 2001; Steponaitis et al. 2011; Walker 2004). General acceptance of the presence of tattooing among ancient Native Americans is perhaps best illustrated at the recently renovated Jones Archaeological Museum at the Mississippian site of Moundville, Alabama, where displays of life-size figures prominently exhibit an assortment of tattooed patterns on their faces and bodies (Figure 2.2).

The available archaeological and iconographic evidence, combined with the presence of geographically widespread and culturally distinct tattoo traditions throughout the entire Western Hemisphere at the time of initial European exploration, leads to two possible conclusions regarding the

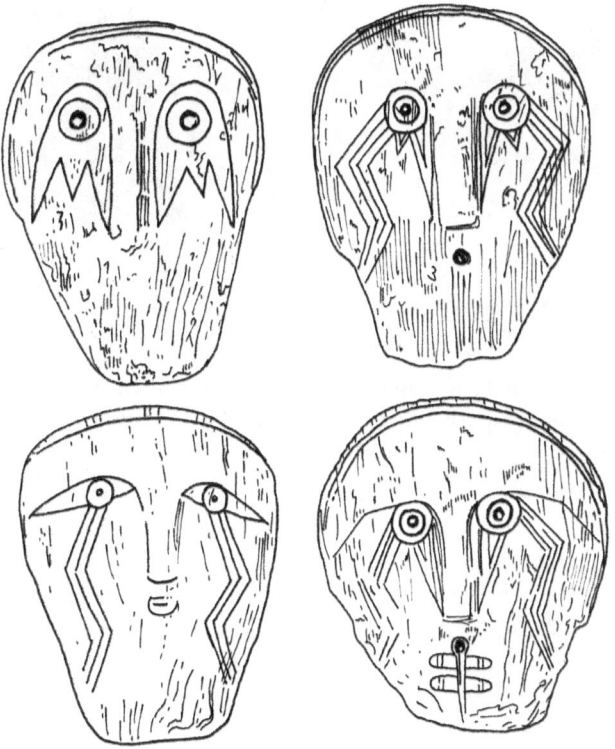

FIGURE 2.1. *Mississippian Marine Shell Masks* (after Holmes 1883: plate 66). Holmes (1883:295) writes: "These lines may . . . represent the characteristic lines of the painting or tattooing of the clan or tribe."

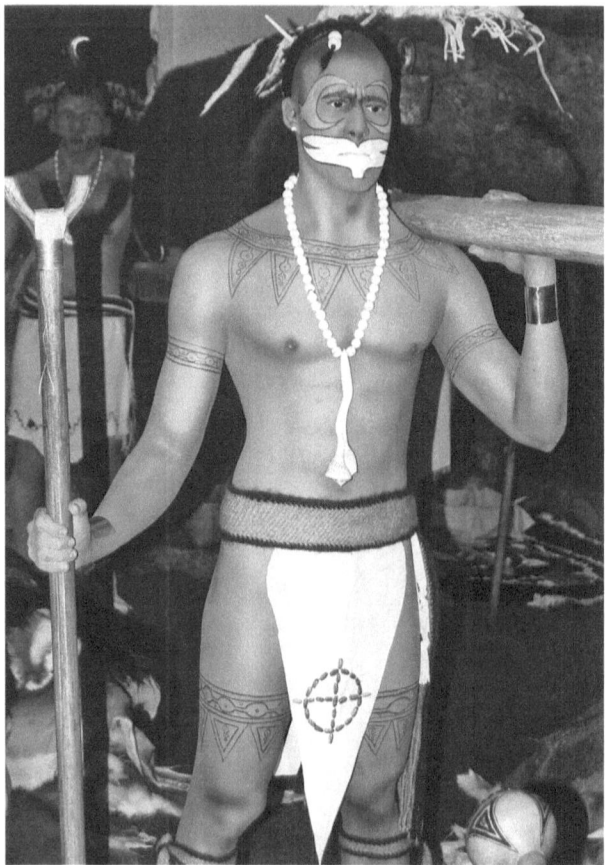

FIGURE 2.2. Tattooing displayed on the torso, biceps, and thighs of a life-size figure at the Jones Archaeological Museum, Moundville, Alabama.

origins of tattooing in the Americas. The first is that tattooing, like ceramics and agriculture, evolved spontaneously and independently in both North and South America, as well as at numerous other locations throughout the world. The second conclusion is that tattooing is one of the "symbolically mediated behaviors" that coincide with the appearance of modern human cognition (Powell et al. 2009). The identification of possible tattoo implements from Magdalenian-era France (Péquart and Péquart 1962) and the Middle Stone Age in South Africa (Deter-Wolf 2013) suggests that the practice existed by at least the Upper Paleolithic, and possibly as early as 84 KYA. If this second hypothesis is correct, tattooing belongs among the essential suite of behaviorally modern adaptations that diffused throughout the Western Hemisphere at the end of the Pleistocene along with the earliest human inhabitants.

Regardless of its specific evolution, the presence of diverse, well-established tattooing practices throughout the entire Western Hemisphere in the sixteenth century AD implies sufficient antiquity for the formation of distinct regional traditions. Although the specific time depth for the development of tattooing in the Eastern Woodlands and Great Plains cannot be conclusively determined, analysis of comparative data from throughout the Western Hemisphere seems to suggest the practice extends at least as far back as the Late Archaic.

/ Existing Archaeological Identifications of Tattoo Implements /

It would be far easier to discuss both the antiquity and material culture of indigenous tattooing practices in the Eastern Woodlands and Great Plains with the support of chronologically sensitive archaeological data. Given the millions of prehistoric artifacts recovered from the region, the ubiquity of early historic tattoo traditions, and the likely temporal depth of Native American tattooing practices, one might expect the existence of a corpus of positively identified tattoo implements in archaeological collections. However, despite thousands of archaeological investigations over the last century and a propensity of archaeologists to pigeonhole all manner of tools into descriptive categories (e.g., awls, projectile points, etc.), only a handful of instances exist from either the study region or North America as a whole where prehistoric artifacts have been identified as potential tattooing tools or tattoo paraphernalia. Those identifications that do exist include both academic and informal sources and span the entire prehistoric sequence, from the Paleoindian through late prehistoric.

Paleoindian assemblages throughout North America regularly produce both single- and multi-spur chert gravers, the function of which remains elusive. Researchers have variously suggested that these tools served to pierce hides, engrave or cut circular patterns in durable materials such as bone, antler, or wood, and most importantly to the present study, to tattoo human flesh (Maika 2010; Tomenchuk and Storck 1997; Weedman 2002). The identification of Paleoindian gravers as possible tattoo implements appears to originate in early reports from the Lindenmeier site in Colorado (Roberts 1936). This interpretation was revisited and substantially expanded by Painter (1977, 1985), who suggested that the presence of gravers at some Paleoindian habitation sites in conjunction with natural pigments such as

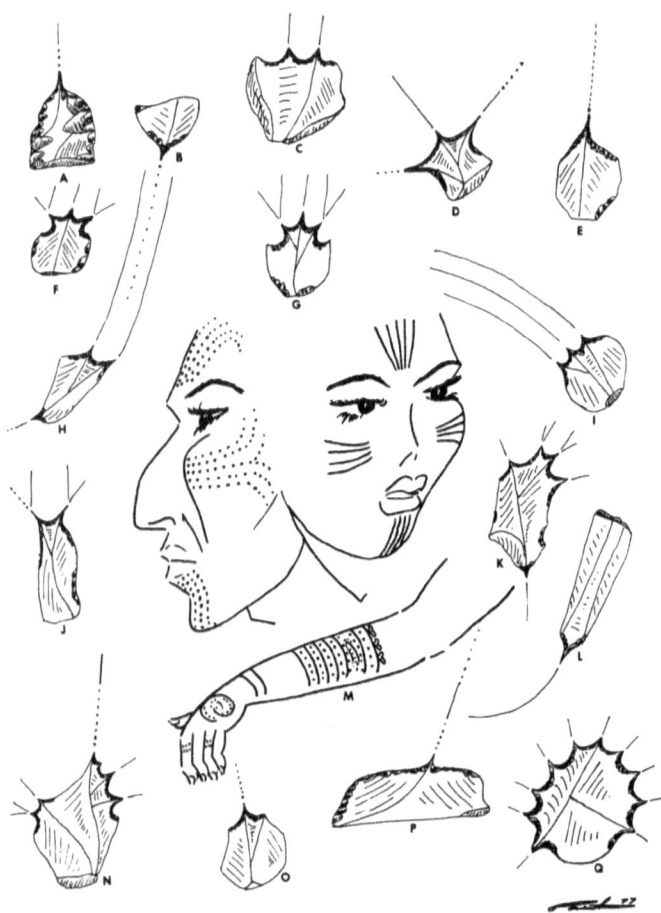

FIGURE 2.3. Illustration by Floyd Painter showing Paleoindian gravers and their possible function as tattoo implements (after Painter 1985: fig. 1). Reproduced courtesy of Rodney M. Peck.

ochre was indicative of their use in tattooing. To illustrate his hypothesis, Painter presented an image of flake gravers surrounding tattoo patterns found on naturally mummified remains from St. Lawrence Island, Alaska (Figure 2.3). Subsequent to the discussion by Painter, the identification of Paleoindian gravers as possible tattoo implements appears to have entered the conventional wisdom of North American Paleoindian scholarship (e.g., Collins 2004; Stafford et al. 2003).

During a 2009 interview with the PBS program *Time Team America*, Goodyear (2009a) exhibited a "bend break tool" from the Topper site in South Carolina that features a graver spur (Figure 2.4) and that he identifies as a possible tattoo implement. That artifact was recovered from the upper portion of the Pleistocene terrace, which has been dated to at least 18,000 BC (Goodyear 2009b; Waters et al. 2009). The graver from the Topper site therefore stands out as the oldest potential tattoo implement identified in the Western Hemisphere to date.

Excavations of late Pleistocene through early Holocene deposits at Hinds Cave, Texas, in the late 1970s resulted in the recovery of various perishable and organic materials, including examples of woven fiber and cordage. In their examination of perishable materials from the site, Andrews and Adovasio (1980) illustrate and describe a 34.5-mm-long sharpened antler tine wrapped in a coiled basket weave (Figure 2.5). The tine is set within the basket weave using resin or sap, and the weave itself shows indications of extensive wear, presumably from being tightly grasped between the fingertips of its user(s). The small (less than 8 mm) sharpened tip of the tine that extends beyond the basket weave exhibits heavy polish. Andrews and Adovasio (1980:61) refer to this implement as a "scarifier or incising tool" and note that it appears to be a unique specimen, unduplicated either within the site assemblage or in the surrounding region. This same tool was illustrated again in a 2000 *National Geographic* article on Paleoindian settlement of the Americas, where it was identified in a photo caption as a "tattooing tool" (Parfit 2000:62). A news

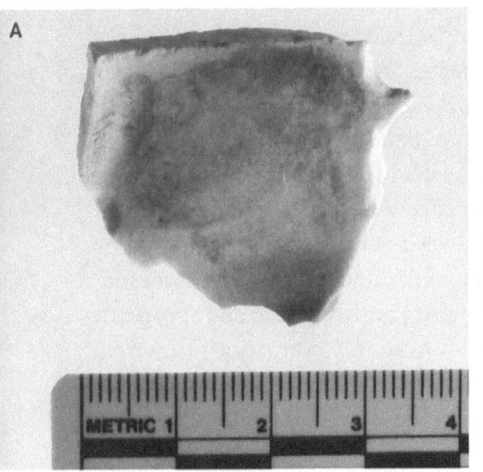
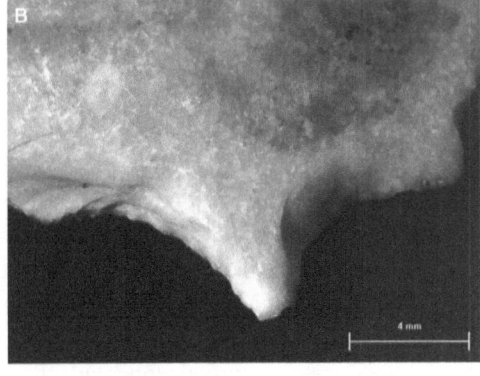

FIGURE 2.4. Chert graver from the Topper site, South Carolina (A, photo by Daryl P. Miller, South Carolina Institute of Archaeology and Anthropology; B, photo by Jim Weiderhold, Texas A&M Digital Imaging Center). Images courtesy of Albert C. Goodyear.

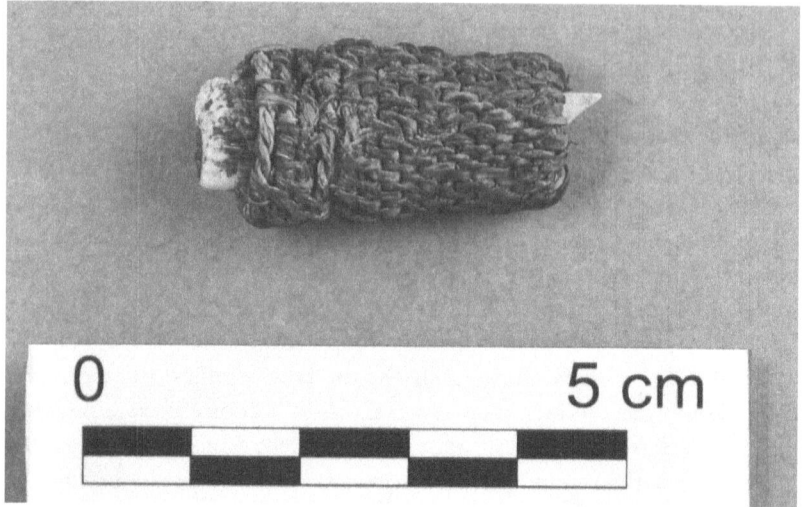

FIGURE 2.5. Antler tine "scarifier" from Hinds Cave, Texas.
Photograph courtesy of Mercyhurst Archaeological Institute.

release from Mercyhurst College (2006) later identified this same implement as a "10,000-year-old tattoo needle."

Between 2004 and 2006, the cultural resources firm of Cumberland Research Associates conducted excavations at the Hermitage Springs site near Nashville, Tennessee, to identify and remove prehistoric and historic graves within a planned development footprint. One loosely flexed Late Archaic internment of a pregnant adult female from that site (Burial 263a) contained a cache of artifacts including various faunal and lithic tools, a gorget made from a human cranium, and a set of four turkey metatarsal awls (Figure 2.6). Allen (2006) tentatively identified these awls as tattoo implements based on their extreme sharpness and the presence of dark discoloration and/or staining at their apical tips. The awls were grouped tightly together and apparently deposited within the grave inside a bundle or bag. All mortuary artifacts from the site were reburied along with the associated human remains shortly after exhumation according to state cemetery laws, and the full results of the burial removal project at Hermitage Springs have not been published to date.

In 1966, Carl F. Miller reported in the Current Research section of *American Antiquity* that work by the Smithsonian Institution–sponsored River Basin Survey in the Smith Mountain Reservoir of Virginia had recovered a "series of bone tattooing needles which corroborates the drawings John

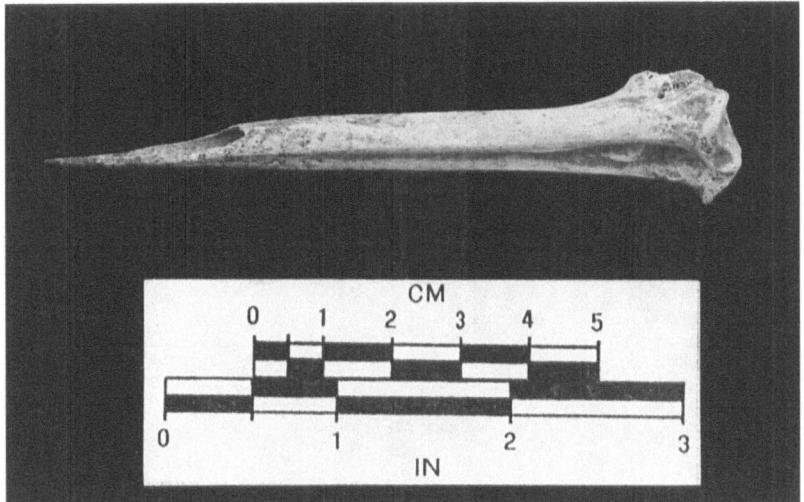

FIGURE 2.6. Turkey metatarsal awl with stained tip, recovered from Burial 263a at the Hermitage Springs site, Nashville, Tennessee. Photograph courtesy of Dan S. Allen.

White made during the early portion of the seventeenth century" (Davis 1966:903). The results of the Smith Mountain project were never published, and materials from the survey are curated at the Smithsonian and with the Archaeological Society of Virginia.

In February 2011, archaeologist Thomas Klatka of the Virginia Department of Historic Resources identified a photograph from Miller's personal papers (now in the collection of the Archaeological Society of Virginia) labeled "Tattooing needles / Smith Mountain Reservoir / 1965" (Figure 2.7). The photo displays six sharpened bone tools, all measuring between 3 and 5 cm long. It is not known what evidence prompted Miller to identify these particular implements as tattoo needles.

The artifacts are labeled with site numbers Miller assigned to the Booth Farm (44FR2) and the Fitzhugh M. Chewing's Farm (44FR3) sites. According to the Smithsonian collections database, that institution curates only two artifacts from Chewing's Farm, neither of which is among the bone needles documented in Miller's personal papers. The Smithsonian holds more than 1,500 artifacts from Booth Farm, including a single bone implement identified in the catalog as a "tattooing needle" (Smithsonian Catalog Number A485093-0; illustrated in the center-left of Figure 2.7). Miller's papers also included a proposed reconstruction drawing of a tattoo implement

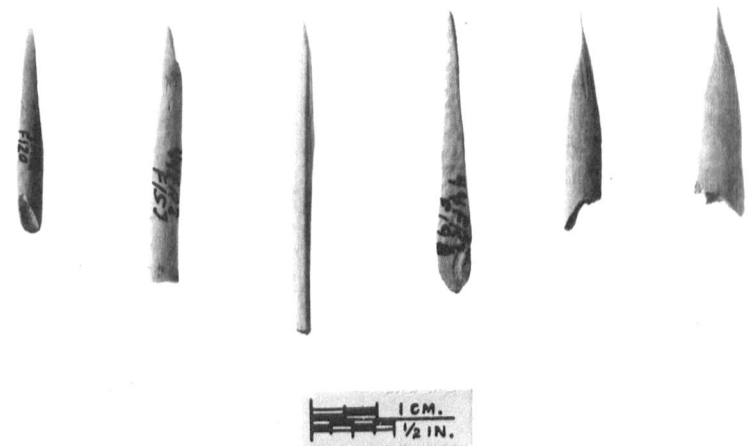

FIGURE 2.7. Photograph of sharpened bone implements from the personal papers of Carl Miller. The photo is labeled on the reverse as "Tattooing needles / Smith Mountain Reservoir / 1965." Image courtesy the Archaeological Society of Virginia's Archaeological Resource Center Library, Charles City, Virginia, and the Department of Anthropology, Smithsonian Institution, Suitland, Maryland.

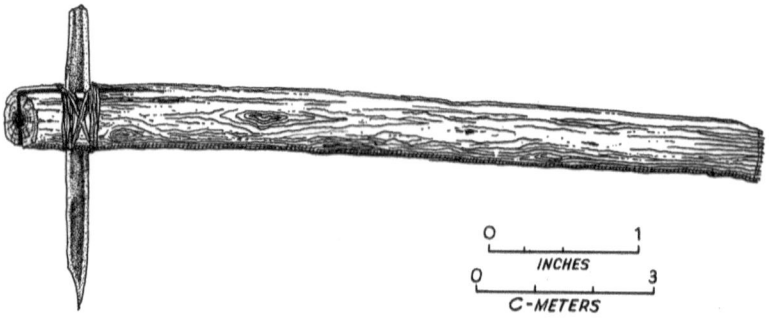

FIGURE 2.8. Drawing from the personal papers of Carl Miller showing proposed perpendicular hafting of a bone tattoo needle from the Smith Mountain Reservoir. Image courtesy of the Archaeological Society of Virginia's Archaeological Resource Center, Charles City, Virginia, and the Department of Anthropology, Smithsonian Institution, Suitland, Maryland.

incorporating that artifact hafted perpendicularly on a wooden handle (Figure 2.8).

A 1975 article by Martha Otto in *Ohio Archaeologist* describes the Low Tablet, a sandstone artifact featuring incised Adena-like designs that was reportedly collected from a mound near Parkersburg, West Virginia. In her report, Otto describes a series of grooves worn into the reverse face of both the Low Tablet and an associated whetstone. Similar grooves appear on the reverse faces of numerous other whetstones and at least three other Adena tablets (the Berlin, Cincinnati, and Wilmington Tablets) (Otto 1975; Webb and Baby 1957; Webb and Snow 1974 [1945]).

Grooved Adena tablets and whetstones are sometimes associated with bone needles, as evidenced by a burial assemblage from the Adena Mound that included a tabular whetstone along with a series of eleven elk and twelve deer bone awls (Mills 1902:471). Finds of hematite and ochre embedded in the grooves of some Adena whetstones (e.g., Dragoo 1963; Solecki 1953) suggest these artifacts also served in manufacturing pigment. Webb and Baby (1957) further postulate that the Adena tablets functioned as stamps with which to mark clothing and/or skin on ritual occasions. Based on these various interpretations, Otto (1975:33) proposes that the grooves that appear on Adena tablets and whetstones are the result of sharpening bone needles used for tattooing. This conclusion also suggests that finds of hematite and ochre embedded in whetstones are the result of manufacturing tattoo pigment.

A final identification of possible tattoo implements in the archaeological record of the region comes from the Mississippian site of Moundville in northern Alabama. Excavations at Moundville's Mound Q between 1989 and 1994 resulted in the recovery of a suite of artifacts that Knight (2004:309) identifies as a "pigment complex." In addition to ceramic pigment containers, stone mixing pallets, painted artifacts, and raw pigments, the pigment complex from Mound Q includes three fish spines that exhibit sharpening and polish on their tips (Figure 2.9A), and three others that appear "suspiciously sharp" (Knight 2004:310). The three sharpened fish spines from Mound Q come from blue catfish, drum, and an unknown perciform, and were initially identified as possible tattoo implements in an unpublished manuscript by Jackson and Scott (1998, as cited in Knight 2004). The spines were included within the formally defined pigment complex from Mound Q because of the possible association of those materials with body decoration. According to Knight (2004:313), "some part of the pigment complex may have been devoted to body paint and tattooing."

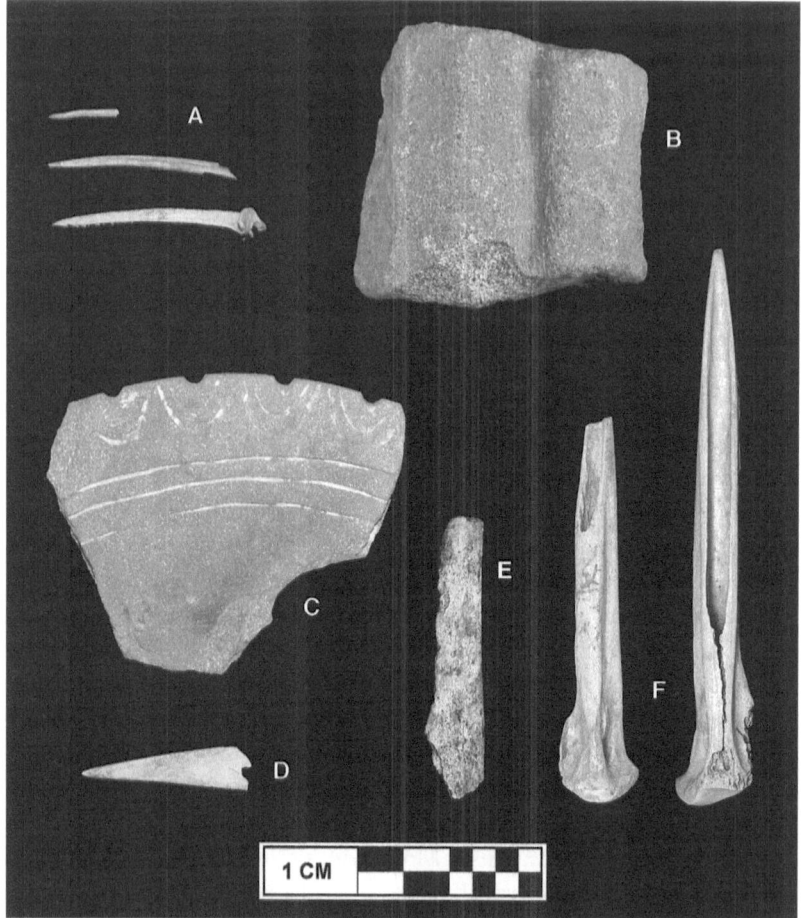

FIGURE 2.9. Selected artifacts recovered from Mound Q at Moundville.
Courtesy of the University of Alabama Museums, Tuscaloosa, Alabama.

/ *Ethnohistorical and Ethnographic Descriptions of Tattoo Materials* /

In lieu of a broad or well-accepted corpus of archaeological identifications
it is necessary to consider alternative lines of evidence when discussing the
material remains of tattooing in the prehistoric Eastern Woodlands and Great
Plains. The specific ethnohistorical evidence for indigenous Native American
tattooing has been compiled by several researchers, most notably Sinclair
(1909), Swanton (1946), Wallace (1993), and contributors to the present volume. In an effort to identify descriptions of indigenous tattooing technology

in the region, research by these scholars was supplemented by searches of additional ethnographies and ethnohistories from the fifteenth through early twentieth centuries. Some early English editions of foreign-language sources provide literal translations that better illuminate the material culture of tattooing and so were employed in lieu of more modern versions (e.g., Bossu 1771 [1768]). Finally, various Native American narratives were also examined for references to tattooing in an effort to provide an emic perspective on indigenous material culture.

Many accounts of Native American tattooing in the Eastern Woodlands and Great Plains document the existence of the practice, but include little expository information. For example, Marquette (1900 [1681]:149) simply notes in passing that the Mosopelea "tattoo their bodies after the Iroquois fashion." John Smith (2007 [1624]:283) records that native Virginians "embroidered" their bodies with images, but makes no mention of the actual items used to achieve this effect. Other sources discuss the social context in which tattooing functioned, but include no information regarding materials or methods of the practice (e.g., Dorsey 1889; Henry 1988).

Fortunately, those sources that do describe the material culture of indigenous tattooing generally include some description of both the tattoo implements and pigments used to create the final image. Ultimately this research identified descriptions of indigenous Native American tattooing technology in thirty-five sources. These accounts are summarized in Table 2.1 and include forty-eight separate identifications of tattoo implements and thirty-seven descriptions of tattoo pigments.

The influx of European trade goods into North America had a dramatic effect on the material culture of indigenous tattoo practices. Following initial contact, Native Americans rapidly abandoned precontact tattoo implements in favor of metal needles, which were "more effective and less painful" (Mallery 1886:49) than indigenous technologies. The exchange of European items also resulted in changes to the composition of tattoo pigments in the region. Several sources identify gunpowder as the postcontact pigment of choice (Filson 2006 [1784]:75; Loskiel 1794 [1789]:50), while others record the use of vermilion (Long 1791:48; Raudot 1904 [1709]:64–65).

Descriptions of Native American tattoo technology are sometimes vague as to whether the author is describing pre- or postcontact materials. All sources containing unclear identifications of tattooing tools and/or pigments were examined for additional contextual clues as to whether the materials represented indigenous or foreign technologies. In one case, an origin narrative for the Iowa Buffalo Clan recounts that a split eagle feather

TABLE 2.1. Indigenous tattoo technology identified in ethnohistorical and ethnographic accounts, alphabetically by source.

SOURCE	TOOL	PIGMENT	PEOPLE/ LOCATION
Adair 2005 [1775]:384	Garfish teeth	Soot of pitch-pine	Chickasaw/ MidSouth
Anonymous (Swanton 1946:535)	Needle A little bone	–	Natchez
Bartram 1996 [1791]:400	Needle	Bluish tinct	Creek or Cherokee
Bossu 1771 [1768]:107	Great needles	Ashes from burnt straw	Quapaw
Bossu 1771 [1768]:163	One or more needles	Black	Osage
Bossu 1771 [1768]:235	Needles	–	Alabama territory
Bressani 1899:251	Awls Needles Thorns	Powdered charcoal Black coloring matter	Huron
Bushnell 1909:10	Needle	Yellow pine soot	Choctaw
Curtis 1907–1930:4:175	Four or five porcupine quills	Powdered red willow Pine charcoal	Apsaroke
Curtis 1907–1930:5:143	Porcupine quills	Charcoal	Mandan
Curtis 1907–1930:19:156	Porcupine quill Turkey bone	–	Otoe
Dièreville 1933 [1708]:169	Needle	Vermilion	Acadia
Dorsey 1890:78	Three or four needles	Charred box elder wood	Omaha
Dumont de Montigny 1753:140	–	Pine charcoal Red cinnabar or vermilion	Louisiana
Fletcher and La Flesche 1911:503	Flint points	Charcoal	Omaha
Gatschet 1882:153	Jaw of a small species of garfish	Pulverized charcoal	Chitimacha
Goodtracks 2002a:8	Split eagle feather	Willow charcoal	Iowa
Harrington (Skinner 1926:266)	Bone points	Willow charcoal	Iowa
Heckewelder 1876 [1818]:206	Sharp flint stones Sharp teeth of a fish	Burned poplar bark	Tuscarora

TABLE 2.1. *Continued*

SOURCE	TOOL	PIGMENT	PEOPLE/ LOCATION
Isham 1949:102	Needle	Coal beat fine	Hudson Bay
James 1905 [1823]:74	Three or four needles	Pulverized charcoal	Omaha
Joutel 1906 [1714]:143	Needles	Charcoal	Texas
Jouvency 1896:279	Awls Spear points Thorns	Pulverized charcoal	Acadia
Lafitau 1977 [1724]:33	Needles Little bones	Red lead Crushed charcoal	Iroquois
La Flesche 1914:68–69	Pelican wing bones	Charcoal mixed with kettle black	Osage
Le Page du Pratz 1947 [1758]:346	Six needles	Charcoal dust	Louisiana
Long 1791:48	Ten needles Gun flint	Vermilion	Ojibway
Loskiel 1794:50	Needle	–	Northeast (?)
Mallery 1886:49	Splinter of bone	–	Hidatsa
Mallery 1893:395	Spicules of bone	–	Ojibwa
Marest 1931:124	Little sharp bones	Wet charcoal dust	Hudson Bay
Pénicaut 1953 [1883]: 110	Needles	Crushed willow charcoal	Natchitoches
Raudot 1904 [1709]:64–65	Fish bones Animal bones	Soft wood charcoal Vermilion Red earth	Eastern Canada
Sagard 1866 [1636]:347	Bone of bird Bone of fish	Black powder	Eastern Canada
Sparke (Payne 1907:56)	Thorn	–	Florida
Talon and Talon (Bell 1987:238)	Thorns	Crushed walnut wood charcoal	Cenis
Garcilaso de la Vega 1993 [1605]:413	Points of flint	–	Caddo
Von Reck (Hvidt 1980:45–46)	Needle	Charcoal dust	Yuchi
Whitman 1938:200	–	Willow charcoal	Otoe

originally used for tattooing was replaced following European contact by a "tied bunch of needles" (Goodtracks 2002a:8). The juxtaposition of materials in this account suggests the adopted needles were metal trade goods rather than indigenous technology. Those accounts that describe tattoo tools only as "needles" but provide no additional clues as to their material type or origin were nevertheless included in Table 2.1.

While sources describing only postcontact tools and/or European pigments were omitted from the table, accounts describing combinations of pre- and postcontact materials were selectively included. In the case of pigments, naturally occurring precontact colors continued to be used alongside European-introduced materials through at least the early twentieth century. Furthermore, European terms for red pigments used by Native Americans were to some extent interchangeable and independent of actual raw material type. Ethnohistorical identifications of vermilion and cinnabar-based tattoo ink may well be misnomers for locally procured, traditional pigment, and so were included in the analysis.

A number of sources specifically reference the technological shift from indigenous to European tattoo materials. When describing metal needles from a late nineteenth–early twentieth-century Iowa tattoo bundle, Harrington (Skinner 1926:266) writes that "in former times the points were made of bone." Similar juxtapositions of pre- and postcontact technologies also appear in Heckewelder, Mallery, La Flesche, and Fletcher and La Flesche (see Table 2.1). In these instances explanations of precontact technologies were included, while references to postcontact adaptations were omitted. The accounts identified in Table 2.1 inform a clearer understanding of indigenous tattooing in the region, including the methods of application as well as the pigments and tattoo implements employed prior to the arrival of European technologies.

< Pigments >

At its fundamental level, tattoo ink consists of pigment suspended in a liquid, which is mixed to form a solution of slurry-like consistency. The liquid functions as a carrier, intended to evenly distribute the pigment and prevent it from clumping. Modern tattoo inks vary widely in composition according to manufacturing company and the recipes of individual artists, and include a variety of metal, salts, and vegetable dyes as pigment bases (De Cuyper and D'hollander 2010). A number of materials identified in Table 2.1 are still incorporated in modern tattoo inks, including soot, iron oxide/ochre, and (although highly toxic) cinnabar.

A basic carbon and water mixture appears to have been the pigment recipe of choice for tattooing throughout North America at the time of European contact. Twenty-seven of the thirty-seven pigment descriptions identified in Table 2.1 specifically reference the use of charcoal, ash, or soot. This material was ground or pounded into dust and then mixed with water to create the final tattoo ink. Several sources indicate a preference for particular species of wood for creating carbon-based pigments. These include box elder (Fam. Aceraceae-Sapindaceae), poplar (Fam. Salicaceae), walnut (Fam. Juglanda-ceae), pine (Fam. Pinaceae), and willow (Fam. Salicaceae), with the last two being the most frequently identified (see Table 2.1).

The preference for carbon-based pigment in the study area corresponds to comparative data from tattooing cultures around the world (e.g., Hose and Shelford 1906; Mathur 1954; Sapir 1907; Schneider 1973; Smea-ton 1937), as well as information from recent examinations of preserved ancient tattoos in both Europe and South America. Electron microscopy of preserved tattoo pigment from the so-called Tyrolean Iceman (Pabst et al. 2009) and of remains from Chiribaya Alta in Peru (Pabst et al. 2010) revealed that the lines inked on these individuals contained concentrations of round carbon particles consistent with soot. Examinations of the Peru-vian mummy also identified tattoo pigments comprised of plant-based ash (Pabst et al. 2010).

Despite an apparent preference for carbon-based ink, there is some indi-cation that precontact Native Americans were not monochromatic in their choice of tattoo pigments. Lafitau (1977 [1724]:33) identifies the use of "red led" and states that the Iroquois would tattoo with "whatever other colour they wish to apply." Dièreville (1933 [1708]), Dumont de Montigny (1753), Long (1791), and Raudot (1904 [1709]) all record the use of red tattoo ink containing vermilion and/or cinnabar (see Table 2.1). Archaeological evidence suggests that red pigments employed prior to European arrival in the Eastern Woodlands and Great Plains relied primarily on a base of iron oxide (ochre), although Lederer (1902 [1672]:19) presents a convincing account of indig-enous cinnabar mining. Support for the use of blue tattoo pigment comes from Bartram (1996 [1791]), as well as historic examples such as the "Blue Spot" women among the Omaha (see Chapters 5 and 8 of this volume).

< Tattoo Implements >

Tattoo implements from throughout the world can be separated into three major groups, consisting of perpendicularly hafted instruments, skin-stitching tools, and in-line needles (Robitaille 2007). Perpendicularly hafted tools incorporate indirect percussion applied with a striker or mallet and are widely recognized by the general public as ancient and/or indigenous tattoo tools (see Figure 2.8). However, perpendicularly hafted tattooing technology is geographically unique, with distribution limited to portions of India, Southeast Asia, and the southwestern Pacific Rim. Skin stitching employs a small needle and pigment-infused thread to "sew" tattoo designs into the skin and was traditionally limited to the Arctic Circle and parts of South America (Krutak 2008b; Robitaille 2007).

The final category of tattooing technology is in-line needles, which include both single and grouped longitudinally hafted needles and unhafted linear implements. Ethnographic evidence from the contact-period Eastern Woodlands and Great Plains clearly indicates that indigenous tattooists in these regions were using in-line needles, as opposed to either perpendicularly hafted tools or the skin-stitching method. No examples of perpendicularly hafted or needle-and-thread tattoo implements appear in ethnohistorical accounts or historic ethnographies from the study area.

A number of ethnohistorical accounts (e.g., Bartram 1996 [1791]; Loskiel 1794 [1789]) document the use of simple, unhafted in-line needles for tattooing. However, the single-needle tattoo instrument does not appear to be a universal adaptation in the Eastern Woodlands and Great Plains. In his letters from eastern Canada, Raudot (1904 [1709]:64–65) writes that tattoos were given using "two or three well-sharpened fish or animal bones, which they bind separate from each other to the end of a piece of wood." The longitudinally hafted, in-line tattoo implement described by Raudot is strikingly similar to tools recorded by Curtis (1907–1930:4:175), Dorsey (1890), Le Page du Pratz (1947 [1758]), James (1905 [1823]), and Long (1791) (see Table 2.1). Le Page du Pratz (1947 [1758]:346) writes that hafting was done "in such a manner that [the needles] only stick out about the tenth part of an inch." Postcontact tools employing grouped metal needles in this same general configuration are identified by Dumont de Montigny (1753) and are documented historically in the Great Plains by Fletcher and La Flesche and Goodtracks (see Table 2.1; see also the discussion of Eastern Plains tattoo kits by Krutak in Chapter 5 of this volume).

Twenty of the ethnohistorical identifications included in Table 2.1 describe tattoo implements only as needles or awls. Thankfully, other sources provide more specific descriptions, including further identification of material type. These sources allow for the identification of three broad categories of tattoo implements employed in the study area prior to the introduction of European metal needles: faunal remains, botanical materials, and stone tools. The following discussion of these categories includes ethnohistorical data from Table 2.1, as well as information from the archaeological record, the natural environment, and the handful of formal and informal archaeological identifications discussed previously to provide more insight into the material culture of prehistoric tattooing in the region (Figure 2.10).

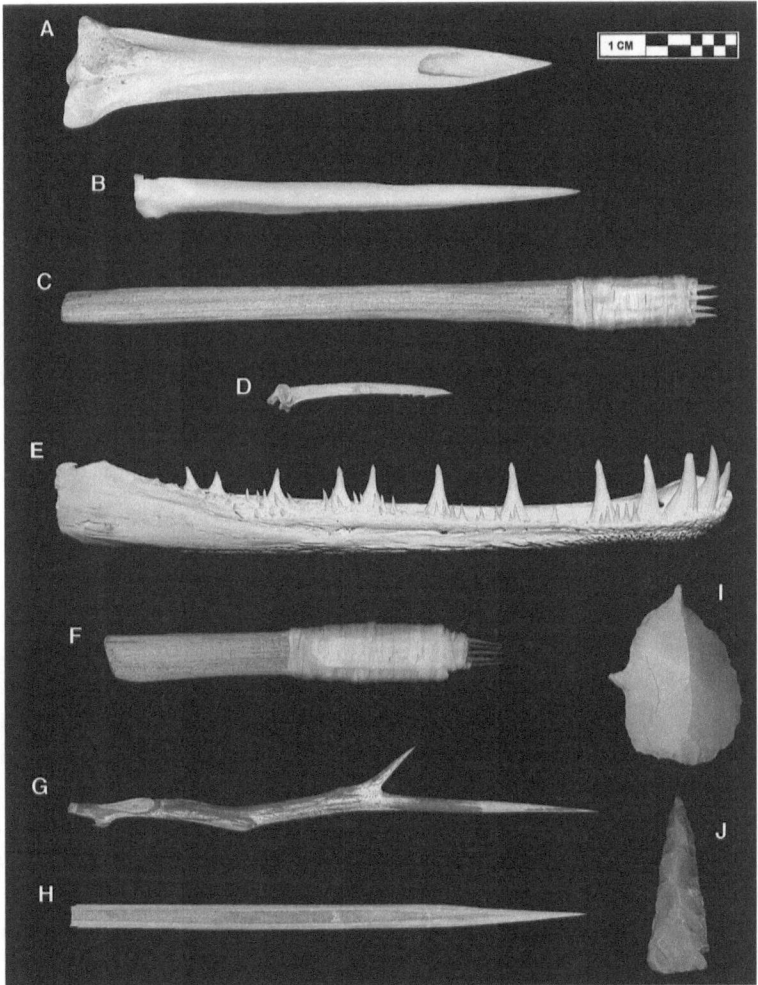

FIGURE 2.10. Reproductions of possible tattoo implements based on ethnohistorical and ethnographic sources: (A) turkey metatarsal awl, (B) deer metapodial awl, (C) hafted splintered deer bone needles, (D) sharpened catfish pectoral spine, (E) alligator gar mandible with partially intact dentition, (F) hafted porcupine quills, (G) honey locust spine, (H) sharpened river cane splinter, (I) chert graver, (J) lithic biface.

– FAUNAL REMAINS –

Nineteen of the ethnohistorical identifications recorded in Table 2.1 specify the use of faunal remains as indigenous tattoo implements. In addition to Lafitau (1977 [1724]:33), who describes tattooing among the Iroquois in eastern Canada with "needles or little bones," six other sources identify the use of faunal material consisting of small bones, sharpened bones, or bone points, albeit without specifying the specific bone employed or the animal of origin. Two other chroniclers (Raudot 1904 [1709]; Sagard 1886 [1636]) identify fish and animal bones used for tattoo implements, while Curtis (1907–1930:19:156) records that the Otoe tattooed with a "turkey bone containing a rattle." Finally, La Flesche (1914:68) notes that although the Osage used metal needles during the early twentieth century, certain portions of the tattooing ceremony suggest the tools were originally made from pelican wing bones, which were "used for doctoring as well as for tattooing."

The obvious candidates for these tools as well as the generalized "needles" identified by Bossu and others are the numerous sharpened bone implements recovered from prehistoric sites throughout the region. These bone tools have generally been classified by archaeologists as needles, awls, or points, and appear throughout the archaeological record, including as mortuary offerings, in residential deposits, and in general midden contexts. In addition to the turkey bone identified by Curtis (Figure 2.10A), raw materials for these tools were procured from a variety of animals including other birds, deer (Figure 2.10B and 2.10C), and fish (Figure 2.10D). Sharpened bones comprise the vast majority of the existing archaeological identifications of tattoo implements from the study area, including those by Allen (2006; see Figure 2.6), Miller (Davis 1966; see Figure 2.7), and Otto (1975). Finally, the fish bones described by Sagard-Théodat (1866 [1636]) and Raudot (1904 [1709]) recall the sharpened spines recovered from Mound Q at Moundville (Jackson and Scott 2002; Knight 2004, 2010; see Figure 2.9A).

Three of the accounts identified in Table 2.1 record that fish teeth were used for administering tattoos, and both Adair (2005 [1775]) and Gatschet (1882) specify the use of garfish dentition. In addition to the family Lepisosteidae (including the longnose, alligator, spotted, shortnose, and Florida gar), there are few other fish from the study area with teeth sizable enough for use as tattoo implements. Exceptions include the bowfin (*Amia calva*) and the northern pike and muskellunge, both members of the family Esocidae. These various species were present throughout much of the prehistoric Eastern Woodlands and to a lesser extent the Great Plains, with one or more species present in Florida and throughout the Gulf Coast, in Texas and Oklahoma, along the Tennessee, Mississippi, Ohio, Missouri, and St. Lawrence Rivers, and throughout eastern Canada (McClane 1978; Tomelleri and Eberle 1990).

The relatively small size of fish teeth suggests they would not have been extracted from the mandible and hafted prior to use for tattooing, but instead were left set in the jaw, which then served as a handle (Figure 2.10E). According to recent ethnographic research by Jesse Dalton (personal communication, June 2011), both longnose and alligator gar jaws with attached teeth continue to be used for scratching rituals at Hitchiti-Creek busks.

Additional faunal materials from Table 2.1 include split eagle feathers (Goodtracks 2002a) and porcupine quills (Curtis 1907–1930) (Figure 2.10F). Contact-period Native American groups throughout North America used both porcupine quills and eagle feathers for a variety of ritual, decorative, and functional purposes, such as needles for both sewing and surgery (e.g., Fortuine 1985). While use of these materials undoubtedly extended to the prehistoric period as well, their biodegradable nature has largely prevented archaeological identification or recovery.

— BOTANICAL MATERIAL —

Four of the sources identified in Table 2.1 record the use of thorns as tattoo implements. Along the Florida coast, Sparke (Payne 1907:56) records that "they use with a thorn to prick their flesh," while the Talon brothers (Bell 1987:238) describe the use of "strong, sharp thorns." Two accounts from eastern Canada identify the use of thorns alongside other tattoo implements. Bressani (1899:251) records that the Huron used "needles, sharp awls, or piercing thorns," and Jouvency (1896:279) describes tattooing with "awls, spear-points, or thorns."

The utility of thorns as tattoo implements is supported by comparative anthropological data from a number of indigenous cultures, including examples from the southwestern United States (Russell 1908), Mexico (Pennington 1963), the western and southwestern Pacific (Ambrose 2012; Krutak 2010), South America (Becher and Schütze 1960; Krutak 2006b, 2008b), and China (Krutak 2006a). The thorns employed for tattooing among these comparative groups were used singly or bundled together and could be either held in the hand or hafted to a wooden handle.

There are a number of thorny trees native to the Eastern Woodlands and Great Plains that may have provided the tools for indigenous tattooing.

These include the honey locust (Figure 2.10G) and other members of the genus *Gleditsia*, black locust (*Robinia pseudoacacia*), Osage orange (*Maclura pomifera*), Washington hawthorn (*Crataegus phaenopyrum*), and possibly some species of native buckthorns (*Rhamnus* spp.). While there are also a number of native vines and bushes with thorns, spines, or prickles, comparative data suggest these smaller and less durable examples were not used for purposes of tattooing.

Another botanical material that may have been used for tattooing is sharpened river cane (*Arundinaria gigantean*) (Figure 2.10H). This species grows along the entire eastern seaboard and west through Kansas and Oklahoma (USDA, NRCS 2011). At least one ethnohistorical source from outside the region cites the use of split or sharpened reeds to tattoo (Major 1870:37), while Adair (2005 [1775]:100) records that sharpened cane was used for ritual scratching and cutting. Sharpened cane slivers could easily be the tools that European chroniclers simply described as "needles" in the ethnohistorical record.

Any of the botanical materials described above would have been readily available to prehistoric inhabitants of both the Eastern Woodlands and Great Plains. However, all of these items are biodegradable and are rarely preserved intact in the archaeological record. Instead, their presence in the prehistoric artifact assemblage is typically limited to the recovery of burned or fragmentary materials from feature and midden contexts throughout the region.

– LITHIC TOOLS –

Including the "spear-points" (presumably chert projectile points) mentioned by Jouvency (1896:279), this research identified only five examples of lithic tools being used to tattoo. In southern Arkansas, Garcilaso de la Vega (1993 [1605]:413) records that Caddoan peoples used "points of flint" to tattoo their faces. Among the Tuscarora, Heckewelder (1876 [1818]:206) identifies the use of "sharp flint stones." Long (1791:48) writes that during his own tattooing by the Ojibwa, "where the bolder outlines occur, [the tattooist] incises the flesh with a gun flint." Finally, Fletcher and La Flesche (1911:503) record that "flint points" were employed by the Omaha prior to the introduction of metal needles.

The prehistoric artifact record of the region is replete with chipped stone tools and the debitage resulting from their manufacture, most of which exhibit at least one sharp point that could have been used to tattoo. Comparative examples of lithic tattoo implements are limited, but include flint or obsidian points once used by the Ainu in Japan (Van Gulik 1982) and obsidian blades from Melanesia (Ambrose 2012; Kononenko 2012).

The points described by Garcilaso de la Vega (1993 [1605]:413) and Fletcher and La Flesche (1911:503) almost certainly refer to bifacially flaked projectile points or knives (Figure 2.10J). Other formal stone tools that may have functioned as tattoo implements include the Paleoindian gravers identified by Painter (1977) and Goodyear (2009a) (Figure 2.10I), and bladelets from Woodland assemblages (see Chapter 3).

Prehistoric lithic debitage also provides numerous potential tattoo implements, and the tools Heckewelder (1876 [1818]:206) described as "sharp flint stones" could be either flakes or flake fragments. Experimental tattooing using lithic flakes has shown that sharp flake edges are better suited for linear cutting (such as butchering or food processing) than for tattooing (Deter-Wolf and Peres 2013). Conversely, the sharp corners and distal tips of flakes performed adequately during experimental analysis.

/ Archaeological Associations and Context for Tattoo Artifacts /

Any of the faunal, botanical, or lithic objects described above are capable of piercing human skin and thereby administering a tattoo, although experimental testing has revealed that these items exhibit varying degrees of relative sharpness and ease of manipulation that could impact their actual utility for that purpose (Deter-Wolf and Peres 2013). Unfortunately, simply recognizing the potential effectiveness of these various tools does not permit conclusive identification of tattoo implements in an archaeological setting. Without additional corroborating data, it would be both unreasonable and irresponsible to suggest that (for example) all sharpened bone awls or lithic gravers contained in the archaeological record functioned as tattoo needles.

At the present time there is not a sufficient library of use-wear data with which to distinguish patterns left on stone or bone tools by tattooing human skin from those created by processing other soft hides (Deter-Wolf and Peres 2013). While use-wear analysis may imply that an item was used for tattooing, such a claim must still be supported by supplementary data. For example, protein residue analysis could determine if an implement with appropriate wear patterns also bore traces of human hemoglobin. These overlapping layers of data might allow researchers to present convincing identifications of tattoo needles, albeit on an artifact-specific basis. Unfortunately such examinations are outside the budget and scope of technology for many archaeological investigations. In the absence of these analyses, convincingly identifying tattoo tools in the archaeological record requires their association with additional tattoo-related artifacts and settings within specific archaeological contexts.

Comparative ethnographic data from tattooing cultures throughout the world reveal that tattoo needles typically exist as part of a larger toolkit that is stored in a specialized context and only handled or deployed by specific individuals (Deter-Wolf 2013). The practice of assembling tattoo equipment and associated ritual paraphernalia within a discrete, culturally identifiable package is also documented historically in the Great Plains, where groups including the Osage, Iowa, Omaha, and Missouria stored their tattoo needles within clan-specific tattoo bundles. These toolkits held cultural significance equivalent to that of war and medicine bundles, and were believed to have been created by the founding ancestors or totemic spirits of the clan (Goodtracks 2002b:1, 2009:18; Skinner 1915b:753). Lars Krutak provides a significant and detailed assessment of traditional tattoo bundles from the Great Plains in Chapter 5 of this volume, and readers should refer to that research for additional information on these items.

Some variation exists among the specific contents of comparative toolkits and Plains tattoo bundles (Bailey 1995; Foster 1994, 2007; Skinner 1926). However, a combination of historic examples from the Great Plains and cross-cultural data allows for the identification of a basic prehistoric Native American tattoo toolkit for the study area. The principal component of the kit consists of one or more in-line implements used to administer tattoos. These might consist of individual devices such as sharpened bones or compound tools comprised of multiple small needles affixed to the tip of a wooden handle. Ethnohistorical sources and the data presented by Krutak in Chapter 5 suggest that Native American tattoo toolkits typically contained multiple tattoo implements, either to provide redundancy in case of a tool failure or to address specific stylistic needs. Along with the needle(s), the proposed toolkit would also likely include items such as stone abraders, lithic tools, or sinew for resharpening and repairing tattoo implements.

The second most essential part of the proposed tattoo toolkit consists of raw materials for creating one or more pigments. These items might include lump charcoal, ochre, and preferred wood, straw, or grasses that could be burned to produce ash. The toolkit would also include utensils for mixing the base material with a liquid to create ink and for applying the pigment to the skin.

Applicators would have consisted of various faunal materials such as bone spatulas and fur, hide, or feathers, while tools for processing and holding the pigment might include a mortar or grindstone, bivalve shells, and ceramic vessels.

The toolkit might also include a variety of medicinal materials and/or ritual accoutrements. Descriptions of historic Plains bundles by Foster (1994, 2007), La Flesche (Bailey 1995), and Skinner (1926) note the inclusion of rattles and feathers used to decorate the tattoo implements, personal adornment worn by the tattooist, incense, numbing agents, bird-bone whistles, and in the case of one Osage bundle, rabbit paws used to brush the irritated skin of the subject (Bailey 1995:55).

The final component of the proposed tattoo toolkit is the storage device itself. Historic tattoo toolkits from the Great Plains were stored inside bundles comprised of one or more wrappings made from woven fiber or the hide or skin of a symbolically important animal. These wrappings were sometimes decorated with designs that mirrored tattoo patterns (see Figures 5.5 and 5.6).

From the hypothetical tattoo toolkit described above, only certain items are likely to survive in the archaeological record. Except under unique circumstances any bundle wrappings, wooden handles, plant-based medicines, and fur, hide, or feather pigment applicators are unlikely to endure in an archaeological setting. Of the entire toolkit, only the actual needles and pigment containers (depending on material type), some vestige of the pigments themselves, and bone or stone materials used for pigment processing, tool repair, or as ritual accoutrements may survive and eventually be recovered through excavation.

The basic materials of the tattoo toolkit that are likely to survive in the archaeological record consist entirely of items that on their own can be assigned a variety of functional interpretations. Therefore, successful identification of tattoo implements within the archaeological record should at a minimum incorporate the presence of one or more potential tattoo tools alongside evidence of raw pigments and pigment storage or processing. Although other elements from the proposed toolkit are not essential to successful identification, they would greatly strengthen any argument for proposed evidence of prehistoric tattooing.

Attempts to successfully identify tattoo implements in the archaeological record must also consider the context from which any potential tools are recovered. Ethnohistorical accounts, ethnographic studies (e.g., Fletcher and La Flesche 1911; La Flesche 1921a; Skinner 1926), and evidence compiled by other authors in this volume reveal that Native American tattooing was a highly structured event that accompanied profound changes in the social and/or spiritual status of the marked individual. Tattooing took place within consecrated spaces; incorporated highly symbolic, ritually prescribed actions; employed powerful ancestral toolkits; and was performed only by specific, elevated-status individuals.

Although many ethnohistorical sources record the presence of body decoration, few chroniclers were witness to the actual act of tattooing. Two notable exceptions are the accounts of Bossu (1962 [1768]:65–66) and Long (1791:47–49), both of whom describe events surrounding their own body marking and tribal adoption (see Chapters 1 and 4). Both authors relate that their tattooing took place within restricted or consecrated space. Bossu recounts being seated on a wildcat pelt and having the floor prepared with animal skins, while Long describes the construction and use of a dedicated sweat lodge followed by tattooing within the chief's hut. Ritual actions accompanying the tattooing of both men included smoking tobacco and the performance of songs and music. While neither Bossu nor Long were privy to the specific symbolism underlying the tattoo rites, their experiences recall ethnographic descriptions of complex tattooing rituals such as the *Hon'hewachi* ceremony, recorded a century later in the Great Plains and discussed in Chapters 5 and 8 of this volume (see also Fletcher and La Flesche 1911:503–509).

Native American tattooing was performed exclusively by ritual specialists who enjoyed elevated social status and were responsible for curation and deployment of the tattoo bundle (e.g., Bailey 1995:22; Long 1791:48). Bundle keepers passed the toolkit on to the next generation once they had become "incapacitated for tattooing work by old age or loss of eyesight" (La Flesche 1921a:73), although La Flesche (1921a:73) records at least one instance of a tattoo bundle being buried with its keeper. As described by Krutak in Chapter 5, bundles that were not in use were stored in specific locations within the lodge of the bundle keeper or within corporate ritual spaces.

The ritual aspects of the tattooing ceremony, importance of the tattoo bundle, and status of the bundle keeper/tattooist described in ethnohistorical and ethnographic sources provide a significant contextual framework for evaluating identifications of possible tattoo implements from archaeological deposits. Specifically, this evidence reveals that tattoo artifacts are most likely to be successfully recovered and identified from within elite or restricted spaces such as mound summits and ritual structures, or as clustered offerings within the grave of an elite-status individual.

/ Discussion /

Several of the existing archaeological identifications of possible tattoo implements approach the above criteria with varying degrees of success. Painter
(1977:30) notes that the presence of ochre and graphite pigments at Paleoindian sites is "of equal value or in fact of most importance" in making an
association between gravers and tattooing. However, Paleoindian gravers are
not universally associated with pigments, and in the absence of specific supporting evidence any discussion of these tools should continue to be circum-
spect regarding a tattooing function.

The bone awls identified by Allen (2006) at Hermitage Springs were recovered from within a Late Archaic mortuary offering and exhibit discoloration
on their tips. These artifacts therefore meet the basic criteria of both association and context necessary for identifying potential tattoo implements.
Unfortunately, the differential coloring on the bone awls is not conclusively
pigment related, and the cache of burial items did not include any additional
materials that could be associated with a tattoo toolkit.

In her discussion of the Low Tablet, Otto (1975) makes a case for Adena
tablets and whetstones being used to process pigment and sharpen bone
needles for tattooing. As part of her argument, Otto cites a burial excavated
by Mills (1902) at the base of Adena Mound. That grave contained multiple
bone awls, a grooved whetstone, and extensive pigment remains.

The grave from Adena Mound included substantial amounts of ochre
around the bones of both lower legs, to the extent that Mills described the
area below the knees as "painted red" (1902:469). A grooved whetstone was
situated between the shins of the individual, along with three beaver incisors,
chert knives and scrapers, and a multi-toothed rib-bone "comb." Eleven elk-
bone awls and a drilled bone needle were deposited beside the exterior of the
left shin (Mills 1902:471). This burial from Adena Mound meets all the criteria for archaeological identification of possible tattoo implements, including
the presence of sharpened bone tools, pigments, and materials for tool repair
and pigment processing, all clustered within an elite mortuary context.

Evidence from Mound Q at Moundville provides the best example to
date of possible tattoo implements recovered from a restricted ritual space
and associated with both pigments and potentially tattoo-related paraphernalia. In addition to the sharpened fish spines reported by Jackson and Scott
(1998), the artifacts of the "pigment complex" include raw coloring material, fragments of stone pallets used to process pigments (see Figure 2.9C),
ochre-stained bone implements, and ceramic sherds with pigment on their

interior surface suggesting they were used to hold inks or stains (Knight 2010).

The Mound Q excavations also produced a series of materials that were not included in the formally defined pigment complex, but that are significant in light of the present research. These include a series of sandstone abraders with distinctive U-shaped grooves (see Figure 2.9B), sharpened turkey metatarsals and splintered bone implements (see Figure 2.9D, 2.9F), two spatulate bone tools made from a deer ulna and a deer rib (see Figure 2.9E), and the remains of large specimens of bowfin, alligator gar, and shortnose gar (Jackson and Scott 2002, Knight 2010).

These additional materials from Mound Q stand out because of their correspondence with ethnohistorical data and items proposed for a tattoo toolkit. As discussed previously, several ethnohistorical accounts from the region identify the use of fish teeth, and specifically gar dentition, as tattoo needles. Gar and bowfin are among the few fish from the region with teeth suitable for use in tattooing, and comprise approximately 20 percent of the relatively small sample of fish remains recovered from Mound Q (Jackson and Scott 2003). No faunal inventory has been published for Mound Q and it is unknown what skeletal elements were represented. Regardless, based on the ethnohistorical data, the small number of identifiable specimens (Knight 2010), and the presence of the pigment complex, it is reasonable to assume that the gar and bowfin remains from Mound Q at Moundville were associated with body decoration (tattooing or scratching) rather than feasting or provisioning of the site's elite residents.

When evaluated in regard to a proposed tattoo toolkit, the sharpened bone implements and bowfin and gar remains recovered from Mound Q suggest the presence of multiple in-line tattoo needles. Sandstone abraders with U-shaped grooves provide tools for needle manufacture and resharpening. Finally, the spatulate deer bone implements are strongly suggestive of horn and bone spatulas, or "rubbing sticks," used by the Iowa and Missouria for applying pigment to the skin during tattooing (Harrington 1913:111, 113; Skinner 1926:265–267). See Figure 5.6 for an illustration of a tattoo bundle that includes these bone tools.

It is important to note that neither the materials of the pigment complex nor the additional artifacts from Mound Q described above originate within a single, discrete context. Instead, proveniences for these materials include summit fill, multiple features, and general midden associations along the mound flanks (Knight 2010). This suggests the finds from Mound Q do not represent a single tattooing event, but rather a long-running association between the mound summit and permanent body decoration. Instead of a cache or bundle of tattoo artifacts, the finds from Mound Q appear indicative of a fully fledged tattoo workshop.

/ *Conclusions* /

Prehistoric iconography and the widespread indigenous traditions documented throughout North America at initial European contact suggest that Native American groups throughout the Great Plains and Eastern Woodlands practiced tattooing beginning by at least the first century AD, and possibly much earlier. However, there have been few identifications of tattoo implements from the archaeological record of the region to date.

Ethnohistorical and ethnographic accounts reveal that indigenous Native American tattoo technology consisted of both individual in-line implements and longitudinally hafted compound needles. Tattoo ink was created principally from bases of carbon and ochre prior to the introduction of European trade goods. The materials used to manufacture tattoo needles, tool configurations, and specific pigment ingredients likely varied by region, and possibly by lineage or clan, although there is not sufficient data to identify those variations at this time.

Comparative evidence suggests that ancient Native American tattoo needles are unlikely to have traveled as individual items, but instead functioned as part of larger toolkits associated with both the functional and symbolic aspects of the tattooing process. The intricacies of differential preservation dictate that only a fraction of the overall tattoo toolkit is likely to survive within the archaeological record and be available for modern identification. To successfully identify a tattoo needle in the archaeological record therefore requires at a minimum the convincing association of that artifact with pigment remains, and if possible with an assortment of supporting materials such as implements for pigment processing and application, artifacts for tool repair and maintenance, and varied ritual accoutrements. This identification can be further strengthened by the context of the find, and specifically the deposition of those materials within a ritual or elite setting.

Ethnohistorical accounts of Native American tattooing beginning in the sixteenth century describe a varied, widespread, and ancient tradition, the material culture of which was rapidly replaced by introduced European technologies. The present research has attempted to use ethnohistorical and ethnographic accounts, and the few existing identifications of potential tattoo implements from the Eastern Woodlands and Great Plains to provide a window into the archaeological footprint of prehistoric tattooing in the region. Careful examination of both existing collections and new archaeological data using the criteria described in this chapter allows us to begin creating a corpus of well-reasoned identifications of potential prehistoric tattoo implements and, in doing so, to acknowledge the material remains of this significant and overlooked aspect of ancient Native American life.

/ Author's Acknowledgments /

Many individuals provided research support that made this chapter possible, including John Broster, Suzanne Hoyal, Tanya Peres, Lars Krutak, Jim Knight, Mary Bade, Teresa Ingalls, Jolene Smith, Tom Klatka, Joey Moldenhauer, James Adovasio, Jeff Illingworth, Dan Allen, Jesse Dalton, and Bretton Giles. This chapter is based on research presented in the 2009 (66th) Southeastern Archaeological Conference symposium, "Tattooing and Body Modification in the Prehistoric and Early Historic Southeast," organized by the author, and the symposia "Tattoos and Body Modification in Antiquity (I and II)," organized by Philippe Della Casa and Constanze Witt for the 2010 and 2011 (16th and 17th) European Association of Archaeologists meetings.

< 3 >

Swift Creek Paddle Designs as Tattoos

Ethnographic Insights on Prehistoric Body Decoration and Material Culture

Benjamin A. Steere

/ / / /

Swift Creek complicated stamped pottery is one of the most elaborately decorated forms of pottery in eastern North America (Figure 3.1). Found primarily in Georgia and adjacent states at sites dating to the Middle and Late Woodland period (ca. AD 100–850), this pottery is distinguished by complex naturalistic and geometric designs that were applied to pots with carved wooden paddles (Broyles 1968; Snow 1998; Wallis 2011; Williams and Elliott 1998). In recent years, great progress has been made in interpreting the meaning of the designs stamped on Swift Creek pots (Saunders 1998; Snow 1998; Wallis 2007), in delineating the movement of Swift Creek pots and paddles across the Southeast (Stoltman and Snow 1998), and in understanding social interaction in the Middle and Late Woodland period through the study of the distribution of Swift Creek pottery designs at multiple spatial scales (Saunders 1998; Snow 1998; Pluckhahn 2007; Wallis 2006, 2007, 2011).

Southeastern archaeologists have long wondered if Swift Creek pottery designs were used in body decoration, especially tattooing (Figure 3.2). In their edited volume on Swift Creek archaeology, Mark Williams and Dan Elliott suggested that the designs found on Swift Creek pots "symbolized ideas that were presumably important to the people" and that "there is no reason not to suppose that these symbols were also painted on a wide variety of items, woven into baskets, and even tattooed onto their bodies" (Williams and Elliott 1998:10).

Using this idea as a point of departure, I looked for ethnographic and archaeological evidence to support this admittedly speculative claim. First, are there cross-cultural data to suggest that people painted or tattooed similar designs on their bodies and on material culture such as pottery, basketry,

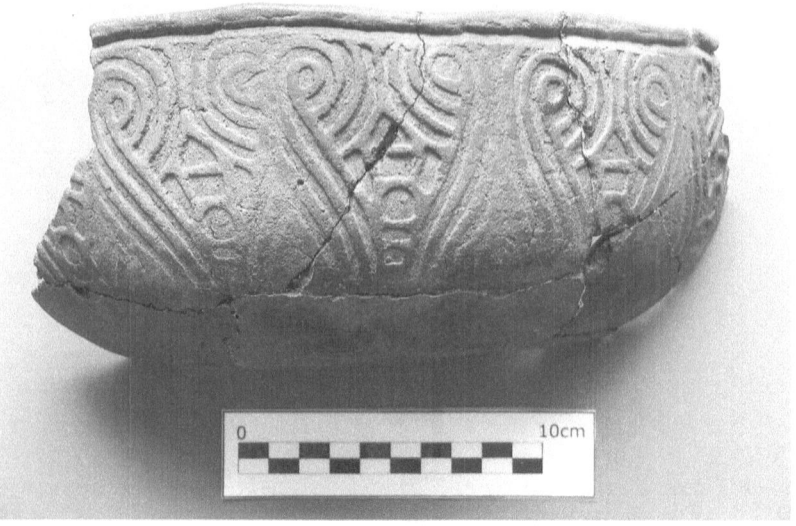

FIGURE 3.1. Swift Creek vessel fragment from the Leake site (9BR663), Bartow County, Georgia. Photograph courtesy of Scot Keith, Southern Research, Historic Preservation Consultants, Inc.

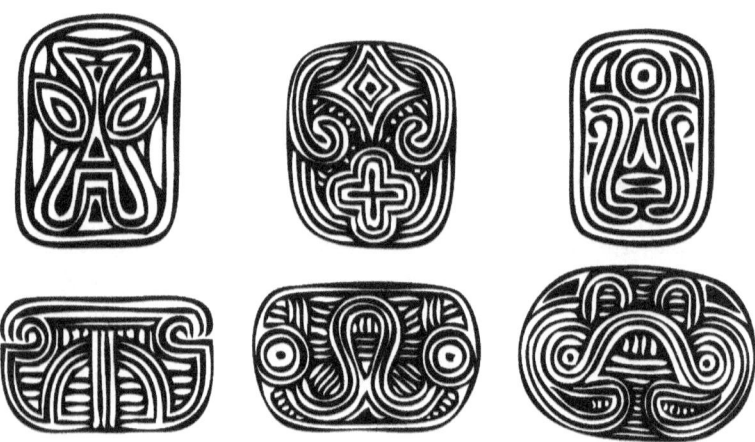

FIGURE 3.2. Swift Creek pottery designs from the lower Ocmulgee River valley in Georgia (redrawn from Snow 1998:64, fig. 6.1). Snow (1998:63) describes the top three designs as "mask-like," while the bottom three may represent "unidentified creatures."

and carved wooden objects? Second, do archaeological data from Middle and Late Woodland period sites with Swift Creek pottery provide any material evidence for tattooing or other body decoration?

In this chapter I discuss the results of my ethnographic research and identify possible archaeological evidence for tattooing in Swift Creek assemblages. There are good historic and ethnographic case studies from Africa, Brazil, Borneo, and Polynesia illustrating the tendency for certain culturally important design elements and motifs to be applied to people, pots, and carved wooden objects. Beyond showing that people will decorate their bodies with the same designs that appear on material culture, these case studies reveal common themes about the connections between body decoration and craft production that offer new insight for understanding social life in the prehistoric Southeast. The archaeological evidence for Swift Creek tattooing is more limited, but three classes of artifacts—bone awls, prismatic blades, and human effigies—point to the possibility of tattooing in the Middle Woodland Southeast.

/ Cross-Cultural Evidence /

Descriptions of tattooing and other forms of body decoration are commonly found in historic accounts of indigenous groups written by European explorers, traders, and missionaries dating from the late fifteenth to the early twentieth centuries. Many of these accounts are sensational and are clearly written with the intent of emphasizing the "otherness" of non-Western societies (Schildkrout 2004:327). However, some of these documents contain useful descriptions and illustrations of body decoration that can be extracted from their ethnocentric context.

Modern anthropological studies of body decoration are more reliable. Until the 1990s, much of the scholarship on tattooing focused on the role of body decoration as a marker of gender, age, and status. More recent work focuses on themes of modernity, authority, authenticity, and representation (Schildkrout 2004:319–321). Fortunately for archaeologists, some researchers have paid close attention to the relationships between body decoration and material culture. Examples include Berns's (1988, 1990) work with scarification and pottery in northeastern Nigera and Gell's (1993) multifaceted study of Polynesian tattooing. These recent studies, combined with the less sensational early documents, provide valuable information for exploring the relationships between body decoration and material culture.

This research began with venerable sources such as the Human Relation Area Files and the Handbook of South American Indians (Steward 1948) and proceeded by following leads into historic accounts and ethnographies. The goal of the investigation was to identify descriptions of body decoration in societies with a well-documented history of pottery making, basket making, or woodcarving. The search was limited to documents that described the cultural context of body decoration and compared the designs used on the human body to designs used on other media. While there is no shortage of descriptive accounts of body decoration in the historical and ethnographic literature, fewer case studies place the practice in a broader context. Geographic coverage was broad, and produced the best examples from Africa, Brazil, Polynesia, and Borneo.

< Africa >

Nicholas David, Judy Sterner, and Kodzo Gavau (1988) found notable similarities in the decoration of pots and people among Mafa and Bulahay potters in northern Cameroon. Mafa and Bulahay potters often compare their vessels to the human body, stating that pots have "mouths, necks, bodies, bellies, navels, lower parts (*vuzi*, i.e. bases), and arms (*ray*, i.e. handles)" (David et al. 1988:371). Two design motifs, spirals and a raised bump or "spike" representing millet, are used in the decoration of both pottery and the human body (David et al. 1988:376). On pots, these designs are incised as bands along the shoulders of the vessel. The motifs appear on people as spiral bracelets worn around the wrists and as raised keloid bumps, also applied in bands, drilled into the skin with a razor or sharp straw (David et al. 1988:370). Potters claim that the designs used in vessel manufacture and body decoration bring good luck and ward off evil (David et al. 1988:374).

The research by David and his colleagues demonstrates that the same symbols are applied to people and pots. Moreover, these protective motifs extend into other categories of material culture. The millet, or "spike," motif adorns the walls of house compounds and iron-smelting furnaces, and appears in ritual costumes (David et al. 1988:375–376). Mafa and Bulahay potters distinguish between male and female vessels, and gendered forms of body decoration may also play out on the surface of pots, although this pattern is less clear.

Berns (1988) documents similar practices in Ga'anda communities in northeastern Nigeria, where abstract geometric designs used in scarification also appear on portable objects and houses. Ga'anda body decoration is strictly gendered, and the practice is intertwined with marriage ceremony. Only women practice scarification, referred to as *Hleeta*. This process begins when a girl turns five or six years old. Older women apply the designs with an iron needle and a razor in a series of six biennial stages over several years (Berns 1988).

Marriages in Ga'anda society are arranged for children before they reach adolescence, and substantial bridewealth payments are expected of the groom's family. Postmarital residence is generally patrilocal, and descent is patrilineal. Each stage of scarification coincides with symbolic exchanges between the families of the bride and groom. For example, after the second stage of *Hleeta* scarification, the groom's family gives a gift of iron hoes to the bride's family, and after the fourth stage, the groom's family provides corn beer in large pots to the family of the bride (Berns 1988:60–62). Girls are not eligible for marriage until they have received the complete body decoration treatment, and sometimes the last *Hleeta* stage is postponed until the groom's family can meet the last of the bridewealth payments (Berns 1988:62).

The design motifs used in *Hleeta* consist of raised dots arranged in rows, arcs, triangles, lozenges, and chevrons (Figure 3.3A). The same design patterns are used by all Ga'anda groups, even though some of the communities have been geographically separated long enough to develop distinct dialects (Berns 1988:57). Similar designs appear on what Berns (1988:68) refers to as "public arts," including beer pots, baskets, armlets and charms, and the exterior walls of houses and granaries. These objects are all involved in marriage exchanges, and the portable utilitarian objects are used primarily in

A B

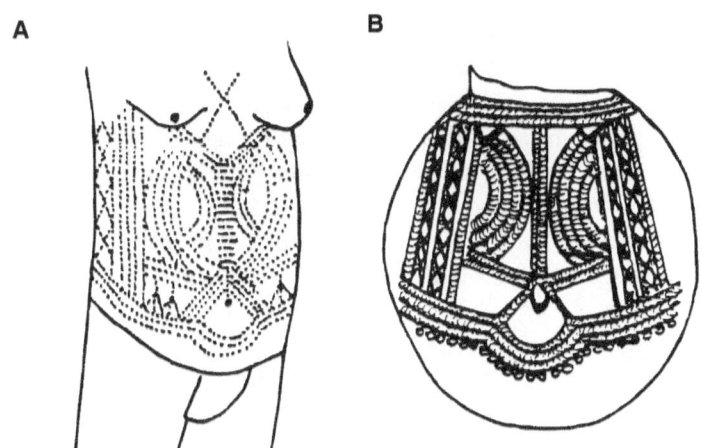

FIGURE 3.3. *Hleeta* designs applied to pottery and female bodies. Note the appearance of lozenges, curves, vertical lines, chevrons, and scallops in both illustrations, and the overall similarity of both compositions (after Berns 1988:73, fig. 18).

women's agricultural activities. Berns (1988:69–71) argues that the shared design elements on women's bodies, beer pots, baskets, houses, and granaries emphasize the importance of women's subsistence contributions and their role in maintaining household stability in a patrilineal society where men wield much of the official political power.

Hleeta designs also appear on anthropomorphic pots used in mortuary ritual. According to Ga'anda cosmology, deceased ancestors can influence the affairs of the living, and special pots play an important role in mediating the relationship between the living and the dead. According to Berns (1988:71), "as the spirit or soul of the deceased does not leave the world of the living immediately, it is temporarily relocated in a ceramic vessel, called a *hlefenda*, so it can be attended and placated for one full seasonal cycle." The pot is placed in the household of the deceased, and relatives drink corn beer from the vessel on special occasions. After one year the pot is broken in a special ceremony, releasing the spirit of the now-appeased ancestor into the next world. The *hlefenda* is a large, long-necked jar whose body is decorated with *Hleeta* designs (Figure 3.3B). Berns (1988:73) argues that the *Hleeta* motifs, and the act of inscribing these markings on people and pots, signal permanent transitions in the Ga'anda life cycle, for example, girl-to-woman and life-to-death. *Hlefenda* pots are the same for both male and female ancestors. While *Hleeta* designs are used strictly for female body decoration, they seem to cross-cut gender lines in mortuary symbolism.

Anthropomorphic pots are used for ceremonies honoring ancestors in Yungur farming communities, also located in northeastern Nigeria (Berns 1990). In Yungur society, anthropomorphic pots called *wiiso* are said to contain the spirit of deceased male leaders (Berns 1990). These pots are a kind of portraiture in that each one is unique and meant to resemble the person it commemorates. The pots are decorated with designs used in Yungur scarification. There are additional symbolic links between pots and people in Yungur mortuary ritual. While *wiiso* are placed in ancestral shrines, the bodies of Yungur chiefs are buried in large cooking pots in sacred areas such as caves (Berns 1990:57). This practice reinforces the concept of *wiiso* as the embodiment of deceased leaders.

< Brazil >

Ethnographic evidence from eastern and central Brazil shows that certain symbols appear in both pottery decoration and tattooing. In a nineteenth-century account of Bakairi communities along the Kulisehu River in central Brazil, Karl von den Steinen described tattooing in several villages. Designs were generally a series of straight or curved lines executed with a sharp thorn or dogfish tooth and a mixture of soot and plant juice dye (Steinen 1894:180–181). He observed similar motifs in tattoos and surface treatment on pottery, especially in the village of Mehinakú. Steinen writes, "The men had as tattooing a line or a double line that followed the inner contours of their shoulder blades, sometimes as obtuse or approximately right angles which have the vertex turned toward the spinal column, sometimes as an arc—a design that . . . appears outside on the *bottoms of the large pots*" (Steinen 1894:181, emphasis added). Mehinakú women tended to have two small curved lines tattooed as armbands, a motif that also appeared in the center of pots made in their village (Steinen 1894:310).

Tattoos in the Mehinakú village varied by gender and were used to mark group affiliation. In a passage that points to one social function of tattoos in a neolocal residence pattern, Steinen (1894:181) claims, "According to the Indian conception, the sons belong to the tribe of the mother, and in every case they visit the tribal village of the mother under peaceful circumstances. It is certain that the Mehinakú women and the Mehinakú pots bore their home stamp."

Among Tupinamba communities along the eastern coast of Brazil, tattoos designs were abstract geometric forms usually applied by rubbing a mixture of charcoal and plant dye into cuts made with sharp rodent teeth or shell (Métraux 1948:108). Although there are few detailed descriptions of the designs, they were apparently very similar to patterns on pottery (Métraux 1948:108). Both men and women were tattooed, and for men, tattoos seem to have been badges of achievement for success in warfare (Métraux 1948:108).

< Borneo >

Ethnographic accounts of indigenous communities in Borneo point to strong connections between tattooing and woodcarving rather than pottery production (Jensen 1974; Sandin 1980). Although a connection between body decoration and pottery decoration may once have existed, imported Chinese pottery had already replaced most indigenous container technology by the time of the earliest historical and ethnographic accounts. However, traditional woodcarving practices continued into the twentieth century (Haddon 1905).

Shared imagery in woodcarving and tattoos is well documented in ethnographic accounts of Kayan-speaking communities from Sarawak in the early twentieth century, and especially in Charles Hose and R. Shelford's (1906) "Materials for a Study of Tatu in Borneo." Kayan tattoo designs were generally geometric and naturalistic. The primary motifs were zigzags, hourglasses, and stylized animals such as dogs and hornbills (Hose and Shelford 1906).

FIGURE 3.4. The Kayan dog motif, used in tattooing
and woodcarving (after Haddon 1905:177, fig. 4).

The stylized dog motif was an important design element in woodcarving
on house beams, wooden tools, and wooden structures erected over tombs
(Figure 3.4), and seems to have had religious significance (Haddon 1905:117;
Hose and Shelford 1906:66).

Kayan tattoo designs were carved in high relief onto wooden blocks (Figure 3.5). These wooden blocks were dipped into ink and applied as stencils
onto the body (Hose and Shelford 1906). The artist would then follow the
outline and tattoo a mixture of soot, water, and sugarcane juice into the skin
with a wooden needle struck with an iron baton. While these wooden tattoo paddles are exciting pieces of evidence for a Swift Creek researcher, the
more salient point is the clear overlap in technical skills and design motifs in
woodcarving and tattooing.

There are good descriptions of the social context surrounding Kayan tattooing, especially with regard to gender. Men generally carved the blocks,
while women performed the tattooing and were considered experts on the
"significance and quality of tattoo design" (Hose and Shelford 1906:68).
Women received extensive tattoos over their forearms, thighs, and feet, often
over a period of years as a rite of passage into adulthood (Hose and Shelford
1906:67). The tattooing of girls was a rite of passage surrounded with ceremony, feasting, and dietary taboos. During a series of tattooing episodes,
the tattoo artist would be paid for her work in food and other commodities.
Women interviewed by Hose and Shelford (1906:69) claimed that it was
"considered bad luck to draw the blood of a friend"; thus the payment seems
to have placed some social distance between the giver and recipient of the
tattoo, but also reinforced social networks in the community via exchanges
of services and goods.

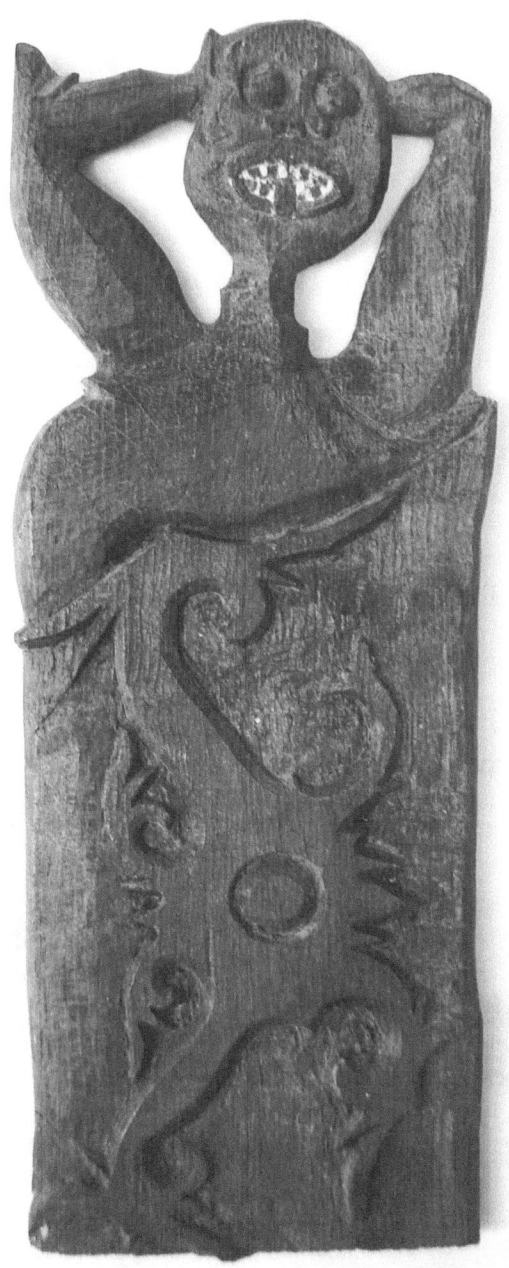

FIGURE 3.5. Carved wooden Kayan tattoo block collected in the early twentieth century. © Trustees of the British Museum, registration number As1905C3.318.

Less ceremony was attached to the tattooing event among men. Tattoos on the upper arms, chest, and back seem to have been for personal adornment and were applied through boyhood into adulthood. However, tattoos on the back of the wrists and fingers, and in some cases the thighs, were badges of achievement in warfare, and could only be applied after taking enemy heads (Hose and Shelford 1906:64–65). This pattern of behavior is reminiscent of Adair's account from the American Southeast of tattooing among Chickasaw, who also used tattoos as markers of male status and would forcibly remove any unearned marks (Adair 2005 [1775]:384).

< Polynesia >

Some of the most vivid historic and ethnographic tattoo literature comes from Polynesia. In Tikopia, Raymond Firth (1937) described tattooing in the late 1920s. Tattoo artists applied designs using a soot-based dye, bone or wood needles, and a baton. Tattoo designs were either geometric lines or naturalistic designs, such as stylized fish, and some were very similar to patterns carved on the hulls of canoes. For both men and women, tattoos served primarily as personal adornment, and the tattooing event was not surrounded by any particular ritual. Tattoo artists were usually male and were considered to be skilled experts (Firth 1937:176). Payment for the service, referred to as "the sharpening of the tattoo" (Firth 1937:176), was rendered to the artist upon completion of the operation and usually took the form of food or a day of agricultural labor.

For the Marquesas, early twentieth-century accounts paint a similar picture of tattooing, but the relationship between tattooing and woodcarving is more clearly delineated. Men and women were tattooed, and tattoos were a marker of adult status for women (Handy 1922:5). As in Tikopia, tattoo artists were male and were given payment for their work. In her 1922 study of tattooing in the Marquesas, Willowdean Handy noted that many geometric designs and specific naturalistic motifs, such as a stylized "brilliant eye" (Figure 3.6), woodlouse, and "underarm curve" appear both in tattoos and on carved wooden bowls, paddles, and housepoles (Handy 1922:19–23).

The use of domestically produced pottery for cooking and storage ceased in Polynesia during the first millennium AD (Rainbird 1999:218). However, the Lapita pottery style, which is found over much of Polynesia between 1500 and 300 BC, is decorated with geometric designs that are nearly identical to patterns on historically recorded tattoos, woodcarving, and barkcloth (Green 1979a, 1979b) (Figure 3.7). Researchers in Polynesia generally agree that there is historical continuity between the designs on prehistoric pots and historic

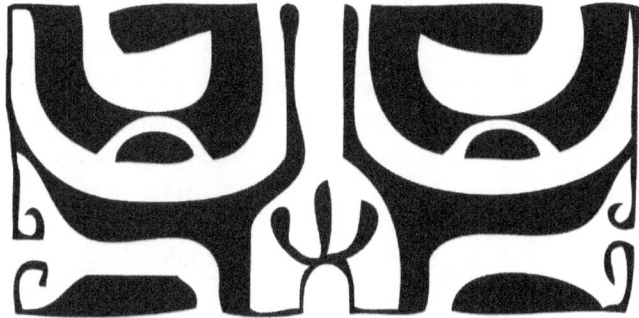

FIGURE 3.6. The "brilliant eye" motif from the Marquesas. In the early twentieth century, this motif was applied to wood carvings and female leg tattoos (after Handy 1922: plate 26e).

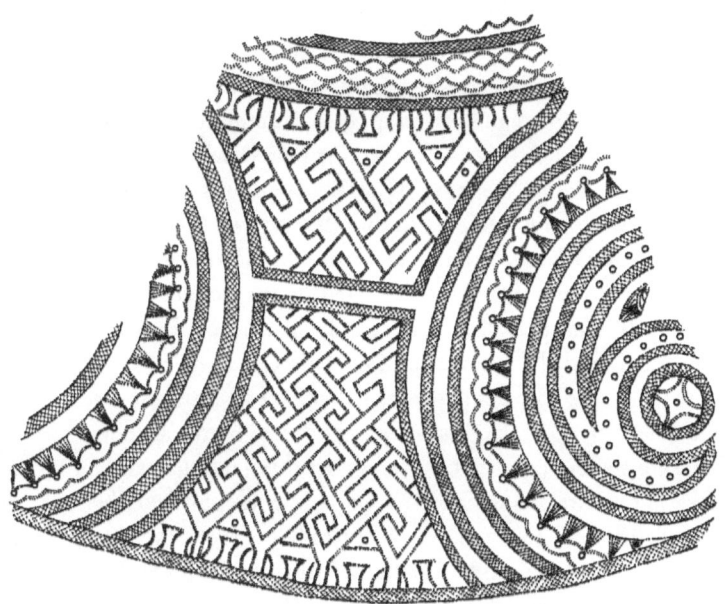

FIGURE 3.7. Lapita pottery designs also used in tattooing (after Green 1979a:57, fig. 1.5).

tattoos (Rainbird 1999:219), although this assumption has recently been critiqued by Ambrose (2012). Patrick Kirch (1997:142) makes the technological argument that Lapita pottery designs were extended to tattooing because "the dominant technique used for decorating the clay was the same as that used for piercing the human skin."

< Swift Creek Pottery Designs >

Several themes that emerge from this review of ethnographic literature support the idea that Swift Creek pottery designs may have been used in body decoration. Across the ethnographic cases, general design elements and specific motifs shared among body decoration, pot making, and woodcarving have common features. They are primarily geometric or naturalistic, and they follow a basic visual grammar. Clearly identifiable design elements are repeated across media and are combined in different ways to create novel forms. In many cases these elements are important cultural symbols. In the Mafa and Bulahay examples, a spiral representing millet is applied to pots, jewelry, and bodies in different ways. However, in each case the spiral element is legible to informed viewers and is understood to be a good luck symbol that wards off evil (David et al. 1988). In Ga'anda communities, a lozenge and triangle symbolizing fertility are common elements in more complex designs found on women's bodies, ceramics, baskets, and houses (Berns 1988).

The same rules of design seem to apply in the ethnographic examples from Brazil, Borneo, and Polynesia, but unfortunately few of the records from these areas discuss the meaning of particular motifs. Haddon (1905) and Hose and Shelford (1906:66) claim that the dog was "venerated" by Kayan, and that the dog motif was a religious symbol. However, in their published accounts they do not show how it is used on carved wooden objects other than tattoo blocks. It is clear that the "brilliant eye" from the Marquesas (Handy 1922), and the geometric designs described by Steinen (1894) and Métraux (1948) are core design elements applied on different media, but the specific meaning of the designs was not discussed by the authors.

There are obvious parallels between these ethnographic examples and Swift Creek design motifs. Most Swift Creek paddle designs are either geometric or naturalistic (see Figure 3.2). According to Snow (1998:63), the less abstract designs can be "recognized as flowers, serpents, birds, insects, and wolf-like and other animal heads, plus human-mask like designs." Moreover, despite their complexity and diversity, Swift Creek pottery designs are composed of a relatively small number of design elements (Saunders 1998:156–158; Snow 1998:74–80). In the ceramic assemblage from the Hartford Mound in south-central Georgia, some of these repeated design elements include concentric circles, a stylized eye, and a spiral (Snow 1998:74). Saunders (1998:166–170) analyzed ceramic assemblages from the Kings Bay site on the Georgia Coast and found that 127 different paddle designs identified from over one thousand sherds could be sorted into ten design groups, each of which contained only one or a few primary design elements. These elements included tear-drops, ladders, circles, scrolls, spirals, triangles, and lobes.

Many Swift Creek researchers contend that these design elements were important religious symbols with parallels to better-understood cosmological symbols from the historic period (Anderson 1998:291; Saunders 1998:156–158; Snow 1998:62–63). Using a direct historical approach, Snow (1998:74–80) argues that the concentric circle and eye element are references to the sun, that the spiral element refers to the wind, and that the common pattern of four-part designs refers to the quartering of the earth. It is a short logical leap to interpret these symbols as references to basic themes in Southeastern Indian cosmology, and similar design elements appear on both Mississippian and historic period Indian pottery (Hudson 1976; Saunders 1998). Saunders (1998) argues the same point using both historical analogy and information theory. Building on earlier theories of the relationship between artifact style and social interaction (e.g., David et al. 1988; Hodder 1977, 1979, 1982; Wobst 1977) Saunders (1998:154–158) argues that the repetition of a few key elements in Swift Creek paddle stamps suggests that those elements are important cosmological symbols.

While their meaning may be obscure, Swift Creek paddle designs share essential features with ethnographically known designs that are applied to multiple media, including pots and people. The complex designs are composed of simple, legible, repeated elements that probably transmitted important symbolic and cultural information. From the cross-cultural information presented above, we might expect to find elements of Swift Creek paddle designs, if not complete designs, used in body decoration.

In many of the ethnographic cases, motifs that appeared on bodies and material culture were symbols of group membership. This was especially clear in the case of women's tattoos in the Bakairi villages of central Brazil (Steinen 1894) and facial tattoos in the Marquesas (Handy 1922:6). Design motifs shared basic design elements and canonical features but showed a wide range of fine variation that could be used to mark identity at the scale of a single village or corporate descent group.

Swift Creek paddle motifs seem to have a similar kind of variation, and hundreds of different designs have already been identified (Snow and Stephenson 1998). The nature of this variation and the role of Swift Creek pottery in group membership and social interaction is an active area of research. Saunders argues that the paddle designs at Kings Bay and Mallard Creek (sites located 1.5 km from one another) are so similar that a single group of people may have inhabited both sites at different times of the year. Wallis

(2007) suggests that the designs may have been totemic, signaling membership in clans or lineages that were bound together through a system of reciprocal exchange. In an analysis of Swift Creek designs from Kolomoki, Pluckhahn (2007) found a greater emphasis on design symmetry in mound context as compared to the village assemblage, and argues that this difference may be causally related to the use of decorated pottery in strategies of social incorporation.

The ethnographic data show that there is overlap in the technical skills used to produce tattoos, pots, and woodcarvings. In Borneo, woodcarvers produced the blocks used for tattooing, and in northern Cameroon and northeast Nigeria, the physical processes of decorating pottery surfaces and human skin are quite similar. Tattooing, pottery decoration, and woodcarving appear to be what Melissa Hagstrum (2001) refers to as "intersecting technologies." This concept, developed from ethnographic studies of Andean farmers, addresses "the different ways crafts may share (or intersect at) technical knowledge, resources, and labor" (Hagstrum 2001:50). For example, in the prehistoric American Southwest, the skills and tools needed to manufacture utilitarian stone tools may have intersected with drilling turquoise beads (Hagstrum 2001:50). This general tendency for technological skill sets to overlap helps explain the historical continuity between designs in Lapita pottery and historic Polynesian tattoo, barkcloth, and woodcarving designs (Green 1979a, 1979b; Kirch 1997). In the context of Swift Creek pottery manufacture, the skills and tools needed to carve the complex and ornate wooden paddle stamps—manual dexterity, sharp cutting tools, stencils, and so on—intersect with tattooing.

There is variation in the social context of tattooing among the groups examined in this study, but a few key trends are especially noteworthy. First, gender always matters. Tattoos themselves can be markers of group identity, badges of status or achievement, good luck charms and religious blessings, or beauty marks. Yet, across the examined groups, tattooing was governed by a set of gendered norms that not only applied to what sorts of tattoos were appropriate for men and women but also dictated the gender of the tattoo artist. Applying this concept to tattooing in the prehistoric Southeast could generate interesting hypotheses. It is worth considering pot making, woodcarving, and tattooing as a suite of related but gendered activities in the societies of the Middle Woodland period.

Second, in many cases the act of body decoration is just as important, if not more important, than the decoration itself. Tattooing and scarification leave the body permanently altered. As a result, these practices often accompany rites of passage, visually signaling to the community that initiates have passed from one important stage in the life cycle to another. In the examples from Ga'anda, Kayan, and Marquesas society, permanent body decoration accompanied female coming-of-age ceremonies. In the Ga'anda case, the act of body decoration played a role in structuring bridewealth exchanges and may have been a strategy for the assertion of female power in a patrilineal society. In the Tipokia example, there was little ceremony surrounding the tattoo event, but there were significant exchanges of goods and labor (Firth 1937).

In his examination of designs applied on both bodies and material culture in the Marquesas, Gell (1998) argues that the act of tattooing and woodcarving carried just as much religious symbolism as the motifs themselves.

> The tattooing of, for example, an *etua* [godling] motif on the body was not a matter of representing an *etua* which existed (as a three-dimensional solid object) somewhere else. The graphic act was a ritual performance that brought into being a protective spirit through the utterance of a "legitimate" (stylistically coherent) graphic gesture. (Gell 1998:191)

During Middle Woodland times and later in the Southeast, the acts of carving wooden paddles, stamping pots, and decorating bodies may have been related performances that reinforced important social and cosmological ideas and beliefs.

/ Archaeological Evidence /

Tattooing is well documented among the Southeastern Indians during historic times (e.g., Wallace 1993, this volume), but as Williams and Elliott (1998:10) were careful to point out over a decade ago, in the absence of remarkable, perhaps bog-like preservation, finding direct material evidence for Swift Creek tattooing is nearly impossible. There are, however, a few lines of indirect archaeological evidence that may point to tattooing in the Middle Woodland Southeast. These are possible tattoo instruments, pigments and pigment containers, and depictions of tattooing on human effigies. Keeping in mind that the people who made Swift Creek pots were participants in the broader Hopewell Interaction Sphere (Williams and Elliott 1998:5–6), I include Middle Woodland sites well beyond the heartland of Swift Creek ceramics in this discussion.

Historic evidence compiled by Aaron Deter-Wolf in this volume suggests that tattoos in the Southeast were applied with various sharp objects, possibly including the sharpened teeth of fish; bird feathers; thorns; sharpened bone implements; flint blades; and later in the historic period, iron needles. Of the likely prehistoric technologies, only a select few artifact types are likely to survive in the ground. As discussed by Deter-Wolf in Chapter 2, potential tattoo implements most likely to be recovered from an archaeological context include sharpened bone awls or needles and lithic items such as gravers and blades.

Sharpened bone implements appear at many Middle Woodland sites, including some sites with Swift Creek pottery. To be perfectly clear, there is no direct evidence that these objects were used for tattooing. However, based on the historical evidence marshaled by Deter-Wolf, these artifacts fit the description of tools that could have been used for tattooing. In most cases these objects were found in special contexts such as burials and mound deposits. This provides additional indirect evidence for their use in special ritual activities, one of which may have been tattooing. Table 3.1 provides a summary of the archaeological evidence discussed below.

TABLE 3.1. Summary of archaeological evidence for tattooing

SITE	ARTIFACT	CONTEXT	REFERENCE
Mandeville	Bone awls, bladelets	Mound	Kellar et al. 1962
Tunacunnhee	Bone awls, bladelets	Burial	Jefferies 1976
Hartford	Stingray spine, worked bone	Mound	Snow and Stephenson 1990
Leake site	Bladelets	Structure/large pits	Keith 2010
Crystal River	Bone awls	Midden	Bullen 1953
Mann	Bone awls, bladelets	Village area	Kellar 1979
Pinson	Bone awls, bladelets	Mound and village	Mainfort 1986
Napoleon Hollow Floodplain sites	Bladelets	Structure	Odell 1994
Napoleon Hollow Hill Slope sites	Bladelets	Burials	Odell 1994
Elizabeth Mound Group	Bladelets	Burials (mostly female)	Leigh 1988
Edwin Harness Mound	Head effigies	Mound	Greber 1983
Hopewell	Head effigies	Mound	Moorehead 1922

Deer or turkey-bone awls were discovered in Mound A at the Mandeville site in southwest Georgia. Two bone awls were found in Layer I of the mound and two more were found in Layer II (Kellar et al. 1962:344, fig. 3m). Layer I was primarily associated with Deptford pottery while Layer II was primarily associated with Swift Creek pottery. Special artifacts generally associated with the Hopewell Interaction Sphere (Caldwell 1964) were found along with these bone awls, including a panpipe, bladelets made of Ohio Flint Ridge chert, copper beads, cut mica, galena, steatite pipes, ear spools, and a human figurine (Kellar et al. 1962:342–345).

At Tunacunnhee, a cache of five bone awls was discovered in Burial 7 (Jefferies 1976:29). Located between two mounds, Burial 7 contains the remains of five individuals. The awls were most likely made from the split tarsometatarus bones of turkeys. No Swift Creek pottery was found at Tunacunnhee, but it was clearly an important Middle Woodland center and perhaps a node in a regional exchange network (Anderson 1998:278–280). The usual suite of Hopewell exchange goods was found at Tunacunnhee, including panpipes, ears spools, copper pins, celts, mica, clay and stone pipes, ground stone celts, gorgets, and bladelets made of Ohio Flint Ridge chert. The bone awls in Burial 7 were found along with caches of chert and greenstone celts (Jefferies 1976:17–18).

The Hartford site was an important center in south-central Georgia during the Early and Middle Swift Creek periods (Snow and Stephenson 1998:100–101). In addition to the large sample of sherds recovered from Hartford, excavations in the submound and village middens also produced a stingray spine and some worked deer bone (Carder et al. 2004; Snow and Stephenson 1990). Stingray spines are not mentioned in historic accounts of tattooing from the Southeast, but they are quite capable of piercing skin and are believed to have been used in Maya bloodletting rituals (Haines et al. 2008).

The Crystal River site is a large Swift Creek mound site on Florida's west-central Gulf Coast. Bullen (1953:18–21, 27) notes that several bone awls were found in association with Swift Creek ceramics in test units excavated in the shell midden north of Mound A. Fancy Hopewell exchange goods have also been found at Crystal River (Pluckhahn et al. 2010:164).

Farther from the Swift Creek heartland, bone needles and Swift Creek pottery have been found at the Mann site in southwestern Indiana (Kellar 1979) and at the Pinson Mounds in western Tennessee (Mainfort 1986). These sites were important Middle Woodland centers with multiple mounds and earthworks as well as the usual suite of diagnostic Hopewell artifacts, including Flint Ridge chert blades, copper objects, galena, and mica. At the

Mann site, deer- and bird-bone awls were found "with some frequency" in excavations in the village area (Kellar 1979:105).

Obviously these tools could have been used for multiple purposes, none of which were necessarily tattooing. Out of all the sets of bone needles and awls recorded here, the cache of tools in Burial 7 at Tunacunnhee may be the best candidate for possible tattoo needles. Their placement together in a burial is reminiscent of tattoo bundles discussed by Krutak in Chapter 5, but this is only a speculative interpretation. The bone awls from Mandeville were found in the mound along with other fancy goods, which suggests they may have served a special ritual function. Ideally we could test these objects for protein residue or wear patterns consistent with tattooing. At Mann, bone needles and awls were recovered from test units in habitation zones and middens, and it is harder to determine the social context in which they were deposited.

Prismatic blades or bladelets appear in ceremonial, mortuary, and domestic contexts at several well-known Middle Woodland sites across the Southeast, and have long been recognized as an important artifact in Hopewell exchange networks (Kellar et al. 1962; Leigh 1988; Odell 1994). Bladelets made of Flint Ridge chert from Ohio have been found in Georgia at the Mandeville, Leake, and Tunacunnhee sites (Jefferies 1976; Keith 2010; Kellar et al. 1962), and also at Mann and Pinson (Kellar 1979; Mainfort 1986).

George Odell (1994) analyzed use wear on chert bladelets from the three sites in the lower Illinois valley and found that most of the bladelets from mortuary contexts were used only for cutting soft materials, such as soft animal or vegetal matter. Such use wear might be consistent with tattooing or scarification (Deter-Wolf and Peres 2012). In a comparative study of four mound groups in the lower Illinois valley, Leigh (1988:202–203) found that prismatic blades were commonly recovered from burials, most often in interments of older females. Considering the gendered nature of body decoration, this is an interesting pattern if the blades were indeed used for tattooing. The inclusion of prismatic blades in ceremonial and mortuary contexts is also suggestive, given that tattooing often accompanies, or is the focus of, group ceremony and ritual.

Human effigy heads from Ohio Hopewell sites provide indirect evidence of tattooing or other body decoration during the Middle Woodland period. A carved stone pipe from the central area of the northern sector of the Edwin Harness Mound appears to represent a human head covered with geometric designs that have been interpreted as tattooing, scarification, or face painting (Figure 3.8) (Carr and Case 2006:198; Greber 1983:33). Effigies from the Hopewell site (Moorehead 1922:169) (Figure 3.9) and Mound City (Squier and Davis 1849:244) (Figure 3.10) also exhibit facial decorations.

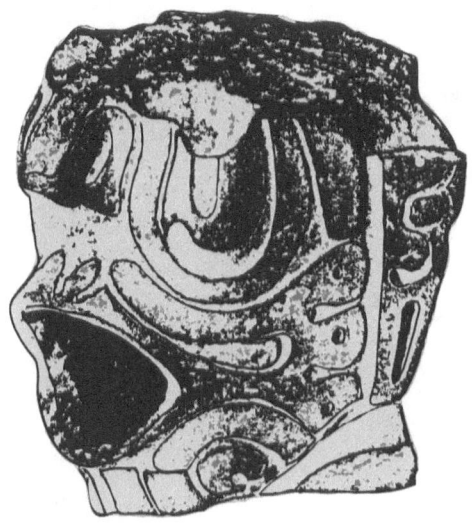

FIGURE 3.8. Human head effigy pipe with facial decorations from
Edwin Harness Mound, Ross County, Ohio. Peabody Museum of
Archaeology and Ethnology artifact catalog no. 84-6-10/35002.

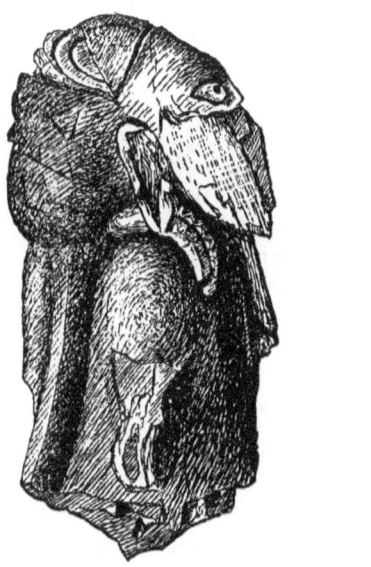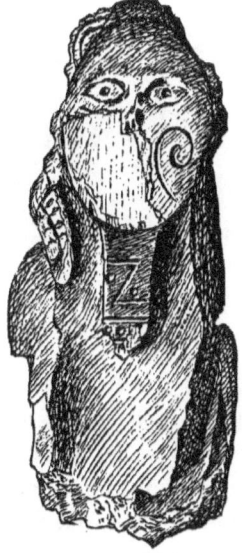

FIGURE 3.9. Human effigy from Hopewell, Ohio. Note the facial decoration visible on the front view (after Moorehead 1922:169, fig. 68).

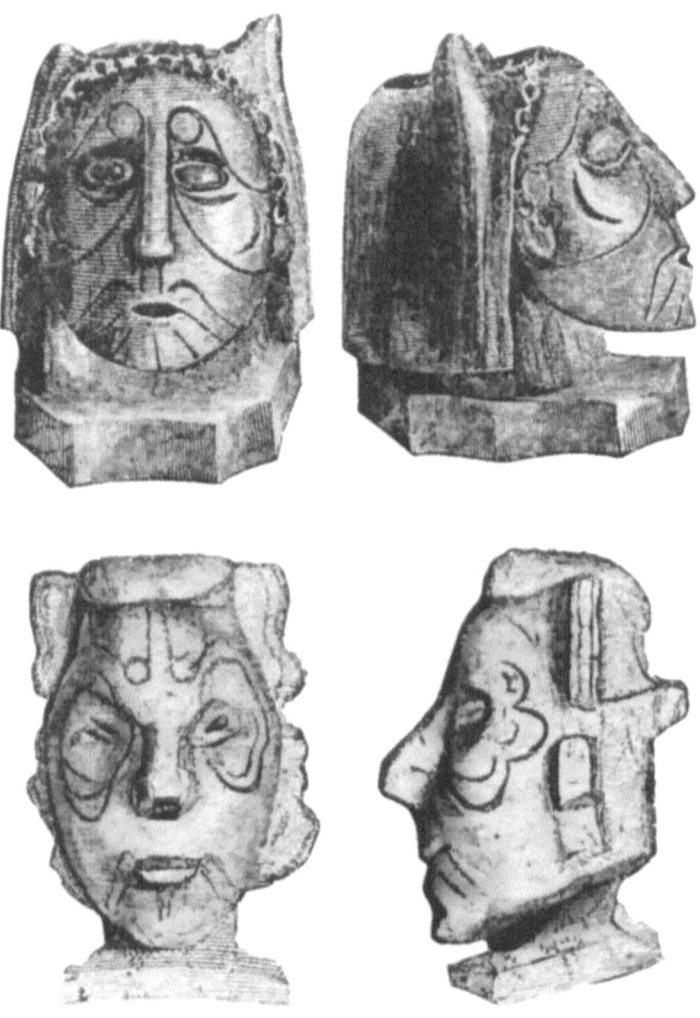

FIGURE 3.10. Human effigy pipe bowls with incised facial decorations from Mound City, Ohio (after Squier and Davis 1848:144, figs. 142 and 143).

Kellar (1979) found several human terra cotta figurines at the Mann site. According to Kellar (1979:105), "rare examples may be embellished with striations on the head to represent hair, and incised lines appear to indicate elements of attire and/or body decoration." Similar ceramic figurines with obvious human faces were found during recent excavations at the Leake site, but there is no evidence for depictions of body decoration on these artifacts (Keith 2010:413–417).

Conclusion

Williams and Elliott (1998:10) were right to tread cautiously in regard to possible Swift Creek tattooing, and I take complete responsibility for this admittedly speculative foray. Finding direct archaeological evidence for Middle Woodland tattooing will be extremely difficult, and the indirect evidence—bone needles, stone bladelets, and human effigies—can of course be interpreted in different ways. However, the comparative ethnographic evidence examined here offers compelling models for how and why the people who made Swift Creek pots during the Middle Woodland period might have decorated their bodies.

Like the tattoos and scarification patterns described in ethnographic and historic accounts from Africa, Brazil, Borneo, and Polynesia, the naturalistic and geometric designs on Swift Creek paddle stamps seem to have carried important cosmological and ideological messages, and they may have been used to symbolize group membership within and between settlements. The ethnographic cases discussed here show a strong tendency for people to draw, stamp, carve, and tattoo the same symbols across multiple media, including human skin. If the people who made Swift Creek pottery decorated their bodies at all, it seems likely that they would have done so with the same design elements and images found on their pots.

Exploring the connections between the decoration of bodies and the decoration of material culture provides insight for archaeological studies of body modification in the Southeast and beyond. Above all, the ethnographic data marshaled here indicate that body decoration cannot be understood solely by analyzing designs. The act of permanently marking the body often plays a vital role in rites of passage and marriage ceremonies, and can be a locus for important economic exchanges. As we see in the Ga'anda case, applying the same set of designs to bodies and objects related to subsistence, such as pots and baskets, can be a strategy for negotiating power and authority along gender lines within communities (Berns 1988). In the prehistoric Southeast, the act of decorating bodies may have had similar social and economic, as well as symbolic, ramifications.

Studies of prehistoric body decoration will be incomplete unless they take gender into consideration. Even in ethnographic cases where there is relatively little ceremony surrounding the tattooing event, there are important gender restrictions surrounding the nature and application of the tattoo. There was a strong division of gender roles between men and women in Creek and Cherokee society, so much so that men and women were practically considered to be different kinds of human beings (Hudson 1976:317–319). Body decoration no doubt played an important role in symbolizing this division. Exploring the interplay between the decoration of bodies and material culture among historically known Southeastern groups may shed new light on gendered activities. The ethnographic examples gathered here suggest that female body decoration is more often tied to rites of passage and marriage ceremony, while male tattoos are more often used as markers of status achieved in warfare.

Given the comparatively poor chances for the preservation of soft tissue and organics in the Southeast, many attempts to understand body decoration will be speculative and will depend largely on argument by analogy. However, thought exercises like these are useful. As Williams and Elliott (1998) pointed out over a decade ago, social life in the Middle Woodland Southeast was vibrant and complex. Swift Creek pottery provides a tantalizing glimpse into this world. Thinking about Swift Creek paddle designs as important symbols that were used on multiple media, including people, may help generate new ideas about what these symbols meant and produce new insight on social processes related to marriage, exchange, and even the negotiation of power along gender lines.

< 4 >

Tattoos, Totem Marks, and War Clubs

Projecting Power through Visual Symbolism in Northern Woodlands Culture

Lars Krutak

/ / / /

When Lewis Henry Morgan published his classic account of Iroquois culture in 1851, tattooing had ceased amongst the people he so vividly described. Although the cultural tradition of body marking was once quite widespread across Iroquoia and the Northern Woodlands, missionization, the cessation of warfare, and the adoption of European dress and less permanent forms of ornament all contributed to the decline of this important custom among the Iroquois, as well their Algonquian neighbors—and sometimes enemies—the Delaware, Illinois, and other groups inhabiting the Great Lakes region.

Traditionally speaking, tattooing embodied several functions. First, as a graphic art form it spoke about the ability and achievements of Woodlands tattoo artists who plied the epidermis with lasting designs long before the arrival of Europeans. Second, among the Iroquois and others, tattooing was employed as a form of medicine and worked to assert and inscribe tribal affiliation, maturity, and social status. Finally, tattoos signified military achievement by warriors who engaged their enemies in hand-to-hand combat on the field of battle. Unfortunately, our knowledge of the complete range of information embodied in these kinds of martial symbols is limited by the paucity of evidence contained in the ethnographic record and by the fact that these historical sources have not yet been properly interpreted.

The purpose of this chapter, then, is to review these extant sources, as well as related early historical portraiture from the Southeastern Woodlands and prehistoric Mississippian imagery, to suggest new interpretations of Northern Woodlands warrior tattoo pictography. My intention is to identify and analyze these highly symbolic and magical expressions by outlining the indigenous patterns of thought that were inextricably bound to the personal imagery of the warrior body.

/ *The Warrior's Path* /

The eighteenth-century Iroquois—Mohawks, Oneida, Onondaga, Cayuga, Seneca, and Tuscarora—called themselves the "United People" to remind each other that their safety and power resided in a strict mutual adherence to their tribal confederacy (Loskiel 1794 [1789]:2). Groups like the Mahican, who were neighbors to the Mohawk, became allies around 1640, although this relationship was often strained.

Members of the Six Nations of the Iroquois were closely linked through marriage, and each nation acquired warriors from one another when the call to arms was given. Collectively speaking, war was not waged in competition for natural resources or to accrue new territories (Williamson 2007:193). Rather, it was part of an ongoing cycle of blood feuds extending back many generations that were settled or avenged with still more violent retaliations.

The Iroquois had many enemies and most could be reached via the "Warrior's Path," a network of trails through the great Appalachian Valley extending from New York to Georgia and branching outward to the Eastern Seaboard and westward to the Great Lakes. Along this path, alliances were made and broken, and the Iroquois monitored the movements of many nations either in league with or against them, including the Delaware, Shawnee, Cherokee, Kickapoo, Potawatomi, Chippewa, Ottawa, Huron, Catawba, Nanticoke, Choctaw, and Chickasaw.

Because victory in warfare was the primary vehicle for becoming a great man in Iroquoia, young men were trained from their earliest days to build their bodies into pillars of strength through rigorous physical exercise, including sports like lacrosse and hunting in the wilderness. These activities not only enhanced a young man's endurance and patience, but also his tracking skills and knowledge of local and distant trails, his capacity to bear extreme fatigue and pain, and especially his ability to conquer the fear of death. Writing from Quebec in 1709, the Jesuit priest Raudot reported: "They do not fear death as we do, regarding life as nothing but a transition; they are convinced that in leaving it they will lead a more agreeable one in a delightful country where they will have all the comforts and all the pleasures they desire" (Kinietz 1965:353).[1]

John Heckewelder, a Moravian missionary to Native Americans in Ohio and Pennsylvania, quoted a Delaware warrior in the 1760s as telling him:

> When we go to fight an enemy . . . we meet on equal ground; and we take
> off each other's scalps, if we can. The conqueror, whoever he may be, is
> entitled to have something to shew to prove his bravery and his triumph,

and it would be *ungenerous* in a warrior to deprive an enemy of the means of acquiring that glory of which he him self is in pursuit. A warrior's conduct ought to be *manly*, else he is *no man*. (Heckewelder 1876 [1818]:215, italics in original)

Taken together, all of these training techniques were incredibly important from the standpoint of warfare, because Iroquois warriors sometimes traveled immense distances—upward of one thousand miles or more—to meet their enemies. As the eighteenth-century Jesuit missionary Joseph François Lafitau related: "One Mohawk warrior who went against the Fox nation had his shoulder fractured by a gunshot during the attack on a Kickapoo village; yet he survived hunger and the discomforts of a journey of 700 leagues (2,100 miles) to be treated by a tribal surgeon" (Fenton 1942:512). Other accounts further illustrate the distances involved in Iroquois warfare, documenting travel over hundreds of miles either to attack specific targets or to pursue enemies (e.g., Beauchamp 1905:226, 227).

/ Manitous and Manitos /

Once an Iroquois adolescent attained manhood his status was enhanced with a new name drawn from a pool of clan monikers held by a chief. About the same time, the young man was encouraged to fast and wander the wilderness until he found a *manitou*, or personal guardian spirit, that would protect him in battle for the rest of his life.[2] Morgan (1922 [1851]:233) wrote that the young warrior waited for a dream, and "whatever he dreamed of became his manitou on which his fortune depended . . . and whatever the totemic object, it accompanied the Indian on his journeys and especially on the warpath. If the manitou were an animal, the skin, or the plumage of a bird, was taken as containing the spirit of the animal."[3] When the young warrior dreamed, it was believed that this sign was a divine message or omen given to him by his spiritual assistant. It was to be followed under any circumstance no matter how absurd it may have seemed.

The assumption of personal spirits by young men was documented among various Eastern Woodlands groups in addition to the Iroquois (e.g., Loskiel 1794 [1789]:40; Cadillac 1947 [1823]:22). The French geographer and mathematician Joseph Nicollet recorded that among the Chippewa, raptorial birds were "the most appropriate" manitous, but there were also

many other gods apt to protect warriors in all the mishaps of battle: climbing birds that shun the hunter by creeping around tree limbs as they are being pursued; aquatic birds famous for their ability to dive and hide under the waters; quadrupeds that escape their enemies by fleeing down burrows. All of them are so many manitos that confer upon warriors under their safekeeping not the power to do what the manitos do according to their instincts but the faculty of appearing to the enemy as these animals appear to theirs.

No wonder that in the wake of these concepts it is so important for the natives to be under the protection of a war spirit. (Nicollet 1970:164–165)

The Jesuit Raudot, writing about all of the many "savage" nations of Iroquoia, commented in 1709 that they

are much given to dreams and are so well persuaded that it is their spirit who gives them to them, that they absolutely must carry them out. It is dreams which oblige them to undertake wars, to make great voyages, to abandon war parties which they have undertaken against their enemies and to return from them to their cabins. It is also these dreams that give them their spirit, or to use their term, their manito, which they imagine takes care of them in all the acts of their lives . . . He takes thenceforth from his childhood for this divinity, for his manito, for his protector, and continues during his life to worship it by sacrifices and by feasts which he gives in its honor. (Kinietz 1965:351–353)

These potent dream messages derived their power not simply from the manitou itself, but from higher beings and deities that communicated with it, such as the Iroquois God of War (Areskoui) and the Creator (also called the "Master of Life"), which were both associated with the Sun, as well as other deities who monitored everything above and below the world of humans (Morgan 1922 [1851]:233–234). As noted by Raudot, a personal manitou had to be propitiated with sacrifices over one's lifetime; otherwise its supernatural gifts might be taken away. Offerings of this type usually consisted of burning tobacco in a fire, but blood sacrifices have also been recorded. The Dutch priest Isaac Jogues, who was held captive by the Mohawk in 1642–1643, witnessed a female prisoner and two bears burned on a pyre as an offering to the God of War (Areskoui) to "render [the Mohawk] ever anew victorious over [their] enemies" (Jogues 1857 [1643]:203) (Figure 4.1).

In such instances, the sacrificial fire symbolized the Sun, which, according to the early eighteenth-century Quebecois merchant and militia captain François Pachot, was worshipped by the Iroquois, Illinois, Ottawa, and

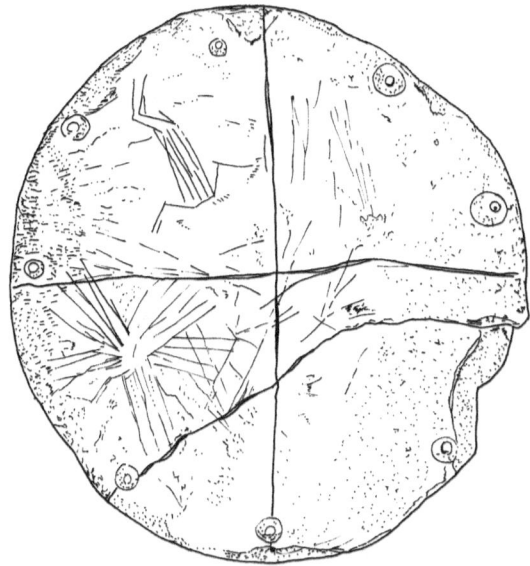

FIGURE 4.1. Rattle fragment, fifteenth century. In the Iroquoian sacrificial complex, prisoners were often slain at sunrise to the accompaniment of rattles that were sometimes constructed of disk-shaped human parietal bones that may have been intended to represent the Sun (Jamieson 1983:166; Williamson 2007:209). Solar symbols and headless figures engraved on some of these rattles perhaps reinforce this connection (after Jury 1941: plate 9, fig. 1).

Sioux "because [it] was attached to the superior being whom they called 'the master of life.'" He continued, "They had confidence in their manitos because they believed that these spirits gave them ideas which came [directly] from the superior being, and that it was he who showed them in their dreams the animals which they took for their manitos, because he wished to use these animals to lead them" (Kinietz 1965:289). Beauchamp reinforced this statement when he wrote:

> The Sun . . . is the chief messenger of the [Iroquois] Creator. It is his duty to observe all the activities of men and nature, and report them to his superior. . . . The sun is especially the patron of war, and lingers as he watches the conflict. Thus days of battle are longer [than others]. (Beauchamp 1922:107)

The Algonquian-speaking Delaware also worshipped the Master of Light, especially in its concrete manifestation of fire, which was called "Grandfather" and the "Sun" (Brinton 1885:65). In the Southeastern Woodlands this relationship existed for both the Yuchi and the Creeks (Hvidt 1980:42–43, 47; Swanton 1946:533). The Sun was adopted as a personal manitou by many native groups throughout the Northern Woodlands, like the aforementioned Iroquois (Loskiel 1794 [1789]:40), as well as the Ottawa (Kinietz 1965:298), Huron (Kalm 1812 [1749]:659), and Chippewa (Kinietz 1965:288). These peoples carved symbols representing the Sun into their personal weapons, placed them upon battlefield markers like trees, or had the emblems tattooed on their bodies as permanent talismans.

/ War Birds /

Before the widespread adoption of the tomahawk and musket, warriors across the Eastern Woodlands employed war clubs of various shapes and sizes manufactured from hardwoods like maple or ironwood. Typically, these were a warrior's most decorated instrument and were sometimes carved with a personal portrait of the owner, clan markings, personal manitous, marks tallying human kills and other martial exploits, and even the owner's "dream of life."

When the German travel writer Johann Kohl encountered an Ojibway warrior in the 1850s with a richly adorned "gunstock" variety of club, this man vividly recounted the deeply personal meanings that his weapon carried, including the vision that provided him with his manitou (Figure 4.2).[4] Kohl (1985 [1854]:296–297) stated that on one side of the warrior's club was a drawing that represented his "dream of life," which came to him on the St. Croix River in Wisconsin when he was a young man after he had fasted for ten days in the wilderness. Two human figures on the club represented himself and his guardian spirit, or guide, who spoke to him in his dream and ordered him to look upward. When he did so, he saw a large, handsome eagle (*kiniou*[5]) sitting in its nest; this was also carved into the club (Figure 4.2B). Above the bird a crown of glistening stars floated, and over them the moon (Figure 4.2D). The owner of the club told Kohl, "I often think of this face, this eagle, and I not only think of it, but I speak to it in a loud voice." When asked if the eagle had aided him, the warrior replied, "Frequently. If it did not help me I should not have taken so much trouble to paint [carve] it on my [club]" (Kohl 1985 [1854]:297). Also etched into the overall design of the club were the number of expeditions against the Sioux (Figure 4.2F), a heart-shaped design, (Figure 4.2C),[6] and a representation of the man's "war birds" (Figures 4.2E and 4.3).

War birds were similar to a personal manitou and were another form of sympathetic war magic.[7] According to the French explorer and trader Pierre

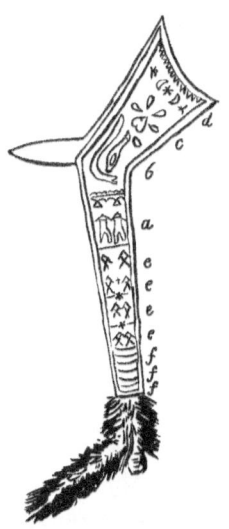

FIGURE 4.2. Ojibway war club, ca. 1850 (after Kohl 1985 [1854]:296).

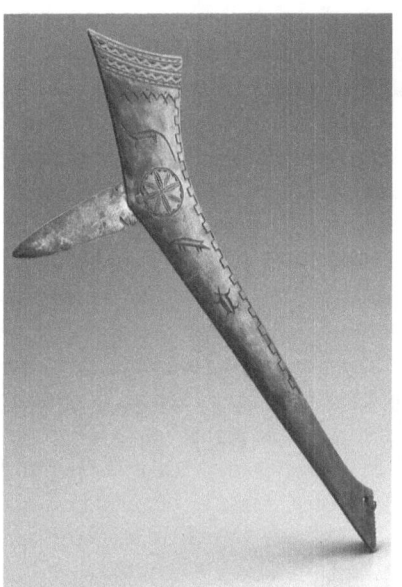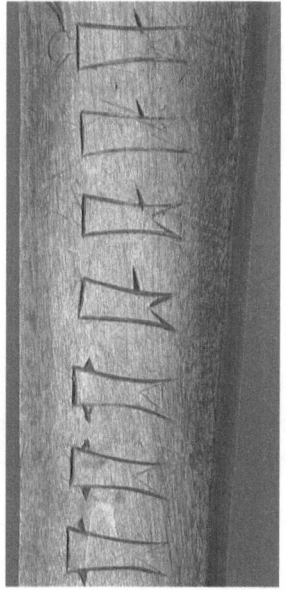

FIGURE 4.3. Eastern Sioux "gunstock" club of maple dating to ca. 1810. The weapon contains numerous chip-carved designs illustrating the biographical history and military exploits of the owner, including one or more personal manitous (e.g., bear, turtle, and an "underwater panther"); a solar motif inscribed in a circle that may refer to the "dream of life" of the owner (or another manitou); campaign marks of six enemies killed (three women, three men) and one man taken prisoner; and three avian symbols that I believe are mistakenly called "thunderbirds" (Brasser 2009:58). In fact, these are more likely the warrior's war birds. Image courtesy of the John and Marva Warnock Collection, www.splendidheritage.com.

Deliette, who spent several decades with the Illinois and other neighboring tribes beginning in the 1680s,

> besides the animals I have already mentioned as manitous, they also have several birds which they use when they go to war and as to which they cherish much superstition. They use the skins of stone falcons, crows, carrion crows, turtledoves, ducks, swallows, martins, parrots, and many others that I do not name. (Deliette 1947 [1934]:152)

Joseph Nicollet, who spent time among the Chippewa in 1836–1837, observed that many of his indigenous traveling companions created headgear from various species of birds. Although he sometimes referred to these plumed bonnets as "manitos," he also variously described them as "a guardian, a genius, a spirit, a manito of war which strangely enough will not inspire courage, bravery, or fighting skill, but will inspire them in what they should do, how they must operate to avoid death" (Nicollet 1970:163). Nicollet stated that each of the birds utilized as ornament was considered "sacred" and that they were invoked in ceremony and named in "all of their war songs." He concluded that the Chippewa were keen observers of nature, and that this belief of superstition "originate[d] in the particular order of their sensory concepts," which he described in great detail (Nicollet 1970:163).

In the late seventeenth century, Sieur Pierre Deliette recorded that during war preparations, an Illinois war chief paid homage to "his birds" so that he would gain many warriors. After his search had drawn to a close and thirty to fifty men had gathered by his side, the men opened their war mats[8] and then spread their war birds upon them. Together they picked up their rattles and began singing a chorus that lasted through the night: "stone falcon, or crow, I pray to you that when I pursue the enemy I may run as fast as you fly, so that I may be admired by my comrades and feared by our enemies" (Deliette 1947 [1934]:153).[9] The Jesuit Raudot (Kinietz 1965:404–405), also speaking about the Illinois in 1709, offered similar testimony.

Deliette reports that after the war party had set off and moved closer to its destination, the war chief gathered his warriors' birds into his own mat, along with medicinal herbs to be used for healing the wounded. "As soon as they stop, the chief takes out the birds, and, after offering a short prayer to them, sends out three or four of the bravest and most active warriors to reconnoiter the enemy" (Deliette 1947 [1934]:155). Once the party had fallen upon their enemy, they immediately began imitating the cries of "their birds" while collecting scalps and attempting to capture prisoners (Kinietz 1965:406).[10]

/ War Clubs and Ornamented Trees /

As noted previously, a warrior's war club was often inscribed with "his birds," personal manitous, and other messages, including his accomplishments on the battlefield (see Figures 4.2 and 4.3). More specifically, warriors often carved their military exploits into the body of these clubs, including the number of enemy engagements and the number of prisoners taken and killed. This military shorthand not only spoke about the courage and skill of the warrior, but also must have had a psychological effect on his enemies. It was customary for men to leave their decorated war clubs as "calling cards" (Meachum 2007:68) on the field of battle, either depositing them near a corpse or leaving them embedded in the victim's body so that "his enemies may know who killed their people and of what nation he was" (Kinietz 1965:351). This practice of leaving behind a personal weapon after a successful engagement was widespread across the Woodlands region.

William Hyde, a British officer speaking about the Iroquois around 1695, wrote: "Now when These Men Goe a Scalping to Cannada, they scratch the markes they have on their faces and bodyes upon their Clubhamers which they always leave behind them with the dead body, that it might be Knowne who did the action" (Hyde 1965, cited in Meachum 2007:68). A French document dating to 1666 notes that when a club was left behind with a corpse, the head of the weapon was deliberately pointed in the direction of the dead man's village: "When they have finished, if they have casse-tetes or clubs, they plant them against the corpse inclining a little towards the village of the slain" (O'Callaghan 1849:5).

Further south, among the Cherokee, Henry Timberlake references the custom in his translation of a "War-Song" he recorded about 1760:

> We'll leave our clubs dew'd with their countries show'rs
> And, if they dare to bring them back to our's
> Their painted scalps shall be a step to fame
> And grace our own and glorious country's name. (Timberlake 2007
> [1765]:31)

Timberlake notes: "It is the custom of the Indians, to leave a club, something of the form of a cricket-bat, but with their warlike exploits engraved on it, in their enemy's country, and the enemy accepts the defiance, by bringing this back to their country" (Timberlake 2007 [1765]:120, note 111). The war song concluded with a final line describing the "boasting place," the location where the battle would be commemorated through markings on a tree. According to Timberlake, "Their custom is generally to engrave their victory on some neighboring tree, to set up some token of it near the field of battle; to their enemies are here supposed to point to, as boasting their victory over them, and the slaughter that they made" (Timberlake 2007 [1765]:120, note 113).

Tree ornamentation was another significant part of the corpus of military pictography across the Eastern Woodlands (Coy 2004). The marking of trees not only added insult to injury by serving as a semipermanent reminder of the losses inflicted by marauding enemy warriors upon local forces, but also had other functions similar to those of a modern-day global positioning system (GPS). As Deliette recalled for the Illinois, "They also mark places for joining each other [on trees] in case they are obliged to go by several routes, different routes, and in such cases those who arrive first take a little of what they have left, if they need it, and leave their marks, which they never mistake. For this purpose, they paint a picture of themselves on the nearest tree. Although several of them have heads of hair that look just alike, their totems identify them. They all have distinctive ones" (Deliette 1947 [1934]:154–155).

In his particularly useful study of Eastern Woodlands war club pictography, Meachum (2007) identifies a series of colonial-era records that allow us to more accurately decipher the precise meanings of ornamented trees and wooden clubs. These documents also represent the keys with which to unlock many of the tattooing symbols worn by Woodlands warriors themselves.

The earliest of these illustrated papers, the so-called Paris Document of 1666, provides the first map from which to chart the meanings of this abstract language of signs (Figure 4.4). An original sketch of the document by Meachum (2007:70, fig. 8) relates a few more graphic details than the version published by O'Callaghan (1849:8), which is illustrated here. However, I use the latter's translation of the French text:

> The Portrait of a Savage on a board in their cabin on which they ordinarily paint how often he has been to war, how many men he has taken and killed.
>
> a. These are the punctures [tattoos] on his body.
> b. This is the way they mark when they have been to war, and when there is a bar extending from one mark to the other, it signifies that after having been in battle, he did not come back to his village and that he returned with other parties whom he met or formed.

c. This arrow, which is broken, denotes that they were wounded in this expedition.

d. Thus they denote that the belts which they gave to raise a war party and to avenge the death of some one, belong to them or to some of the same tribe.

e. He has gone back to fight without having entered his village.

f. A man whom he killed on the field of battle who had a bow and arrows.

g. These are two men whom he took prisoners, one of whom had a hatchet, and the other a gun in his hand.

g.g. This is a woman who is designated only by a species of waistcloth.

h. This is the way they distinguish her from the men.

Such is the mode in which they draw their portraits. (O'Callaghan 1849:9)

The Jesuit missionary Lafitau, who spent many years proselytizing the Iroquois, also left us with a lengthy description of their tree-carving practices.

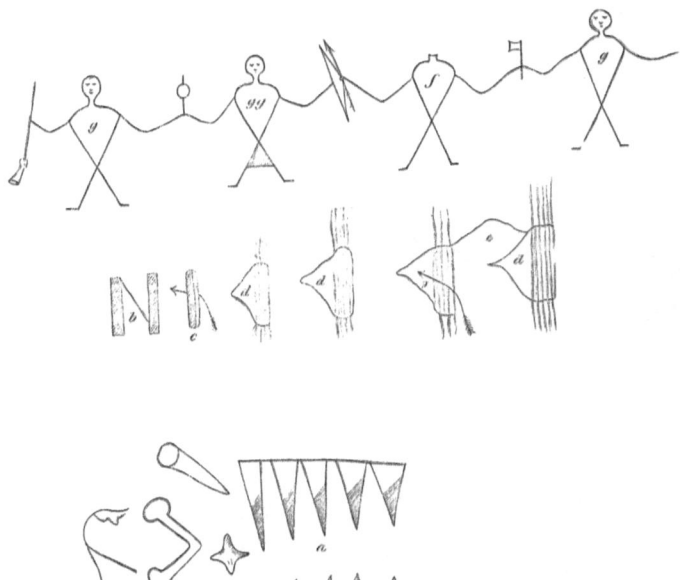

FIGURE 4.4. The Paris Document of 1666 (after O'Callaghan 1849:8).

He seems to have been familiar with the Paris Document (see Fenton 1977:36, note 3) and perhaps that provided him with the initial impetus to study the "hieroglyphic" systems of the Iroquois in more detail. Lafitau also keyed his original account (published in 1724) with two very important detailed drawings of Iroquoian tattooing (Figure 4.5).[11] These sketches will serve as a baseline for later comparisons. Lafitau touches upon other themes I have discussed previously, including the use of war mats. Moreover, he explains that these customs were common throughout the Woodlands region from the headwaters of the St. Lawrence River extending toward Louisiana, but that each tribe had their own hieroglyphic "method" and variations existed amongst "all the Indian tribes who know each other" (Lafitau 1977 [1724]:37).

One final example of tree pictography I will describe comes from a written journal account produced by American Colonel Adam Hubley during the Revolutionary War in 1779 (Figure 4.6). The inscriptions produced on the tree were said to belong to the great Mohawk war chief Joseph Brant (1743–1807), who may have been a distant relative of the heavily tattooed Mohawk war chief Brant Saquainquaragton (1673–1710) (Sivertsen 1996:69). The elder Brant was painted in 1710 during a trip to England and Queen Anne's court (Figure 4.7).

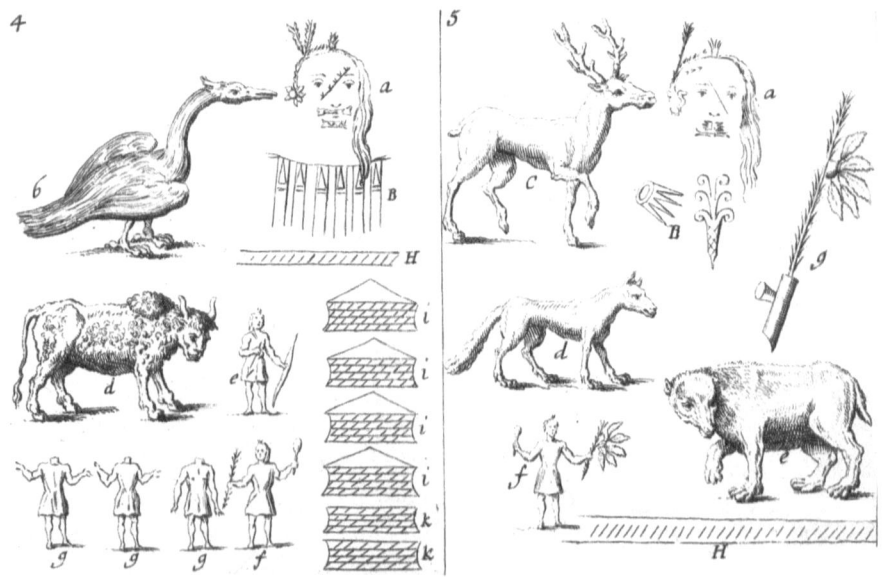

FIGURE 4.5. Tattooed Iroquois warriors Two Feathers (left, 4A, 4B) and Two Arrows (right, 5A, 5B) (after Lafitau 1977 [1724]:43, plate 3).

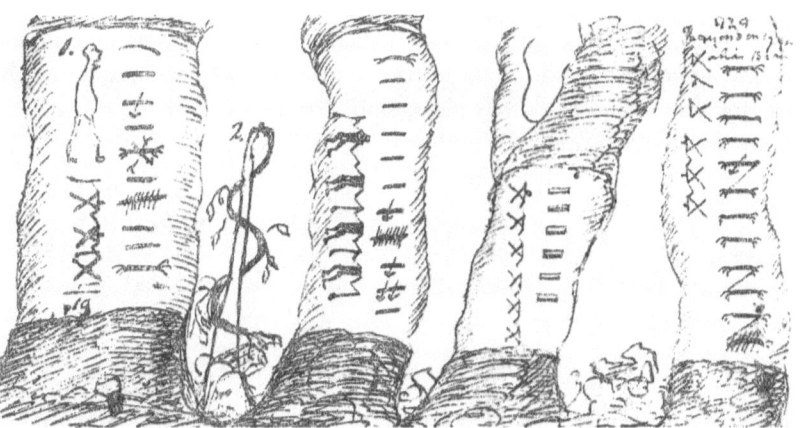

FIGURE 4.6. Mohawk tree pictograph, 1779 (after Hubley 1909).

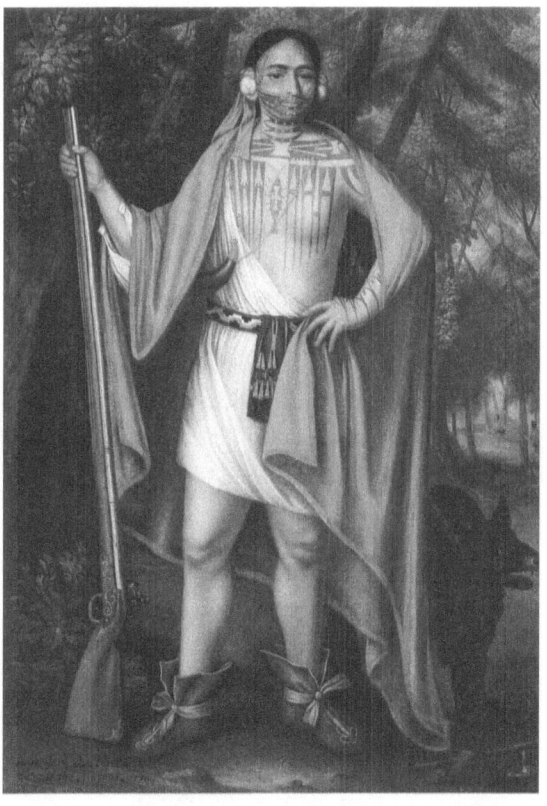
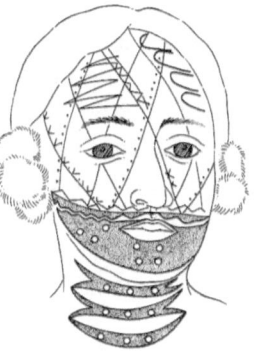

FIGURE 4.7. *Tattooing of the Great Mohawk War Leader Brant* (painting by John Verelst, 1710) and illustrated reconstruction of his facial markings (after Fenton 1978:310).

Although Hubley's sketch does not include any body markings, it is nonetheless important to the study of Woodlands tattooing because it reveals still more subtleties in the way pictographic war symbols could be depicted. Cross strokes (/////) represented the number of losses that year; simple Xs or hourglass figures with black heads holding each other's arms signified how many white enemies with weapons had been scalped; X figures not holding hands and without heads represented scalped noncombatants; and small rectangles tallied the number of times at war (Hubley 1909:294).

/ Totems, Marked Graves, and Warrior Tattoos /

Because manitous and a man's war exploits were so inextricably bound to his sense of personhood, it should not be surprising that they also accompanied a warrior to his grave. Among the Potawatomi, the manitou of a warrior was painted in red, the color of war, on top of his grave post (de Smet 1905:1091–1092). One early Dutch account from 1634 describes that at an Oneida burial place, "[the graves] were painted with red and white and black paint; but the chief's grave . . . at the top [had] a big wooden bird, and all around were painted dogs and deer, and snakes and other beasts" (Beauchamp 1922:236). These creatures likely represent the manitou or manitous of the buried individual. The fur trader Alexander Henry the Elder, who was captured by the Ojibway and later adopted by them, witnessed the funeral of an Assiniboine warrior around 1770. Henry describes the end of the event:

> The eulogium finished, the [grave] post is painted, and on it are represented the number of prisoners taken, by so many figures of men; and of killed and scalped, by figures without heads. To these are added his badge, called, in the Algonquin tongue, a *totem*, and which is in the nature of an armorial being. (Henry 1809:305)

The trader and interpreter John Long, who lived and worked among the Ojibway and Potawatomi in the eighteenth century, wrote about the bear manitou, calling it a "*totam*." Long was the first writer to publish the term *totem* and described it in this way:

> One part of the religious superstition of the Savages, consists in each of them having his *totam*, or favourite spirit, which he believes watches over him. This *totam* they conceive assumes the shape of some beast or other, and therefore they never kill, hunt, or eat the animal whose form they think this *totam* bears. (Long 1791:86; italics in original)

A number of ethnohistorical sources from the Northern Woodlands confuse or do not differentiate between individual totemism (e.g., manitous) and group totemism (clan symbolism) when discussing Native American beliefs.[12] For example, Kohl (1985 [1854]:159) illustrates the tombstone of an Ojibway warrior that imparts information, including a tally of his conquests, the number of relatives mourning his death, and an inverted bear, purported to be his "family name" or clan symbol. In light of the accounts presented above, the bear may instead have been the personal manitou of the deceased.

In a recent paper by Fogelson and Brightman (2002:311), the authors argue that the dissociation between individual and group totemism "may be more an analytic dream, and anthropological nightmare, than a native reality." Instead, Fogelson and Brightman provide evidence suggesting that individual and hereditary/clan totemism overlapped in the Northern Woodlands and that Native Americans here may have originally derived their clan totems from guardian spirits (manitous). For example, in his brief 1644 description of the Mohawk, the Dutch priest Johannes Megapolensis correctly describes the three clan animals of this tribe: turtle, bear, and wolf. In his dealings with a local warrior, however, he unknowingly stumbles upon what I also believe is his personal manitou, the bear, which probably doubled as his clan's namesake. Megapolensis writes:

> Each of these tribes carries the beast after which it is called (as the arms in its banner) when it goes to war against its enemies, and this is done as well for the terror of its enemies, as for a sign of its own bravery . . . When he opened his budget there appeared in it a dried head of a bear, with grinning teeth. I asked him what he meant? He answered me that he fastened it upon his left shoulder by the side of his head . . . and did not fear anything. (Megapolensis 1857 [1644]:159–160)

As noted previously, a warrior's manitou was often tattooed upon his body to make it more lasting and sacred. According to the Jesuit Claude Dablon, who wrote at the end of the seventeenth century, Ottawa and Chippewa boys received their first tattoos after they had discovered their manitou. Around the age of ten,[13] a child

> was given instructions by his father and then made to fast for several days in order that something divine might appear to him in his sleep. In the morning after the fast, the father questioned him secretly on what has happened during the night. If nothing had appeared to him, the fast had to be recommenced; but usually the sun, the thunder, or something else he had often

been talked to about appeared to him. A representation of this manito was tattooed on his skin. (Kinietz 1965:288)

After this feat had been accomplished, the boy moved one step closer to becoming a warrior.

For the Delaware, tattooing was a tradition "with those who had distinguished themselves by their valour, and acquired celebrity" (Heckewelder 1876 [1818]:205). In 1762, Heckewelder observed that a valiant Tuscarora war chief desired to have another name attached to him and "had the figure of a water-lizard engraved or tattooed on his face, above the chin, when he received the name, the water-lizard"[14] (Heckewelder 1876 [1818]:206). The Rev. David Brainerd's (1822:347) account of the Delaware indicates that such animals were perhaps derived from dreams and were manitous themselves: "[The Delaware] give much heed to dreams, because they suppose these invisible powers give them directions at such times about certain affairs, and sometimes inform them what animal they would choose to be worshipped in."

Loskiel (1794 [1789]:49–50) provides further evidence that personal appellations were associated with particular tattoos among the Iroquois. "The most singular part of their ornaments is displayed in figures made by scarification, representing serpents, birds, and other creatures . . . Sometimes by these decorations, they acquire a particular appellation, by which their pride is exceedingly gratified."

Perhaps this tradition applied to the heavily tattooed Mohawk war chief Brant Saquainquaragton. As late as 1696 he was called Thowariage, and by 1700 he had acquired a new name that roughly translates to "Disappearing Smoke" (Bryant 1889:5; Sivertsen 1996:64).[15] Whether or not this cognomen was transferred to his body (e.g., face) via a permanent tattoo is not known, although the area above his chin is nearly black with markings (see Figure 4.7).

John Long remarked that his Ojibway adoption ceremony culminated in the receipt of a tattoo and new name. This highly descriptive account speaks about not only the technique employed to execute the tattooing but also the ritual preparations that were performed before it. To my knowledge, this account is without parallel and thus is quoted at some length here:

When the pipe has gone round, a sweating-house is prepared with six long poles fixed in the ground and pointed at the top; it is then covered with skins and blankets to exclude the air, and the area of the house will contain only three persons. The person to be adopted is then stripped naked, and enters the hut with two chiefs; two large stones made red hot are brought in, and thrown on the ground; water is then brought in a bark dish, and sprinkled on the stones with cedar branches, the steam arising from which puts the person into a most profuse perspiration, and opens the pores to receive the other part of the ceremony.

When the perspiration is at the height, he quits the house, and jumps into the water; immediately on coming out a blanket is thrown over him, and he is led to the chief's hut, where he undergoes the following operation. Being extended on his back, the chief draws the figure he intends to make with a pointed stick, dipped in water in which gun-powder has been dissolved; after which, with ten needles dipped in vermilion, and fixed in a small wooden frame, he pricks the delineated parts, and where the bolder outlines occur, he incises the flesh with a gun flint; the vacant spaces, or those not marked with vermilion, are rubbed in with gunpowder, which produces the variety of red and blue; the wounds are then seared with pink wood, to prevent them from festering.

This operation, which is performed at intervals, lasts two or three days. Every morning the parts are washed with cold water, in which is infused an herb called *Pockqueesegan*, which resembles English box, and is mixed by the Indians with the tobacco they smoke, to take off the strength. During the process, the war songs are sung, accompanied by a rattle hung round with hawk bells, called *chessaquoy*, which is kept shaking, to stifle the groans such pains must naturally occasion. Upon the ceremony being completed, they give the party a name; that which they allotted to me, was *Aniik*, or Beaver. (Long 1791:47–49)

Most historic chroniclers are in agreement that tattooing among warriors was a mark of distinction that had to be earned, not given.[16] As success on the battlefield increased with additional scalps, prisoners, or human lives being taken, so too did the tattooing of the Woodlands warrior. Early eighteenth-century accounts from the Southeast by Le Page du Pratz (1947 [1758]:346) and Catesby (1747:9) document that young men who had performed bravely in combat would receive tattoos commemorating their victories and depicting their personal manitous (see also Chapter 1).

Adair visited the Chickasaw in the late eighteenth century and also referred to tattooing. He related that the Chickasaw could immediately tell which prisoners held the highest military ranks by the blue marks spread across their chests and arms, "they being as legible as our alphabetical characters are to us" (Adair 2005 [1775]:384).[17] He also noted that if any Chickasaw warrior wore "false marks," these were erased in a public ceremony with the juices of green corn (Adair 2005 [1775]:384; see also Chapter 1).

In the Northern Woodlands, the Jesuit Relations of 1662–1663 attest that a "captain General" of the Iroquois, nicknamed "Nero" by the French because of his notorious cruelty, sacrificed eighty men by slow fire to the "shade" or ghost of a brother killed in combat. This individual was also said to have killed sixty more men by his own hand. According to the French account, Nero kept a tally of his exploits on his thigh, which "consequently appears to be covered with black characters" (Lalemant 1899:169–171).

In reviewing the ethnographic literature focusing on tattooing amongst historic Eastern Woodlands peoples, most writers suggest that the fullest expression of this art form was probably extinct before the start of the Revolutionary War, with the deaths of the last generation of tattooed warriors and other tribal leaders about that time. I believe instead that the most symbolic and complex forms of tattooing probably died out even earlier, and that the last vestiges of prehistoric-era tattooing were produced only as late as the seventeenth century. This conclusion is supported by ethnographic accounts such as that of Bartram, who during his visit to the Creeks in the mid-eighteenth century wrote that the most ornate tattooing "is found on the skin and bodies of their ancient chiefs and *micos*"[18] (Bartram 1996 [1853]:533).

Philip Georg Friedrich von Reck, who in 1736 left us with some of the most important illustrations of Yuchi drawn from life, depicted their "supreme [military] commander" Kipahalgwa (see Figure 1.10) and the Yuchi "King," or mico Senkaitschi (see Figure 1.11), with elaborate facial and body tattooing consisting of vertical bands, which I believe are raptorial bird plumes, running across their chests (see also Chapter 1). Based on their important positions in Yuchi society, both men must have been approaching or had already reached middle age, and in all likelihood were tattooed around 1700 or just before. The similarly tattooed Yamacraw-Creek mico Tomochichi, whom von Reck interacted with on his journey to Georgia, was portrayed in a 1734 oil painting by William Verelst commemorating his trip to England and the court of King George II (see Figure 1.12). It was said that Tomochichi was born in 1650, and that at the time of his sitting he was almost ninety years of age (Foreman 1943:57).

/ *Tattooed "Bodyes" of Evidence* /

One of the most useful, and surprisingly overlooked, accounts of tattooing in Iroquoia is that of an elderly Delaware warrior who joined a Moravian settlement in Bethlehem, Pennsylvania, and was baptized as Michael in 1742. The Moravian missionaries Heckewelder and Loskiel knew Michael well. From the details that can be gleaned of his facial tattooing and heavily scarred body, we can reconstruct, perhaps for the first time in hundreds of years, some of the hitherto forgotten secrets of the indelible arts of the Northern Woodlands.

In his discussion of Native American dress and ornamentation Heckewelder (1876 [1818]) provides a description of Michael's extensive tattoos at the time he joined the Moravian settlement:

> This man, who was then at an advanced age, had a most striking appearance, and could not be viewed without astonishment. Besides that his body was full of scars, where he had been struck and pierced by the arrows of the enemy, there was not a spot to be seen, on that part of it which was exposed to view, but what was tattooed over with some drawing relative to his achievements, so that the whole together struck the beholder with amazement and terror. On his whole face, neck, shoulders, arms, thighs and legs, as well as on his breast and back, were represented scenes of the various actions and engagements he had been in; in short, the whole of his history was there deposited, which was well known to those of his nation, and was such that all who heard it thought it could never be surpassed by man. (Heckewelder 1876 [1818]:206)

Heckewelder's superior, Moravian bishop George Loskiel, also knew Michael and attended his funeral in 1756. Looking over the brave man's eighty-year-old body in death, Loskiel reported invaluable information concerning Michael's facial tattoos. With this information, I now believe we have the key with which to unlock some of the meanings behind several famous portraits of tattooed personages and engraved war clubs from the Eastern Woodlands region. Loskiel writes:

> The serenity of [Michael's] countenance, when laid in his coffin, made a singular contrast with the figures, scarified upon his face when a warrior. These were as follows: upon the right cheek and temple, a large snake; from the under-lip a pole passed over the nose, and between the eyes to the top of his forehead, ornamented at every quarter of an inch with round marks, representing scalps: upon the left cheek, two lances crossing each other; and upon the lower jaw, the head of a wild boar. (Loskiel 1794 [1789]:189)

Loskiel's statement regarding scalp-tally tattoos makes perfect sense because this is an exceedingly common tattoo motif amongst the Iroquois, and possibly the Cherokee and Yuchi.

The Iroquois also engraved scalp tallies on their war clubs, as evidenced by a rare seventeenth-century example housed at the Fenimore Art Museum in Cooperstown, New York (Figure 4.8). This war club, believed to have been left at the scene of an Iroquois engagement with a coastal Algonquian group during King Philip's War (1675–1676), displays an exceedingly rich body of facial tattoos that belonged to the club's owner, who may have been Seneca or Mohawk based on the style of tattooing.[19] A close-up view of the club clearly shows a series of approximately fifteen carefully carved circles running along a band that crosses the ridge of the warrior's nose. These circles likely

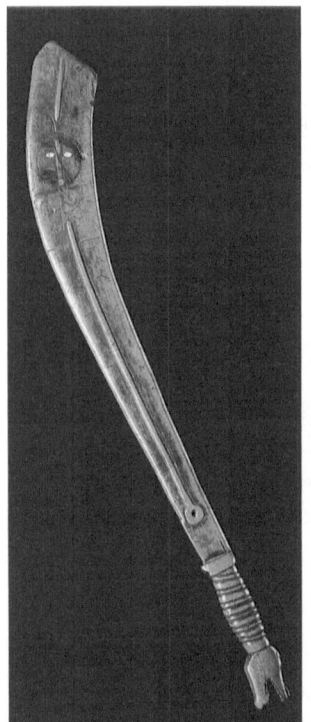
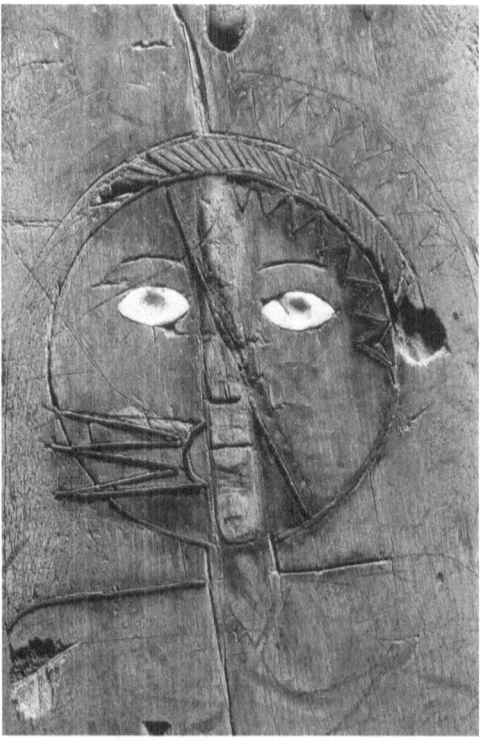

FIGURE 4.8. Iroquois war club from King Philip's War (1675–1676) showing scalp and wound tallies, manitou tattoo near the mouth, and inverted bird on the sternum of the warrior. The backside of the club shows two headless figures that represent slain enemies. Image courtesy of the Donald Ellis Gallery, Dundas (Ontario) and New York City.

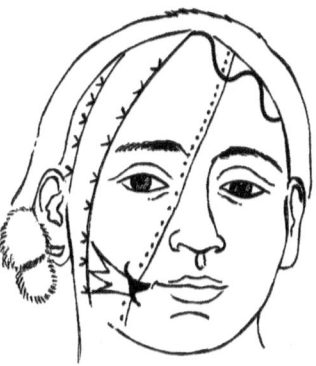

FIGURE 4.9. Illustration of Mohawk warrior
Onigoheriago's facial tattoos (after Fenton 1978:311).

represent a scalp tally and fit nicely with Loskiel's account of the Delaware
war chief Michael's scalp-tally tattoos.

Similar scalp-tally bands appear on the faces of individuals in various historic imagery and portraiture, including the drawing by Lafitau (see Figure
4.5), in the portrait of Mohawk war chief Brant Saquainquaragton (see Figure 4.7), and on the face of Mohawk warrior Johannes Onigoheriago, who
accompanied Saquainquaragton to England in 1710 (Figure 4.9). Onigoheriago proudly displays approximately twenty scalp-tally marks, a manitou
design beside his mouth, and fourteen cross-hatches or V-shaped markings
that probably denote the number of times he had been wounded in battle.

The face on the war club has several other tattoo markings. A series of
zigzagging lines (or seven conjoined triangles) at the hairline could indicate a
tattooed serpent, an extremely common facial tattoo found across the entire
Eastern Woodlands region,[20] although I think this motif relates other information. Upon closer inspection, another series of similar zigzagging lines is
faintly carved above the first set and resembles ten conjoined arrowheads. This
second set of symbols seems to have been added to the club after the owner
first marked his facial portrait upon it. Furthermore, the bottom (or seventh)
triangle terminating the original zigzag design on the owner's face looks as if
the carver attempted to redraw an arrowhead at this place. This suggests to me
that both design elements stand for another kind of tattooed tally mark, one
record being placed upon the club at the time of construction, and another
added later, after some additional feat had been accomplished.

In Heckewelder's (1876 [1818]:206) account of Michael, he stated: "His
body was full of scars, where he had been struck and pierced by the arrows

of the enemy." Similar information was also carved, with slight variations, into ornamented trees. As previously noted, the Paris Document (see Figure 4.4) specifically identifies symbols indicating wounds received on a military expedition. At another place, the document states that a man receiving a wound will "paint a broken gun which however is connected with the stock, or even an arrow" (O'Callaghan 1849:6). Woodlands war clubs also displayed this information in varying forms, and several examples contain bent or broken arrows to indicate that members of the war party had been wounded (Meachum 2007:70).[21] Therefore, I believe the owner of the club from King Philip's War had been wounded at least ten times before deciding to leave his club at the scene of the battle.

Another intriguing tattoo motif, which resembles a sunburst streaking off the face, adjoins the warrior's mouth on the lower jaw. The location for this tattoo seems to be a preferred one across the Woodlands; eighteenth-century portrait art from the Yuchi, Cherokee, Yamacraw-Creek, Delaware, and Mohawk (see Figures 1.11 and 1.12) shows similar placement of facial tattoos. The Delaware warrior Michael also was reported to wear a "boar" design in this region. I believe the boar was one of Michael's personal manitous, because the boar was not a clan animal of the Delaware (Miller 1996:157).[22]

Earlier in this chapter I noted that solar, avian, and other animal designs were commonly adopted as manitou spirits and were usually tattooed on the face. Placing such powerful beings on the face or near the mouth was not a haphazard choice, because the mouth (and perhaps the eyes) was considered to be a passageway into the soul. This ideology may be embodied in the art of the late prehistoric Mississippian period (AD 900–1600), including on representations of the "Birdman" character (Figure 4.10) and in individualized and "tattooed" prehistoric Pecan Point–style human head effigy vessels (Figure 4.11). Avian symbols seem to emerge from the mouths of many of these objects or "grapple" their eyes. The facial markings accompanying several of the Pecan Point vessels resemble early eighteenth-century facial tattooing shown on portraits of Senkaitschi (as depicted by von Reck; see Figure 1.11), Tomochichi (see Figure 1.12), and the Mahican warrior Etow Oh Koam (Figure 4.12). These motifs may have operated as personal manitous and perhaps helped carry the warrior safely through life and into the afterworld at death.

This meaning can be further illuminated through other examples of material culture, including both the club from King Philip's War and an Iroquois war club at the National Museum of the American Indian (Figure 4.13). This later item features a sinuous carving pattern representing a serpent (likely the manitou of the owner) moving along the handle of the club towards its

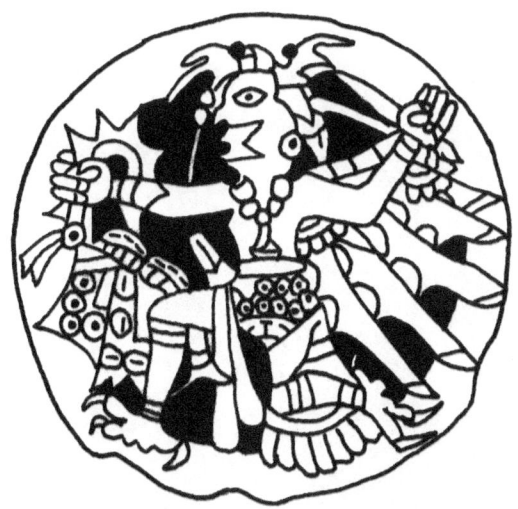

FIGURE 4.10. Marine shell gorget from the Etowah site in Georgia showing the Bird-man with sunburst motif beside the mouth (after Knight and Franke 2007: fig. 6.2).

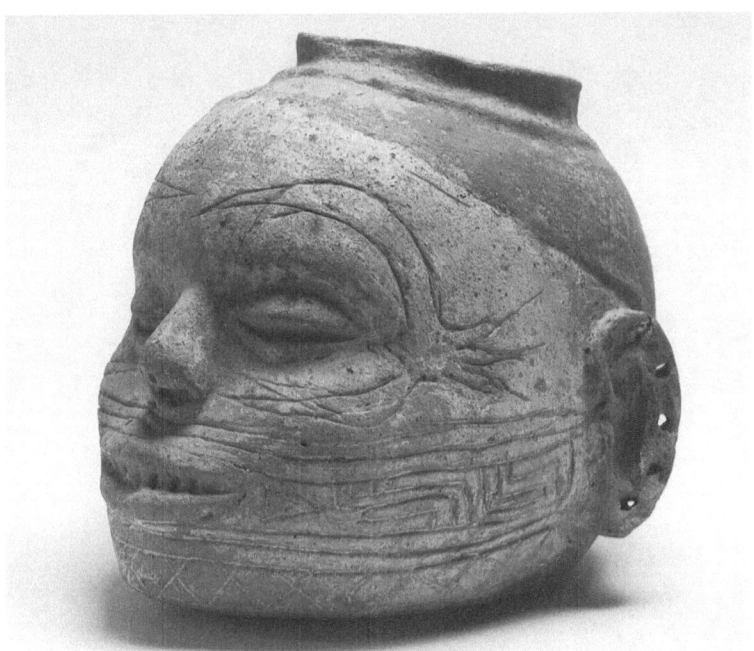

FIGURE 4.11. Human head effigy vessel of the Pecan Point style. Pecan Point site, Poinsett County, Arkansas, AD 1350–1550. Catalog number A91298, Department of Anthropology, Smithsonian Institution, Suitland, Maryland. Photograph by Jane Beck.

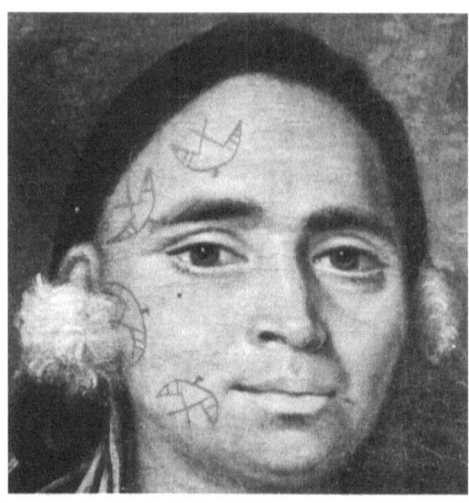

FIGURE 4.12. Detail of Etow Oh Koam's facial
tattoos from painting by John Verelst, 1710.

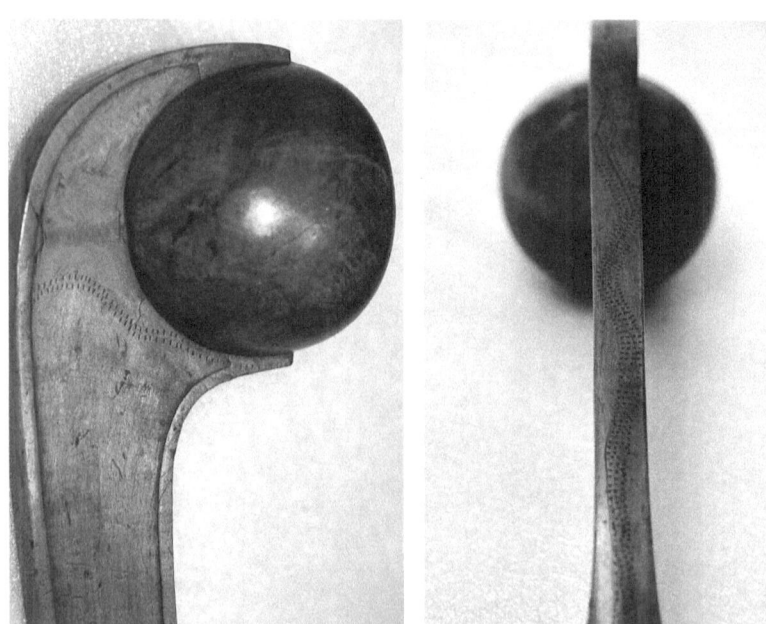

FIGURE 4.13. Iroquois war club with serpent manitou, eighteenth century. Catalog number 11/1317, National Museum of the American Indian,
Smithsonian Institution, Suitland, Maryland. Photograph by Lars Krutak.

"mouth." As Carpenter (2005:86) has observed, "In Woodland[s] cosmology, death swallows its victims."

On the club from King Philip's War, a thin "spirit" or "power line" emanates just above the tattooed sunburst at the mouth (see Figure 4.8) and connects with a turtle design on the opposite side. Inscribed within the body of the turtle is a "star" that Carpenter (2005:85) indicated was a clan design that could double as a personal manitou. I believe instead that the star motif from the war club represents a cruciform or "cross" tattoo such as that which appears on the necks or sternums of Iroquois warriors in the Paris Document (see Figure 4.4A) and on Mohawk warriors like Brant (see Figure 4.7), who wore on his chest several forms of cross tattoo patterns including one circumscribed by what appears to be a crayfish.[23]

Similar cross designs appear as neck motifs in the widely reproduced engraving of three Cherokee leaders who visited England in 1762 (see Figure 1.14).[24] These men also wear facial tattoos that resemble Loskiel's (1794 [1789]:189) descriptions of cross-hatches, or "lances," while zigzagging designs that originate at the mouth may also signify some kind of spirit line. This engraving and other Cherokee portraits of the era do not lend themselves to great detail, but it is reasonable to assume that circular scalp-tally marks were also a feature of Cherokee facial tattooing. Among the Yuchi, von Reck composed a pencil sketch of the mico Senkaitschi that prominently displays several tattoos aside both corners of the mouth, and a serpentine motif moving across the forehead that ends in at least three circles sloping down the left side of his face (Figure 4.14).

The cross motif, which appears on Brant's chest and the necks of the Cherokee, may have its origins in prehistoric shell gorgets from the Mississippian Art and Ceremonial Complex (Reilly 2004). These ornaments were worn suspended over the throat and sternum, and often a cross adorned the center. In several examples, the cruciform, as a representation of the cardinal directions, was encompassed by a solar motif or sunburst pattern that probably signified the Upper World. Sometimes both the cross and sun emblems were surmounted by the heads of birds interpreted as crested woodpeckers (Figure 4.15) (Krech 2009:98). Among the historic Osage, shell gorget pendants were considered to be "life symbols" of particular clans (La Flesche 1932:361). They symbolized the sun and longevity, or in the words of the Osage: "It is a god of day who sitteth in the heavens. By pressing this to his breast, he shall be free from all causes of death" (La Flesche 1932:383).[25] According to La Flesche (1921a: plate 13), the pileated woodpecker (*wa-zhi^n-ga pa stese-dse*) "is a life symbol of the Tsi'-zhu Wa-non^n ["Elder Sky" clan], the principal war gens of

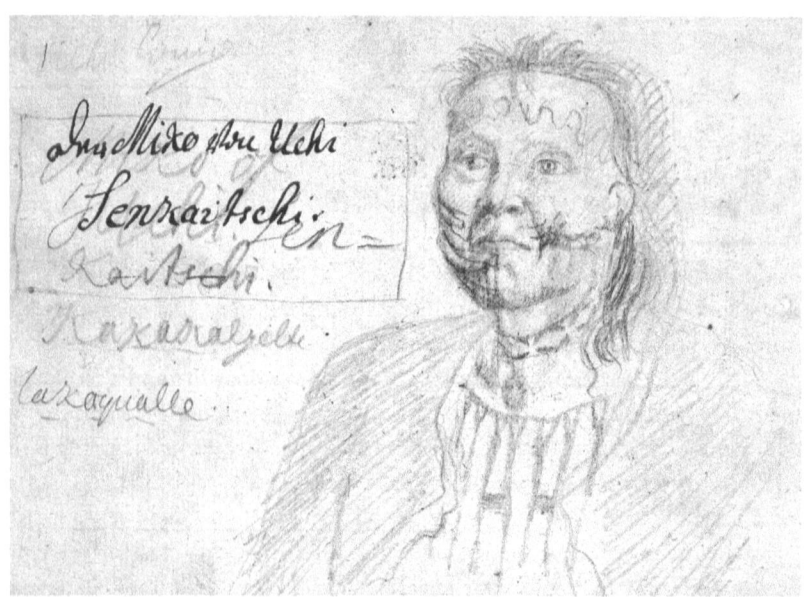

FIGURE 4.14. Facial and body tattoos of the Yuchi leader Senkaitschi of Georgia, 1736. A series of interlocking neck tattoos closely resemble a ring of conjoined birds. Image courtesy of the Royal Library of Denmark (Det Kongelige Bibliotek), Copenhagen: NKS 565 4°, 47.

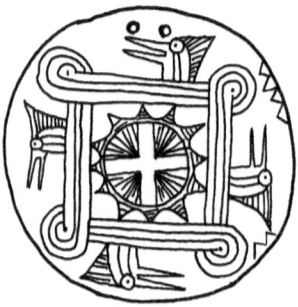

FIGURE 4.15. Late prehistoric Cox Mound–style marine shell gorget from Mississippi exhibiting central cross motif and sunburst pattern (after Holmes 1883: plate 68).

the [Tsi-zhu] tribal division.[26] This bird symbolizes the sun, the moon, and the morning and evening stars. These stars have the power of granting to the warriors trophies and spoils."

One final motif present on the club from King Philip's War can be related to tattooing of warriors in the Northern Woodlands, and so bears mention here. A large inverted bird (the tail and wings of which are visible in Figure 4.8) is positioned on the sternum of the warrior, and perhaps indicates yet another manitou of the owner. As the pictorial record indicates, V-shaped sternum tattoos are a common tattoo symbol throughout Iroquoia, the Great Lakes (Figure 4.16), Choctaw territory (see Figure 1.18), and the Yuchi region (see Figures 1.10 and 1.11). Sternum tattooing seems to have persisted longer than facial tattooing, and one of the latest examples, a miniature oil painting of the seventy-five-year-old Oneida chief

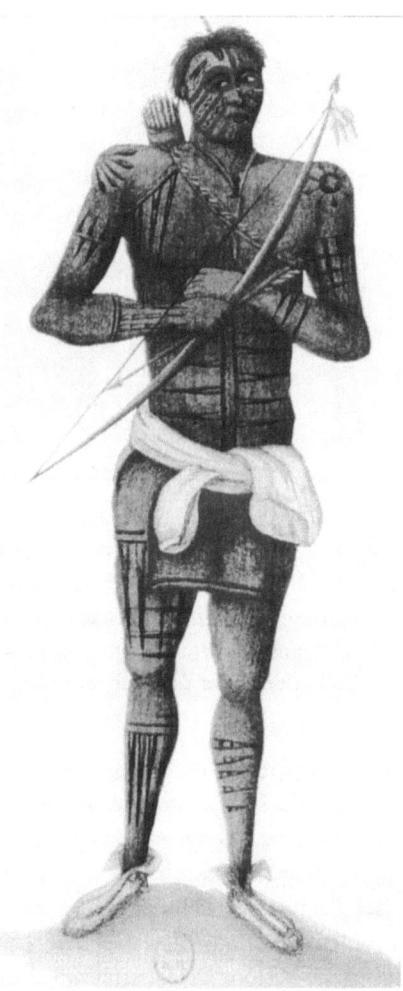

FIGURE 4.16. The tattooing of a Fox or Mesquakie warrior of Wisconsin (ca. 1710) provides evidence that the horizontal placement of elongated triangular torso markings was a widespread cultural tradition spanning the western Great Lakes region to the Eastern Woodlands. Image courtesy of the Bibliothèque Nationale de France, Paris.

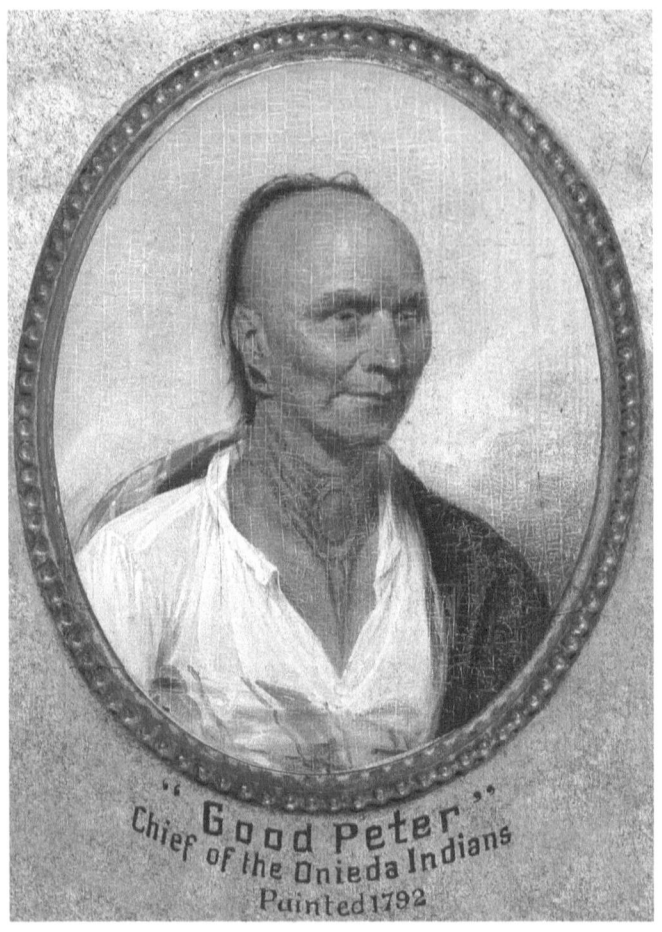

"Good Peter"
Chief of the Onieda Indians
Painted 1792

FIGURE 4.17. *Tattooing of the Elderly Oneida Chief "Good Peter."*
Painting by John Trumbull, 1792. Image courtesy of the John
Trumbull Collection at the Yale University Art Gallery.

Good Peter, dates to 1792 (Fenton 1978:312) (Figure 4.17). However, it is
not known if these V-shaped sternum markings carried avian symbolism
(e.g., a predatorial bird swooping downward; Figure 4.18) or were related to
sacred ancient weaponry (e.g., flint knife), as they were among peoples of
the Eastern Plains (see Chapter 5). Perhaps future research may shed light
on this important problem.[27]

    Nearly all Iroquois men's tattoos were distinct to them. According to the
account book of Dutch trader Evert Wendell, dated August 13, 1706, a young
Seneca brave named Tan Na Eedsies visited Wendell in Albany, New York,
and completed his transaction by drawing a pictograph next to his order

(Figure 4.19). This drawing identified Tan Na Eedsies specifically, and the tattooed patterns on his face, neck, and chest were considered equivalent to his personal signature. Evert's account books contain several other drawings of his customers' tattoos, which he and his clients used to decipher their financial activities. As the British officer Hyde (ca. 1695) stated: "They have neither Learning or letters but trust all to their Memory, and this way of figuring their faces and bodyes they use as an Ornament" (Hyde 1965 cited in Meachum 2007:68).

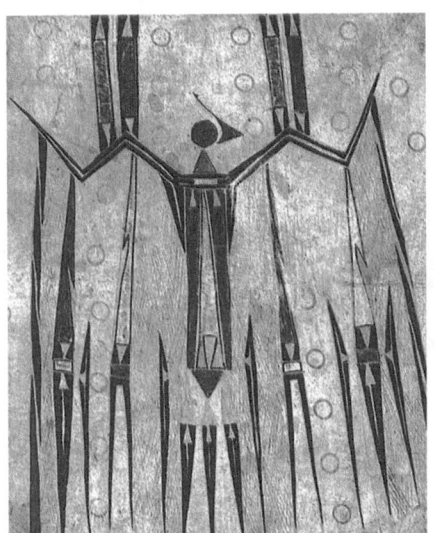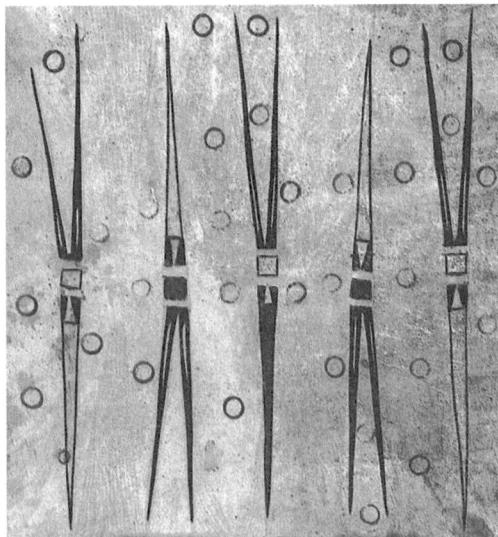

FIGURE 4.18. Details of two ornamented eighteenth-century deerskins attributed to the Illinois and featuring avian motifs with similarities to warrior tattoos. The skin on the left portrays a thunderbird or other raptorial bird with plumes closely resembling the chest tattoo patterns of Iroquois, Yuchi, and Yamacraw-Creek warriors (redrawn after Horse Capture 1993:121). The skin on the right shows circular hailstones and abstract forked-tail bird designs (redrawn after Horse Capture 1993:117) that also resemble warrior tattoos of the Eastern Woodlands. Among the Delaware, the "forked eagle" (*chauwalanne*), or rather, the swallow-tailed kite (*Elanoides forticatus*), was said to rise so high in the sky that the human eye could not perceive it. Bad weather, thunder, and rain were said to follow when it approached a village. Among indigenous peoples of the eastern plains, the swallow-tailed kite was specifically associated with war dances, war bundles, Thunder clans, and the Creator. These raptors are great acrobats and powerful fliers, able to devour their prey while on the wing. These and other unique characteristics may have contributed to their adoption as a form of tattooing by Woodlands warriors.

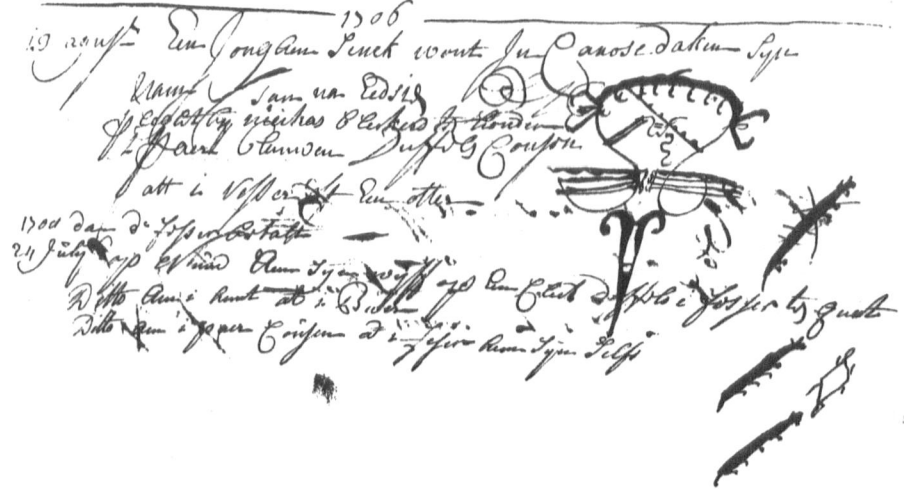

FIGURE 4.19. Corporal tattoos of the Seneca warrior and trader Tan Na Eedsies, 1706. Image courtesy of the New-York Historical Society.

Tan Na Eedsies's facial marks are consistent with the ethnographic record and include a serpent manitou, a series of birds skirting his hairline, scalptally markings running along a bar that crossed his nose, and other neck and sternum designs presented elsewhere in this chapter. In his drawing of Two Arrows, Lafitau presents a similar tendril-like or "double-curve" (Fenton 1978:303; Speck 1914) sternum design. This motif is commonly employed in Iroquois embroidery at or on the borders of leggings, shirts, breech-clouts, headbands, hair ornaments, and moccasins. According to the noted indigenous Seneca scholar Parker (1912:616), this design had deep significance for the Iroquois "and [e]ven the Yuchi [were] familiar with it." This design symbolized the celestial tree, its branches piercing the heavens and its roots extending into the Beneath World, and may have held secondary meanings associated with life, living, and light, as well as continuity of life in the world beyond (Parker 1912:616–617). Thus, as a symbol that represents the passageway between the worlds, this mark may have provided psychological benefits to its owner.

Sternum tattoos of this sort were also engraved on war clubs. A particularly fine Onondaga example said to have been gifted to Sir William Johnson (1715–1774), the superintendent of Indian Affairs for the State of New York, clearly illustrates the full-body tattooing and war exploits of a mideighteenth-century Iroquois warrior (see Meachum 2007:71) (Figure 4.20). A V-shaped sternum tattoo appears below the man's face, followed by sunburst designs resembling bird talons inked upon his shoulders, and a series of eight vertically oriented triangular markings. Also depicted are four balls carved into the abdomen of the figure that, according to the Paris Document, represent war wounds: "If there be only wounded . . . and if it be a gunshot they make the mark of the ball on the body" (O'Callaghan 1849:6). Although the owner of the club neglected to depict any of his facial tattoos in great detail, the adjacent sides of the club are replete with war symbolism numbering engagements, captures, wounded, losses, and a tally of enemies killed and or scalped (Carpenter 2005:98; Meachum 2007:71–72).

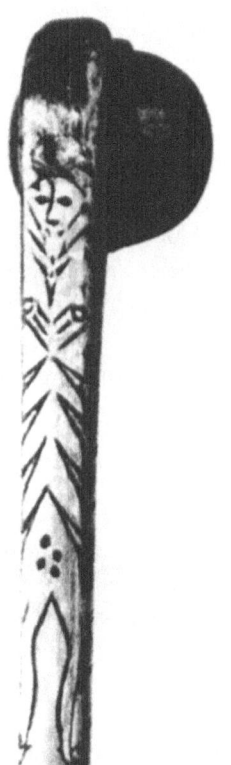

FIGURE 4.20. Decorated Onondaga war club of a great war captain, ca. 1760. The back side of the club provides an image of the warrior based on the tattoos worn on his neck, shoulders, and chest. One side of the club displays thirteen armed human figures. They represent the number of enemies the club owner had taken prisoner, scalped, or killed. The opposite side of the club details how many war campaigns were waged, whether there were wounded at these battles, and whether a death was avenged or the owner raised a war party (after Meachum 2007:71).

/ *Conclusion* /

With this essay, I have attempted to direct a spotlight on the largely neglected study of warrior tattooing in the Northern Woodlands through a comparative review of ethnographic sources and material evidence drawn from within and outside of the region. Through several examples I have shown that tattoos were not simply ornamental devices, but instead were meaningful conduits through which supernatural power and esoteric knowledge flowed. Moreover, as physical manifestations of mythological and highly spiritual entities, tattoos were embodied with life-preserving forces that granted their owners some level of psychological influence and control over their adversaries.

Although it has been argued here that tattooed warriors across the Northern Woodlands were participants in a magico-religious complex of shared belief and experience, the exercise of looking for other cultural patterns and symbolic implications indicates that there is still much more research that needs to be conducted before we can firmly codify this corpus of permanent visual representation. Nevertheless, my purpose is to call attention to these problems, to sharpen our focus, and to stimulate interest in other investigators in the hope that they will establish new ways of seeing and reading the messages encoded in the indelible arts of Woodlands warrior tattoo.

/ *Author's Acknowledgments* /

This contribution is the product of several collaborations with collectors, galleries, and institutions that supplied visual resources that greatly enhanced my overview of Woodlands tattoo. I would like to extend my deepest gratitude to John and Marva Warnock, the Donald Ellis Gallery, the Royal Library of Denmark (Det Kongelige Bibliotek), the Bibliothèque Nationale (Paris), the National Anthropological Archives of the Smithsonian Institution, and the New-York Historical Society. Considerable thanks should also be offered to publisher Matthias Reuss for allowing me to reproduce here material previously published in my book *Spiritual Skin: Magical Tattoos and Scarification* (Germany: Edition Reuss, 2012). Additionally, I would like to thank Jane Beck (Repatriation Office, National Museum of Natural History) for her photographic efforts and Aaron Deter-Wolf and Carol Diaz-Granados for their insightful editorial comments.

/ Notes /

1. Compare with von Reck's (1736) observation of the Yamacraw-Creek and Yuchi of the Southeastern Woodlands. "But the reason they are so cruel [to their prisoners captured in war] is that they hold death itself to be no punishment and do not fear it" (Hvidt 1980:47).

2. These personal symbols can be considered as an extended type of kin because the individual is adopted by the manitou spirit during his vision quest and a new kinship relation is established, one that lasts a lifetime (Fogelson and Brightman 2002).

3. Speaking about the Ottawa, the Jesuit missionary Father Sebastien Rasles wrote in 1723:

> An Ottawa wishing to acquire a manito usually took the first animal that appeared to him during sleep. Afterward, he killed an animal of this kind, put its skin or its feathers in the most conspicuous part of his cabin and made a feast in its honor, during which he addressed it in most respectful terms. From that time on it was recognized as his manito, and he carried its skin to war, to the hunt, and on journeys, believing that it would preserve him from every danger and cause all his undertakings to succeed. (Kinietz 1965:288)

De Smet (1905:1093) provides similar evidence for the nineteenth-century Potawatomi: "The animal which presents itself to him will become his manitou or totem (*dodeme*), and all his long life he will carry about him a badge of it, whether a claw, a tail, a feather, it matters not."

4. The origin story of a nineteenth-century Chippewa war club housed in the National Museum of Natural History (E359606) is also attached to a vision of its owner and creator. Joseph Nicollet (1970:163) revealed that the adoption of the rifle before 1836–1837 compelled Chippewa warriors to increasingly abandon more "ancient" weapons like war clubs in combat. To the Chippewa, however, the club was "still of a sacred character and [was] classified as [an] object which women, children, and strangers may not profane by their touch."

5. This is perhaps a misspelling. The Iroquois and other peoples of the Great Lakes call the golden eagle *kiliou*. Amongst many Woodlands groups, the golden eagle was the most powerful bird of prey, capable of killing other large birds and even small mammals such as fawns. Krech (2009:111) writes about the importance and use of eagle feathers amongst the Caddo, Creek, Chickasaw, and Cherokee of the Southeastern Woodlands.

6. King (1999:60), speaking about a very similar war club (before 1821) at the British Museum, writes that the heart motif seen carved into these clubs is patterned after Montreal-made silver brooches used in the Indian trade. The British Museum club also contains the heart design, but it is instead punched into the steel blade of the weapon.

7. In the Great Plains, these objects were variously called medicine bundles or war bundles. For a detailed discussion of these implements, please see Chapter 5 of this volume.

8. Deliette (1947 [1934]:152) states that the warrior's mat was fabricated by women. For a discussion of similar objects (e.g., "portable shrines") employed by tribes of the Eastern Plains, please see Chapter 5 of this volume.

9. Before an Illinois war leader employed his war birds, he fasted up to a week, daubed and painted his face black, prayed to his manitous, and pondered his dreams. According to Cadillac (1710–1716), the French explorer, adventurer, and future governor of Louisiana: "If during their sleep they see visions of their enemies at certain times and places, and if the vision has appeared favorable during their fast, they take it as a good omen and conclude that they will be victorious over their enemies" (Cadillac 1947 [1883]:22).

10. Creek warriors whooped when scalping their enemies with the cry turning into "several tremulous throat tones in imitation of a turkey's gobble" (Krech 2009:121).

11. Whether or not Lafitau was providing us with a lesson in deciphering Iroquois pictography or actually representing the true exploits of known warriors in these sketches can only be a source of conjecture. The heavily tattooed warrior named Two Feathers is stated to have been a war leader that participated in six campaigns, "and at the fourth where he commanded the [war] party" (Lafitau 1977 [1724]:6). His chest markings are consistent with those of a military leader as well as with the Mohawk (e.g., Brant) and with Southeastern Woodlands groups like the Yuchi (e.g., Kipahalgwa) and Yamacraw-Creek (e.g., Tomochichi), who wore slight variations of a similar design. Although this could be a matter of coincidence, the numbers of triangular elements that comprise Two Feathers's chest design also match the number of war campaigns he participated in. They do not correspond, however, to the number of arrow marks on his face (five), which may provide additional evidence that these marks contained different information; that is, they may have tallied the number of his war wounds or something else.

12. John Long, who was adopted by the Ojibway and had a working knowledge of their language, recognized in his book that descent group or hereditary totemism existed among the Iroquois, and so "presumably recognized the presence of both among the Ojibwa" (Fogelson and Brightman 2002:308).

13. Pope (1792) reported that very young Creek boys, some just four years of age, were tattooed. After the painful ordeal was completed, one child exclaimed, "Now, I'm a man, and a warrior too" (Swanton 1946:533).

14. Among the Iroquois, according to Morgan (1922 [1851]:95), only war chiefs "could earn the right to names that were not hereditary to the tribe or an individual clan or his family . . . [R]ather these were purely elective and a reward of merit in combat." Conversely, Iroquois civil-administrative chiefs, or sachems, received their

names from a pool of fifty select titles that had been handed down for such purposes (Morgan 1922 [1851]:95).

15. According to Sivertsen (1996:64), Brant was "the first known holder of this important name."

16. Iroquois women were rarely tattooed. But when they were, the purpose was usually medicinal, as a remedy to cure toothache or rheumatism (Lafitau 1977 [1724]:34). For more information on women's tattooing in the Southeastern Woodlands, see Swanton (1946).

17. Cadillac (1947 [1883]:28–29) recorded that Illinois prisoners were able to recite the names of those men they had killed in combat. Whether they gained this information from deciphering the tattoo marks or "alphabetical signatures" of their enemies is not known but is perhaps implied.

18. Foreman (1943:57) writes that the term *mico* is analogous to *chief*.

19. Evidently, the Mohawks continued their aggressions against Native groups in Massachusetts even after the treaty ending King Philip's War was finally signed. "In 1680 the Massachusetts commissioners said the Mohawks had killed or captured 60 of their friendly Indians in three years" (Beauchamp 1905:226).

20. In their review of sources for the Natchez, Fundaburk and Foreman (1957:58) indicate the relationship between serpents, tattoos, and warfare: "Among the Natchez, the serpent seems to have held a place very near to the sun, for Tattooed-serpent was evidently the hereditary title of the great war chiefs" (Fundaburk and Foreman 1957:58).

21. There are reports of Northern Woodlands warriors who possessed arrow tattoos on their faces. In 1749, the explorer and naturalist Peter Kalm witnessed a group of tattooed Hurons on a trip to Quebec. He wrote: "Many of them have figures on the face, and on the whole body, which are stained into the skin, so to be indelible. These figures are commonly black; some have a snake painted on each cheek, some have several crosses, some an arrow, others the sun, or anything else that imagination leads them to. They have such figures likewise on the breast, thighs, and other parts of the body; but some have no figures at all" (Kalm 1812 [1749]:659).

22. Of course, the boar tattoo may have referred to a new namesake that Michael earned in war.

23. The crayfish is not a clan symbol of any Iroquois tribe, and it may have been one of Brant's manitous. The Mohawk were comprised of three clans (turtle, bear, wolf) and Brant himself was a member of the bear clan. For this reason, a bear stands to his left in his 1710 portrait.

24. Similar tattooing also adorned the sternums of Hidatsa and Mandan warriors of the plains. A related motif was worn by the Yankton Sioux. See Chapter 5 of this volume for more details.

25. Speaking of the Kansa or Kaw, Dorsey (1894:372) wrote: "They often wear a shell which is in honor or in representation of Him [The Creator, or Wakanda] . . . Some addressed the sun as Wakanda."

26. Feathers of these birds were used in Osage tattooing bundles as paintbrushes to apply pigment (see Chapter 5 of this book).

27. This symbolism may have originally been derived from ancestral Mississippian Art and Ceremonial Complex "birdman" forms of iconography. Analogs drawn from other scalping and headhunting societies around the world support an avian origin for many forms of chest tattooing (see Krutak 2007:195, 203).

< 5 >

The Art of Enchantment

Corporeal Marking and Tattooing Bundles of the Great Plains

Lars Krutak

/ / / /

*While these bundles were in my house it seemed as if
the old people were still with me in spirit, the forefathers
who made them. But now they are gone. The dreams
of men long dead lie wrapped within those covers.*

OTOE ELDER (HARRINGTON 1913:110)

Rock art panels in Missouri provide evidence that tattooing probably has been an indelible feature of Great Plains culture for at least one thousand years (Diaz-Granados 2004:147), if not longer. In the historic period, ethnographic records reveal that tattooing was practiced amongst most groups inhabiting this vast culture area, with the tradition reaching its apex amongst Siouan groups including the Hidatsa, Osage, Ponca, Omaha, Otoe, and Iowa. Although each tribal society employed specific abstract designs in ritualistically mandated patterns, the religious structure of belief behind the origins of these corporal symbols was remarkably similar.

Fundamental to such concepts was the creative and actively controlling force of all things, called *Wakanda* (also *Wakonda*, *Wa-kon-da*, or *Wako^{n}da*), from *Wakán*[1] (Sioux, "holy") (Foster 1994:71). Sometimes glossed as the "Great Spirit" in literature focusing on other Plains tribes that tattooed (e.g., Plains Cree and Prairie Potawatomi) (Light 1972:13; Skinner 1924:66), *Wakanda* was the invisible, mysterious, and sacred power that permeated all things, including the sacred bundles that housed tattoo instruments, which were derived from the "Mysterious Power" itself (La Flesche 1930:532). This divine supernatural energy was revered and also feared because it was believed to animate the cosmos, as well as the spiritual and ancestral worlds of the people.

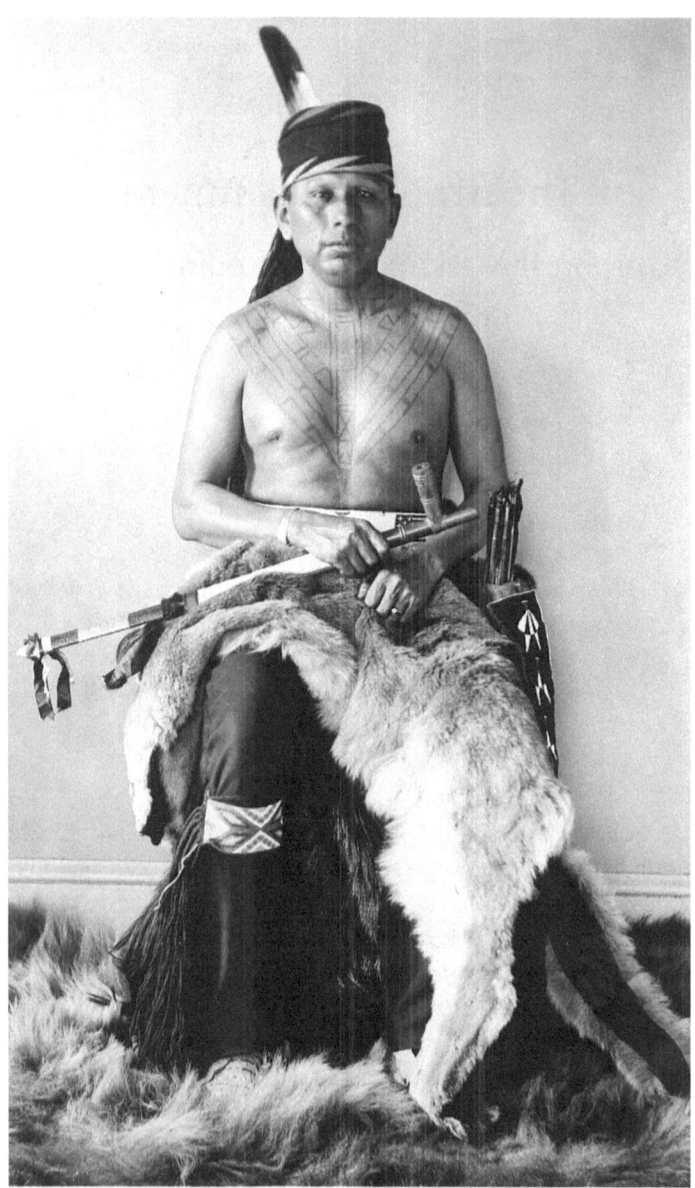

FIGURE 5.1. The tattooed Osage chief Bacon Rind (1860–1932). Bacon Rind was about seventeen years old when he received the ancient markings, but they were not received as a result of successful combat. He stated that the markings were made "to make him faithful in keeping the [sacred] rites." These rites included seeking visions with the aid of the sacred pipes of his clan "in order that his children might have long life" (Fletcher and La Flesche 1911:220). Manuscript collection 4993, National Anthropological Archives, Smithsonian Institution, Suitland, Maryland.

The motifs used in tattooing were also related to this all-encompassing power, and among the Osage many were considered to be "life symbols" (*zho'-i-the*) of the particular clans who employed them (Figure 5.1). Life symbols were derived from natural and celestial objects whose supernatural faculties were transmitted in primordial times by *Wakanda* to sacred religious leaders called "little-old-men" (*non-hon-zhin-ga*) through visions and dreams (Bailey 1995, 2001). More specifically, these symbols were believed to embody the forces of life, death, and renewal, and Osage clan names were taken from the most important of these symbolic objects and sentient creatures. According to one of the last Osage tribal priests, Saucy Calf (Tse-zhin'-ga-wa-da-in-ga), "the symbolic marks ceremonially put upon the body stand as a supplication to a higher power [*Wakanda*] to bestow these blessings upon the person tattooed" (La Flesche 1930:532).

Although the practice of tattooing was ubiquitous across the plains, tattoos could not be worn by just anyone. Warriors had to prove themselves on the field of battle by winning specific war honors to merit the right to be tattooed (Figure 5.2). Women traditionally earned their "marks of honor"[2]

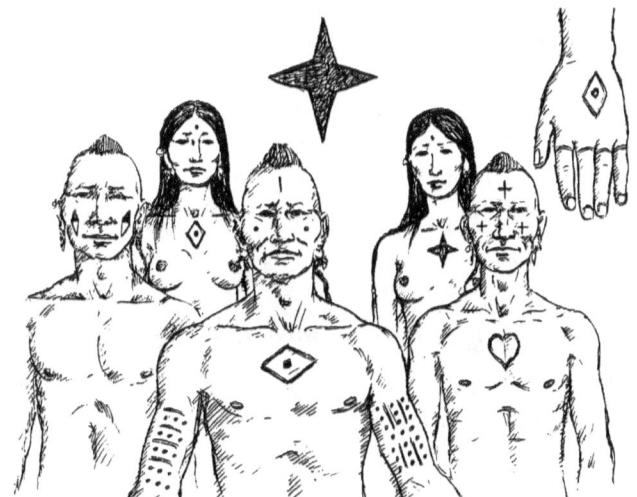

FIGURE 5.2. Iowa men wore tattoos reflecting their status as warriors on the field of battle. The corporal designs of the Iowa were less complex than those of the Osage. Veteran warriors displayed single eagle feathers on each cheek, while stripes or circular motifs on the arms symbolized warlike exploits or scalps taken. Men could also have a star, cross, or line on the forehead, or a star, circle, or cross on the cheek. Torso tattoos may have included diamond- or heart-shaped figures. Original art by Lance Foster (1994:115). Reproduced courtesy of Lance Foster.

through their fathers, who, upon lavishing large quantities of gifts on those individuals who witnessed the ceremony, reserved their progeny's place among families of high social standing. Because the costs associated with female tattooing were so great, it followed that only those individuals who were members of particularly wealthy families (i.e., of chiefly descent) could ever hope to receive the sacred marks. Among the Omaha, for example, a tattooed girl was called a "woman chief"[3] (Fletcher and La Flesche 1911:494), and the Osage named the tattooing ceremony "The Making of Young or Honorary Chiefs."[4]

Tattooing across the Great Plains provided a ritual means by which to enhance one's status and access to supernatural power. This spiritual energy was embodied in specific forms of corporeal iconography, the human bodies that absorbed it, and especially the tattooing bundles from which such designs were created. Because these ancestral toolkits served as the primary repository for the transfer of sacred power, this chapter will examine the properties, significance, and use of tattooing bundles with specific reference to traditional Eastern Plains religion and society through an exploratory narrative based on studies of associative material culture and ethnographic sources. My focus on this geographical region of the plains is guided by necessity, since it is here that we find the most detailed records of tattooing preserved in long-neglected published and unpublished sources. Through describing this largely understudied world of material and visual culture, I seek to expand not only our knowledge of traditional tattooing instruments from the plains but also indigenous body art and the belief systems that inspired it.

/ *Tribal Origins and Contents of Tattooing Bundles* /

Tattooing bundles are one class or category of "sacred" (*waxobe*, Osage; *waxube*, Omaha) or "medicine" bundles that, following Hanson (1980:200) and Foster (1994:7), may be roughly defined as an object (or cadre of objects) that is stored in a woven container or skin cover and that functions as a repository for the transfer of supernatural power. These sacred objects had their origins in individual visions or tribal myths wherein ritual rules of use and care were stipulated. Harrington (1913:108) observed that the first Otoe bundles were "given" to an unnamed man through visions transmitted by *Wakanda*. It was the Great Mystery himself who provided the instructions for making these bundles, including the meaning and significance of each component. In unpublished field notes, Harrington also recorded that Kansa, or Kaw, clan bundles were originally created by a personage called *No piu wa* ("afraid to be seen in the light") who proclaimed to the Buffalo, Deer, and Bear clans that these items "would give them great power in battle" because the contents of these objects "charmed" or "mesmerized" the enemy.[5] Harrington, who collected numerous clan bundles for George Gustav Heye's Museum of the American Indian, the University Museum of Pennsylvania, and other institutions, acquired an Iowa tattooing bundle (*wigrêxê*) that was said to have been given to the people by the Air Spirit, or "Person Above" (*mungri wancike*) (Foster 1994:253; Skinner 1926:267).

One of the last Plains Cree tattooing bundles, the Four Sky Thunder bundle, was transferred into non-Native hands in a private ceremony in September 1953. Simon Bluehorn, the last indigenous keeper of this bundle, told the story of the bundle's creation and its relationship to a vision provided in a dream:

> Long ago, in the buffalo days, a man had a dream. A buffalo spirit came to him and said, "My Grandson, I am the most powerful spirit of the Plains Cree. If you follow my instructions I will give you a great gift; it is a tattooing bundle."
>
> This spirit was called the "Buffalo that Walks like a Man" and under his instructions the man made the bundle. When the spirit gave this gift, he also taught the first owner the proper tattooing procedures, songs and prayers. Because of this gift, the man was considered to be one of the most influential medicine men of the Cree. (Light 1972:13)

Other detailed information concerning Plains tattooing bundles and their contents was recorded by the pioneering Native American ethnologist and linguist Francis La Flesche (Omaha) among the Osage.[6] The Osage are divided into two exogamous moieties, the *Tsi-zhu* (symbolic of the sky, peace, East, and left) and *Hon-ga* (symbolic of the earth, water, war, West, and right), which are comprised of twenty-four patrilineal clans of which the tribe was originally formed. According to Bailey (2001:481), "the unity of the sky and earth peoples was symbolized in the form of a perfect man who faced east [left] in times of peace and west [right] in times war." As a model of the universe, this symbolic man "united the people into one ever-living body [because] the inseparable unity of the sky and the earth made possible the continuity of the life that proceeded from them" (La Flesche 1916:278). This idea of bringing together the two symbolic divisions of the tribe to form one body was further carried out in village planning,[7] by the ceremonial

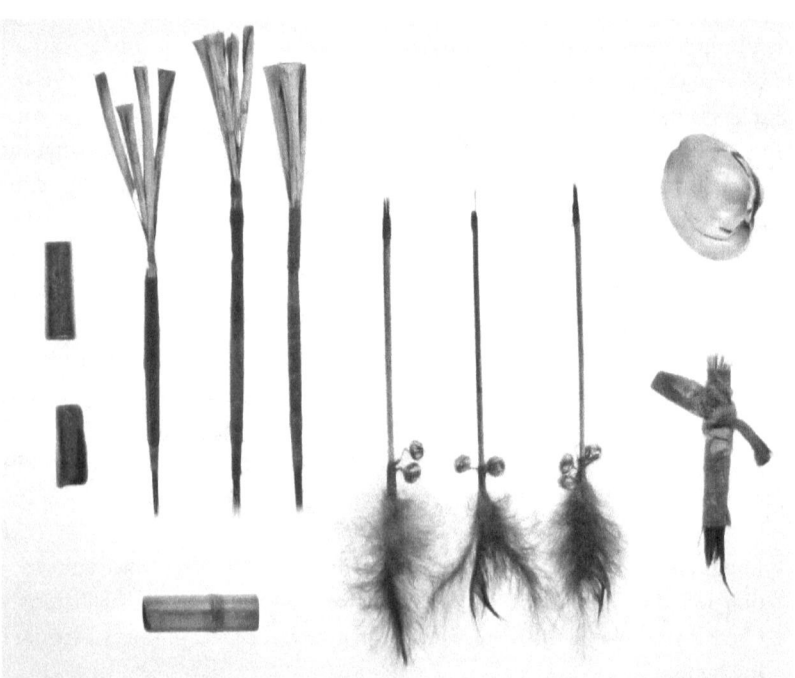

FIGURE 5.3. Osage tattooing bundle. Catalog number E263122, Department of Anthropology, Smithsonian Institution, Suitland, Maryland.

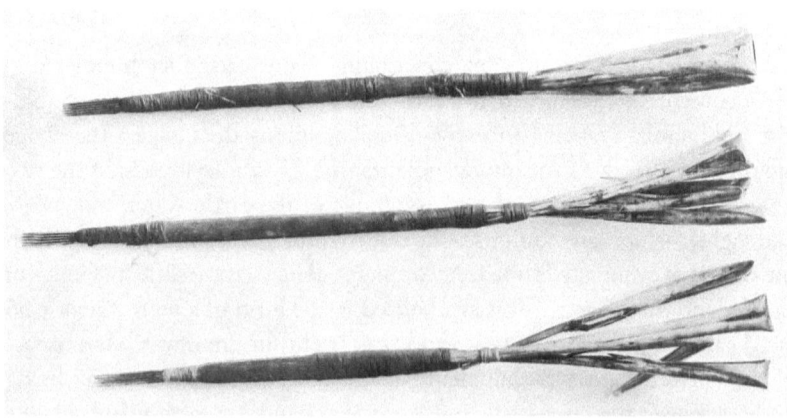

FIGURE 5.4. Detail of needles from an Osage tattooing bundle. Manuscript 4558, Box 33, National Anthropological Archives, Smithsonian Institution, Suitland, Maryland.

positions and actions of moiety members in tribal rituals (e.g., La Flesche 1916:286), and the construction and manipulation of ceremonial objects like tattooing bundles (Figures 5.3 and 5.4).

Osage tattooing bundles were *wa-xo'be ton-ga* ("great bundles") imbued with life-giving powers. The Gentle Ponca clan of the *Hon-ga* moiety served as the symbolic keeper of these objects, but because they were considered to be tribal bundles, any of the other Osage clan bundle priests could wield them (Bailey 1995:54–55; La Flesche 1921a:72).[8] It is likely that specific moiety and clan members were responsible for constructing the various parts of these objects.

Tattooing bundles, like war bundles, were manufactured and stored with reference to the position of the two great Osage moieties. The outer case was made of woven buffalo hair (La Flesche 1921a:72). This "wallet," which was used to hold the bundle's sacred contents, was presumably made by a member of the *Tsi-zhu Tho-xe* ("Buffalo Bull") clan, who were also responsible for making similar cases for other great bundles. As with other clan bundles, if the tattoo bundle holder was of the *Hon-ga* moiety it was stored to the right of his lodge door entrance, or to the left if it resided with a bundle keeper of the *Tsi-zhu* division.[9]

Within the buffalo hair bag were a series of other compartmentalized bags, usually three in all, that together constituted what La Flesche (1916:281) called a "portable shrine." The innermost bag consisted of a symbolically decorated case of woven rush (*Eleocharis interstincta*) called *ça-zhi^n'-ga* that was considered to be "the holiest" of the inner compartments (La Flesche 1930:682) (Figure 5.5). The *ça-zhi^n'-ga* held the tattooing instruments, sacred birds (see below), and other objects of power. It was probably constructed by a selected female member of the *Hon-ga Mi-ké-stse-dse* ("Cattail") clan, "which represents the water part of the earth" (La Flesche 1930:682).

The rush bag's sacredness stemmed from the fact that its upper side represented the sky and the lower side the earth. The inner receptacle of the case (*i'-o-ga*) symbolized the space between the sky and the earth, or the expanse into which all life comes through birth and departs only at death (La Flesche 1916:282). More specifically, the inner case

was woven in one piece but divided by the symbolic designs into two equal parts, one part representing the sky, the other part the earth. The two parts also represented night and day. The part that represented the earth and the sky had conventional designs woven into the matting and symbolized the clouds that moved between the sky and the earth. The portion of the matting that symbolized the day is left undyed and is of a very light color. Across the entire width of this portion of the mat are woven, equidistant, narrow dark lines that represent night. The pocket in which were to be placed the [tattooing tools and other objects] was made by doubling that part of the matting having on it the symbols representing the sky and earth, and was fastened at the ends with cords made of the nettle [*ha'-do-ga*; *Urtica gracilis*] fiber, the same consecrated material that had been used for the warp. (La Flesche 1930:683)

The rush bag of the tattooing bundle displayed additional moiety signatures in the form of woven fasteners or knots that distinguished the right (*Hon-ga*) and left (*Tsi-zhu*) sides of the container. As La Flesche (1930:541, 683) observed, seven knots were tied at the right end of great bundles and six knots were tied at the left. These corresponded to the Seven Songs of the

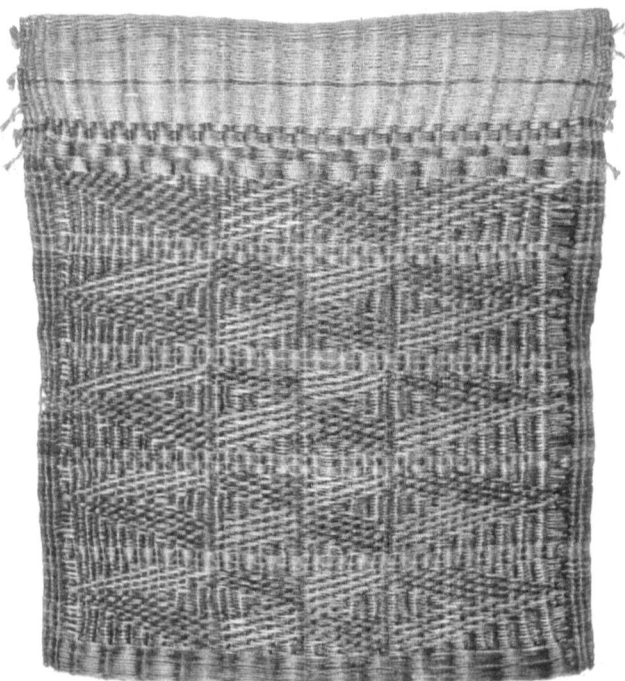

FIGURE 5.5. Osage rush bag used to hold the sacred tattooing bundle. Catalog number E263122, Department of Anthropology, Smithsonian Institution, Suitland, Maryland.

Hon-ga and the Six Songs of the *Tsi-zhu*, which were performed during the ceremonial unfolding and opening of the bags.

As already noted, the holy rush receptacle contained the tattooing implements and associated objects. The origins of these items have been documented in a deeply symbolic and lengthy Osage myth that, in short, recognizes the adoption of tattooing and the particular life symbols associated with it as a means to combat old age and disease, increase fertility, and maintain the numerical strength of the tribe (La Flesche 1921a:71). The primary objects associated with the tattooing bundle were two water birds, the cormorant and pelican,[10] and a mussel shell. According to Osage elder Charley Wa-hre-she, the pelican was called *"Do'-tse-ton-ga* (Big Throat), a symbol of long life."[11] The pelican is featured prominently in the "Legend of the Tattooing Custom" because it lived longer than other birds and became associated with old age.[12] The mussel shell, or that which "harden[s] against death," is also equated with longevity amongst the Osage and neighboring Dhegihan peoples like the Kansa, or Kaw.[13] Wa-hre-she, speaking about the tattoo myth of the Osage, added: "it is said when a man was out fasting, the bird came to him and spoke to him, giving him the secret of living long. The bird appeared to him in the guise of a very old man."[14]

La Flesche (1921a:72) collected an Osage tattooing bundle in 1911 for the U.S. National Museum (now the National Museum of Natural History) and offers a detailed listing of its contents. I provide this inventory below, but also include additional pieces of information in brackets that are found in his unpublished field notes.[15] These documents are currently housed at the National Anthropological Archives, Smithsonian Institution, and reveal new insights into the symbolism and meaning of these sacred objects.

> The outer case . . . was made of woven buffalo hair. The inner case, within which are kept the pelican and the cormorant and the other sacred articles, was made of woven rush, with symbolic designs similar to those on the rush cases of the hawk [or war] wa-xo'-bes.
>
> The two wa-xo'-bes were folded one inside of the other, so as to make one roll. The tattooing wa-xo'-be, which is the skin of a cormorant, is split down the entire length of the back. Around the base of the tail is wound a string of scalp locks, 10 or 12 in number, that hang down like a shirt. Within the body of the skin are placed eight tattooing instruments, the points toward the head and the tops toward the tail. The shafts of some of the instruments are flat, others round, and about the length of a lead pencil. To the lower ends of the shafts are fastened steel needles, some in straight rows

[for the straight lines] and others in bunches [for the spots on the forehead of the woman]. [The small leather figure is a pattern for the eagle tattooed on the wrist of a woman with the head positioned towards the hand. It is buffalo leather. The Tsizhu women are tattooed with an eagle at the left-inner wrist, if a Honga woman on the right-inner wrist.[16]] To the tops of some of the shafts are fastened small rattles made of pelican or eagle quills. The needle parts of the shafts are covered with buffalo hair to protect them against rust. The skin of the cormorant was folded over the tattooing instruments, the neck of the bird doubled over the back and tied down. The skin of the pelican, split down the back, is wrapped around the cormorant and tied around the middle with a band of woven fiber. The bill, head, and neck of the pelican are missing.

Within the woven rush case, placed without any particular order, are seven weasel skins [these are taken on the warpath]; one tobacco pouch made of a buffalo heart-sack; bits of braided sweet-grass; half of the shell of a fresh-water mussel for holding the coloring matter; four tubes, one of bamboo and three of tin, worn by the operator on his fingers as guides for the instruments when he is at work [a skillful operator does not use them]; two bunches of the wing-feathers of small birds [pileated woodpecker[17]] used in applying the coloring matter; an old burden-strap; four wing-bones of a pelican or an eagle, tied together with a twisted cord of wood or nettle fiber [the four bones tied in a bunch are eagle bones[18] and are whistles carried on the warpath]; two rabbits' feet [they symbolize invisibility, no one can see the rabbit's house or his tracks], used for brushing the skin [—the palms of the hands, soles of the feet and top of the head—] that have been gone over with the instruments when the subject becomes nervous by the irritation of the wounds; [the plant tied up in a piece of calico is what is called *mon'-zhi-pa-giton*—and is poison. Arrows are poisoned with the leaves by putting them in the bottom of the quiver. This does not belong in the bag. Has nothing to do with tattooing. Sometimes use with cedar for incense. There is a ritual relating to the rabbit's feet; also two little pieces of wood having a strong smell[19]—(probably) yellow willow or redbud.[20] Either these or the leaves were charred for pigment;] and a large brass ring [that "symbolizes the sun"] worn by the operator around his neck as part of his symbolic paraphernalia. (La Flesche 1921a:72).

Other tattooing bundles from Siouan and Plains Cree groups contain similar articles. The tattooing bundle of Iowa chief Tohee, collected for the Milwaukee Public Museum (Skinner 1926:271, 342, plate 50), consists of a needled wooden baton tipped with split heron-quill rattles, pieces of plaited sweetgrass used as incense, a small leather bag containing red pigment with attached rabbit's foot brush, bone cylinders used as stencils for a woman's dot-like honor mark placed in the center of her forehead, and a small decorated woven vegetable fiber bag (four zigzag trails and six hourglass elements) used to hold the blue-black tattoo pigment and deadening medicine.[21] All of these items were placed within a large decorated mat case divided into five zones (Foster 1994:213), each with one large diamond-shaped lozenge that closely resembles those that adorned the woven rush cases of Osage tattooing bundles.

Foster's (1994:213–219) reexamination and reassociation of Tohee's tattoo outfit revealed more details and additional components, the most important of which are as follows: one willow stick, charred to obtain black pigment; lumps of charred wood; four circular wooden stamps, each one larger than the smaller bone cylinders and perhaps used to make men's tattoo designs (e.g., spots on the arms of warriors representing scalps taken); a cloth bundle containing tobacco; several additional packets of "medicine" comprised of roots, plant stems, and flowers; one packet of bird down in a skin wrapper; and one pair of antique spectacles.

Harrington's (in Skinner 1926:265–267) description of the Iowa tattoo bundle he collected for George Gustav Heye's Museum of the American Indian includes the indigenous names for each component of the sacred object. In this inventory, amongst other things, are a buffalo wool swab and hide rag used for soaking up excess blood released during the rite, deadening medicine (*ma^{n}ka^n*), lumps of willow charcoal pigment, a species of duck (*mi^{n}xe*) with head removed,[22] and two rubbing sticks or spatulas of an unnamed material, bearing split quill rattles used for "laying out the patterns and applying the pigment (*wikuntê*)."

The "unnamed" material for the spatulas was buffalo horn. Rubbing spatulas of buffalo horn were also included in the Missouria tattoo bundle Harrington collected in 1912 for the University Museum of Pennsylvania (Harrington 1913:111, 113). This remarkable kit was enclosed within a beautifully woven purse adorned with "thunderbird" figures that probably were symbolic of Sky Powers[23] and the celestial deities associated with warfare (Figure 5.6).[24] Among the Menominee, the "tattooing needles [were] said to have been given to mankind by the Thunderbirds, and represent their spears or lightning" (Skinner 1921:135; see also Figure 4.18).

Returning to our discussion of the contents of these bundles, some additional details should be noted regarding the purpose of particular objects

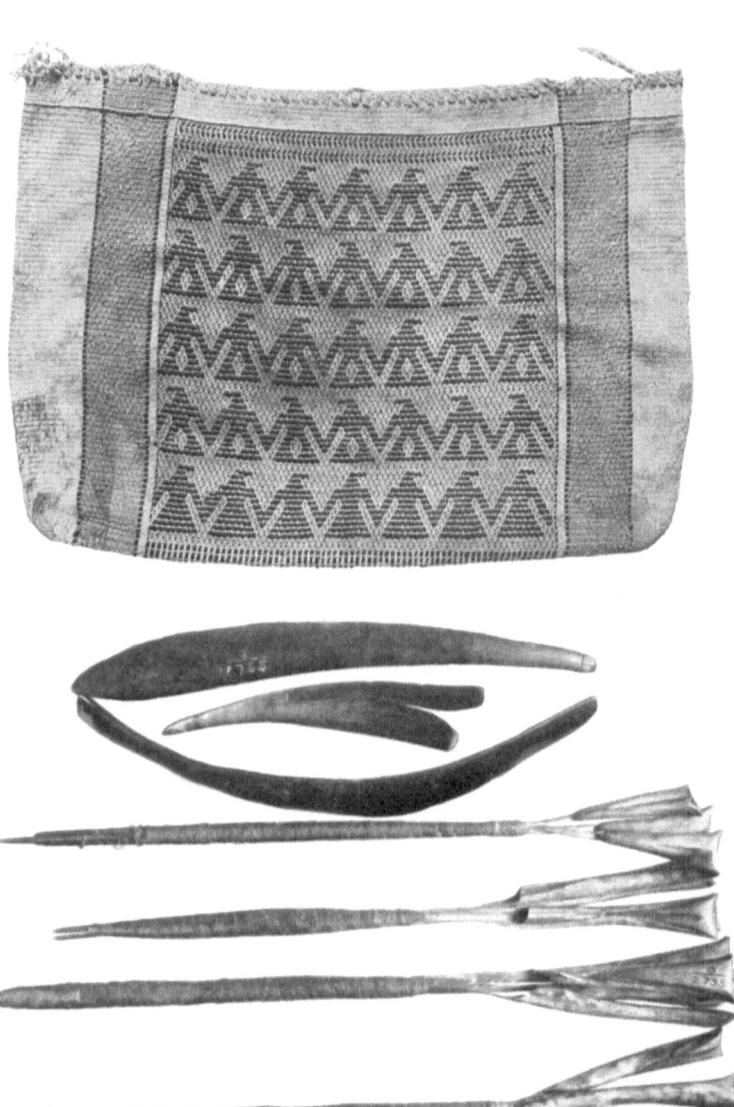

FIGURE 5.6. Missouria tattoo bundle bag and
implements (after Harrington 1913:110–111).

within them. Sweetgrass and tobacco were important to the overall function of tattooing (and other) bundles because they were offered as "prayers" (e.g., through ascending smoke or as physical gifts) to those unseen forces who animated tattoos with their life-giving and life-preserving powers. Simon Bluehorn, the last Plains Cree keeper of the Four Sky Thunder tattoo bundle, said: "Whenever the bundle was opened or actually used, a cloth offering was added to the outer wrappings. Tobacco was left inside the bundle for the use of the spirits. Sweet grass was always burned to enable the prayers and songs to be carried aloft to where the spirit would be watching" (Light 1972:13). Similarly, during the Iowa tattooing ceremony for a virgin girl, Harrington reported:

> Two men, who must be of blameless life, who never have been known to kill or injure anyone [i.e., they are ritually pure], then light the sacred pipes with hot coals and take them around. Everybody smokes, even little children, for they say this will bring good health to the girl who has been tattooed. This may be because the holes through the pipestems symbolize the "straight path" of the sun [associated with *Wakanda*]. While this is in progress, the chief makes a speech, or prayer, and talks to Wakanda saying something like the following: "We have marked a girl, and now we are burning tobacco. We beg that you drive away all sickness and disease." During the [tattooing] ceremony the songs and speeches contain petitions to Wakanda for the girl's future life—that she may be good herself, get a good man, and have good children, and finally that she may live to be old. (Harrington, in Skinner 1926:270)

Other objects, like the poison included in the Osage tattooing bundle, were said to not belong there. However, I believe that poison was appropriate for inclusion in the Osage bundle, as many Plains tattooing bundles contained powerful medicines and other items related to warfare. Such objects would have been extremely important when males were tattooed by the bundle keepers of the tribe. I stake this observation on the fact that Plains war bundles contained many of the same objects of power as those found in tattooing bundles (e.g., scalps, weasel skins, whistles, birds, and herbal medicines), and these objects enhanced a warrior's abilities on the battlefield. Harrington makes this distinction quite clear in his discussion of an Otoe war bundle he collected for the University Museum of Pennsylvania, an object he said bore a close "resemblance to those of the Osage and Kaw":

This is well brought out in a bundle belonging to the Bear clan, which contained among many other things a fetish, the dried skin of a hawk[25] attached to a deerskin strap to sling about the neck. To the hawk's tail were tied pieces of nineteen scalps, each one of which represents a successful war expedition. The hawk fetish was supposed to protect the entire war party and to endow them with the bird's predatory powers. This, together with a weasel skin amulet carried by scouts to give quickness and ease of conceal-ment, and an eagle foot, used as a magic wand to symbolically claw[26] at the enemy to get them within one's power—into the claws of the eagle, as it were—all find their counterparts in the bundles of the Osage[27] and Kaws. The bundle also yielded an enchanted sash to wear across the shoulder, a bird-skin amulet to tie upon the wearer's scalp-lock, a magic whistle, blown to hypnotize the enemy, a buckskin sack containing herbs which, chewed and rubbed on the body, were supposed to act as a charm for turning away bullets[28] and arrows, and another packet containing an herb mixture for poisoning one's own missiles against the foe. (Harrington 1913:110–111)

In unpublished field notes, Harrington adds still more details regarding similarities that existed between the war and tattooing bundles. Some Kaw war bundles contained a "sacred shell" symbolizing long life or a "powerful bird" (i.e., a hawk) associated with lightning/thunder[29] and war deities of the sky. These great bundles were carried by warriors during military expedi-tions. The man carrying such objects stayed, as a rule, behind the others, and wore the bundle by a cord tethered to his neck. However, in the beginning of the campaign he was compelled to serve as the scout to discover the where-abouts of the enemy:

When he is sent out he must go, no matter what the distance, and [if] he does not do as he is told he is killed by his own tribe. They say to him: "If you can get an enemy's head, bring it to us quick." Or they may say: "That shell will change life for us, it will make us live longer. That is why we gave it into your care." As he advances he must keep right on going until he hears the guns fired, even if the enemy is in plain sight. When guns are fired he throws the shell [or bird] around to his back, and turns to rejoin his party . . .

When scalps are taken they are given to the man with the shell [or bird], who carries them until they can be tied to the bundle . . . Scalps tied upon a new bundle were thought to give it strength.[30]

Harrington recorded that when Kaw war bundles were opened during ceremonies in preparation for a new battle, "whistles" were always blown toward the sky.[31] Tobacco was smoked in a sacred war pipe and as the clan war leaders exhaled they said, "*No ne Wakanda*, we are going to ask you to open these bundles." After they decided who would carry the bundle into combat, they stopped addressing that individual by his regular name and from that point forward they called him "*Wa ho be*" (in Osage, *waxobe*,[32] or "made sacred"), which is the same name applied to the bundle.

Dorsey (1885a:674–677) documented similar rituals for the Kaw, or Kansa, especially those that pertained to war expeditions held to end ceremonial periods of mourning.[33] One highly detailed account was provided to him by a "war captain," "chief," and "principal sacred man or doctor" of the tribe. Because several new details emerge here concerning the symbolism and ceremonial functions of Kaw war bundles, I quote some passages again here:

> When the sacred pipe is smoked by a Large Hanga (Black eagle) or a Small Hanga (Chicken-hawk) man, he must hold it in his right hand, blowing the smoke into the clam shell,[34] which is held in his left. The smoke is supposed to ascend to the thunder-god, the god of war, to whom it is pleasant. (Dorsey 1885a:674)

Once the bundle containing the shell was brought forward, the individuals in the ritual joined the bundle owner in singing. A kind of pictographic chart was used by the singers as a mnemonic device to assist them in singing the appropriate songs.[35] Dorsey (1885a:675) stated that the songs were "very sacred, never being sung on ordinary occasions, or in a profane way, lest the offender should be killed by the thunder-god."

As the sacred bundle was opened, three songs were sung to the sacred war pipe (Dorsey 1885a:675). Additional song cycles followed, and each performance was accompanied by offerings and addressed to specific entities including *Wakanda*,[36] "the maker of all songs," the wind "deities," Venus (or the Morning Star, which was a manifestation of *Wakanda*), and all other deities above and below. The specific types of offerings varied. For example, Kaw warriors used to remove the hearts of enemies and place them in the fire as offerings to the four winds. It was said that in former times they made a personal flesh offering to each direction while also stating: "That I give to you, O Wakanda!" (Dorsey 1885a:676).

Other songs paid homage to specific animals, the night, the moon, and other creatures and objects. Once the singing had been completed, all individuals who were present smoked the war pipe and then slept until just before sunrise. At that time everyone rose to their feet and began weeping until the sky became light, whereupon they mounted their horses and departed to make war.

/ *The Price of Honor* /

The expenses associated with tattooing among the Iowa, Ponca, Osage, and other Chiwere and Dhegiha Sioux tribes were extremely high. For the Iowa, tattooing "was above all the badge or sign of honored and respected people, men or women, and naturally, due to the great expense of the process was seen only among the well-to-do. 'The Ioways wore tattoo marks just as the whites wear diamonds,'" as one tribal chief exclaimed (Skinner 1926:268).[37]

Omaha men who wished to have their daughters tattooed had to present a *wathin'ethe* ("long count") of gifts or respectable actions to earn membership into the order of honorary chieftainship known as *Hon'hewachi* (*Hon'he*, "in the night"; *wa'chi*, "dance"), or what has been called the "Night Blessed Society" (Fortune 1932:148). Men who achieved membership originally were required to present or accomplish one hundred or more *wathin'ethe*, because these sacred gifts or personal sacrifices "have relation to the welfare of the tribe by promoting internal order and peace, by providing the chiefs and keepers, by assuring friendly relations with other tribes" (Fletcher and La Flesche 1911:203). As "something done or given for which there is no material return but through which honor is received" (Fletcher and La Flesche 1911:202–203), *wathin'ethe* publicly solidified an individual's social ranking and the position of his family with respect to others in the milieu. A partial listing of prescribed *wathin'ethe* included

> eagles, eagle war bonnets, quivers (including bows and arrows), catlinite pipes with ornamented stems, tobacco pouches, otter skins, buffalo robes, ornamented shirts, and leggings. In olden times, burden-bearing dogs, tents, and pottery were given; in recent times these have been replaced by horses, guns, blankets, blue and red cloth, silver medals, and copper kettles. (Fletcher and La Flesche 1911:203)

Successful entrance into the *Hon'hewachi* was due in large part to the accomplishments of a man's wife, since "the ornamentation [of the objects] was the woman's task. Her deft fingers prepared the porcupine quills after her husband or brother had caught the wary little animals. [She presided over] the slow task of dyeing the quills and embroidering with them" (Fletcher and La Flesche 1911:202). Speaking of the Otoe, Whitman (1937:73) noted that traditionally only the eldest daughter of a chief could be tattooed.[38] These markings were directly associated with her father's prowess in battle; as one Otoe informant stated: "In the old days, war deeds, recited by the father, validated the right to be tattooed. Later the pattern changed to recitation of benevolent acts: how many people a man had helped; how much money he had given away" (Whitman 1937:73–74, note 3). Whitman (1937:73) added that within the last two centuries, this "privilege was extended to any father who could afford it, and a very rich man might not only tattoo his own daughters, but also the daughters of close relatives" because it added to his prestige.

Among the Ponca, Skinner (1915b:684) observed that there were hereditary chiefs and chiefs whose position was acquired through social and military merit, but "these latter were privileged to have their daughters tattooed and did so at great expense in a public ceremony. The tattooed women had their own dancing society and special privileges." This was also true for female members of the Fish clan of the Prairie Potawatomi who were "well born" and the "only" women allowed to receive tattoo markings (Skinner 1915b:684).

Ridington (1998:193–194) interviewed the last generation of Omaha tattoo bearers in the late twentieth century. These "Blue Spot" women and their relations recalled that there were many social obligations that were required of tattoo bearers (see Figure 8.6). This is because tattoos were "marks of honor" linked to a moral code that newly marked persons were compelled to follow throughout the remainder of their lifetime. Ramona Turner, whose mother wore the mark and who was the granddaughter of the prominent Omaha leader Little Chief (Oliver Turner), stated:

Person that's got that blue mark has to be like a, like clergyman, you know.[39] They got their doors open for you to talk to you, counsel them, whatever problems like that. That's the way these people are supposed to be, I guess. They're supposed to be good people. They're supposed to have love and caring. Anybody that needs help. They're supposed to be humble. That's the role they're supposed to play. Because that's what, we mentioned at times, you know: "That lady's got a blue mark. She's supposed to have the wisdom and knowledge and have compassion for everybody." That's the way I was told. (Ridington 1998:193)

Mabel Hamilton, who owned a blue spot, recalled that she was about four years old when she received the mark. She was extremely proud of her tattoo because

> everybody respect me. They ask me, "What's you got that spot on you for?" "That's a church member," I said. "I'm supposed to be good to you orphan kids. When you see orphan child, take him in your house and feed him. Do good things to him. Talk to it when you see them," he says. That's what this spot is for. (Ridington 1998:194)

/ *The Chosen Few: Men's Tattooing Motifs and Cosmological Implications* /

Most Plains warriors were not charged for their tattooing, as the right to wear the markings had to be earned on the battlefield through the performance of a series of ritually mandated acts that varied between tribes.[40] Because men had to confront death every time they attempted to distinguish themselves from their fellows, "few persons ever attained the honor" of receiving a tattoo (Skinner 1915a:754) (Figure 5.7). Once marked, however, these men of honor were required to fulfill specific social obligations to their communities, just like their female counterparts.

Skinner (1915a:753), writing about the Kansa, observed that men who had killed seven enemies or who had captured or stolen six horses were entitled "to the greatest honor that could befall a Kansa, that of being tattooed on the breast." He wrote:

> This was the summit of a warrior's ambition, and, though he might do many brave deeds thereafter, they could only add to his general reputation, and no more honors could be shown to him. He might even retire on his laurels if he desired. The privileges and honors enjoyed by the tattooed warriors were numerous and important. Among them were:—the right to act as a go-between in marriage contracts; the right of ear piercing; the right of presiding at naming ceremonies. When a tattooed man died, it was customary to raise another to fill his place, provided he had killed at least five or six foes, otherwise only the regular count was accepted. (Skinner 1915a:753)

Among the Iowa, only "very brave men had the right to be tattooed on the breast" (Skinner 1926:206), and those who earned the honor "had accomplished so many brave deeds that they were publicly tattooed . . . at no

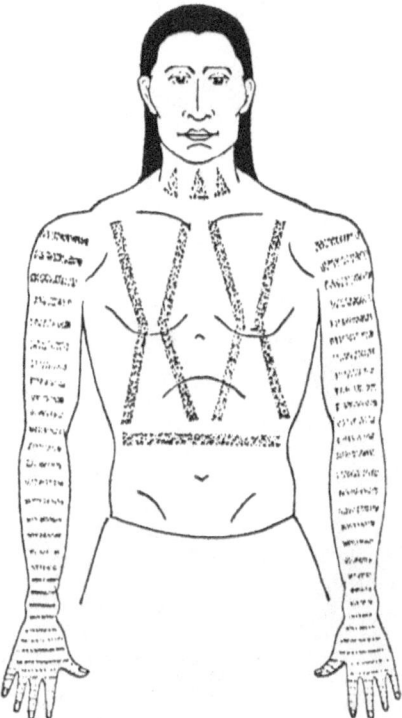

FIGURE 5.7. Illustration of Plains Cree honor
markings, ca. 1910 (after Skinner 1914:76, fig. 10).

expense . . . by the bundle owner of their" clan (Skinner 1926:221). Men of
such standing strove to achieve as many graded titles in the Iowa war honor
system as possible, because each one was associated with desirable social
benefits. Skinner (1915b:684, note 1) wrote that tattooed braves "served as
soldiers, or police, [who] were noted for their generosity, or had received the
pipe dance, etc. They were also permitted, like the chiefs, to contract polygy-
nous marriages, to eat with the chiefs at their feasts, and to have their daughters tattooed. As a title was attached to each of these achievements, progres-
sion up the scale was called 'building up one's name.'" Because there is not
enough space here to list the many other privileges and duties associated
with these titles, I refer the reader to Skinner's (1926:206–207) inventory.

On the northern plains, the Hidatsa and neighboring Mandan also
earned tattoos for brave deeds on the battlefield. Bowers (1965:280) related:
"Striking a live enemy was considered a higher honor than striking one

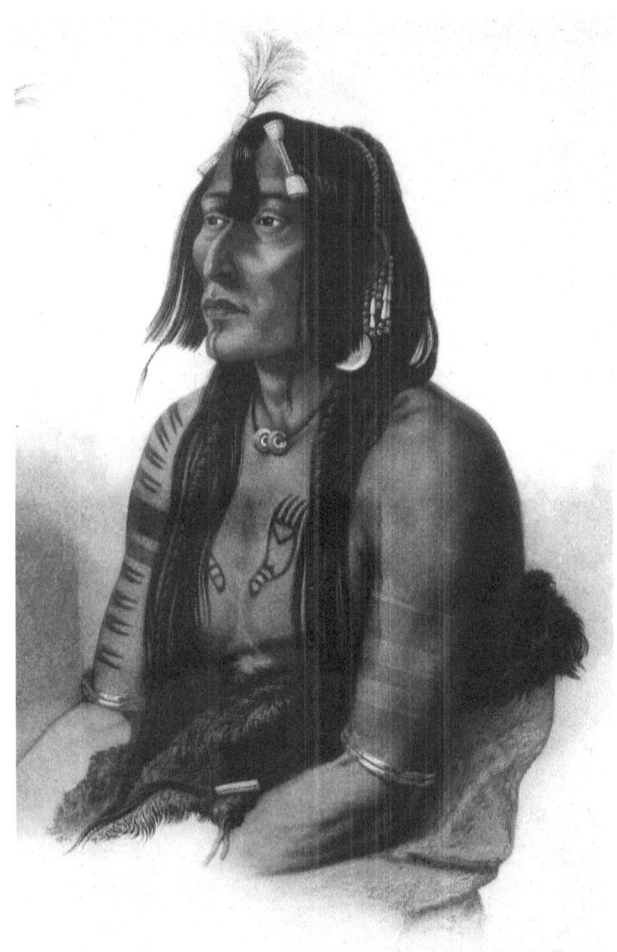

FIGURE 5.8. The Yankton Sioux warrior Psíhdjä-Sáhpa with tattooed "hand" honor markings. Detail of *Noápeh, an Assiniboin Indian, and Psíhdjä-Sáhpa, a Yanktown Indian.* Art by Karl Bodmer (after Wied-Neuwied 1840–1843: tab. 12). Courtesy of Smithsonian Institution Libraries, Washington, DC.

who had been killed. One could paint two hands on one side of the chest to show that a live enemy had been struck or one could have two hands tattooed on his chest" (Figure 5.8). Similarly, an indigenous informant of the American photographer Edward Curtis told him in 1927 that tattooed hands were part of the Woods Cree repertoire of permanent body designs. This man also revealed that other tattooed symbols were associated with warrior culture in the tribe and that men were tattooed on their chests with the same design:

A pair of vertical lines on each half of the thorax, with sloping lines . . . was a good-luck symbol. A certain man had on each side of his chest a tattooed hand, in commemoration of a fight with the Blackfeet, in which an enemy actually laid hold of him but nevertheless was killed. Some men had themselves ornamented with figures representing their dream-animals [or *manitous*]. (Curtis 1907–1930:18:67)

Assiniboine men were marked for having struck their first enemy (Denig 1930:592) and the design, which has not been documented in detail, was said to have occupied the entire chest and arms. The noted Swiss artist Rudolph Kurz, who spent the years 1846 to 1852 at western trading posts on the northern plains, encountered Assiniboine warriors but did not describe their tattooing. However, his sketches did include imagery of tattooed Sioux and Hidatsa braves (Figure 5.9), and a journal entry discusses these indelible traditions as follows:

A soldier is in every case a brave man who has already distinguished himself—counts several "coups." He is always more or less tattooed; i.e., figures, lines, or points are made with a needle on his skin and then rubbed over with powder or coal dust, so that the tattoo marks assume a blue-black color. Indians in this region are not tattooed over the entire body, but usually on the throat and breastbone or over the chest and shoulders, sometimes on the shoulders and arms or merely on the forearm or on the shin, the latter, however, being decorated only with large dots, hoofprints, or spear heads. They never tattooed their backs, for a warrior, as you know, does not manifest by his hinder part that he is brave. (Kurz 1937:173)

Kurz's predecessor, the Swiss artist Karl Bodmer, sketched several tattooed northern Plains warriors of the Yankton Sioux, Cree, Mandan, and Hidatsa during his travels (1832–1834) with the Prince Maximilian von Wied expedition to the Missouri River (see Figures 5.8, 5.10, and 5.11). One of his most famous images was of the longstanding Hidatsa chief, warrior, and tattoo artist Road Maker (Addíh-Hiddísch), who marked the last known Hidatsa man to have worn the traditional tattooing of his tribe (Figure 5.12). This warrior, Poor Wolf (or Lean Wolf), was over ninety years of age when he was interviewed about his tattooing in 1909 (Figure 5.13). He said that he was tattooed at nineteen years of age, and in preparation for the ritual he fasted in the cold hills for four days and nights.[41] Poor Wolf recalled the ordeal:

Part of the time I stood erect on a buffalo skull with no means of support. No matter how hard the wind blew, nor how difficult I found it to keep my balance, I was compelled to stand erect.

On the fifth night, I ate and drank. That night, too, I cut three strips of skin from my breast. Then, my father came. As a sacrifice, he cut four strips of skin below the elbow and the shoulder of the same arm . . .

No pattern was drawn on my body before the men began pricking me. While some sang, two men always came forward to do the pricking. The group had four drums.

Many stones were prepared for a sweat bath. After the day's pricking which made me bloody,[42] I had to go into a sweat bath to wash off the blood. It required a whole day to finish less than a foot of the pattern. After I had been pricked for a day, I rested about two days, until the wounds were partly healed. On the third day, I was ready to continue. Each night preceding the resumption of tattooing, I went out into the hills and cried. In the morning, when the men were ready, they sent for me. They worked a long time before the whole pattern was completed. (Weitzner 1979:224)

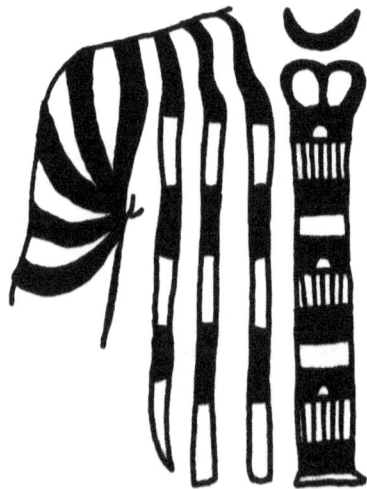

FIGURE 5.9. Rudolph Kurz sketched this tattoo design on December 27, 1851, and it was placed on a sheet of paper with illustrations of "Cree" men. However, this chest pattern more closely resembles those documented for the Mandan and Hidatsa (redrawn after Kurz 1937: plate 9).

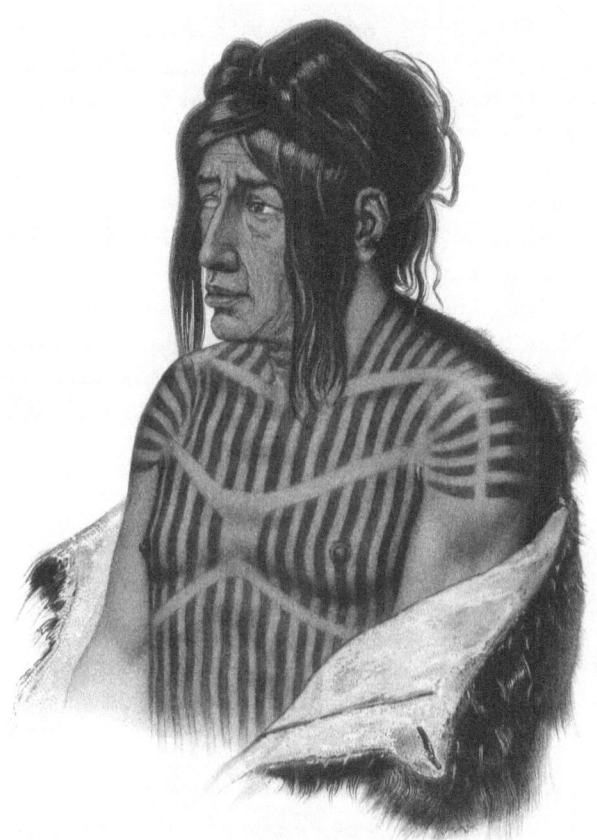

FIGURE 5.10. *Mähsette-Kuiuab, Chief of the Cree Indians*. Art by Karl Bodmer (after Wied-Neuwied 1839–1841: fig. 22. Courtesy of Smithsonian Institution Libraries, Washington, DC.

Another Hidatsa elder, Hairy Coat, remembered Poor Wolf's tattooing session as a boy and recalled many important details that the old man could not, including the source of inspiration for his wrist and hand designs: eagle plumes and a claw. The eagle claw and plume tattoos originally were given to Road Maker by his "god," or guardian spirit during a vision quest. I would like to believe that these feathers also encircled his arms, stood upright on his chest, and that the forked tail of the eagle, or another bird (e.g., swallow-tailed kite or thunderbird), adorned the bottom of Poor Wolf's torso.[43] Hairy Coat stated that Poor Wolf was tattooed by his uncle Road Maker because he was unmarried, did women's work, and was living with another man before he was tattooed. Hairy Coat detailed the events that unfolded during the tattooing session and concluded by stating that Poor Wolf eventually became a great warrior (Weitzner 1979:226–228).

An elderly woman also recalled a few additional details regarding Hidatsa tattoos, the most significant being that warriors were only marked on the right side of their torso (Weitzner 1979:224, 226). This observation seems to be confirmed in some of Bodmer's illustrations, and in the sketch of Poor Wolf, although individuals such as Road Maker were profusely tattooed on the breast, arms, hands, and legs (Hunt and Gallagher 1984:315). I would suggest that a plausible reason why chest tattoo variations existed among the Hidatsa was because not every warrior could claim the exact same war

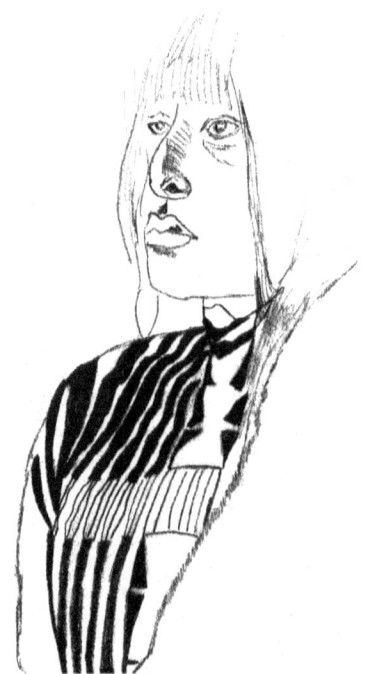

FIGURE 5.11. *The Mandan Warrior Máhchsi-Níhka.* Original art by Karl Bodmer (redrawn after Hunt and Gallagher 1984:303, fig. 312).

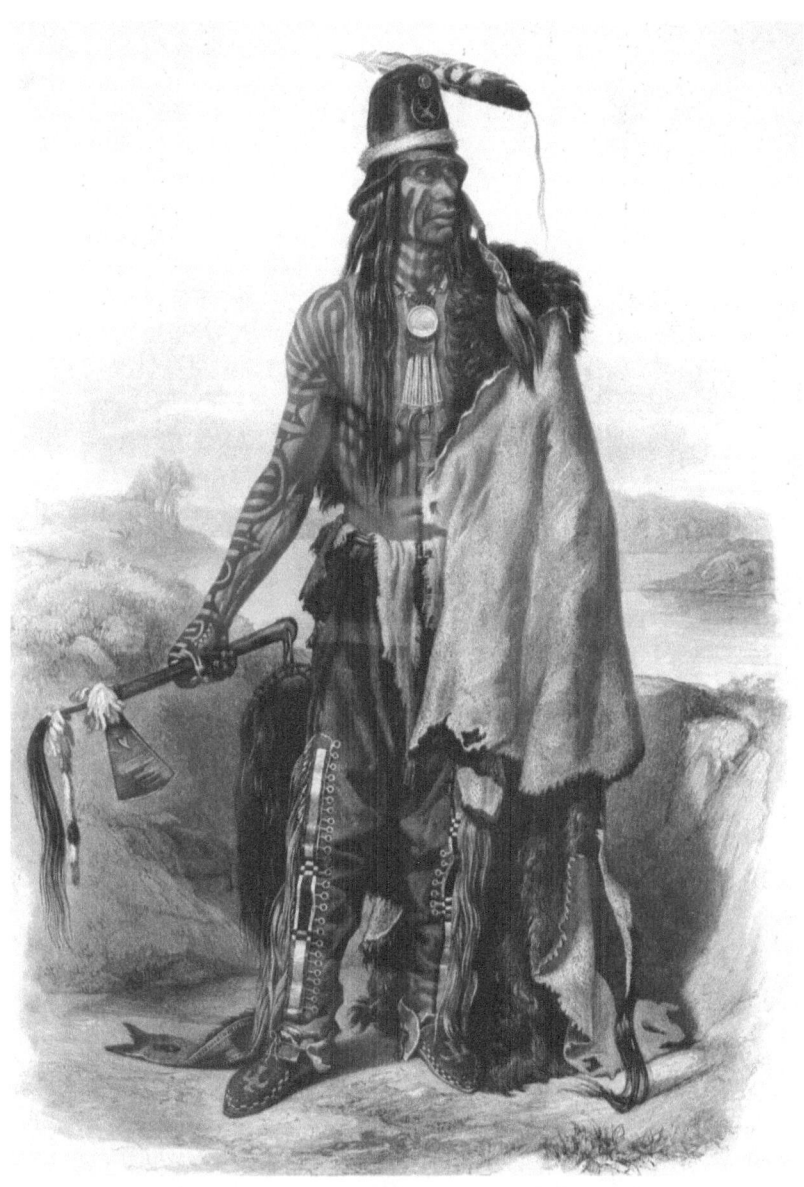

FIGURE 5.12. *The Hidatsa Chief Addih-Hiddísch or Road Maker.*
Art by Karl Bodmer (after Wied-Neuwied 1840–1843: tab. 24).
Courtesy of Smithsonian Institution Libraries, Washington, DC.

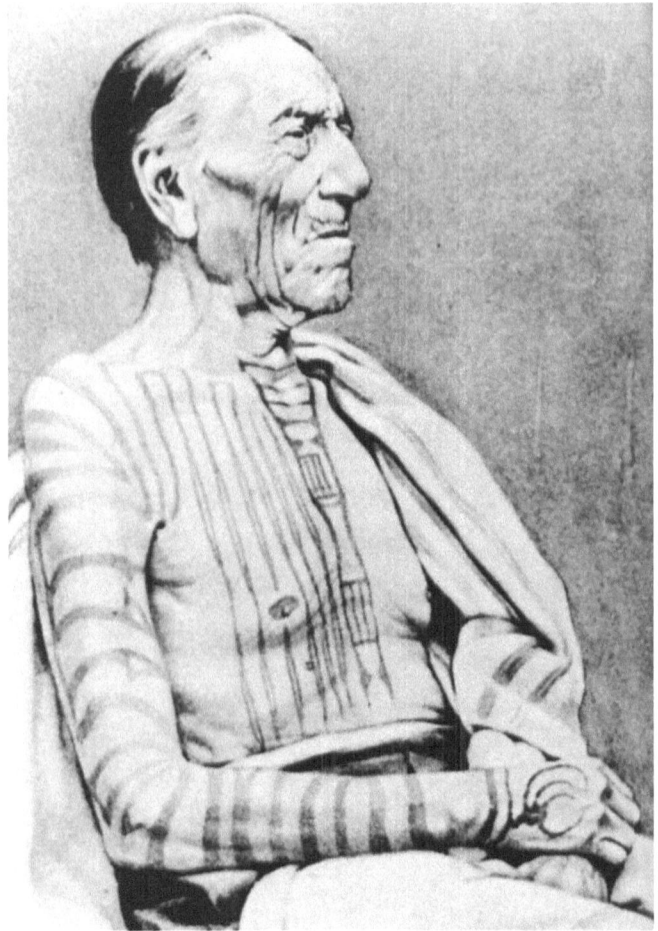

FIGURE 5.13. The Hidatsa warrior Poor Wolf. Original untitled art by Frederick N. Wilson. Courtesy of Minnesota Historical Society, St. Paul.

honors, since each man had performed a different degree, series, or number of exploits that were expressed in his body ornamentation. Some men, like Road Maker, also received visions from spirit protectors, which may have inspired other unique designs.

Further south, among the Osage, the central component in men's chest tattooing was based upon a weapon—the sacred flint knife. This motif closely resembles that worn by a Yankton Sioux chief illustrated, but not described, by Bodmer in the 1830s (Hunt and Gallagher 1984:187) (Figure 5.14) and a tattooed Illinois warrior depicted by de Batz in 1735 (Bushnell

1927:9) (see Figure 1.17). In myth, it is said that the flint knife "shall always" be used when the Osage "go forth toward the setting sun against their enemies" (La Flesche 1921a:208).[44] For Osage men, the honor of receiving a warrior tattoo was fraught with extreme difficulty because only those men who had achieved all thirteen sacred war honors (*o-don*)[45] could ever hope to be tattooed. The actual process of tattooing was a deeply symbolic rite that was considered to be "greater than any of the [other] ceremonies" because it combined "all the sacred rites."[46]

The knife motif was just one of many sacred Osage "life symbols" that were incorporated into the overall warrior tattoo. Every element of a warrior's chest tattoo, including the pigment, was stated in myth to have been

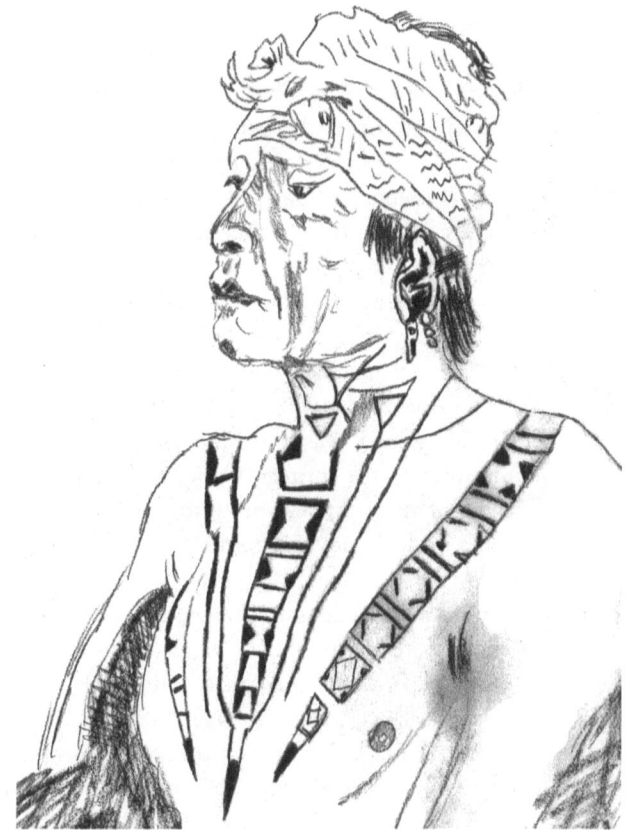

FIGURE 5.14. The Yankton Sioux chief Tukán-Hätón. Original untitled art by Karl Bodmer (redrawn after Hunt and Gallagher 1984:187, fig. 189).

derived from supernatural powers that were given and "belonged" to particular Osage clans. The sacred chest piece was a composite design drawn from primordial sources, and therefore was a unifying tribal symbol representing the Osage's ability to meet and overcome their enemies in order to perpetuate their existence on earth. What Osage body marking tells us from this perspective is that the whole (the tribe) could not function without its constituent parts (moieties and clans), and that this complimentary logic was the ultimate basis from which Osage tribal organization and tattooing emerged. This was because "the safety of the people as an aggregate body must always be regarded as of the first importance, [and] the perpetuity of tribal existence must depend upon the bodily strength and valor of the warrior," who was the ultimate protector of Osage tribal life (La Flesche 1921a:248–249).

These and other distinctions are made explicit in La Flesche's various published works, as well as previously unpublished notes focusing on Osage warrior tattoos. The majority of information contained in these unpublished records was provided to La Flesche by Charley Wah-hre-she (or Waxrizhi), a priest of the Puma clan and son of the last "great bundle" keeper (Bailey 1995:21–23) (Figure 5.15). In his field notes, La Flesche lists those clans to which particular tattoo elements "belonged."[47] In presenting this information, I adhere to La Flesche's spelling of the clan names and other tribal words, but I also add moiety designations.

It is apparent from La Flesche's field notes that many of the tattoo elements described here are polysemous, having multiple symbolic referents. One example of this is the V-shaped tattooing that runs from the chest back over the shoulders of the *Tsi-zhu Wa-no*[n] ("Elder Sky") clan of the *Tsi-zhu* moiety. Their primary life symbol was the thirteen rays of the sun, which are war symbols and represent the thirteen Osage war honors (La Flesche 1932:378).[48] The outline of these rays ran upward from either side of the center chest design like bird plumes and terminated behind the warrior's shoulders.[49]

The inner line (or pipe-shaped) design belonged to the *Wa-zha-zhe Non-ni-on-ha-zho-i-ga* ("Elder Water") clan of the *Hon-ga* moiety and represented the *wa-zha-zhe*, or sacred pipe, which was carried into battle. The pipe was equated to a living body—ultimately the Osage tribe writ large—and its hollow channel was the path of the sun or the path of life. This pipe was the medium through which the Osage communicated with *Wakanda* and was an enduring symbol (La Flesche 1921a:61, 1939:252).

The midline (or knife) motif belonged to the *Ke'-kin* ("Carrier of the Turtle") clan of the *Hon-ga* moiety and the *Mi-kin-wa-non* ("Elder Sun Carrier")

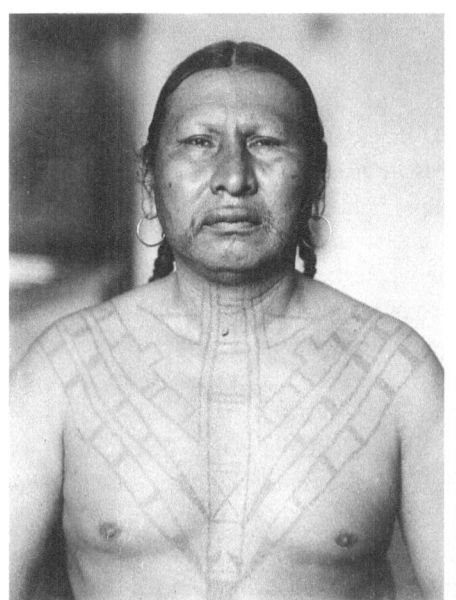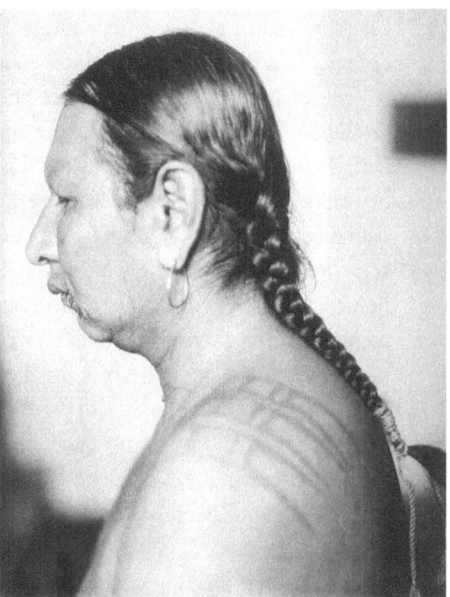

FIGURE 5.15. The Osage priest Charley Wah-hre-she or Wax-rizhi (?–1923). Negative number GN4109a, National Anthropological Archives, Smithsonian Institution, Suitland, Maryland.

clan of the *Tsi-zhu* moiety. The six lines (or "rays") tattooed on the left side of the man also belonged to the latter clan, as the sun was also one of their life symbols (La Flesche 1939:361–362). These lines were used to count a man's war honors. Interestingly, "The Otoes say that the lines tattooed under the chin of Osages represent knives and the cutting of the throats of the enemies."[50]

The sharp point of the knife belonged to the *Wa-ca-be-ton* ("Black Bear") clan of the *Hon-ga* moiety and the *In-gthon-za* ("Puma") clan of the *Hon-ga*.[51] This tattoo was colored entirely black, like the noses and various other body parts of the puma and bear (see Figure 8.9). Black also was symbolic of the sacred redbud (Judas tree) charcoal that warriors used to paint their faces before engaging their enemies. It has been recorded that if a warrior did not adorn himself with this pigment before combat, he could not claim any war honors (*o-don*) even if he achieved them.[52] The redbud charcoal was emblematic of the sun and the relentless fire that destroys everything (La Flesche 1939:118, 361). Carbonized redbud was also used as tattooing pigment for Osage men and therefore carried these and other meanings. In turn, the black bear and puma were also associated with the sun, relentless fire, and charcoal (La Flesche 1921a: plates 10 and 11).

The two lines running under the chin to the back of the ears (called *i'bashabe*) (Fletcher and La Flesche 1911:219) belonged to the *Tho-xe* ("Buffalo Bull") clan of the *Hon-ga* moiety. La Flesche stated in his notes that "W[a-hre-she] does not know what it represents."[53] However, in another unpublished source found in La Flesche's documents, these lines are said to "represent the dark line of the western horizon when the sun has set. This symbol belongs to the black bear gens and is used by their permission."[54] This seems to make perfect sense because the west was associated by the Osage with the direction where their enemies dwelled.

Fletcher and La Flesche (1911:220) also observed that a triangle was traced at the root of the neck, on each side of the stone knife design. These were said to represent "tents." Other symbols were sometimes placed between the forked lines on the shoulder:

> If the keeper had cut off heads in battle, skulls would be represented between the pointed ends of the bands which fall over the shoulders. It was explained that the pictured skulls would draw to the tattooed man the strength of the men he had killed, so that his life would be prolonged by virtue of their unexpended days. (Fletcher and La Flesche 1911:220)

Reporting testimony provided by Black Dog in 1898, La Flesche also stated that round marks placed in the location of the skulls represented scalps taken, and these signs brought similar powers to the victor.[55] Black Dog also noted that the practice of tattooing for men became "empty" once tribal war ceased, but it could still be purchased.

Osage elder Charley Wa-hre-she described the procedure as "painful," noting that the individual "operated upon [was] forbidden from the use of salt as it would irritate the parts tattooed and bring on inflammation."[56] The Osage tribal priest told La Flesche that warriors or men who had successfully raised children were chosen to accompany the male tattoo client. These visitors were said to "amuse" the young man, presumably in an attempt to keep his mind off of the pain. Wa-hre-she specified that warriors would entertain the tattoo recipient "with stories of attacks and hardships endured on war excursions."[57]

As shown above, Osage warriors were honored with sacred tattoos because they had risked their lives to defend their people. They had survived death many times and were what I would call "the chosen few," because they had been blessed by *Wakanda* to carry on the lineage and spread their knowledge. They were distinguished from ordinary men by sacrosanct symbols that channeled the life power of the universe into their bodies and eventually to their wives and offspring.

/ *Women's Marks of Honor and Sacred Skins* /

Only the wife, or wives, and daughters of tattooed Osage men who had achieved all thirteen war honors could be tattooed (Bailey 2010:34).[58] These tattoos also were believed to be imbued with life-giving powers, which was significant because it was through the act of childbirth that "the continual existence of the tribe" depended (La Flesche 1921b:113). The tattoos of Osage women were even more complex than those of men, especially in their symbolic and cosmological implications (see Figures 8.2 and 8.3). Women were compelled to fast for a period of four days while their extensive tattooing was completed.[59] As with other Siouian groups of the eastern plains, dot-like marks tattooed upon the foreheads of Osage women represented celestial bodies. For example, the Osage two-dot motif represented the "double stars" of Theta and Iota of the constellation Orion. Originally this design was said to have belonged to the *Mi-kin* ("Sun Carrier") clan of the *Tsi-zhu* moiety. In naming rituals, this star cluster was called "Stars-Strung-Together" and addressed as "Grandmother" (La Flesche 1939:138, 395). The line of diamonds running up and down from the navel to the throat represented four stars (female symbols) that also belonged to the Sun Carrier clan. Large designs flanking these stars symbolized a turtle and belonged to the *Ke'kin* ("Carrier of the Turtle") clan. Some of the projecting elements on the breast were said to depict "the projecting points of clouds," like the design that appears on the woven rush bag of the Osage tattooing bundle. However, in another La Flesche notebook this area was labeled the Milky Way galaxy.[60] All of these designs were associated with lengthy *wi'-gi-es*, ceremonial recitations, by which old age was believed to be reached.

The two large diamonds appearing on the back of the tattooed woman belonged to the *Tsi-zhu Wa-no*ⁿ ("Elder Sky") clan of the *Tsi-zhu* moiety. To this group, the motifs represented the sun (male symbol) and were associated with *wi'-gi-es*, by which old age was said to be reached. The row of diamonds running up and down the back belonged to the *Mi-kin* clan and was a continuation of the line running up and down in front.

The five stripes on either side of the shoulder belonged to the *Tsi-zhu Wa-no*ⁿ clan, and also had *wi'-gi-es* that spoke about long life. The row of diamonds running up and down the arms belonged to the *Mi-kin* and represented stars, as did the half-diamond design at the elbow. The straight lines running from the shoulder to the wrist were called "animal paths" and represented "life descending from the sun and stars to the earth," which was symbolized by the spider design (*Tse'-xo-be*) on the back of the hand (La Flesche 1921b:113). The forked lines below the elbow represented the tracks of these animals. These and the "paths" belonged to the *Ta'I'ni-ka-shi-ga* (or "Deer People") clan and had *wi'-gi-es* associated with long life.

The spider design on the back of the woman's hand belonged to the *Hon-ga U-Tah-No'n-Dsi* ("Isolated Earth") clan (see Figure 8.4). This tattoo also represented the "house" of this clan, the earth, which "like a snare draws to itself all living creatures, whosoever they may be" (La Flesche 1921a:102), from the "two great fructifying forces—namely the sky and the earth" (La Flesche 1921a:48).

It appears that in the ancient tradition of Osage tattooing, the conceptual organization of tribal society was intimately bound to a web of life forces and life symbols residing in the natural and supernatural environment. According to La Flesche (1921a:48), "This arrangement did not arise from idle thought, but from a belief, born of a long study of nature, that such was the means employed by *Wa-ko*ⁿ*-da* to bring forth life in bodily form." This "great unit," as it has been called, issued from the combined forces and influence of various objects that comprised it, including personified complementary pairs of visible bodies like the sky (male) and earth (female), and the sun (male) and stars (female) that, when combined together, implied a procreative relationship (La Flesche 1921a:50–51).

It is important to note that the Osage were not the only group to employ such beliefs. Although Omaha men were rarely tattooed, Blue Spot women of the Night Blessed Society were adorned with a solar (male) symbol on their forehead, the four-pointed star (female) at the base of their throat, a crescent moon (female) on their neck, and a turtle motif on the back of the hand symbolizing "a long, well-protected, and fruitful life" (La Flesche 1930:506, 531). Ponca women of the *Ni kagahi EshonGa* ("Chief's Daughters Dance Society") also received a sun dot on their forehead, and like their Otoe and Iowa[61] counterparts, a four-pointed star on their chest (see Figure 8.6). Circumscribed within the center of this Ponca star mark was a circle, perhaps symbolic of the sun, and other stars were tattooed on the top of the woman's hand, across her shoulders, and on her back (Figure 5.16; see also Figure 8.7). Interviewed Omaha and Ponca women stated that the star was emblematic of the night, the great mother force of creation, and that the four points of

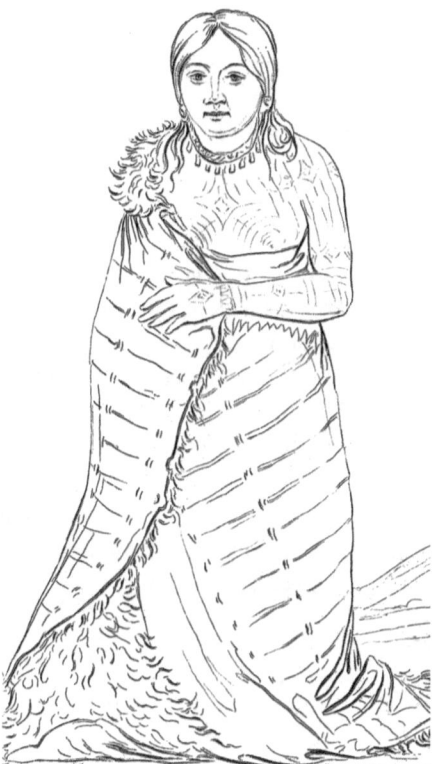

FIGURE 5.16. Pure Fountain, a Ponca woman
(1832) (redrawn after Catlin 1973: plate 88).

the star represented the "life giving winds" (Fletcher and La Flesche 1911:505; Rice 1988:105–106). The Osage also appealed in *wi'-gi-es* to the "goddess of darkness" because she was believed to "possess the power of reproduction" and to enable those who beseeched her "to reach maturity successfully" (La Flesche 1939:376).

Another composite Ponca tattoo design brings forth additional associated meanings that are embodied within female tattoo symbolism of the Eastern Plains (Figure 5.17). The text that accompanies the illustration relates:

Here are the emblems of day [sun] and night [star] and between them stand the forms of children. By the union of Day, the above, and Night, the below, came the human race and by them the race is maintained. The tattooing on this figure was said to be "an appeal for the perpetuation of all life and of human life in particular." (Fletcher and La Flesche 1911:507, fig. 106)

Fletcher and La Flesche's vivid descriptions of the Omaha tattooing rite dramatically reinforce these transformative and inscriptive processes, and they are worth repeating here. First they speak about the etymology of the word *Hon'hewachi*, where *Ho^{n}he* means "in the night," and *wa'chi* means "dance." But they say that the word *dance* has a veiled meaning, because in the Omaha sense of the term it refers to the "rhythmic movements for the expression of personal emotion or experience, the presentation of mythical teachings, and to creative acts, for through the mysterious power of *Wako^n'da* night brought forth day" (Fletcher and La Flesche 1911:493–494). That is: "Night was therefore the mother of day, and the latter was the emblem of all visible activities and manifestations of life." In turn, the "feminine cosmic force was typified not only by night but by the heavenly bodies seen by night, as the masculine cosmic force was symbolized by day and the sun" (Fletcher and La Flesche 1911:494).

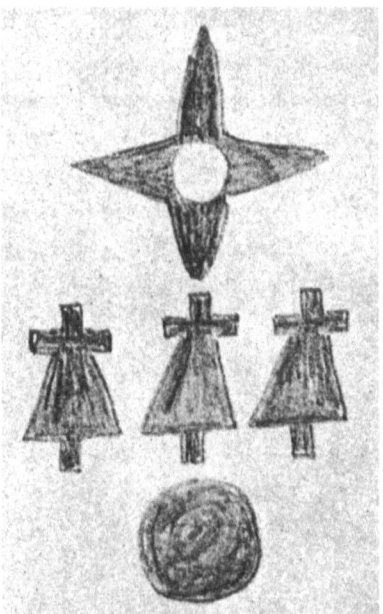

FIGURE 5.17. Ponca hand tattoo drawn by an indigenous woman (after Fletcher and La Flesche 1911:507, fig. 106).

On the morning of the Omaha tattooing rite, many kinds of preparations were performed and eventually the girl to be tattooed was made to recline facing west so that her head would lie closest to the sunrise.[62] The tattooist then readied his implement, which before the advent of hawk's bells was traditionally adorned with a rattlesnake rattle that would rustle as the blue mark was placed upon the girl's forehead. As this was being done, the following song was performed: "The Sun, the Round Sun; Comes, Speaks, or Says; Yonder Point; When It Comes; Comes, Speaks, or Says" (Fletcher and La Flesche 1911:504). This ancient tune referred to the sun as it rose to its highest point in the sky. When it travels to that location, it "speaks" as its symbol descends upon the girl with the "promise of life-giving power" (Fletcher and La Flesche 1911:504).

After the blue mark was completed, the four-pointed star was placed on the initiate's chest to the accompaniment of another song: "Night Moves, It Passes; and the Day Is Coming." After the cosmic symbols of Day and Night were applied to the skin of their new owner, a final song was performed: "Yonder Unseen Is One Moving; Noise; for That Reason; over the Earth; Noise; the Cry of the Living Creatures" (Fletcher and La Flesche 1911:504).

The latter song symbolically referred to the serpent, or as Fletcher and La Flesche (1911:506) explained, the serpent was "the representative of the teeming life that 'moves' over the earth. Because this life is 'moving' it makes a noise. Even the sun as it 'moves,' it is said, 'makes a noise,' as does the living wind in the trees." This noise also can be associated with the rattling of the tattooing implement, which dramatized the awakening of the feminine element—"an awakening everywhere necessary for a fulfillment in tangible form of the life-giving power" (Fletcher and La Flesche 1911:502).

/ Conclusion /

For over a millennium, the ritual of tattooing on the plains was a sophisticated genealogical system used to illustrate and declare tribal origins within the great cosmic chain of being. These bold patterns enabled communities and individuals to trace their ancestry back to the Creator from which all life proceeded, and upon which all life depended, while also mapping the ways in which to achieve tribal rebirth. Because tattooing was governed by a cultural complex of specific rules, rights, and roles, however, it also worked as a conduit through which ceremonial prerogatives, pedigrees, obligations, and esoteric knowledge were exchanged across moieties, clans, families, and individuals. Seen from this light, tattoos were alive and literally pregnant with meaning. And as enchanted symbols derived from the primordial Source, they allowed individuals to capture, condense, and then release this power back into the world as a sacred blessing to the people.

/ Author's Acknowledgments /

This chapter greatly benefited from imagery provided by individuals and institutions without whose support the words I have written would remain lifeless and shallow. In this regard, the photographic and/or illustrative resources of Lance Foster, the National Anthropological Archives, the Smithsonian Institution Archives, the Smithsonian Institution's Cullman Library, the Smithsonian's John Wesley Powell Library of Anthropology, and the Minnesota Historical Society deserve special attention. I am also indebted to Dr. Andrea A. Hunter and the Osage Traditional Cultural Advisors for providing guidance with respect to the proper display of the sacred Osage tattooing bundle featured in this essay, and the National Museum of the American Indian Archive Center of the Smithsonian Institution for allowing me to reproduce documentary records. Finally, I thank Aaron Deter-Wolf and Carol Diaz-Granados for their careful readings of earlier drafts of this chapter.

/ Notes /

1. Jonathan Carver (1778:309), who spent several months with the Dakota in Minnesota in the mid-eighteenth century, may have been the first European observer to record the Siouan term *Wakon*. Carver spoke about how the Dakota venerated these "spirits" as personal assistants and properly recognized that Algonquian groups living to the east (e.g., Chippewa) employed the term *manitou* to refer to such entities. See Chapter 4 for a more detailed discussion of *manitous* (or *manitos*) among the indigenous peoples of the Northern Woodlands.

2. Several Plains tribes that practiced this form of tattooing either are not discussed in this chapter or only receive a little attention because of space constraints. However, honor marking among women also was practiced among the Assiniboine (Denig 1930:592), Plains Cree (Skinner 1914:77), and Kansa (Skinner 1915a:754), amongst others.

3. Omaha men were rarely tattooed.

4. "Tattooing. *Wa-je-pa-in*, Pawhuska, OK. Sept. 10, 1910," p. 1, MS 4558, Tattooing Ceremony Notes 1898, 1910, 1918, Box 23, Alice Cunningham Fletcher and Francis La Flesche Papers (1873–1939) [FLP], National Anthropological Archives, Smithsonian Institution, Suitland, MD [NAA].

5. "Notes on Kaw Sacred Bundles," pp. 1–2, Folder B239.12, Box 239, Mark R. Harrington Papers [MHP], National Museum of the American Indian Archives, Smithsonian Institution, Suitland, MD [NMAI].

6. The contemporary Osage consider tattooing bundles to be some of their most sacred objects. I only include old photographs of these objects in this discussion because they should not be handled by anyone except spiritual practitioners of the tribe who are versed in the traditional ceremonies and protocols.

7. For example, the central village path or street represented the surface of the earth that divided the *Tsi-zhu* lodges (above, north of the path) from the *Hon-ga* residences (below, south of the path).

8. For information concerning the transfer of Osage bundles, see Bailey (1995:55) and La Flesche (1921a). See Light (1972:18) for an eyewitness account of a Cree tattooing bundle transfer ceremony.

9. Unpublished letter from La Flesche to Willoughby, December 14, 1916, Correspondence, Sacred Bundles, 1911, 1915–1917, Box 23, FLP, NAA. Bundle keepers across the plains adhered to rigid ceremonial protocols with regards to bundle storage; otherwise they risked supernatural danger (Fortune 1932:30, 49, 68, 164–165; Light 1972:13). Harrington revealed additional details for the Kaw ("Notes on Kaw Sacred Bundles," Folder B239.12, Box 239, MHP, NMAI).

10. The pelican is the life symbol of "the Chief of the *Ho^n-ga* tribal division" (La Flesche 1932:362).

11. Unpublished letter entitled "*Wa-xri'-zhi*," Tattooing Ceremony Notes 1898, 1910–11, 1918, Box 23, FLP, NAA.

12. "Legend of the Tattooing Custom," Tattooing Ceremony Notes 1898, 1910–11, 1918, Box 23, FLP, NAA.

13. "Notes on Kaw Sacred Bundles," Folder B239.12, Box 239, MHP, NMAI.

14. "*Wa-xri'-zhi*," Tattooing Ceremony Notes 1898, 1910–11, 1918, Box 23, FLP, NAA.

15. These notes are found in a handwritten letter entitled "Tattooing Outfit" with information apparently provided by the Osage informant Charley Wa-hre-she of the Puma (*In-ghton-ga*) clan. (Tattooing Ceremony Notes 1898, 1910–11, 1918, Box 23, FLP, NAA.

16. Undated letter entitled "The Tattoo," p. 8. Tattooing Ceremony Notes 1898, 1910–11, 1918, Box 23, FLP, NAA.

17. According to La Flesche (1921a: plate 13), the pileated woodpecker (*wa-zhi^n'-ga pa stese-dse*) "is a life symbol of the *Tsi'-zhu Wa-non^n* ["Elder Sky"], the principal war gens of the [*Tsi-zhu*] tribal division. This bird symbolizes the sun, the moon, and the morning and evening stars. These stars have the power of granting to the warriors trophies and spoils." The red plumage on its head "symbolizes persistency and perseverance" (La Flesche 1939:231), and is symbolic of the sun and never-ending life. Ponca informants interviewed by Whitman (1937:122) said that the ivory-billed woodpecker was an important tribal symbol: "His strong beak breaks into wood and

digs food out. He is a good bird since he seeks only food. It is his qualities that God gave the Indians."

18. The eagle is regarded as sacred by the Osage, "because it was the bird, according to myths, that led the people from the sky to the earth" (La Flesche 1939:205).

19. Letter entitled "Pawhuska OK. Feb. 18, 1911," Tattooing Ceremony Notes 1898, 1910–11, 1918, Box 23, FLP, NAA.

20. Undated letter entitled "Tattoo (Man) and Tattoo (Woman), (*Wa-xthi-zhi*)," Tattooing Ceremony Notes 1898, 1910–11, 1918, Box 23, FLP, NAA.

21. The "roots gathered for the purpose are chewed into pulp, and rubbed on the spot to be tattooed. This deadens the pain" (Skinner 1926:270).

22. According to Iowa chief Tohee (in Skinner 1926:267), the duck "was probably put in the bundle in obedience to someone's dream, as strictly speaking it does not seem to belong [there]." In another account, an Iowa man received a vision from a duck and gained the ability to "walk on water" (Skinner 1915b:706–707). Whitman (1937:122) cites testimony from Ponca informants that "the duck is always in the water, and water is life."

23. For information regarding Plains thunderbird symbolism and tattoos, see Fortune (1932:49, 146–147), La Flesche (1921a:61), and Light (1972:6–8).

24. Prior to the advent of firearms on the plains, all warriors carried wooden war clubs as their primary weapon in hand-to-hand combat. Harrington (1913:112) describes the contents of an Otoe war bundle he collected, stating that one "of the best things was tied on the outside of this [object], a fine old war club, symbolizing the power of the thunderbolt." Elsewhere, in his discussion of the Big Iowa War Bundle, Harrington states that the point of the club included in this bundle "represents lightning which strikes and destroys everything" ("Tattooing Bundle," Folder B241.9, Box 241, MHP, NMAI).

"Thunder-beings" were invoked by Omaha warriors as they readied to head out on the warpath. If the war party was large, a preparatory feast was held and the sacred bundle keepers sang thunder songs, amongst others. In one instance a singer stated that he could not continue with the song because it was *waqube*, or sacred: "As my grandfather is dangerous, As my grandfather is dangerous, Dangerous when he brandishes his club, Dangerous" (Dorsey 1894:382).

Among the Iowa, *Wakanda* (or *Ma'oⁿ*, The Earthmaker, as he was originally known) was assisted by several deities, including the "Thunderers." Possessing both human and avian form (i.e., eagle), these divine beings were associated with war and fertility and included Thunder Man, Rain Man, Lightning Man, Little God, and Little Thunder (Skinner 1926:253).

25. In Osage myth, the hawk is associated with "dauntless courage" used to "attack [its] foes" (La Flesche 1939:10). According to Black Dog, former principal chief of the Osage, the hawk was adopted "as the god of war" ("Honor Packs of the Osage Tribe, Black Dog, March 10, 1898," Tattooing Ceremony Notes 1898, 1910–11, 1918, Box 23, FLP, NAA).

26. Harrington also states that when "an eagle claw is seen attached to a [Kaw] bundle it is said that the owner belonged to the Eagle clan. When such a man is tattooed he talks to the claw as if he were talking to an eagle, saying 'I hope that after I am tattooed it will not make a sore on my neck'" ("Notes on Kaw Sacred Bundles," p. 4, Folder B239.12, Box 239, MHP, NMAI).

27. In an unpublished letter to Charles C. Willoughby of Harvard's Peabody Museum, La Flesche describes in great detail the contents of an Osage war bundle recently acquired by that institution ("Dec. 14, 1916," Correspondence, Sacred Bundles 1911, 1915–1917, Box 23, FLP, NAA).

28. The French geographer Joseph Nicollet (1970:163–164) documented the contents of Chippewa hunting and war "bags," or more appropriately their bundles, that were constructed of bird skins "in which the natives place their herbs, thus increasing the power of the [bag]" itself. "[They] contain mainly those remedies that heal wounds, that give flexibility to the limbs, and that prevent bullets from penetrating the body. This particular kind they grind and chew, spitting out the resulting froth onto the parts of the body they wish to soften and preserve." It should be noted here that the Chippewa were sworn enemies of the Dakota Sioux.

29. La Flesche, writing about Osage war bundles, states: "The *Gdhe-don*, Bird hawk, and the *Ni-shku-shku*, Sand martin, control the war parties, they pertain to Thunder. These birds are carried in a buckskin bag. In taking the birds out when about to go to battle, the birds are withdrawn from their covering by degrees, while ritual songs are sung. The Leader is given the bird to wear about his neck, and the 'scabbard' or ba[g] is given to the next in common to wear in like fashion" ("Notes on the Birds in the Honor Packs of the Osage by Conner," March 1898," Sacred Bundles, Notes, 1898, Box 23, FLP, NAA). Of the hawk, La Flesche (1916:282) adds that when placed in an Osage war bundle this "bird represents life and death—life for the Osage and death for all their enemies."

30. "Notes on Kaw Sacred Bundles," pp. 1–4, Folder B239.12, Box 239, MHP, NMAI.

31. "Notes on Kaw Sacred Bundles," p. 3, Folder B239.12, Box 239, MHP, NMAI.

32. In La Flesche's (1932:208) Osage dictionary, the word *waxobe* is variously defined as (1) a whistle used as a sacred symbol after victory; (2) a talisman, or something worn about the person to ward off evil; (3) anything consecrated for ceremonial use; and (4) a portable symbol, like the hawk, that represents or symbolizes the courage of a warrior.

33. Bowers (1965:279), speaking of the Hidatsa and Mandan, stated that the highest military honors that could be attained by men were those given to individuals who sought to avenge the death of a sibling, clan member, and particularly a "blood brother." Only those men "who went out alone far from home to kill and scalp an enemy unassisted" were eligible. The Osage also counted such activities as one of their thirteen war honors, but La Flesche (1939:87) added that such war parties were formed "for the purpose of slaying a member of some enemy tribe in order to secure

a spirit to accompany that of a dead Osage to the spirit land. There is a belief among the Osage that the path of the spirit land is a lonely one and he who travels upon it craves company, therefore a man who has lost by death his wife, son, daughter, nephew, or other loved relative" desires to be avenged.

34. The clam shell was said to have been brought "from 'the great water at the east' by the ancestors of the Kansa. This was the case with all the sacred objects of the tribe, including the pipes and sundry roots used as medicines" (Dorsey 1885a:673). A number of the shells included in Kansa war bundles (including the "clam shell" discussed and illustrated by Dorsey) were in fact Mississippian "masks" manufactured from marine whelk (Howard 1956; Peres and Deter-Wolf 2012).

35. "The Osages have a similar chart, on which there are fully a hundred pictographs" (Dorsey 1885a:675). Harrington added that one Kaw war bundle contained a piece of paper "on which were rude pictures recalling the song records of [his] lodge. The pictures in this case represent songs of different birds and animals. Before he started to war, the owner used to pick out each picture, and sing its appropriate song. The belief that these songs had frequently helped him to victory impelled him to put the record of them in his bundle" ("Notes on Kaw Sacred Bundles," pp. 4–5, Folder B239.12, Box 239, MHP, NMAI).

36. One of the most detailed accounts of a ritual petition to *Wakanda* is that of an Otoe woman who vividly recounted her experiences under the needle (see Whitman 1937:74–76, 79). Her statements not only complement those recorded for the Iowa, but also contain significant details regarding the contents and possible functions of items within tattooing bundles, as well as information on the ceremonies performed in conjunction with Otoe body marking itself.

37. The artist Rudolph Kurz (1937:173) observed that the families of Iowa girls parted with ten horses (one mark) or twenty horses (two marks) depending on the number of dot-like honor tattoos they received.

38. Helen Grant Walker, one of the last tattooed Omaha women, proclaimed that she was the "first daughter [and] that is why my father put it [the tattoo] on me . . . And he give it away for a hundred horses" (Ridington 1998:193).

39. Pauline Tindall, a respected Omaha elder, believed that these women were above all "recognized for their saintliness . . . They were people who were supposed to be good to the poor and sick . . . and went about doing good deeds. They were an order that were recognized for that, and their character had to be above reproach" (Ridington 1998:193).

40. It has been recorded that a Plains Cree man "who desired to be thus marked had to fee the tattooer well unless he dreamed that he must be tattooed, in which case the work was done free of charge" (Skinner 1914:77).

41. Skinner (1915a:689) noted that Iowa men, in the common fashion of earlier times, "had to sit down four days before it [tattooing] was done to them." This statement may refer to a vision quest performed before the actual tattooing took place, but no additional details are provided.

42. The Hidatsa tattooing tool resembled that already described for other groups like the Osage, Iowa, Otoe, Plains Cree, and so on. However, as amongst the Assiniboine, a small thin piece of an old skin tent was used as a kind of blotter to soak up excess blood that ran from the wounds. In her account of Assiniboine tattooing, the Hidatsa elder Buffalo Bird Woman said that this sponge was smoke-soiled and probably cut from near the smoke hole of a tent or tipi cover (Weitzner 1979:226). In turn, the soiled membrane may have added an additional layer of sooty pigment.

43. Bird symbolism that parallels this style of tattooing can be seen in an illustration of a Fox or Mesquakie warrior ca. 1710 (see Figure 4.16), and in several painted animal hides attributed to the Illinois dating to the eighteenth century (Brasser 1999:52, figs. 3–6). This should not be surprising, since a large segment of the Siouan people originated from the East in prehistoric times.

William Bartram noted in 1789 that the animal hide paintings created by the Illinois "were much like those inscriptions [tattoo] or paintings on the bodies of the chiefs and warriors" (Bartram 1996 [1853]:534). For additional information regarding Illinois hide paintings and tattoos, see Chapter 4 and Figure 4.18.

44. One of the sacred Osage war honors was earned when a warrior beheaded an enemy with "his own knife or a borrowed one" (La Flesche 1939:16). "To this day children are named for this ancient ceremonial weapon" (La Flesche 1939:14). The sacred knife also stood as a metaphor for societal strength and cohesion (La Flesche 1921:237). In antiquity, flint knives probably were suspended from the neck for use in combat. For a discussion regarding the survival of this practice into the historic period, please see Feest (2002).

45. Bailey (2010:70–72) and La Flesche (1939:15–16, 86) provide listings of these war honors.

46. Undated field note entitled "Number of Tattooing Packs," Tattooing Ceremony Notes 1898, 1910–11, 1918, Box 23, FLP, NAA.

47. Undated field note entitled "Tattoo (Man) and Tattoo (Woman), (Wa-xthizhi)," pp. 1–2, Tattooing Ceremony Notes 1898, 1910–11, 1918, Box 23, FLP, NAA.

48. In a myth that speaks about the origins of the thirteen prescribed war honors of the Osage, the black bear, beaver, and sun are believed to be the source of inspiration for setting this ritual mandate (see La Flesche 1916:283–284).

49. In Osage cosmology, the "sun pillars," or beams of light that emerge at sunrise, are likened to eagle plumes because, like feathers, "they stand upright and never droop for want of strength" (La Flesche 1916:279). Plumes always stand upright, no matter their age, and this everlasting quality (longevity) was likewise equated to the sun's rays, which "never fail to appear at the beginning of [each] day" (La Flesche 1932:387). The Osage called the sun "the God of Day," and it was associated with *Wakanda*. Because the Osage were said to "depend" on *Wakanda* for "continued existence," they appealed to this entity at sunrise, at noon, and at sunset every day (La Flesche 1921:49).

Late prehistoric Mississippian rock art depicts a mythical warrior hero called

"Morning Star," who is typically portrayed with stripes, or perhaps the sun's rays, presumably tattooed across his torso (Diaz-Granados 2004:147–148; Diaz-Granados and Duncan 2004:149). Morning Star also is associated with what are called "Long-Nosed God" maskettes, which, when worn upon his head (e.g., on the back of his head or turned sideways), resemble chief's headdresses (*watha-ge*, Omaha and Osage) of a similar projecting form utilized by Omaha, Osage, Ponca, Pawnee, Otoe, Iowa, Fox, and other historic leaders (Callender 1978:642, fig. 7; Fletcher and La Flesche 1911: plates 36, 49, etc.). Striped or rayed tattoos of this type also find their counterparts in portraiture of historic Eastern Woodlands warriors (see Chapter 4).

50. Unpublished letter entitled "Notes on Tattooing," Tattooing Ceremony Notes 1898, 1910–11, 1918, Box 23, FLP, NAA.

51. La Flesche stated in unpublished notes that the "straight lines of the tattoo symbolize the stripes on the opossum" ("Tattoo," p. 2, Tattooing Ceremony Notes 1898, 1910–11, 1918, Box 23, FLP, NAA). Looking at the overall design, I believe this observation is possibly related to the series of three small horizontal lines that occur at intervals along the knife design. The opossum is a nocturnal animal and is featured on twentieth-century Osage Roadman's staffs for use during the Big Moon peyote ceremony (Swan 1999:37, 39). However, it is possible that these bands may refer to a more ancient symbolic animal, the raccoon (i.e., its banded tail), which is associated with the prehistoric Mississippian striped-center-pole motif of the sacred World Tree, the axis mundi of the universe (Duncan and Diaz-Granados 2004:208–209; Reilly 2004:127). Similar lines also adorned the indelible sun rays and pipe motifs seen on the tattooed chests of Osage men, but these may be "joint" or "body" markings. As noted, the sacred pipe symbolizes the Osage people as a tribal body, and each segment of lines may refer to a specific part of that body (e.g., neck, spine, etc.), since the pipe bowl is equated to a mouth.

52. Osage warriors who claimed war honors had to participate in a lengthy ritual. See La Flesche ("Notebook, May 1918," Tattooing Ceremony Notes 1898, 1910–11, 1918, Box 23, FLP, NAA).

53. Undated letter entitled "Tattoo (Man) and Tattoo (Woman), (Wa-xthi-zhi)," Tattooing Ceremony Notes 1898, 1910–11, 1918, Box 23, FLP, NAA.

54. Undated letter entitled "Tattoo," Tattooing Ceremony Notes 1898, 1910–11, 1918, Box 23, FLP, NAA.

55. Unpublished letter entitled "Notes on Tattooing among the Osage. Black Dog, March 1898," Tattooing Ceremony Notes 1898, 1910–11, 1918, Box 23, FLP, NAA.

56. Unpublished letter entitled "Notes on the Tattooing," Tattooing Ceremony Notes 1898, 1910–11, 1918, Box 23, FLP, NAA.

57. Undated letter entitled "The Tattoo," p. 8, Tattooing Ceremony Notes 1898, 1910–11, 1918, Box 23, FLP, NAA.

58. Skinner (1915b:754) observed similar traditions amongst the Kansa: "When a man had been very successful in war it was his privilege to have his wife tattooed. He

would gather many presents, including a full suit of Indian clothes and give them to the owner of the tattooing bundle. The tattooing was done on the woman's chest, her arms as far as the wrist, and her calves. A round spot was also made on her forehead between the eyes."

59. Undated letter entitled "The Tattoo," Tattooing Ceremony Notes 1898, 1910–11, 1918, Box 23, FLP, NAA.

60. "Notebook, May 1918," Tattooing Ceremony Notes 1898, 1910–11, 1918, Box 23, FLP, NAA. According to Lankford (2004:211–212), the Milky Way was viewed by indigenous Eastern Woodlands people as the "path traversed by the souls of the dead." An Otoe tattooist interviewed by Whitman (1937:76) said that the four-pointed star he tattooed on women symbolized the "Big Star" (Venus?) through "which we enter into Heaven."

61. Harrington's Iowa informants said that this "pointed" star is the Morning Star, "and its use is said to be of some help to the wearer, through the supernatural power of the star itself" (in Skinner 1926:269).

62. Iowa and Otoe women were tattooed at sunrise (Skinner 1926:269; Whitman 1937:78).

< 6 >

Identifying the Face of the Sacred

Tattooing the Images of Gods and Heroes in the Art of the Mississippian Period

F. Kent Reilly III

/ / / /

The ethnographic data informs us that paint itself can have deep symbolic meaning and that the art work is not an end product, but is only part of a process that proceeds and follows it.

SALZER AND RAJNOVICH (2000:69)

Within all cultures the images of gods and heroes carry specific markings, colors, or tattoos to allow the initiated to recognize their identities, their ritual objects, and the practitioners who were dedicated to serving and worshipping these extraordinary beings. The forms and styles of body modification and tattooing, in effect, function as templates that identify the cosmic realm or realms that these "Other-Than-Human-Persons," or supernaturals, inhabit. Tattooing also identifies the human ritual practitioners who can access these preternatural entities through sacred rituals and objects.

For this study, body decoration and modification among ancient and modern Native Americans is classified into three categories. The first category is body decoration, which uses color or pattern—as opposed to tattooing or scarification—to identify the decorated individual as engaging in a specific act such as war or ritual. Since these acts are not permanent, paint as the medium of identification likewise is impermanent and may be removed once the war or ritual has been terminated.

On the other hand, tattooing, the second category, permanently modifies the body, marking the individual with a specific identity and designating the person as a member within a specific kinship system, lineage, or moiety (Hambly 2009 [1925]; Wallace 1993). As we shall see, tattooing also can indicate specific honors won in war, achieved through specific rituals or derived from political offices the individual has held.

For many cultures, tattooing visualizes an individual's effort to approach what Hambly characterizes as

> non-human forces by positive rites carried out with meticulous accuracy, and at the same time . . . Association of such ceremonial with body marking is a sure indication of its importance. When, in addition to caution, secrecy, and ritual, there are definite beliefs relating to the value of tattoo marks in heaven, dedication to a deity, the evidence for a religious dynamic force in body markings is incontrovertible. (Hambly 2009 [1925]:25)

Piercing, the third category, establishes points on the individual's body to ensure the proper placement of hanging ornaments, which often is ritual or lineage specific. The scarification caused by piercing also can visually attest to and identify the rituals during which the piercing and scarification occurred. This certainly is the case for the scarring participants carry out during certain rituals, for instance, in the Sun Dance. Both tattooing and piercing often serve as scripts and mnemonic devices recorded on the manuscript of the human body. The information that body modification conveys functions as links in a chain of memory important to the tattooed individual as well as to viewers who read the encoded markings (Roberts and Roberts 1996:85–116).

In this chapter I first will identify the imagery or body decoration that certain painted anthropomorphic figures display on their bodies, from the art in caves and rockshelters in Missouri and Wisconsin, dating to the Early or Proto-Mississippian period (AD 750–1100) (Diaz-Granados 2004). Second, I will link this body decoration to the Classic Braden style of art (Brown 2007b, 2011). Finally I will discuss those anthropomorphic figures who bear Braden-style symbols and motifs on their bodies, thus identifying them as Other-Than-Human-Persons.

The beginning of this essay discusses the methodology appropriate to recover meaning from ancient works of art. A brief discussion of Native American body decoration follows, as it is described in European accounts of the sixteenth through eighteenth centuries. After contextualizing this body decoration within demonstrably identifiable motif complexes, I will present specific data within a Mississippian period motif complex. The existence of this broad but detailed motif complex supports the several hypotheses presented here. Finally, I will conclude with examples that illustrate the validity of those hypotheses.

/ *Methodology* /

Erwin Panofsky (1939) pioneered an art historical technique for categorizing image groupings by means of their formal visual components. As part of his threefold theoretical approach, Panofsky presented motif complexes as tools or keys to better understand the iconographic and, more importantly, the cognitive function of works of art. Analyzing the body decoration of the specific anthropomorphic figures painted in caves will show that these traits also exist within a motif complex that flourished on shell engravings executed in the Braden style, discovered in or looted from the Great Mortuary at the Craig Mound at the Spiro archaeological site in Oklahoma (Brown 2011). Some painted anthropomorphic images from Missouri and Wisconsin can be linked to the Oklahoma shell engravings by means of the testable investigative process known as "upstreaming."

Ethnohistorian William N. Fenton (1953) first developed upstreaming as a theoretical approach that provides an understanding of cultural stability and conservatism:

> The functioning present society becomes the model for critically examining the past. It would appear that the internal structure of a society remains relatively stable over long periods of time. And so the ethnographer turned cultural historian—or social historian, if you will—finds the same basic cultural patterns functioning at both ends of the time-stream, and [with] his own observations confirmed by earlier observer[s], he knows that he has found stability and he trusts his sources. (Fenton 1953:170–171)

Fenton's arguments for the survival of traits at "both ends of a time-stream" certainly have been applied successfully to the study of ancient Native American cultures and their art, as well as to the art of contemporary Native American cultures. James A. Brown, in his extensive study of the Red Horn stories (Radin 1948), has argued convincingly for a connection between Red Horn (or Morning Star) imagery from fireclay figurines and shell engravings from the Mississippian period and ethnohistorical data on Morning Star collected among the Osage and other Dhegihan peoples (Brown 2005). If such links can be established further, through Panofsky's method of structural analysis as well as through the use of upstreaming between ethnohistorical collections of Native American stories and folklore with prehistoric visual imagery, then the same method of linking styles can be applied to contemporaneous prehistoric imagery, even that which has been recovered from widely separated archaeological sites.

In this chapter, I will expressly examine painted imagery from Picture Cave, Missouri (Diaz-Granados 2004), and from the Gottschall Rockshelter located in southwestern Wisconsin (Salzer 1987; Salzer and Rajnovich 2000) in order to link these two sets of pictographs with a third group of depictions engraved on shell artifacts recovered from the Great Mortuary, Craig Mound, Spiro, Oklahoma. I will concentrate on painted and incised imagery that clearly seems to reflect ancient tattooing practices and contexts. Undoubtedly, by recording specific Other-Than-Human-Persons, artists and ritual practitioners depicted actual tattooing and body decoration to identify these beings, as well as to cue the ancient stories in which the supernaturals acted their major dramatic and symbolic roles. These images thus triggered memories of those rituals that dwelt within the public collective memory of these supernatural entities and diagrammed their place in those cosmic events that established the Native American world as it then was understood to exist (Duncan 2011; Reilly 2011).

/ Evidence for Native American Tattooing and Body Decoration in Early European Sources /

Archaeological evidence strongly suggests that Native Americans were practicing the art and rituals of tattooing as early as the Adena cultural period (1000–200 BC) in the central Ohio River valley (Penney 1982:257–277; see also Chapter 2 of this volume). Likewise, from the earliest extant accounts of European exploration (ca. 1500–1790), observers and artists alike recorded that many inhabitants of the Americas practiced body modification, in particular tattooing (see Wallace, this volume).

French artist Jacques Le Moyne de Morgues (ca. 1533–1588) and the English explorer John White (ca. 1540–1593) left some of the most dramatic evidence of Native American body modification in their accounts and illustrations. Some scholars now doubt the validity and accuracy of both Le Moyne's and White's depictions of Native Americans and their lifeways, at least insofar as they were later reproduced by the Flemish engraver Theodore de Bry (Milanich 2005; see also Chapter 1). However, we must consider that each artist was employed specifically to record the landscapes, native inhabitants, and flora and fauna of these newfound lands. Each was contracted by the official or commercial factors that financed these early expeditions. Allowing for Renaissance and Mannerist stylistic conventions and tropes used within those artworks, there must have been a core of credible, even empirically scientific, accuracy within these drawings and paintings. Indeed, their creators would have been held accountable by witnesses, as well as by their patrons and investors, who would have challenged their accuracy if these early artworks were total fabrications.

As described in Chapter 1 of this volume, Le Moyne and some three hundred French Huguenots landed in La Florida at the site of what would become Fort Caroline on the St. John's River in 1564. Le Moyne was primarily responsible for recording the wonders of Florida and its native peoples with paint and pen. Unfortunately Le Moyne's paintings and drawings only survive mediated through a series of engravings executed by the Flemish printer and engraver Theodore de Bry (Lorant 1965). Nevertheless, de Bry's prints of Le Moyne's artwork provide truly wonderful windows onto the daily lives of both the elite and plebeian Native Americans of Florida. Many of these depictions clearly show these people's bodies adorned with elaborate body paint or tattoos (see, e.g., Figures 1.1 and 7.7).

In the modern American mind, the English artist and investor John White is identified strongly with Sir Walter Raleigh and the Lost Colony of Roanoke. White is thought to have originally been a painter of miniatures who sailed in 1585 to the shores of North Carolina with the responsibility of painting the peoples, plants, and wildlife of the newly named English colony of Virginia. White's surviving drawings are noted for their meticulous attention to detail (Hulton 1984, Sloan 2007) and often illustrate the elaborate body painting and tattooing of the Native inhabitants of coastal North Carolina (see Chapter 1).

By the mid- and late eighteenth century, several other Euro-Americans were observing and recording Native American tattooing and body modification. For instance, James Adair (ca. 1703–1789), in his monumental *History of the American-Indians* (2005 [1775]), describes Chickasaw tattooed symbols as blue in color, with the color itself prepared from pine-pitch soot. He further describes the original tattooing instrument as the sharp-toothed jaw of the garfish. The tattoo marks were inscribed on the arms and chests of warriors and described as being as "legible as our alphabetic characters are to us" (Adair 2005 [1775]:384). Thus, a credible source directly informs us that for the colonial Chickasaw, and certainly other Southeastern tribes, tattooing functioned as a symbolic information system that could be read and understood by an individual trained in this system.

In 1791, when botanist and explorer William Bartram noted that Muscogee Creek elite bore tattoos that served as records of their tribes or families or of memorable events, he was observing a tradition with roots deep in the Mississippian period, if not earlier. As will be shown, iconographic investigations of body modification or decoration, perhaps including tattooing, in the several examples of Braden-style art (Phillips and Brown:1978) reveal patterns suggesting that the tattoos referred to specific cosmological events and preternatural beings. Of Muscogee or Creek art, William Bartram states that

> the most beautiful painting now to be found amongst the Muscogulges is in the skin on their bodies of their ancient chiefs & micos which is of a bluish lead or indigo color. It is the breast, trunk [,] muscul[ar] or fleshy parts of the arms & thighs & sometimes almost every part of the surface of the body that is thus beautifully depicted or wrote over with hieroglyphics—commonly called the Sun, Moon & Planets—occupies the breast. Zones or belts, beautiful fanciful scroles wind round the trunk of the body, thighs, arms, legs, dividing the body into many Fields or Tablets, which are ornamented or filled up with innumerable figures as representations of animals of the chase. A sketch of a landscape representing an engagement or battle with their enemy, or some creature of the chase; & a thousand other fancies. These paintings are admirable well executed, & seem to be inimitable. It is performed by exceeding fine punctures & seems like merzitinto or a very ingenious impression from the best executed engravings.
>
> There is no doubt hieroglyphics or mystical writings, or records of their tribe, family & memorable events &c &c. (Bartram in Waselkov and Holland Braund 1995:144)

For this discussion, Bartram's most important observation is that the bodies of Creek political and religious leaders were used as a pictorial canvas or an informational slate. This canvas was divided into "Fields or Tablets," containing lineage, warfare, hunting, and cosmological information. Bartram's reader is left with the impression that this tattooing not only enhanced the status of the individuals who were tattooed but also served to record and display information that was important to both the tattooed individual and those who observed the executed tattooing.

By the mid-nineteenth century, information concerning Native American tattooing was being recorded regularly and published in several sources. One noteworthy source was "The Omaha Tribe," which Alice C. Fletcher and Francis La Flesche presented in the *Twenty-Seventh Annual Report of the Bureau of American Ethnology*. La Flesche himself was not only the first professional Native American ethnographer but was also the son of Iron Eyes, the last Omaha head chief. Fletcher and La Flesche (1992:2:495) recorded that the act of tattooing was linked to prestigious membership in sacred, and sometimes secret, societies. Importantly, they also observed that the act of tattooing recorded esoteric knowledge and was coupled with memorizing sacred songs (see Chapter 5). Thus tattooing, as well as the esoteric knowledge it recorded, became critical to the performance of the sacred, or those rituals that embodied and visualized the sacred within Omaha secret societies. Fletcher and La Flesche (1992:2:495) further recorded that other members of the Dhegihan-speaking family also practiced tattooing as marks of honor that identified the individual's society membership and also proclaimed the one so marked as a prestigious individual who belonged to important lineages and clans (see Chapter 7).

This selection of ethnographic literature, across 350 years, documents that tattooing served several functions within a wide range of Native American cultures. Tattooing was a medium for recording individual war honors, as well as lineage and tribal histories. Tattooing also served as a medium to display prestigious marks of honor, such as tribal offices, as well as membership in important secret societies. We can characterize tattoos as near-heraldic devices, publicly identifying the status of an individual, male or female, within the overall social structure of his or her tribal and cultural affiliations.

With this varied evidence, let us return to the fundamental questions asked earlier. First, can prehistoric decoration displayed on the bodies of certain painted anthropomorphic figures from caves and rockshelters in Missouri and Wisconsin (Early or Proto-Mississippian period, AD 750–1100) be linked to the later, Braden-style, artistic conventions (Brown 2005, 2007b, 2011)? Second, through the patterns of tattooed imagery that they display on their bodies, can we identify such anthropomorphic figures as those Other-Than-Human-Persons who were the major protagonists in ancient Native American primordial, or dream, time?

/ *The Braden Style* /

Meyer Schapiro (1953) succinctly defines the general concept of style as the formal qualities and visual characteristics of a work of art. To Schapiro's definition one should add that style also consists of those specific qualities within any work of art that bridge or link one work of art to other works of art (Reilly 2011). Within his critically important effort to define style, Schapiro demonstrates that style can be deployed as a major diagnostic tool to link the individual work of art to specific artists and workshops, as well as to the culture at large. Likewise, stylistic elements can be linked to specific beliefs and artistic concepts of displaying the sacred, or displaying attributes that cannot be seen materially.

Objects created in the Braden A, or Classic Braden, style of the Mississippian period were crafted from a variety of media, including flint clay, copper, and shell. However, the largest corpus of Classic Braden-style objects is the large quantity of incised shell cups and gorget fragments recovered (or looted) from the Great Mortuary of the Craig Mound at Spiro, Oklahoma, after 1933. Even though the greatest number of these artworks come from the Great Mortuary, scholarly research over the last two decades points to the region surrounding ancient Cahokia as the heartland of the Braden style (Brown 2004; Hall 2004). Currently, the earliest known examples of the Braden style do not occur on shell, but rather on rock art and in polychrome compositions painted on the walls of caves and rockshelters (Brown 2007b; Diaz-Granados 2004, 2011; Duncan and Diaz-Granados 2000, 2004).

The formal qualities of the Braden style have been discussed extensively in the first volume of the *Pre-Columbian Shell Engravings from the Craig Mound at Spiro, Oklahoma* (Phillips and Brown 1978:ix–xi). Among those qualities, anthropomorphic representations within Braden exhibit realistic qualities and depictions, and most Braden narrative compositions involve multiple components emphasizing paired figures. Human heads can be depicted independent of bodies. Most heads of anthropomorphic figures are rendered in profile with diamond—or rhomboid—shaped eyes outlined by eye-surrounds. The mouths of these Braden figures are depicted as slightly open, teeth showing within, with parted lips and accented by a second line-surround.

These figures are often referred to as being in a "tiptoed" position, with high arches along the bottoms of the feet. Often one leg is raised and bent at the knee. This posture most likely represents aspects of narrative movement and perhaps dance postures. Although regalia and other accoutrements are often schematized, they can be elaborate and rendered in great detail. Among these accoutrements are high-crested headdresses, the bi-lobed arrow, the agnathous or jawless head, long-nosed maskettes (also known as Long-Nosed God maskettes) worn as ear ornaments, and columella pendants and necklaces. The hair of Braden figures usually is coiffured as a bun gathered in the back, while a long beaded forelock hangs in the front.

The rendering of body decoration or tattooing in the Classic Braden style is important for this discussion:

Allover body decoration in striated and "Akron modes." . . . Forked-Eye surrounds superimposed on striated body decorations . . . Bands of Davis

rectangles as body decoration . . . "Akron" grid as allover background treatment with various motifs superimposed: undulating forked eyes, spud-like
figure, ogee. Minor elements of Akron grid such as crossbars, T-bars, and
triangular oar-like line terminations occur in other contexts. (Phillips and
Brown 1978:x)

As we shall see, many specific aspects of Braden-style body decoration are
present on the drawn figures from the Gottschall Rockshelter and the polychrome paintings from Picture Cave in Missouri. The existence of this Allover
Braden-style body decoration is the crucial element that supports the hypothesis identifying these painted and drawn figures as depicting Early Mississippian Other-Than-Human-Persons. The body decoration these figures bear, as
specific tattooed symbols, serves as a heraldic badge, identifying their painted
and drawn images to human viewers as well as to other supernaturals.

The major themes of Braden-style art first appear in the rock art of Missouri and other regions comprising the earlier Braden, or Cahokian, heartland
(Diaz-Granados 2004, 2011; Hall 2004). Current research strongly suggests
that the Braden themes were manifested in specific cults and their attendant
rituals (Reilly 2007a; Smith and Beahm 2011). The Braden-style cults that
can be identified to date include Creation and Cosmological Establishment,
Morning Star (or Birdman), and Corn Maiden and Old Woman (Reilly
2007a). Of these cults, the one that is identified most certainly through cave
imagery is that of Morning Star, or Birdman. This anthropomorphic imagery bears the Allover Braden-style body decoration and presents a narrative
that identifies these figures as images created in the Braden style.

/ *The Gottschall Rockshelter (AD 900–1000) and Picture Cave*
(AD 800–1000): The Braden Style and the Tattooed Figural Template /

The Gottschall site (47IA80) is a shallow sandstone rockshelter located in
southwestern Wisconsin and famous for its pictographs (Figure 6.1) and
the sandstone sculpture of an anthropomorphic head (Figure 6.2) (Salzer
1987; Salzer and Ranovich 2000). Of particular interest to this discussion is
a painted narrative, Panel 5, rendered in blue-gray paint, dating to ca. AD
900–1000 (Salzer 1987:463) (see Figure 6.1). Robert Salzer describes Panel 5
as follows:

The group includes three highly detailed and carefully wrought human
forms. Facial features and items of wearing apparel and ornaments are

depicted in the figures. There is also a depiction of a large bird. These four figures and possibly a fifth—a turtle-like figure above two of the humans—are believed to be a planned composition because they share many details of design and motif and because they were painted on a surface that had been deliberately prepared by smoothing. (Salzer 1987:441–445)

The overall composition of Panel 5, which I call the Gottschall Figural Template, is not unique. Panel 5 shares stylistic and iconographic attributes with parietal art from Picture Cave, Missouri, and the Thruston Tablet, found near the Castalian Springs site in Sumner County or in the adjoining Trousdale County, Tennessee (Figure 6.3) (Steponaitis et al. 2011). Specifically the Gottschall tableau and the Thruston Tablet both feature a headdress ornament that is round or semi-circular with rays emanating from it.

For this discussion, however, the most significant similarity is between the painted images at Picture Cave and those at the Gottschall Rockshelter. At both sites the painted figures are arranged in tableau and share Braden-style attributes. Both sites are roughly contemporaneous, although the paintings at Picture Cave are earlier, dating from AD 800–1025 (Diaz-Granados et al. 2001).

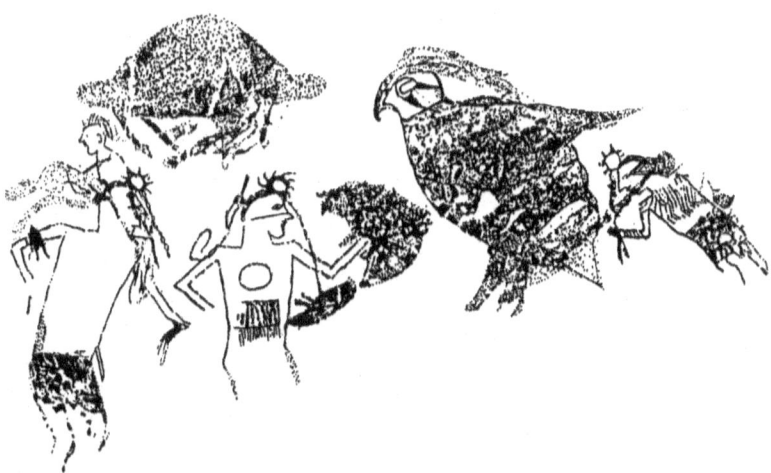

FIGURE 6.1. Detail of figural tableau from the Gottschall Rockshelter, Wisconsin, AD 900–1000 (after Salzer and Rajnovich 2000: fig. 23).

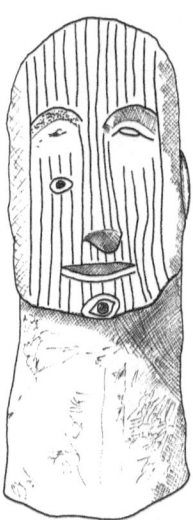

FIGURE 6.2. Anthropomorphic sandstone head from the Gott-schall Rockshelter (after Salzer and Rajnovich 2000: cover).

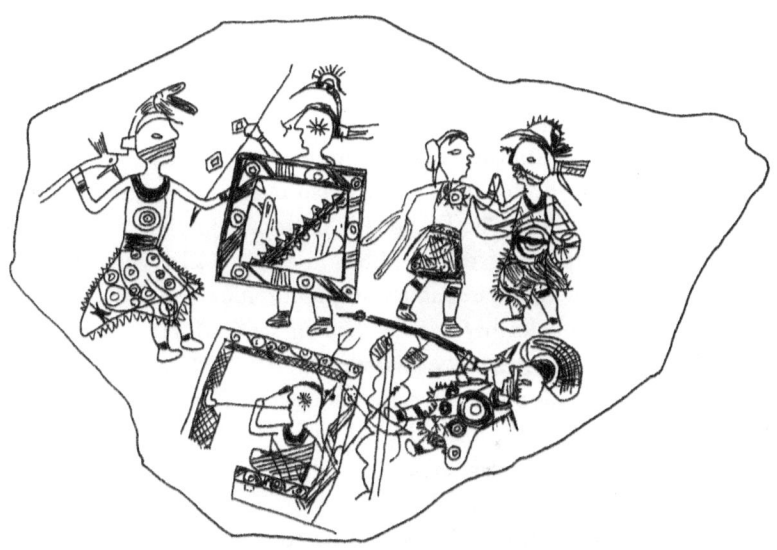

FIGURE 6.3. The foreground of the Thruston Tablet (after Steponaitis et al. 2011: fig. 7.7), which shares stylistic attributes with Gottschall Panel 5 (see Figure 6.1). In particular, both works of art show figures wearing a headdress that takes the form of circle or semicircle with emanating rays.

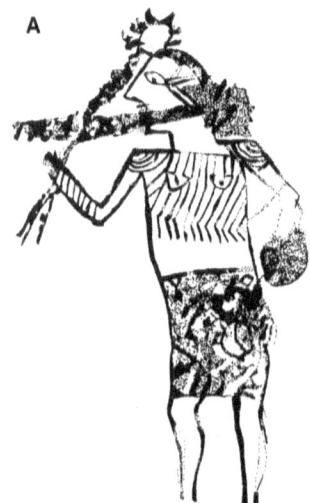
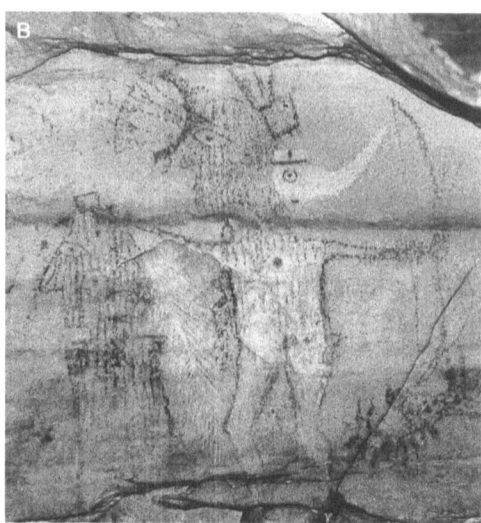

FIGURE 6.4. Detail of Red Horn from Panel 5 at Gottschall Rockshelter (A; after Salzer and Rajnovich 2000: fig. 23) and Morning Star (B; after Diaz-Granados 2004: fig. 20. Image republished by permission of the Art Institute of Chicago).

In this comparison the individuals most likely to display aspects of Braden-style tattooing and at least body paint are the Tattooed Man, or Red Horn, who is depicted in Panel 5 at the Gottschall Rockshelter (Figure 6.4A), and the painted image of Morning Star in the Morning Star Panel at Picture Cave (Figure 6.4B). Both figures are depicted interacting with other images in their respective panels. The Tattooed Man from Gottschall follows closely behind the avian image identified as Storm-as-He-Walks, while at Picture Cave Morning Star dominates an anthropomorphic figure he holds by the hair with a long white feather attached (see Figure 6.4B). This dominated or captured individual may lack both arms and lower limbs. All three figures appear to be either tattooed or wearing body paint. The tattooing or body paint at both sites takes the form of a motif set that Phillips and Brown identify as the Akron Grid (Figure 6.5):

> The Akron Grid is [described as] sets of closed-space parallel lines broadened at intervals by elongated blocks of excision. Lines are terminated by T-bar or triangular oar-like elements, or both. Line-sets form an overall background upon which various independent motifs are superimposed . . . The same treatment is also used as body and facial decoration . . . and,

without excised blocks. . . . Clearly related to the simpler striated mode of body decoration, all occurrences, including the Akron cup and the Cahokia fragments, are clearly assignable on other grounds to the Braden A style phase. (Phillips and Brown 1978:146)

The tattooing or body decoration of the Tattooed Man from Gottschall assuredly echoes the description of the Akron Grid. Specifically, the tattooing falls into what is perhaps a simpler form of the Akron Grid resembling a striated grid variant (see Figure 6.5B). But as in the more complex grid patterns, these gridlines, either parallel or vertical, form an overall background upon which an independent motif set is imposed. In this case that independent motif set is comprised of two "spud" forms with surrounded dots, perhaps indicating the anthropomorphic figure's nipples (see Figure 6.4A). Interestingly, a close examination of the image of the Tattooed Man reveals a diamond- or rhomboid-shaped eye motif positioned prominently on his wrap-around or skirt (see Figure 6.4A) (Salzer and Rajnovich 2000: fig. 28).

Like its Gottschall Rockshelter counterpart, the Morning Star image from Picture Cave (see Figure 6.4B) also bears a variant of the Akron Grid either as body paint or tattooing. Certainly the over-rendering of the Picture Cave

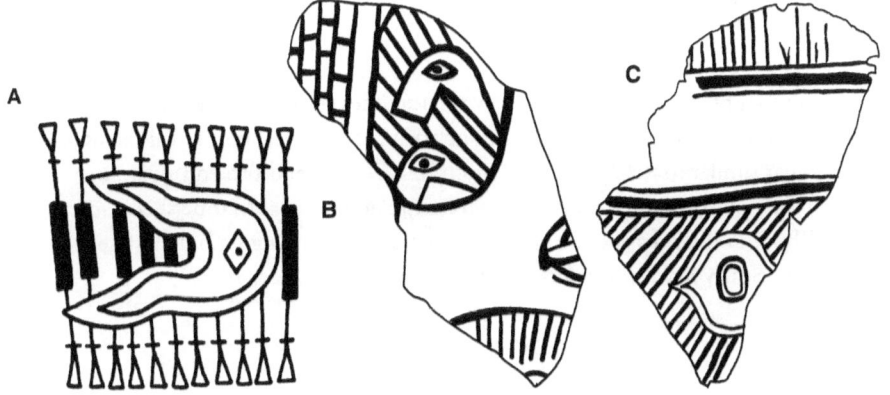

FIGURE 6.5. The Akron Grid (A; after Phillips and Brown 1978:146) and its striated variant (B; after Phillips and Brown 1978: plate 3) both appear as sets of closely spaced parallel lines broadened at intervals by elongated blocks of excision. The lines are terminated by T-bar, triangular oar-like elements, or both. Line sets form an overall background upon which various independent motifs are superimposed. These include the forked-eye-surround motifs (A and B) as well as the spud motif and the ogee motif (C) (after Phillips and Brown 1978: plate 16).

Morning Star figure ranks as one of the most dramatic and powerful images in the prehistoric Native American artistic tradition. This Morning Star figure wears long-nosed maskette ear ornaments (Duncan and Diaz-Granados 2000), as well as a unique headdress element consisting of a concave, bow-like object bossed with five arrow motifs. In his left hand the Morning Star figure holds a strung bow, while in his right hand he grasps a captive, or dominated figure, by the hair. Morning Star and his captive bear the simpler striated variant of the Akron Grid, which serves (as its Gottschall Rock-shelter counterpart does) as an overall background against which to display independent motif sets. In the Picture Cave example of Morning Star, these independent motifs are eyes.

Before leaving the depictions of figures at both Gottschall and Picture Cave bearing Akron Grid tattooing or body decoration, we should examine the sandstone head discovered at the Gottschall Rockshelter in 1992 (see Figure 6.2). Measuring 26 cm long by 9 cm wide, this sculpture is painted with the same blue-gray pigment used on Panel 5, while its mouth is painted with an orange-red pigment (Salzer and Rajnovich 2000:41–43). In a pattern recalling the striated variant of the Akron Grid in general and that of the Picture Cave Morning Star figure in particular, this anthropomorphic sandstone sculpture bears a diamond- or rhomboid-shaped eye painted on its chin, lying over the parallel lines of the grid. According to Salzer and Rajnovich:

> A series of roughly parallel narrow vertical lines adorn the face. The eyes are outlined in the same pigment and interrupt this vertical motif. This is somewhat similar to the Akron Grid motif that Phillips and Brown (1978:146) have isolated in their analysis of Mississippian engraved Marine shell cups. The Akron Grid appears as body decoration or tattooing on human figures that clearly have elite status. (Salzer and Rajnovich 2000:41)

/ *Possible Ideological Interpretations* /

The questions now arise: What is the meaning or interpretation of the figural tableaux found at the Gottschall Rockshelter and Picture Cave? What role does tattooing play in interpreting both complex sets of images? Several researchers have linked the tableaux at each of these rock art sites to what Paul Radin (1949) has identified as a fundamental foundational narrative of Native American religion, that of "the Twins."

In a recent discussion of the previously discussed Thruston Tablet, several researchers suggested that another foundational narrative, "The Children of the Sun," also may be represented on that artifact (Steponaitis et al. 2011). Other scholars have presented persuasive arguments that the individuals depicted at the two rock art sites, as well as on the Thruston Tablet, may depict actors and episodes from the Red Horn or Morning Star stories. Considering the antiquity of the imagery, however, one could argue that they may depict episodes from an original meta-, or Ur-, myth from which the stories of the Twins, the Children of the Sun, and Morning Star all derive. Certainly the Morning Star image in Picture Cave that wears long-nosed maskette ear ornaments resembles the "Seated Warrior" statuette recovered from the Great Mortuary at Spiro (Duncan and Diaz-Granados 2000). This Missouri flint clay statuette is executed in the Classic Braden style and dates to ca. AD 1000–1100. The statue has been interpreted repeatedly as depicting Morning Star or Red Horn (Brown 2005; Duncan and Diaz-Granados 2000; Hall 1997, 2004; Reilly 2004). Whatever the specific tableaux at Gottshall Rockshelter and at Picture Cave represent, both the Morning Star and Panel 5 imagery are linked by the simpler striated variant of the Akron Grid noted above.

Undoubtedly, the images rendered in an Early Braden style from Gottshall Rockshelter and Picture Cave depict heroes, supernaturals, or Other-Than-Human-Persons. When combined with the striated variant of the Akron Grid and attached independent motifs, the overall composition specifies a symbolic cluster that announces Other-Than-Human-Persons.

How then does the striated variant as well as the more complex Akron Grid imagery function on those marine shell cups? What connects this carved imagery from a mortuary context with the body art of tattooing? Analyzing several cups recovered from the Great Mortuary at Spiro yields important clues that well may answer these questions and link the cups to the previously discussed anthropomorphic imagery.

Marine shell cups certainly served as important ritual objects for Native Americans for hundreds of years. Comparing specific shell masterpieces from Spiro with the imagery at Picture Cave and at the Gottschall Rockshelter yields dramatic results. The fact that the imagery is combined with the striated variant of the Akron Grid and its independent motifs means that these cups were used ritually and were thus associated specifically with Other-Than-Human-Persons. When the Akron Grid itself serves as a background or field against which to display emblematic information, it literally wraps the wearer in the aura of the primordial sacred. At the same time,

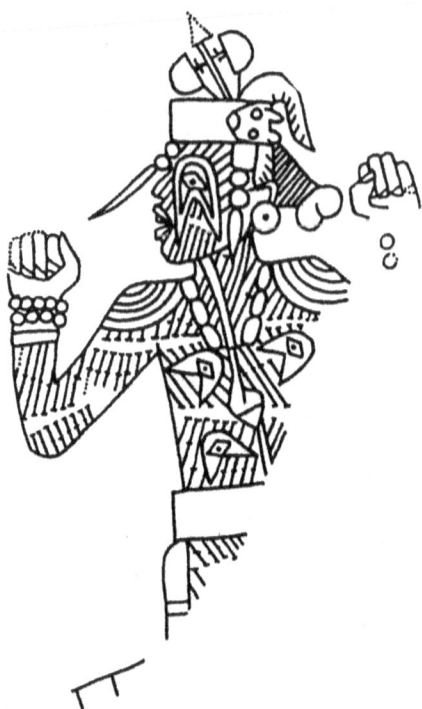

FIGURE 6.6. Detail from the Stovall Cup showing an individual tattooed or painted with the Akron Grid (after Phillips and Brown 1978: plate 6).

independent motifs such as the spud motif (see Figure 6.4A), the forked-eye surround (see Figure 6.5A, 6.5B), the ogee (see Figure 6.5C), and the petaloid motif symbolically identify specific supernaturals.

Among the important artifacts that support this hypothesis is the Stovall Cup, which bears carved or incised imagery clearly depicting elaborately garbed individuals with the Akron Grid tattooed or painted on their faces and bodies, leaving only the hands unmarked (Figure 6.6) (Phillips and Brown 1978: plate 6). In this instance the independent motif carried on the grid is a forked-eye surround. The overall composition of the Stovall Cup strongly recalls the Morning Star image from Picture Cave (see Figure 6.4B). Like the images on the Stovall Cup, the Morning Star image bears several eyes (without the forked surround) as an independent motif superimposed on a grid. Furthermore, the figure with the white plume that Morning Star holds by the hair also carries the eye motif on its overall body grid.

Another possible example of the use of the Akron Grid as a format for the identification of either emblematic or Other-Than-Human-Persons is the striations displayed on the face of the flint-clay "Rattler Figure" from the Gilcrease Museum collection (Figure 6.7) (Robert Sharp, personal communication May, 2012). Certainly, this identification would help to further support a linkage between these various facial striations and the Braden style.

Other examples of carved marine shell cups also reveal vital information on how these important ritual objects functioned. In particular, both the Harrisburg Cup (Figure 6.8A) and shell fragments from Cahokia (Figure 6.8B) carry the spud motif superimposed on an Akron Grid, as seen at Gottschall Rockshelter (Phillips and Brown 1978: plate 15). Other cup fragments (Phillips and Brown 1978: plates 15 and 16) also carry petaloid and ogee motifs, but in these instances the independent motifs may function as locatives identifying the cosmic location of ritual actions, such as indicating activities occurring in the Above World or in the Watery Beneath Realm, or even serving as portals between the cosmic levels (Reilly 2004, 2007b; Sharp 2008, 2009).

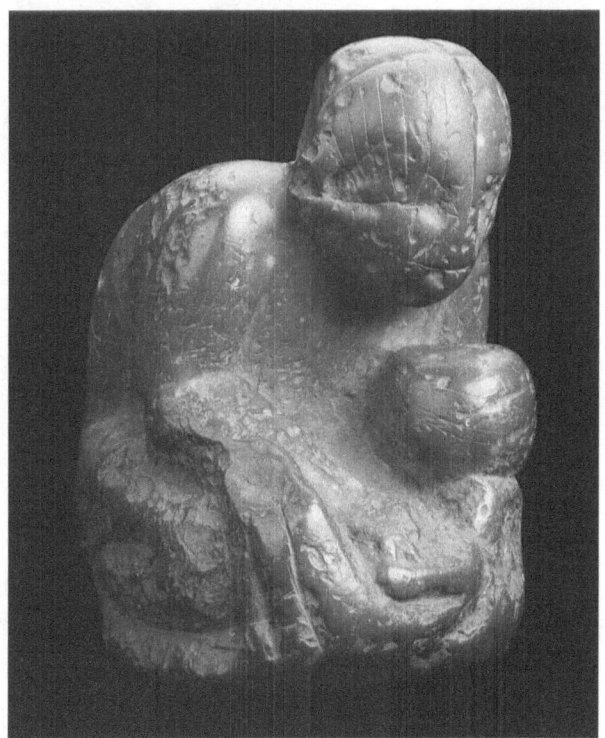

FIGURE 6.7. Flint-clay "Rattler Figure" exhibiting vertical striations. Image courtesy of the Gilcrease Museum, Tulsa, Oklahoma.

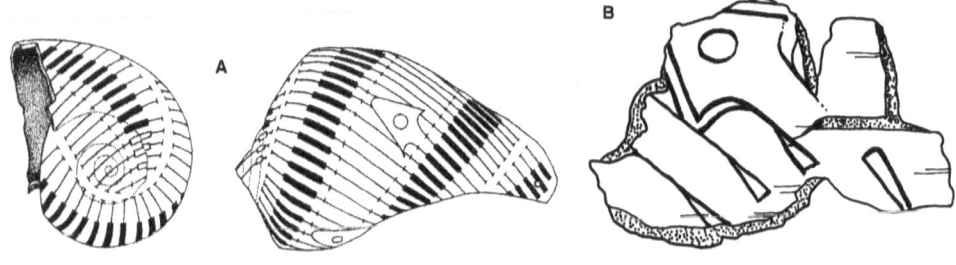

FIGURE 6.8. The Akron Grid and independent spud motif as they appear on the Harrisburg Cup from Arkansas (A; after Holmes 1883: plate 23) and a shell fragment from Cahokia, Illinois (B; after Phillips and Brown 1978: plate 15).

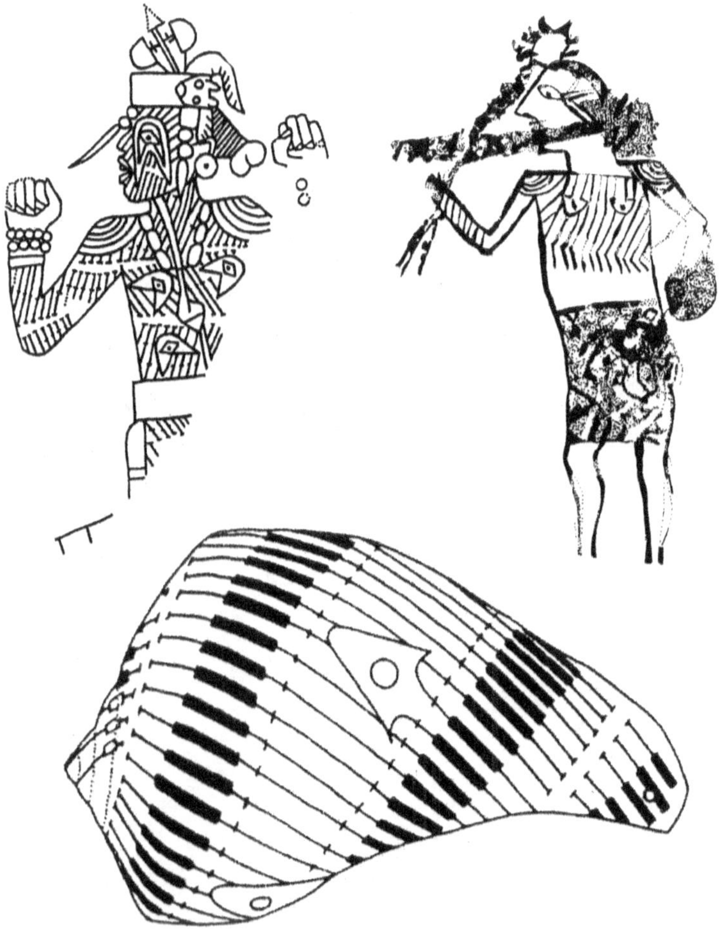

FIGURE 6.9. Shared motif sets between human body decoration (tattooing) and ritual objects.

/ Conclusion /

We see, therefore, that close iconographic analysis demonstrates that within the Classic Braden art style and canon a corpus of shell art existed that, when compared with the paintings in Picture Cave and the Gottschall Rockshelter, confirms that motif sets were shared between human body decoration or tattooing and valued ritual objects (Figure 6.9). When this system of Braden-style symbols is displayed upon the Akron Grid and accompanied by a group of independent motif sets, the motif clusters serve as analogues of the tattooing that conveys ideological and esoteric information on an individual's body, or anthropomorphic canvas. These shared motif sets, or clusters, seem to have emerged from the Braden artists' need to produce an open system of symbolic communication. This open system visually conveyed to the viewer the presence of nonhuman forces whose requisite rites, rituals, and ceremonials identified a metaphysical hierarchy of powers that acted in primordial, or dream, time.

Not only did this open, artistic communication system continue to function in the ideology of the Braden-style craftsmen who created it, but it continues to function today among many traditional practitioners of Native American belief systems. Thus, in the early Mississippian period, artists and ritualists identified the face of the sacred through tattooing and body decoration. Likewise, by covering the surfaces of ritual objects with the same tattooing used to identify specific Mississippian Other-Than-Human-Persons or deities, it signaled that the objects were used to propitiate those preternatural beings themselves.

< 7 >

Dhegihan Tattoos

Markings That Consecrate, Empower, and Designate Lineage

James R. Duncan

/ / / /

Tattooing is defined as indelible marks made by placing pigment beneath the skin. The standard definition also refers to "scarification." As discussed by Antoinette Wallace in Chapter 1, the earliest visual record of the use of tattooing by the Indians of North America is from the artists Jacques Le Moyne and John White in the late sixteenth century, both of whom depicted Indians of the southeastern coastal region, then called Florida. Some but not all of the males and females depicted by these artists were shown tattooed and painted. Throughout the remainder of the sixteenth, seventeenth, and eighteenth centuries there were many illustrations of tattooed American Indians on maps and in contemporary European travelogues and journals. Portraits of visiting Eastern Woodland Indian dignitaries, especially the Iroquois delegation to Queen Anne, show extensive tattooing (Krutak 2005). As shown in Chapters 4 and 5, these tattoos seem to be a representational method of relating military or war honors and expressing the lineage of the person who bears the tattoos. There seem to be some commonalities among the various Indian groups regarding tattoo symbolism. The focus of this chapter is the interpretation of the iconography of the tattoos and a possible explanation of the ideology expressed by a portion of that iconography.

Along the lower Missouri River and the central Mississippi River valley or corridor there is a substantial archaeological record of what appear to be tattoos on late prehistoric figural art. Figures, most of them representing supernatural entities existing in a complex cosmos, are engraved on shell and pottery, painted on cave walls, and incised and painted on pottery and stone.

Early European journals and maps identify the principal inhabitants and largest population at the confluence of the Missouri and Mississippi as the

Dhegihan Sioux. On Marquette's map of the Conception River (Mississippi) and its largest tributary, the Pekittanei (Missouri River), the Osage Indians are located east of the Missouria Indians (Din and Nasatir 1983:27) (Figure 7.1). In 1687 Father Douay wrote that there were seventeen villages of the Osage (Ponziglione 1897:30). Iberville's census of 1702 lists 200 Missouria (Chiwere) families and between 1,200 and 1,500 families of Crevas (Osage-Dhegiha) (Henning 1970:22). The Dhegiha represent the dominant

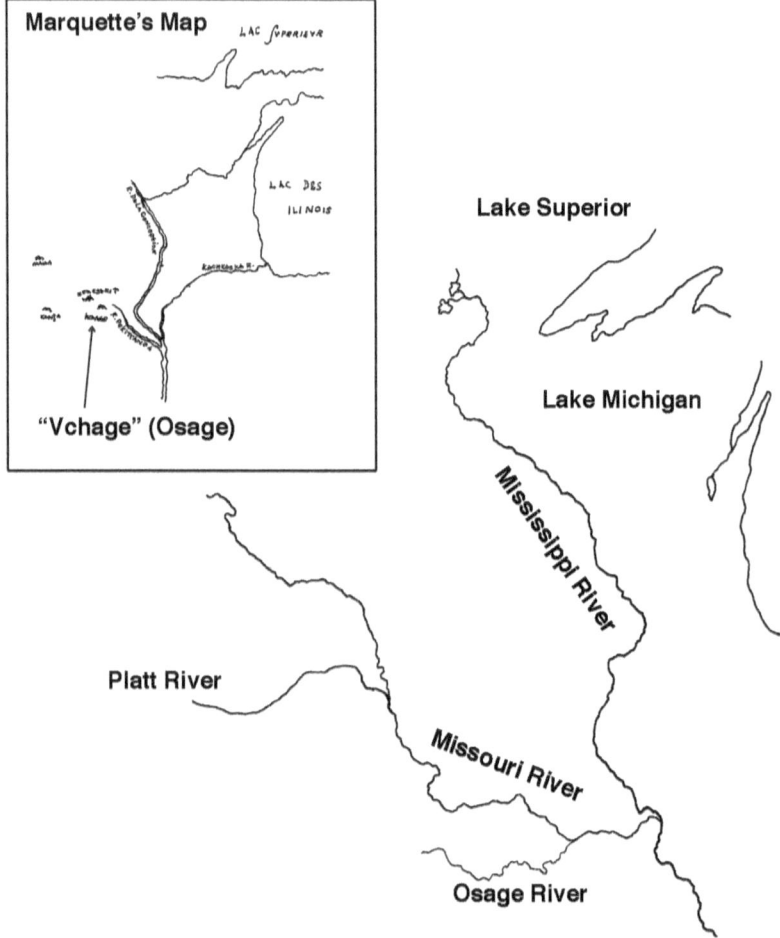

FIGURE 7.1. The map at the upper left is Marquette's, a facsimile drawn from the example given by Din and Nasatir (1983:27). The Osage are east of the Missouria. The lower-right map shows a modern distribution of the Osage and their neighbors.

population from the lower Missouri River just north of the mouth of the Niobrara River, east to the confluence of the Missouri River with the Mississippi River and along the Mississippi corridor south to the mouth of the Arkansas River at the time of European contact, 1670–1760.

Tattooing among these Dhegiha Sioux—the Arkansas (Quapaw), Omaha, Ponca, Kansas, and Osage—was not described as an artistic endeavor; there is no term for "art" in the Dhegihan language. What we do find is the term *xthe-xthe'*, "to tattoo," or "to attach symbolism to a person or an object." This was an important ritual among the Omaha and the Osage. The "Great Sacred Bundle"—the *Wa-xo'-be Ton'-ga*, or "Great Shrine"—contained a tattoo kit encased in a cormorant skin. The scant ethnological record for the Arkansas (Quapaw), Ponca, and Kansas suggests that their bundles and rites were similar to those possessed by the Omaha and Osage in the late nineteenth century. In some cases two distinct Dhegihan groups possessed parts of fragmented rites that formerly represented a single great ceremony. Such fragmented rites, recorded by Francis La Flesche, are present among the Omaha and Osage (for additional insight concerning the origins and relationship of the Dhegiha, see Fletcher and La Flesche 1922).

The universal appeal of tattooing among the Dhegiha and the Prairie/Plains Indians in general is well documented by early explorers and ethnographers. The purpose of the tattoos among these Dhegihans was to insure a long life and many descendants, to consecrate or sanctify the individual, to enumerate military honors, and to demonstrate the tattooed person's role and place in the cosmos (Bailey 1995:54–55; Fletcher and La Flesche 1992:219–221; see discussions by Dye and Krutak, this volume).

Among the Osage, tattoos had to be both earned and "truthful." One interesting account from a Jesuit journal dated 1863 told of a band of twenty-five mounted Osage encountering a detachment of thirty mounted Confederate irregulars who were intent on stealing horses and food near the Kansas–Indian Territory border. The Osage gave chase to the Confederate horsemen and intercepted them near the Verdigris River. The Osage demanded their surrender, to which the Confederates replied with a volley that killed a young warrior, Sunta-Sape. The ensuing melee lasted about fifteen minutes and covered a distance of around three miles. Riding among the Confederates, the Osage knocked them off of their horses with gun butts and war clubs, and then shot or tomahawked the horseless men as they tried to flee. The dead Confederates were stripped, scalped, and beheaded, and the bodies were mutilated. When the Osage warriors returned home, they carefully washed and combed the heads and scalps, to the chagrin of the Jesuits.

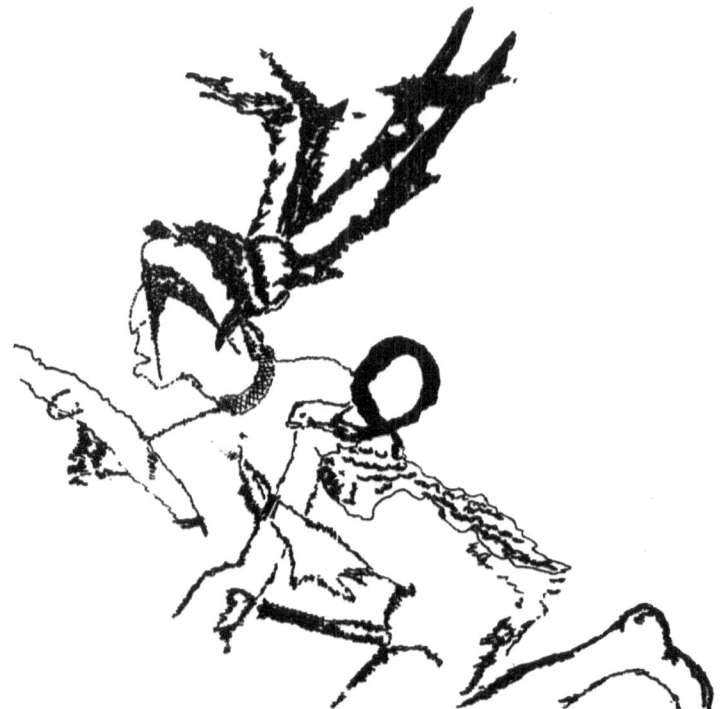

FIGURE 7.2. "Snakehide," Picture Cave, lower Missouri River valley. This figure is on the lower panel and is an outstanding example of the earliest Braden style.

In the aftermath of the war celebrations, a young Osage man who had not taken part in the fighting had a war club tattooed on his arm in honor of the event. The *Non-Hon-Zhinga*, or "Little Old Men" (the priestly decision makers), having been told of the tattoo, ordered it flayed from the young man's arm since he did not participate in the engagement (Ponziglione 1897:345–347). The forcible removal of false tattoos among the Osage is also documented by Jean-Bernard Bossu (Bossu 1962 [1768]:95–96) and described in Chapter 1 of this volume.

The earliest expression of the impressive late prehistoric artistic style known as "Braden" is found at the confluence of the Missouri and Mississippi Rivers and includes evidence of body art, or tattooing. James A. Brown has presented a convincing argument that the Braden style of art best fits the Dhegihan model (Brown 2011:37–63). The earliest dated examples of Braden style are found in Picture Cave on the lower Missouri River, in the general region of three major mound sites: Mound City, East St. Louis, and

Cahokia. The cave contains more than four hundred figures, most of which are drawn or painted, some with stark realism. Many of these figures probably portray the spirit ancestors of the Dhegiha.

One of the two largest figures at Picture Cave is the character called "Snakehide" (Figure 7.2). His profile is skillfully rendered and shows a haughty, hook-nosed male with a hair bun and a fantastic array of four immense antler-like feathers. He has an erect penis. His back is covered with a jaguar pelt, the symbol for the night sky. With his sensitively drawn foot and his distinctive profile, he is the earliest known example of the Braden style (Phillips and Brown 1978:70–72). The imagery at Picture Cave has been radiometrically dated to AD 1025 (Diaz-Granados et al. 2001).

The depiction of Snakehide at Picture Cave includes a delicate cross-hatched band encircling his lower throat. This design is seen on Braden shell cups from Spiro (Phillips and Brown 1978: plates 24–34) (Figure 7.3) and was used by an Omaha artist in the early twentieth century to identify Beneath World beings (Fletcher and La Flesche 1992:515). These beings, who are the inhabitants of the Beneath World and the winter night sky, have a chief, the Great Serpent. They are often depicted as serpentine and may also embody some of the attributes of waterbirds and water-dwelling mammals such as the otter. These beings with reptilian characteristics are drawn or painted with such attributes as the scaled, or cross-hatched, skin. Their serpentine nature allows them to be reborn. Just as the snake sheds its skin, so they can outwit death by shedding theirs, thereby becoming eternal. Like the

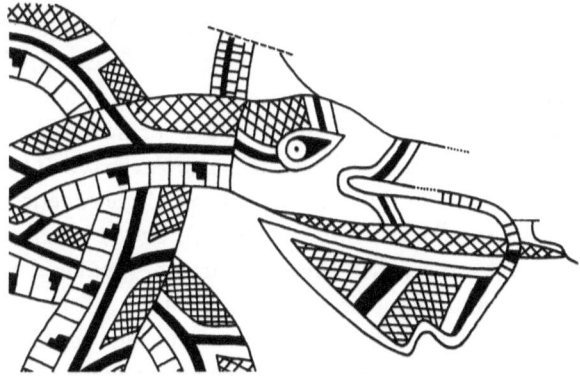

FIGURE 7.3. Detail of a Braden shell cup from Spiro showing the use of cross-hatch designs on serpentine figures (after Phillips and Brown 1978: plate 24).

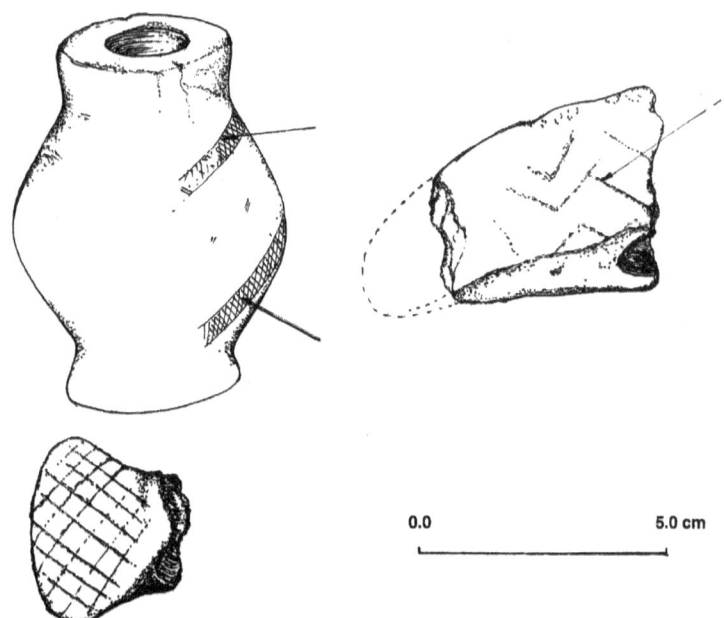

0.0   5.0 cm

FIGURE 7.4. *Atlatl* weights with cross-hatched or chevron designs from near the confluence of the Mississippi and Ohio Rivers. Top left, Mississippi County, Arkansas; top right, Big Muddy Creek drainage, southern Illinois; bottom left, Mississippi County, Missouri. All examples are surface finds. The Mississippi County weight is probably from the Burkett/Weems sites (23MI20 and 23MI25).

rattlesnake, they can kill with one fatal bite of their fangs, and so allegorically they have the power of life and death.

This iconography must be very old in the Eastern Woodlands, especially near the central Mississippi corridor. The earliest "shorthand" method of assigning the salient characteristics of these Beneath World dwellers is the application of cross-hatched designs to an object or a body, thereby endowing it with the power of the Great Serpent or attaching to it a locative symbol. The earliest examples of this cross-hatched motif are found on delicately engraved *atlatl* weights from Middle Archaic, Late Archaic, and Early Woodland archaeological sites in the southern portion of the American Bottoms and the Missouri Boot Heel region (Figure 7.4). By the Middle Woodland period the horned, cross-hatched Great Serpent is depicted in the round as a horned being with multiple attributes (Knight 1989:207).

A jaguar pelt similar to the one worn by Snakehide appears in a nineteenth-century drawing of a Dhegihan (Osage) male by the French medical doctor Victor Tixier, who traveled among the Osages on the Kansas prairie in 1839–1840 (Figure 7.5). Tixier witnessed the Medecine du Charbon

(Charcoal Dance), which was the principal war dance of the Osage and the prelude to an organized and sanctioned military expedition. In Tixier's drawing, the dancers follow an individual who is facing them and dancing backward, and who seems to be choreographing their movements. The first dancer bears what appears to be a staff with an attached bundle, has a raptor head attached to his headband, and is blowing a cane war whistle. Behind this first dancer, the left dancer of a pair holds a pipe in his right hand and an arrow in his left, and wears an unusual neckband reminiscent of that depicted in the Snakehide image, as well as a jaguar pelt with the head attached (see Figure 7.5) (Tixier 1940:225). Being positioned on the left and wearing a jaguar pelt denotes the "savage feline nature of the Beneath World

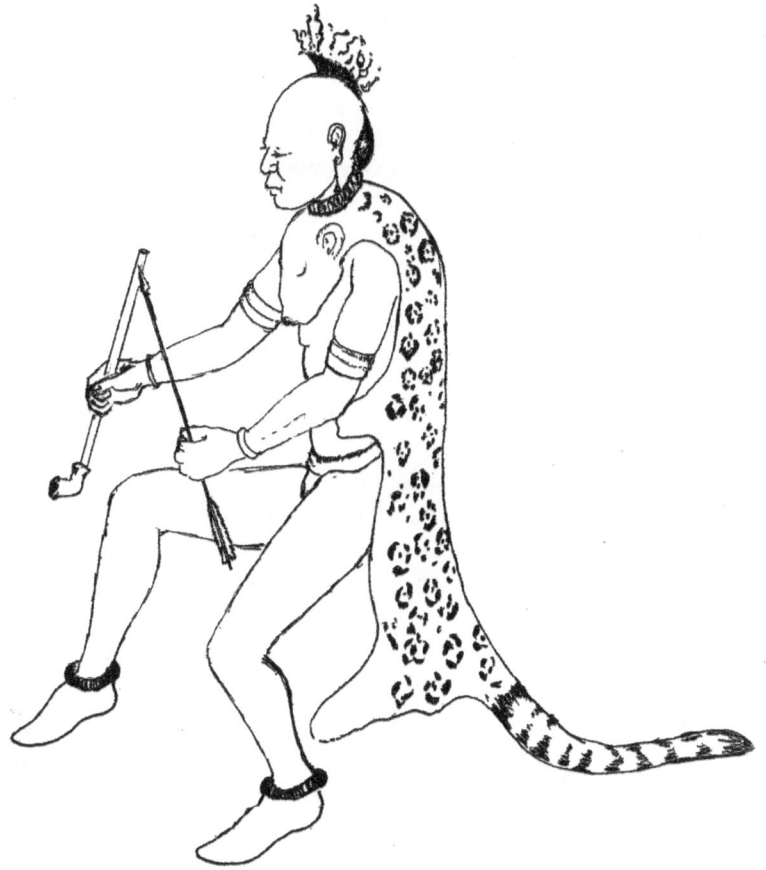

FIGURE 7.5. An Osage participant in the Charcoal Dance (after Victor Tixier's drawings from life, 1840).

chief, the Milky Way as well as the dancer's clan; he embodies the warlike qualities of the *Wah-Sha-She*, whose bodies represent all of the waters of the earth and who are unconquerable" (Mathews 1961:12).

When Fletcher and La Flesche were collecting ethnological material among the Dhegiha, they found that the Omaha had a shrine called the "Tent of War" in which resided the *Waxthe-xe*, the ancient cedar pole. The Omaha related that this pole was a source of power and could endow deserving persons who had engaged in impressive hunting exploits with tattooed honor marks. The Osage, by contrast, tattooed honor marks only on warrior candidates, in a carefully prescribed manner, on the neck and upper torso. One of the Osage men (Wa-Shin-Ha, George Bacon Rind) whom they interviewed had the extensive honor marks of an important hereditary keeper of the Honor Packs of War. Bacon Rind was tattooed when he was seventeen years of age; he was photographed in 1897 (see Figure 5.1). His tattoos included four encircling, diagonal bands alluding to successful military expeditions, above which are the two sacred pipes of war, which he never "laid on the ground." Above the pipes are designs that represent the tents of the pipes of war, symbolizing that the tents have descended to earth and the pipes are in them. The central motif running from his throat down his chest was the sacred stone knife (Fletcher and La Flesche 1992:219–221).

Bacon Rind's tattoos represent the survival of Mississippian symbolism relating to war and warfare. Some of the elements are clearly inherited, and several ancient icons are present, including raptor symbolism, along with thunder and lightning, as well as the motif depicting a conventional Mississippian stone knife affiliated with the "Ramey Knives" and "Dallas Swords" of the archaeological record. Most important is the conclusion by Fletcher and La Flesche that these symbols were complementary components of an ancient ritual and that together they represented a whole and complex ritual, the rites of the Omaha Tent of War Shrine and the Osage honor marks, or tattoos (Fletcher and La Flesche 1992:219).

This symbolism was widespread throughout the southeastern quadrant of North America. In 1585 the Englishman John White began producing a folio of watercolors, including one of a "Warrior of Florida" who exhibits five feather-like designs encircling his torso and a similar motif around his throat (see Figure 1.2A). John White's folio of watercolors has long been recognized as an invaluable insight into the lifeways of the southeastern coastal Indians in the late sixteenth century. While these tattoos are not identical to the nineteenth-century Dhegihan examples, there is still great similarity.

In 1897 the Jesuit priest Paul M. Poziglione wrote his memoirs of more than thirty years among the Osage in Kansas in the mid-nineteenth century. Those documents include an interesting account about the successor of the last grand chief, George White Hair, or Paw-Hiu-Sk'a. We know from Ponziglione (1897:41–49) that there was always a grand chief who bore the name of Paw-Hiu-Sk'a, or White Hair. The name is difficult to translate, as it is an archaic form of Dhegiha and has multiple meanings, one of which loosely translates to "His Countenance Is Too Bright to Look upon." It can also mean something akin to "He Is the Great Trunk of the Tree." It is a complex name and implies various levels of meaning. La Flesche states that it refers to the sacred buffalo (La Flesche 1932:125; Quintero 2004:86, 202).

The importance of an inherited lineage is reinforced in an Osage animal story known as "The Coyote and the Woodpecker," collected by La Flesche when he was working with Fletcher. In this story the woodpecker gives a feast for his coyote friend. During the course of the meal, coyote admires woodpecker's beautiful red head. Woodpecker explains that he inherited this from his father and that his sons will inherit it from him. The coyote then invites woodpecker to his own feast and tries to emulate the woodpecker's red head by tying on a burning brand. The foolish coyote sets fire to his home, and while the woodpecker escapes, the coyote is burned to death. The moral of this little story directly points to inherited "labels" and the fate of those who try to imitate an inherited label without the lineage to go along with it (La Flesche, in Bailey 2010:147–148).

Ponziglione wrote that in 1850, George White Hair, because he had no son to succeed him, adopted his nephew, Anthony Nivale (Ne-Wallah) (Ponziglione 1897:209). The young man was baptized and sent to the mission school, where he was given a conventional mid-nineteenth-century parochial education. About young Ne-Wallah's education and how it proceeded, Ponziglione wrote the following:

As long as Anthony was at school with us he was proud of wearing tidy clothes, but now being continually flattered by his friends, who keep telling him, that he should come out and stay with them, for he was in age to be a Brave, he gives way to the temptation! To please his friends he quits the school, puts off the White man's cloths, and resumes the Indian custom. He no longer calls himself Anthony, but simply Ne-Wallah. He shaves his head, paints his body all over, according to the fashion of the wildest Indians, and starts on the war path with several Braves . . . In his appearance Ne-Wallah shows a true type of a genuine red man. His face is all besmeared with vermillion, a few lines of white color are running horizontally under his eyes,

and a green spot, as large as a dollar, stamped on his right cheek, gives feroc-
ity to his countenance. Nice fish bones, in the shape of small spokes, hang
from his ears. His hair is all shaved off, with the exception of a tuft on the
top of his head, crested with red bristles, a large royal eagle's feather stuck
in his scalp, completes his head gear . . . his body is all tattooed with such
symbolic figures as chiefs alone are allowed to be marked with. (Ponziglione
1897:209–213)

Although we have a very good description of a grand chief's facial paint
and his headdress, we have no information concerning the tattoos, the "symbolic figures as chiefs alone are allowed to be marked with." It is a pity that
Ponziglione did not make a sketch or describe the symbols that he saw. We
do know from Ponziglione's writings that the grand chief is a direct descendant of First Man, or Sun. With this information we can examine several sets
of Braden figures for what might be the chiefly symbols.

There are several good examples of First Man figures to examine. The first
and the oldest is the figure of First Man and his son Morning Star, the "Symbolic Man" at Picture Cave (Figure 7.6; see also Figure 6.4B). In Osage oral
traditions, the Symbolic (or Ideal) Man is a complex spirit being with several
levels of meaning. Simply stated, he is the eldest son of the sky and the earth

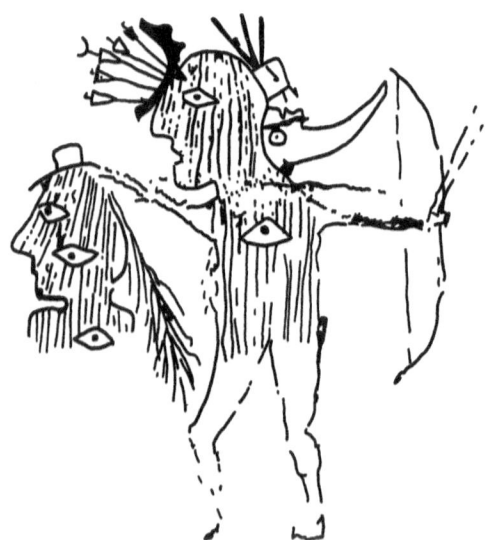

FIGURE 7.6. The Symbolic Man, Picture Cave. This figure has the vertical markings of the First Man lineage.

and represents the valorous Osage Nation (Louis F. Burns, personal communication 1997; La Flesche 1932:206). This image is one of the most enigmatic of all of the images in the cave. The rendering technique is unique in that the composition was first outlined by engraving into the sandstone with a fine (chert?) burin. The torso, arms, and legs of the primary figure, Symbolic Man, as well as the head and upper torso of the second figure, were then carefully scraped or abraded to expose the underlying white, unpatinated sandstone, on which the remaining details such as tattoos were then painted with a delicate brush using a black pigment. The principal motif, which is identical for both figures, consists of thirteen fine parallel vertical lines that cover the face and the torso. On the chest of each figure is an eye.

According to La Flesche, the thirteen vertical lines symbolize the thirteen rays of the rising sun, as well as the thirteen war honors (Bailey 2010:59). In the case of the figures at Picture Cave, the solar connection seems most appropriate. There is little doubt that these parallel lines are prototypical of a later group of shell cup engravings found in the great mortuary at Spiro, Oklahoma, and attributed to Cahokia (see Figure 6.6) (e.g., Phillips and Brown 1978: plates 2, 6, 7, 13, 14, and 15). It would be reasonable to infer that the Picture Cave image of Symbolic Man and his father, Sun, are the ideological anchor and template for the later Braden depictions on shell cups, shell gorgets, flint-clay sculptures, and copper plates.

Another candidate for the tattoos "that only the chief bears" is from the engravings of Flemish artist Theodore de Bry, who is said to have based his depictions of Florida Indians on watercolors by Jacques Le Moyne, a member of the Huguenot expedition to Florida in 1563–1565 (see Chapter 1). In volume 2 of *Grands Voyages*, de Bry includes a depiction of a tattooed chief witnessing the execution of Indian sentinels (Figure 7.7). The engraving shows the chief's torso, neck, arms, and legs covered with a unique solar design. This same motif appears in a second de Bry engraving titled *The Natives of Florida Worship the Column Erected by the Commander on His First Voyage* as the tattoos of Chief Athore of the Timucua. A remarkably similar design is found on Braden shell cups from Spiro (Phillips and Brown 1978:155, plates 36–45), and is referred to by Phillips and Brown as a "Rayed, Concentric Barred Oval, and Davis Rectangle Combination" (Figure 7.8). The historic evidence suggests this complex design is not fictitious, as are some of de Bry's other depictions of Native American tattoos, but instead that the tattooed chief is accurately rendered from Le Moyne's lost original.

Recent work by F. Kent Reilly III's iconography workshops indicates that the symbols and motifs of the Cahokia area, the Cumberland corridor,

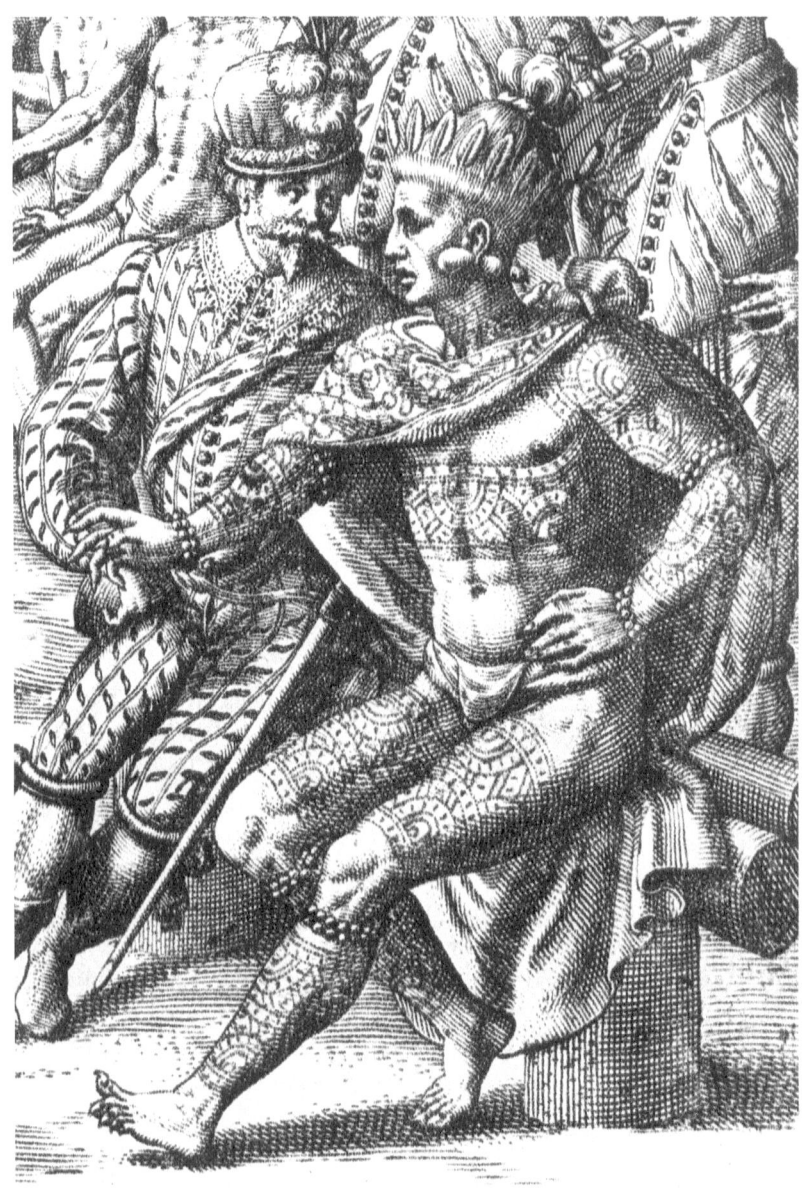

FIGURE 7.7. Detail of *How Sentinels Are Punished for Sleeping at Their Posts*, by Theodor de Bry. This engraving shows a chief witnessing the execution of two guards who fell asleep while on guard duty. The chief's torso and limbs are covered with the rayed concentric barred oval design found on Braden-style engraved shell cups.

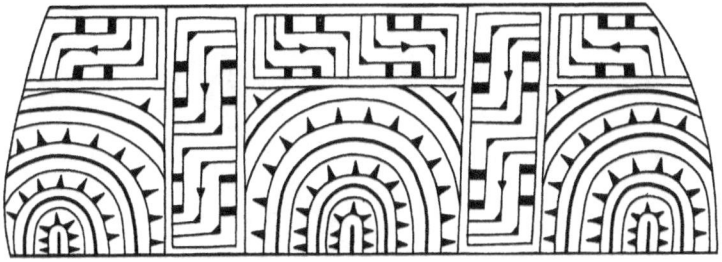

FIGURE 7.8. The rayed concentric barred oval design found on several engraved shell cups from the Great Mortuary, Craig Mound, Spiro, Oklahoma (after Phillips and Brown 1978: plate 36).

Etowah, Georgia, and the Florida area share many commonalities. This corridor extends from the confluence of the Missouri and Mississippi Rivers and stretches from north of Cahokia to Florida's eastern coast. This area of dynamic movement of ideology and symbolism has been designated the "Braden Corridor" (Reilly et al. 2011: map 1).

The most unusual description of the early Dhegihan tattoos is found in the "Genesis Story" of the reunion of the Osage Nation. This oral tradition has been recounted by La Flesche, Mathews, and Burns. While none of the three accounts is credited to a specific Osage informant, it is safe to state that this was a widely known oral tradition among the Osage. Mathews's version is the most lengthy, and its poetic quality suggests that it is closest to the original. Here are a few extracts:

> They resumed their wanderings, the Water People leading, the Land People behind them, and behind the Land People, the Sky People, but this time they had a definite objective; the finding of the U-Tah-No'n-Dsi, the Isolated Earth People . . . even though the houses or lodges were never described.
>
> The essentials that had to be brought out to characterize these people of the village were startling, stark and realistic . . . being afraid to approach the village, they stopped at a distance and sent a messenger forward . . . He saw some of the people, the men had bangs and were tattooed about the eyes and mouth . . . The women were almost naked wearing only an apron of deerskin . . . their breasts were tattooed. (Mathews 1961:12–15)

This passage offers an important clue regarding the appearance of the Isolated Earth people: both men and women were tattooed, and the men had their faces tattooed. Osage men and women were tattooed, like all

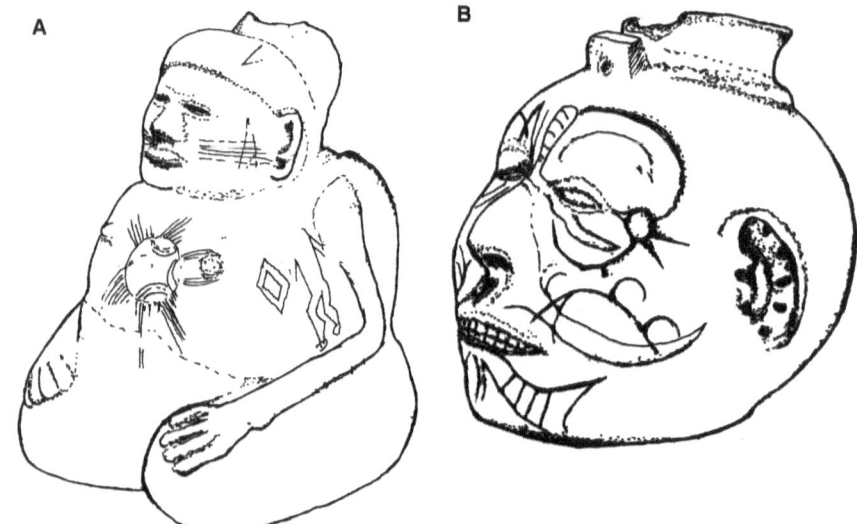

FIGURE 7.9. Armorel Phase pottery vessels: (A) a female figure from northeastern Arkansas, First Woman with a Dhegihan pectoral honor mark; (B) a head pot with elaborate tattoos from 23PM5, the Campbell site, Pemiscot County, Missouri.

Dhegiha, but, according to this narrative the Water, Land, and Sky people did not tattoo the faces of the men, while the Isolated Earth people did. We have evidence of the earlier facial tattooing in Braden art—but where did it survive? The answer is simple: in the southeastern-most part of Missouri and northeastern Arkansas, particularly along the Pemiscot Bayou (Walker 2004). There is ample evidence from this area in the form of effigy pottery, both male and female, with engraved and incised tattoos (Figure 7.9).

The account in Mathews presents a reunification story told by the Dhegihan inhabitants of the Big Bend region of the Missouri River—the more than thirty towns between the mouth of the Lamine River in the east and the Kansas River in the west. This oral tradition gives an account of the reunification of two separate and distinct groups of Dhegihans sometime between 1600 and 1700 that formed the historic Osage Nation. These reunited wanderers then traveled to the three forks of the Osage River and founded a new group of towns, far removed from the Mississippi River and the pestilence-ridden trade with the Europeans to the north, south, and east. Only a few towns of the Little Osage and their attendant Missouri allies remained on the Missouri River after 1700.

The archaeological record for the Osage is not well understood. The late prehistoric towns along the Mississippi River were recognized as Siouan by Williams and labeled "Armorel Phase" to set them apart from the Nodena Phase to the south (Williams 1980:109, 1990:174). While Bray did not specifically assign a large Osage population to the most heavily excavated part of the Utz site (23SA2), he did hint that there was a substantial adjacent population (Bray 1991:140–141). Morse describes the large size of the mound centers and accompanying populations during the population expansion southward from the American Bottoms along the west side of the Mississippi flood plain (Morse 1990:133; Morse and Morse 1989:41–44). These large southeastern Dhegihan populations dominated the Mississippi River floodplain from Cape Girardeau to the mouth of the Arkansas until the "entrada" and the introduction of European diseases forced their migration and reunification.

An excellent marker for the last historic occupations at the Campbell site (23PM5) and the Utz site (23SA2) is the presence of *circarch*, cast brass "sleigh" bells at both sites, and the cast brass "Dog Head" hilt from an English-made hanger or sword from the Utz site (23SA2) (Bray 1978:48; Cherry 2009:177) (Figure 7.10). These artifacts came onto the frontier west of the Mississippi River with the establishment of Carolina governor Colleton's Indian trade

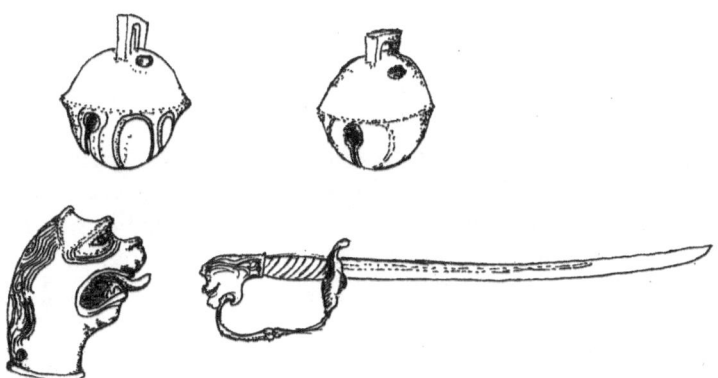

FIGURE 7.10. These early English manufactured goods link the Mississippi valley Dhegihan populations, including the Isolated Earth Division, with the Missouri River populations at the Utz site (23SA2). The top-right circarch bell is from the Campbell site (23 PM5). The cast brass dog head was found at the Utz site (23SA2); to the right is a drawing of a complete hanger or light, curved sword. The Isolated Earth Division is described in Osage oral tradition as being much tattooed. These English goods can be no earlier than 1685 (see text).

regulations, establishing trade with distant nations to the west, especially the Choctaw and Chickasaw. Colleton's regulations came late in his tenure, shortly before he was banished in 1690 (Gallay 2002:92).

During the second half of the eighteenth century, the reunified Osage continued to expand their territory westward, especially to secure land for hunting. The Caddoan-speaking Pawnee and their relations were singled out as the focus of Dhegihan military expeditions. This "pushing away" of Caddo groups had a long history with the Dhegiha. In the early expansion of the three large mound centers at the confluence of Mound City, East St. Louis, and Cahokia, the populations of southwestern Missouri included Caddoan people, as demonstrated by ceramics in the archaeological record. These Caddoan-speaking people were driven out of the southwestern Ozarks of Missouri very early, and with the newly established towns on the three forks of the Osage River, the push continued (Bailey 2010:87).

A great deal has been written about the Osage after 1700. What has not been clearly stated is the stability of the ideological roots of their and other Dhegihan cultures. The institutional use of tattooing persisted until the end of the nineteenth century. Interviews with modern Osage, particularly elite women, have uncovered some interesting pieces of information. The use of the spider motif on the backs of the hands was still evident until recently (see Figure 8.2). The Osage Nation Museum and Library preserves several Osage portraits made after 1930, and the hands of at least two women display these spider tattoos.

According to modern Osage women, the spider is an important Dhegihan life symbol; that means it is a chartering symbol—an essential allegorical concept and an integral part of the visible and invisible Dhegihan cosmos. The antiquity of the spider symbol stretches back to Cahokia, as demonstrated by the archaeological record. The symbol is found clustered along the central Mississippi River valley north up the Illinois River and south to northwestern Tennessee, and east to eastern Tennessee and Etowah (Brain and Phillips 1996:109, 111, 138).

As discussed by David Dye in Chapter 8 of this volume, the spider tattoo was placed on the backs of the hands of elite first-born daughters, at a great cost, and symbolized their role as "Sun Carriers." Elite first daughters were chosen as wives by members of the First Man lineage, and they spiritually carried the Sun across the upper level of the Beneath World, similar to the spider in the lower portion of the constellation Orion. It was the power and prayer of tattooed women, members of an elite secret society, that sustained the sun during a portion of the night passage, and insured that the sun would rise to begin a new day and continue an unending cycle, for the Dhegiha and all of humankind.

The Jesuit priest Ponziglione was witness to a principle that was probably the main reinforcement of the power of the elite, or First Man, faction to govern and direct the behavior of their "children." In 1858, Ponziglione watched the distribution of goods, including dried buffalo meat, buffalo robes, deerskins, garments, and horses to the warriors who had taken scalps during sanctioned war expeditions, and also to the eldest sons, orphans of gallant warriors lost in battle. This process was presided over by the chosen successor of George White Hair, a man called "Gratamantze." The hoard was collected, in part, from the members of the Osage Nation at rites such as funerals, visits, and naming ceremonies. It was also made up of the annuities from the federal government, and most of all from the payment of grazing fees from Texas cattle drovers pasturing their herds on Osage grazing lands. The men, the warriors in all of their finery and regalia, gathered in a large grove of timber, sitting in a large circle while the goods were distributed by the grand chief, Gratamantze, aided by senior war captains. The distribution was carefully regulated; speeches were made and the war records of the recipients were recited by the war captains. The priests of the "war honors" pack verified the validity of the honorees' claims to the tribute. Here we can see how the tattoo symbolism and the merits of that symbolism interact to regulate the flow of wealth throughout the society (Ponziglione 1897:263– 264). Oral tradition mandates that such a rite should take place on or near the spring equinox.

/ Conclusion /

The use of tattoos is an ancient tradition among the Indians of North America. The use of complex designs as indicators of a person's lineage and military prowess is an essential and foundational principle within the iconography of the Western Mississippians. Among the Dhegihan people and their Siouan relatives, tattoos charter and sanction specific ritual behavior. Tattoos also indicate where the bearer of the tattoos exists in the multilayered cosmos. It is not surprising that tattoos have an economic impact upon the individuals who bear them. Among these Western Mississippian societies, members of the First Man lineage were recipients of tribute, and they then redistributed those goods. While evidence of tribute in the form of artifacts made of nonlocal materials (e.g., "fancy goods" from distant sources such as marine shell and copper) can be recovered from the archaeological record, the mechanism for the disbursement of such wealth is not so easily recovered. When such records are found, it becomes evident that many factors are at play. A primary factor would be that the tattoos were an integral part of the complex "labeling system" employed by Mississippian societies to channel goods and guarantee that the honor of tattooing was bestowed where it was deserved. The labeling also insured that the bearer's honor would be readily known to all members of the society. Tattooing would also indicate the cosmic placement of the bearer.

Europeans wishing to establish economic and military ties with the Eastern Woodland people recognized these visual symbols of authority early in their encounters. The earliest journals mention specific gifts, such as a "crown" granted by the Virginia Company to "King Powhatan" (Axtell 1992:188) and red woolen coats with flashy buttons and braid given to prominent war captains. Swords with fancy hilts and guns with attractive inlays and embellishments were given as gifts for chiefs and prominent men. It was through these gifts that diplomacy was advanced, and certainly the tattoos of the prominent men were subject to examination.

Happily, artistic evidence from de Bry/Le Moyne has preserved a record of the tattoos of at least one high-ranking chief, a man with a lineage extending back to the "Sun." Although this does not solve the riddle of the Dhegihan chiefly tattoos, it does support the conclusions of Johann Sawyer and other members of Kent Reilly's iconography workshops who see a Southeastern Woodlands "corridor" along which a complex set of symbols and the attached ideology traveled. While it is not possible to gauge the amount of change in the ideology as it traveled with the motifs, it was probably not too pronounced. Was this man pictured in the late sixteenth century a descendant of the lineage that bore these distinct tattoos at Cahokia, four hundred years earlier? We may never know, but we can assume that some of these Braden symbols were long enduring, if only because we would expect the elite members of these societies to be more conservative. These elite persons would preserve their ancient labels simply because of the advantages and obligations that these marks and icons bestowed on them.

We do have the "Great Sun," his brother the Tattooed Serpent, and all of his tattooed relations extant in the literature about the Natchez, a "simple chiefdom" (Bailey 2004a: 86). While the deference paid to these labeled individuals by their subjects in the early eighteenth century is well known, we must ask if this was the case in the Cahokia model. The complexity of Cahokia, which is actually three immense mound sites linked ritually and surrounded by a plethora of satellite communities and farmsteads, makes answering this question difficult. Although many Prairie/Plains societies had sophisticated governmental systems, the Dhegihan Osage have preserved a unique one—a likely candidate for Cahokia. Each clan is represented by priests/warriors who have attained all seven priestly degrees. This body, deeply rooted in theocratic oral traditions, works like a parliament, advising and balancing the grand chief, or hereditary executor. Add to this the hereditary clan officials working together in all rites, and we see additional egalitarian reinforcement.

Another small piece of the puzzle would be the Dhegihan model for Cahokia, where one would certainly find an elite lineage, particularly that of the First Man. Comparisons of the early Braden images from Picture Cave with the Braden imagery attributed to Cahokia, particularly the engraved marine shell, suggests the images are likely those of other-world supernatural beings, especially personified natural forces. At this time it is not possible to connect any of the motifs found on the Braden images, with the probable exception of the rayed concentric barred oval and the Davis rectangle, as candidates for the tattoos of the First Man lineage.

< 8 >

Snaring Life from the Stars and the Sun

Mississippian Tattooing and the Enduring Cycle of Life and Death

David H. Dye

/ / / /

> *The process of creation is ongoing through the union of male and female principles in the cosmos at large.*
>
> RIDINGTON AND HASTINGS (*In'aska*) (1997:109)

Body painting and tattooing in indigenous eastern North America is illustrated by a wealth of striking images and portraiture. In addition to drawings and photographs from the late nineteenth century, archaeological and ethnohistorical evidence point to body painting and tattooing as once being embraced by numerous peoples who spoke widely different languages. Such depictions are particularly abundant in the Midwest and eastern plains, where extensive ethnographic fieldwork was undertaken among Siouan Chiwere and Dhegiha as well as neighboring Algonquians and Caddoans. Some of this fieldwork was conducted by native researchers, such as Francis La Flesche, an Omaha who produced detailed volumes on Omaha and Osage religion and ritual from an emic, or "insider's," perspective (Bailey 1995).

Body painting and tattooing among these prairie-plains groups was a critical and vital component of religious ideas, especially of appeals for the perpetuation of life through fertility and reincarnation. Studies of human body iconography in eastern North America have received limited attention as a component of religious interest by archaeologists, ethnographers, and ethnohistorians. To aid understanding of eastern North American religious institutions and practices, body art analysis must shift from a perspective where painting and tattooing is envisioned as one component of decorative design or temporal and spatial markers to an approach that investigates fundamental religious concepts. Such an approach could provide the basis for detailed cross-cultural analysis within eastern North America and also within a worldwide interpretive and methodological framework enabling a more nuanced appreciation of the religious significance of indigenous body art. Various forms of iconography illustrate painted and tattooed body imagery in a wide variety of media, including cave walls, ceramic vessels, copper plates, marine shell cups and gorgets, rock art, stone figurines, and wooden sculptures. Body painting and tattooing has received little attention, however, especially as a guide to understanding indigenous religious beliefs.

Body designs and motifs reflected clan affiliation, social ranking, sodality membership, and war honors, in addition to religious beliefs, but they were primarily an integral component of ritual supplication by men and women for continued life and rebirth. The hypothesis presented here embraces the idea that tattooing was critical to religious beliefs associated with men engaging in warfare and women giving birth. Indigenous people reasoned that life could be channeled, snared, controlled, manipulated, and recycled in an unending chain of death and rebirth through painted and tattooed imagery.

/ Recycling Life: Death and the Awakening /

Indigenous beliefs concerning cycles of rebirth may be found throughout eastern North America (Fletcher and La Flesche 1911; Hall 1997; Hultkrantz 1973). Men and women had balanced but opposed roles in life recycling. For women tattooing was a supplication to receive and give life, while for men combat provided the means for acquiring and reallocating enemy souls by trophy taking, including decapitation, dismemberment, and scalping. Therefore, women gave life through childbirth and plant cultivation, while men captured life through hunting and warfare (Bailey 2004c:59). Various figures of speech, including metaphors, similes, symbols, and tropes, in addition to artistic motifs, ritual regalia, and ceremonial paraphernalia, conveyed religious ideas concerning beliefs in souls and the afterlife. Body painting and tattooing provided one component of the visual expression of cosmological and sacred beliefs.

An important example of the visual significance of tattooing and cosmology is seen in an Osage cosmogram given J. Owen Dorsey in January 1883 by William Mathews (Dorsey 1885b:377–378). James Duncan was provided a similar chart in 1998 by Andrew "Bud" RedCorn (Duncan 2011). Both charts, and Duncan's composite cosmogram, explicitly detail the structure of the Dhegihan cosmos (Duncan 2011: figs. 2.1–2.3), part of which was tattooed on the throat and chest of secret society members (Dorsey 1885b:377, fig. 289). Duncan (2011:30) notes that "tattoos would reinforce the accuracy of the cosmic diagram and ensure its survival as a two-dimensional entity."

According to the sacred Osage cosmogram, the universe is composed of a multilayered Beneath World, Middle World, and Upper World. All levels are connected by an axis mundi, a pole that centers the universe to a ritually consecrated sacred spot on earth at one end and a celestial portal in the sky, such as Polaris or the sun, at the other end (Figure 8.1). This sacred pole, also known as the reincarnated "First Man," could take the form of a cottonwood, red cedar, or red oak tree (Duncan 2011:26; Fletcher and La Flesche 1911:217–218, 229). The axis mundi, "the great unifier, forms a bridge between the sky with the male sun and Morning Star and the female earth with her attendant Evening Star. Joining First Woman—the earth and the mother of all things—was an unavoidable episode in a Dhegihan's death and 'awakening'" (Duncan 2011:31). One's death and later "awakening" was facilitated through the ascent and descent of life forces moving along sacred

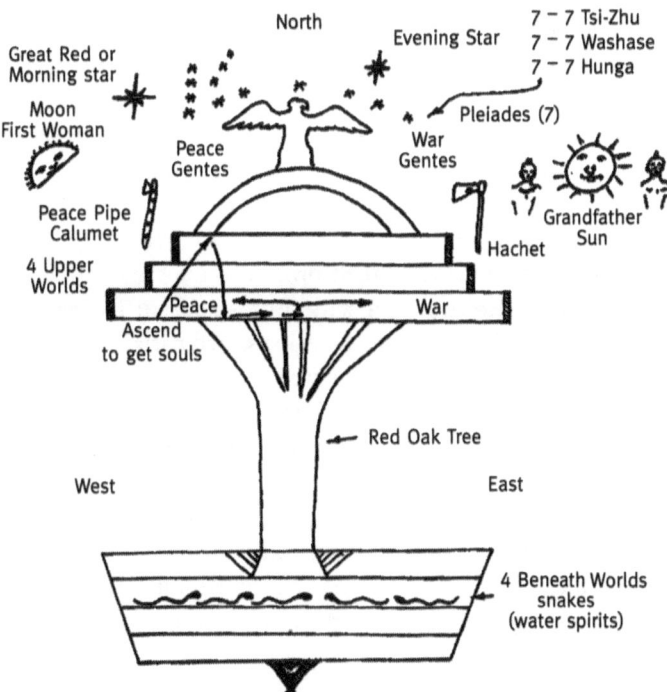

FIGURE 8.1. Osage cosmogram (after Duncan 2011: fig. 2.2).

poles during sun dances and mourning rituals throughout the plains and prairie regions (Hall 2004:98–100). Thus, sacred poles served as conduits or pathways for souls, providing access to portals or gateways at specific terminals, connecting sacred places on earth to those in the sky, including the sun in the daytime sky and constellations or single stars in the night sky. The sacred pole as an axis mundi also allowed deities and mortals to traverse the various cosmic layers (Duncan 2011:31) as they ascended to the Upper World or descended to the Beneath World. Tattooing not only drew life forces to an individual but also channeled those forces along pathways in much the same way as did sacred poles.

Mathews explained to Dorsey how the spirit people traveled about the levels of the Upper World and how they were given souls and human form by powerful spirits who inhabited these Upper Worlds. His narrative related not only the initial creation of the Dhegiha but also the "path of awakening," or the way of rebirth and reincarnation (Duncan 2011; La Flesche 1932:294–295). The journey taken by souls cycled in a pattern similar to the movement of the stars and sun along their nightly or daily routes. The path of life therefore was symbolized as the path of the sun and stars, and was reflected in tattooing.

The sun entered the earth in the west as it began its journey into the Beneath World, the female embodiment (La Flesche 1932:361–362). The celestial parents, sky and earth, sun and moon, are the parents of the stars, and the stars in turn are the Dhegiha's ancestors (Duncan 2011:25; Duncan and Diaz-Granados 2004:204; Fletcher and La Flesche 1911:63–64; Mathews 1961:8–9). As Duncan (2011:28) points out, no other indigenous groups in the Eastern Woodlands trace their origins to the stars, but all Dhegiha groups believe they descend from stars (Burns 2005:21; Dorsey 1885b:379; Mathews 1961:11). According to the Dhegiha sacred narratives, First Woman gives birth to the sun and all her progeny each morning. She embraces all her children as they come into her vulva, just as she receives the impregnating sun in the west as it enters earth at dusk. As the sun sets, she turns her body around and upside down, revealing the night sky and its feminine life forces. She returns to her original position as she gives birth to the sun at dawn. On a daily basis then, the earth inverts at dusk as it enters Earthmother and reorients itself again at dawn, thus placing the Beneath World overhead at night, and returning the Upper World to its familiar daytime position at dawn (Duncan 2011:29).

An example of the belief in rebirth is seen in the case of Crashing Thunder, a Ho-Chunk (or Winnebago) who related to Paul Radin an account told him by his brother-in-law, Thunder Cloud, of being reincarnated and of the events of his various lives (Radin 1913). Thunder Cloud remarked that he was "now on earth for the third time, I who am repeating experiences that I well remember from my past existences" (Radin 1973:7). Among the Dakota, a person was thought to have four souls, one of which after death "passes into the body of a child or some animal" (Neill 1872:293). The Yuchi believed the journey from the realm of the dead to the world of the living took four days and that children were "looked upon as the reincarnation of some ancestral spirit from the spirit world" (Speck 1909:93). The Kansa believed that many people "have become reanimated, who had been, during their apparent death, in strange villages; but as the inhabitants used them ill, they returned" (James 1905 [1823]:195). The idea that rebirth could take place after death was a major theme in a widespread belief system that embraced multiple incarnations of death and rebirth (Hall 1997; Hultkrantz 1953; Radin 1973).

Adoption could also serve as a mechanism for rebirth (Hall 1997). Hultkrantz (1953:326) notes that "in eastern North America we have several instances of reincarnation in connection with the act of adoption after a death. The rite of adoption may in many cases be regarded as a kind of dramatic reincarnation through the conferring of a name." Winnebago parents believed a captured child who had undergone the appropriate adoption rituals became their own reincarnated offspring (Radin 1923:139). Indigenous philosophies of reincarnation and rebirth often included tattoo rituals. Tattoos snared life created in the cosmos; through ritual the breath of life could then be placed within newborns or adopted children.

Additional forms of spirit manipulation are also evident in eastern North America. The concept of spirit trail servants was widespread in the Mississippi valley and Great Lakes area. A spirit companion could be taken through a scalp or some other body part. The life force could then be assigned at the grave of a mourned kinsman to accompany that individual as he journeyed on the spirit trail (Hall 1997:64–67). Radin (1923:97) notes for the Winnebago that every warrior who killed someone was in control of the slain individual's spirit and was "supposed always to be willing to put the spirit at the service of any member of his tribe who had just died." The Osage organized war parties after a death "to kill an enemy so that the spirit of the enemy could accompany that of the deceased" (Bailey 2004c:66; La Flesche 1939:137–141). To this end, a bereaved Omaha father

was apt to join the first party that proposed to "go upon the warpath;" if he had lost a little child he would tuck its small moccasins in his belt. On slaying an enemy he laid the moccasins beside the slain in the belief that the dead man would recognize and befriend the little child as it slowly made its way toward its relatives in the other world. (Fletcher and La Flesche 1911:594)

The belief that souls, or spirits, could be manipulated was a fundamental religious concept throughout eastern North America, where spirit trail servants were ritually assigned to the dead as recently as the early post–World War II period (Lurie 1966:136). A person's life could also be extended by taking someone's spirit and adding it to his or her own. Tattoos were believed to have the ability to draw the life force from the person killed and bestow it upon the successful warrior, whose life would be prolonged by appropriation of the victim's unexpended days (Fletcher and La Flesche 1911:220).

In 1913 Francis La Flesche visited the Osage reservation and recorded the last remaining fragments of the tattooing rite (La Flesche 1914). He observed that Omaha and Osage tattoos shared a number of similarities, especially their ability to supplicate a higher power for old age, many children, and an endless line of descendants (La Flesche 1930:531–532). These essentials of the Dhegiha belief system and cosmology associated with tattooing and the desire for long life were widely shared and had considerable time depth, as seen in western Mississippian iconography. The principles embodied in requests for life forces are linked visually to the fluorescence of the thirteenth-century Braden art style (Brown 2011:63; Diaz-Granados 2011; Duncan 2011) and are associated thematically with the Mississippian Birdman (Brown 2007a), Earthmother (Prentice 1986), Great Serpent (Lankford 2007a), and Spider (Wyatt 2002) deities.

The Dhegiha constructed their conceptions of gender on complementary relationships, rather than inequality (Bailey 2004b; Gangloff 1995). The union of masculine and feminine forces underscores the lack of hierarchical differences between men and women. Although men took life and women created life, they cooperated to ensure tribal fertility, perpetuation, and success (Edwards 2010:11). Life was conceived and brought forth in bodily form between the great fructifying and procreative forces of the universe: the sky and earth, night and day, the sun and moon/constellations, and the morning and evening stars (Duncan 2011; La Flesche 1921a:48). All life resulted from the union of the two greatest physical forces, the masculine sky and the feminine earth, which when combined gave life to all living things on earth. Thus, it was incumbent upon men and women to personify and replicate these creative forces through metaphor, ritual, and supplication. Body painting and tattooing were crucial components of the ritual supplication for life forces.

To achieve an oppositional balance through social organization and marriage, the Osage divided themselves into two grand divisions, or moieties: *Tsi-zhu*, Sky People, and *Hon-ga*, Earth People. The continuity and fertility of tribal life was ensured through their continued union. Exogamy symbolically bound the two tribal divisions: *Tsi-zhu* men married *Hon-ga* women and vice versa. Men and women were perpetually united, just as the sky and earth were inextricably bound together (La Flesche 1920:69–70). Each sunrise symbolized the birth of the masculine day from its union with the feminine night during the previous dusk (Duncan 2011; La Flesche 1921a:49–50). Just as night symbolized death, mystery, and the female power of the moon and stars, so day symbolized life and the vital male power of the sun (Bailey 2001:480). So the rising sun symbolized to the Dhegiha the continuity of human beings, the rebirth of life forces, and the revitalization of all living things (La Flesche 1921a:47–50, 1930:566–570).

Two fundamental aspects of the universe's life-giving forces ensured tribal perpetuity: warriors, who took life; and women, who gave life (La Flesche 1930:681–682). The Osage continually requested divine aid through supplication for continued tribal success and existence (La Flesche 1921a:49). Tattooing was one form of solicitation for a long life, many descendants, and fertility. The Osage recognized that women were channels, or pathways, "through whom all human life must proceed and continue" (La Flesche 1925:238). While men were associated with death in hunting and warfare, women were creators of life forces through childbirth and agriculture. Tattoos provided the conduit for channeling life forces, or souls, from the sun (day sky) and the stars (night sky) to earth. Indigenous eastern North Americans believed in multiple souls, but two basic forms were the life soul and the free soul (Lankford 2007b). The life soul, associated with the functioning of the body, is a person's life force. The free soul, on the other hand, may leave the body during visions or sleep. This free soul also may be taken from the body through scalping or dismemberment and reassigned for a variety of purposes. For example, as already noted, the free soul could be appropriated in the form of a scalp and dedicated at the grave as a spirit trail companion for a recently deceased kinsman (Hall 1997).

Our best information on tattooing and its relation to souls comes from the Dhegiha Siouans, especially the Omaha and Osage, and cognate tribes. Unlike groups east of the Mississippi, who had undergone considerable culture change by the late seventeenth century, many prairie and plains groups maintained a lifestyle well into the 1870s that was much like that of a hundred or more years earlier (Bailey 2004c:67; Brown 2007a). The religious values recorded in the late nineteenth century reflect conservative and well-established Siouan cosmological beliefs concerning life forces. Based in part on La Flesche's pioneering ethnographic work (La Flesche 1914, 1917, 1920, 1921a, 1921b, 1930, 1932, 1939), coupled with recent research on indigenous belief systems (Hall 1997; Hultkrantz 1953, 1973; Lankford 2007b), tattooing (Ridington 1988, 1990; Wyatt 2002), and western Mississippian iconography (Brown 2011; Diaz-Granados 2004, 2011; Diaz-Granados and Duncan 2004; Duncan 2011; Duncan and Diaz-Granados 2004), new insights are being revealed concerning the continuity of religious tattooing throughout the Mississippian and Protohistoric periods.

/ Dhegiha Women and Tattooing /

Tattooing was pervasive among southern Siouan women well into the twentieth century. Various accounts cite tattooing as continuing well into the late twentieth and early twenty-first centuries for the Omaha (Awakuni-Swetland 2008:30), Osage (Wyatt 2002), and Ponca (Howard 1995). While the Kansa (James 1905 [1823]) and Quapaw (Bossu 1962 [1768]) are known to have practiced tattooing, it had disappeared by the time of intensive ethnographic fieldwork during the late nineteenth century. Unfortunately, many of the details about the religious significance of tattooing for the Kansa and Quapaw are now missing. Due to the efforts of Francis La Flesche, the basic outline of supplicatory tattooing has been recorded for Omaha and Osage women, however, and may be extrapolated to other southern Siouans and cognate groups.

< Osage Women >

From the early nineteenth century, travelers noted the extensive amount of tattooing observed on Osage women. For example, in 1840 Victor Tixier stated that nearly all Osage women had blue tattoos on "their necks, chests, backs, arms, the backs of their hands, their stomachs down to the hips, the lower part of their thighs, and their legs" (Tixier 1940:138–139). He witnessed the Scalp Dance, in which "the women and the girls painted red or yellow colors between the lines of tattooing that covered their bodies" (Tixier 1940:227). Visiting the Osage in Oklahoma in 1908, Frank Speck found that tattooing was "common on both sexes. Men have it chiefly on the throat, neck and breast; women on the forehead, forearm, wrist and back of the hand as far as was observed. The designs seen were quite varied and all have reference to membership in and initiation into the different grades of the religious secret societies" (Speck 1907b:163). Unfortunately, Speck was unable to secure information on either the interpretation or symbolism of the tattoos, but five years later Francis La Flesche (1914, 1917), a Dhegihan speaker, obtained drawings, photographs, and interpretations of the tattooing symbolism for men and women. His work informs present knowledge concerning the overall context and structure of female Dhegiha tattooing.

An Osage warrior who had won war honors was entitled to the privilege of tattooing either his body or that of his wife or daughters as a mark of distinction (Fletcher and La Flesche 1911:221). But more than honor or status, tattoos for Osage women reflected their supplications for long life, fertility, and many descendants. The tattooing ritual involved performance, recitations, and songs, not only for the individual being tattooed, but also for the community. Tattooing a woman publicly demonstrated that she, like her husband, had personally undergone pain and suffering on behalf of the people and that she had sacrificed herself in a symbolic prayer for everyone (Bailey 2004c:64). Suffering is inherent in the metamorphosis and constitutes its essential essence (Balvay 2008:9; Fletcher and La Flesche 1911:62).

Tattoos on Osage women were far more elaborate and extensive than those on men. Also, only women at this time had tattoos of cosmic animals, such as spiders and turtles. Tattooing was restricted to the eldest daughters of the best families. Only they might have a spider tattooed on the backs of their hands (Mathews 1961:325). Women's tattoos covered most of their bodies, making their tattoos more expensive and painful than those of men. Many gifts had to be paid to the Great Bundle priests who performed the tattooing.

In May 1918, Francis La Flesche recorded the allegorical story of the Osage governmental organization's four experimental stages. The religious tattoo rite was developed during the second and third stages. The tattoo rite was transferred to the Gentle Ponca clan chief when the fourth stage of the tribal government was completed (La Flesche 1921b:110–112). In 1921 La Flesche published the drawing of an Osage woman that illustrated a variety of body tattoos (Figure 8.2). Two small circular tattoos, one above the other, were centered between the eyebrows (Dorsey 1890:78; La Flesche 1921b: fig. 119), representing the sun and moon. Her chest, back, shoulders, arms, hands, and lower legs were tattooed with geometric designs that were stylizations of the earth, moon, stars, and sun.

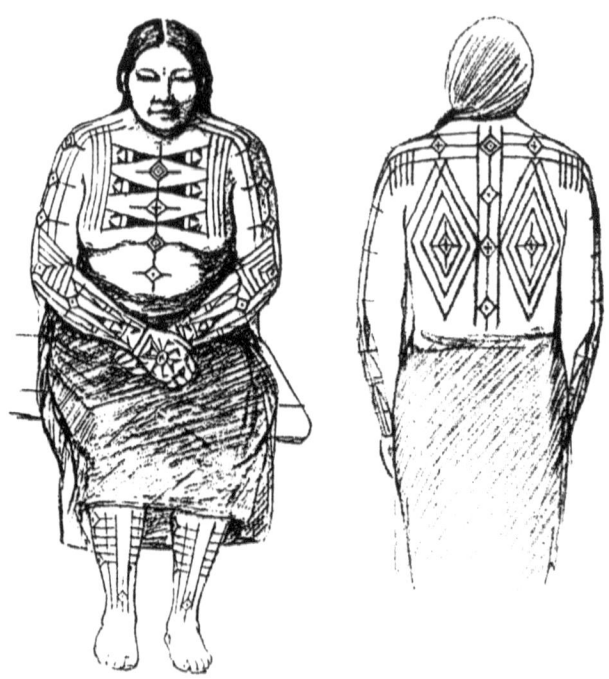

FIGURE 8.2. Tattooed Osage woman (after La Flesche 1921b: fig. 119).

The tattoo motifs channeled and snared life in all forms as it descended to earth. These designs ran from her shoulders down her arms and to her wrists, along the "paths of animals," a Dhegiha metaphor for the "path of life" (Figure 8.3). It was along this path that the four winds brought the breath of life to humankind. The tattoo design on the back of her hands, the spider, snared life from the sky and was the terminus for the tattooed pathways on her arms (Bailey 2004c:64; La Flesche 1921b:110–113, fig. 119). Nested diamonds over most of her body comprised a dominant tattoo motif typically occurring in sets of four, especially along the four pathways leading to the spiders on her hands. The tattoos on her forehead, chest, and back solicited life forces from the sun, stars, and various other astral elements of the sky that would be snared by the cosmic spider. The tattoo motifs as a group represent life descending from the sun and the stars to the earth, where it is drawn along the pathways and finally ensnared by the symbolic spiders on the backs of her hands (La Flesche 1921a:102, 1921b:113). The suite of tattoos thus acted in unison to channel life forces into her body, ensuring fertility and the group's long-term continuity.

Spiders wove webs to trap and ensnare their prey, so they became a life symbol representing the earth and its ability to attract, snare, and hold life (La Flesche 1921a:102). In a sacred recitation the spider is portrayed as a vital life force for the Isolated Earth people:

Verily, this house, like a snare, draws to itself
All living creatures, whosoever they may be.
Into it they shall throw themselves and become ensnared. (La Flesche 1921a:102)

The term *house* in this context is a trope for earth as a snare. Thus, the Osage saw spider webs as metaphoric traps that both attracted and snared life forces from the sky (Figure 8.4).

The Osage believed life was conceived through the interaction of the sky and the earth and that it descended to earth to be snared and to take material form (La Flesche 1921a:277, 1925:302). It was the space between the earth and sky that acted as a snare into which all life came through birth and departed through death (Bailey 1995:31; La Flesche 1930:683). Thus, the woman being

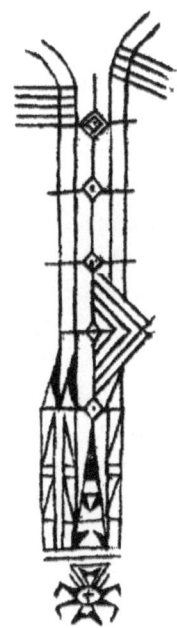

FIGURE 8.3. The four paths of life (after La Flesche 1921b: fig. 119).

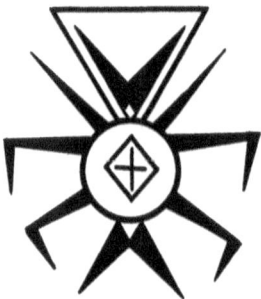

FIGURE 8.4. Conventional Osage spider tattoo (after La Flesche 1921a: fig. 8).

tattooed is a metaphor for the earth, an axis mundi, and a snare for attracting, channeling, and capturing life forces. An axis mundi is a reciprocal channel that connects and allows movement for deities, humans, and life forces
between the earth and the sky (Farrer and Williamson 1992:281). The spider
tattoo anchored the earth end of an axis mundi that was represented by the
lines drawn on the woman's arms. Along this path, life forces descended to
the earth, where they were trapped. The direction that the spider faces represents moiety affiliation and the direction for the flow of life forces, as well as
their movement along the axis mundi. A downward-, or earthward-facing,
spider symbolized the earth moiety and earth life forces ascending from the
earth, while an upward-, or skyward-facing, spider represented the sky moiety and the descent of sky life forces earthward (Wyatt 2002).

Jason Wyatt interviewed Sean Standingbear in 2001 and gained additional
information concerning the various spider motifs (Wyatt 2002:51). The triangle on the lower part symbolized female genitalia and denoted proliferation
of children and great numbers of descendants (Wyatt 2002:51). The cross at
the center of the spider tattoo symbolized the four winds, and the diamond
enclosing the cross was a lightning or sky symbol (Wyatt 2002:52). Osage
women were associated with spiders because both were weavers and channels
for ensnaring life (Hall 1979:262). Therefore, Osage spider tattoos became
a means of supplication for ensnaring life and ensuring fertility. These tattoos also ensured that the recipient would be the subject of a desired match
with a young man of a wealthy, elite family (Mathews 1961:325). Hence, spider designs were widely distributed among the elite first daughters of Osage
families (Duncan 2011:29).

The Osage associate the spider with the Orion constellation (Duncan
and Diaz-Granados 2004:203; La Flesche 1928:73, 1930:531), a life symbol for
the Elder Sky and Gentle Sky clans of the Sky People (Bailey 1995:38–39).

The diamond on the stylized spider's back may reference the diamond shape formed from Orion's principal stars, Betelgeuse and Rigel, with the two outermost belt stars, Alnitak and Mintaka. By connecting these four stars, one can perceive a large, luminous diamond shape in the winter night sky (Figure 8.5). Rigel, a blue supergiant, is the brightest star in the Orion constellation and the sixth brightest star in the night sky, with a visual magnitude of 0.18. Betelgeuse, a red supergiant, is the second brightest star in the Orion

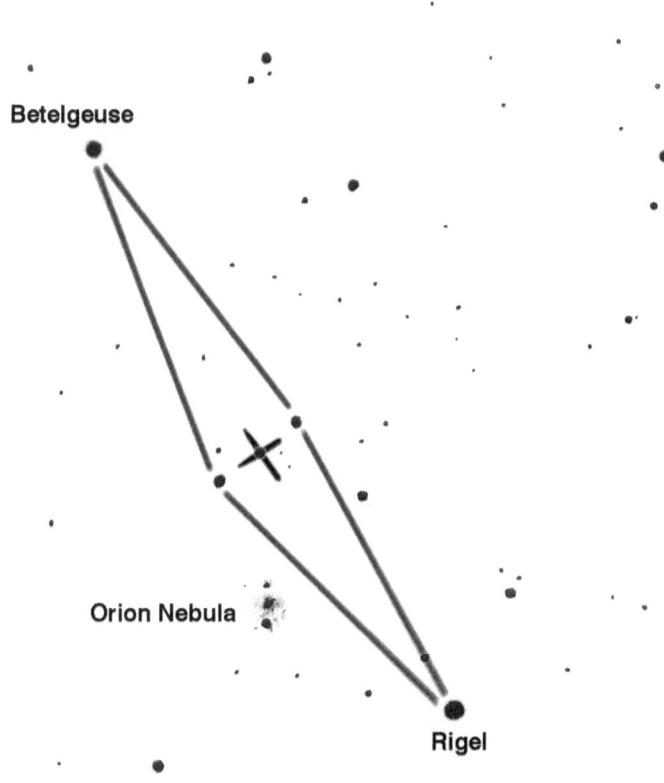

FIGURE 8.5. The Orion diamond.

constellation and the eighth brightest star in the night sky, with a visual magnitude varying from 0.2 to 1.2.

The three "belt" stars, Alnitak, Alnilam, and Mintaka, are seen by the Osage as the "Three Deer" (Duncan and Diaz-Granados 2004:203; La Flesche 1928:73, 1930:531). They are closely associated with the Earthmother, because she can transform herself into Deer Woman (Diaz-Granados 2004:144; Duncan and Diaz-Granados 2004:198–199). Linking Osage female genitalia with Orion suggests that Orion's diamond may be viewed as a sky symbol standing as a portal for life forces or souls. Lankford (2007c:238) notes that Caddoan and Siouan speakers saw Orion as a portal that provided access to the path of souls. The spider asterism is a component of the Orion constellation and is where "Old Woman Spider" waits to take "First Man" or his successors on a journey into the Beneath World (Duncan 2011:30; Lankford 2007c:230). Orion also symbolized First Woman as Grandmother Spider, weaving the web or snare of life, the Middle World.

Osage women were conduits for life forces that descended from the stars and sun along an axis mundi, where the life forces were channeled by various lines on their arms and snared by vulvaform spider motifs into their bodies. Tattoos directed these life forces and aided women's supplication for long life and many descendants. Thus, the tribe's continuity was assured through female fecundity and fertility. In addition, her ability to trap life forces through an Osage woman's femininity promoted her personification as the Earthmother, who metaphorically gave birth to the sun each morning and insured the continuing path of life.

< Omaha Women >

As is the case with other Dhegihan speakers, the religious concepts of the Omaha are represented in the language of ritual performances that dramatize the cosmic union of life forces. The union of complementary opposites, such as male and female, sky and earth, day and night, summer and winter (Ridington 1998:184), is symbolized as sunlight streaming through trees with the mixing of light onto an earth that is "mottled as by shadows" (Ridington 1990:23). The mottled shadow motif or metaphor served as a powerful symbol for fertility. To achieve symbolic union, Omaha women were tattooed on their foreheads, chests, backs, and wrists as one component of the dramatic fertility ceremonies.

One such ceremony, the *Hon'hewachi*, or Night Blessed Society, celebrated the union of complementary opposites as a ritual of fertility and renewal based on supplicatory tattooing. The ritual dramatized the cosmic creative acts through which "night brought forth day," that is, those acts that brought about life through the union of feminine and masculine forces (Fletcher and La Flesche 1911:494). The Omaha tattooing ritual concluded four days of ceremonies that took place in the summer, perhaps including the summer solstice, when the sun reached its most northern and potent place in the sky.

The *Hon'hewachi* was the culmination of a man's initiation into an order of honorary chieftainship as well as a puberty rite for his daughter (Fortune 1932; Gangloff 1995:87, 102–106). The tattooing component of the ceremony illustrated the fundamental principles of creation and fertility on which Omaha society was organized (Ridington 1998:186). While membership was predicated on success and valor in warfare and generosity in gift giving, the main privileges were chiefly office and having one's virgin daughter tattooed with the "mark of honor" (Fletcher and La Flesche 1911:503; Ridington 1988, 1990).

Women who bore the mark of honor were regarded as high-status potential marriage partners who could transfer sacred power from their fathers to their future husbands (Gangloff 1995:104–106). Membership in the *Hon'hewachi* underscored a man's recognition of the creative force inherent in the night sky, a metaphor for the feminine force (Fletcher and La Flesche 1911:507). Together, the *Hon'hewachi* songs, ceremonies, and symbols "refer to the creative cosmic forces typified by night and day, the earth and sky" (Fletcher and La Flesche 1911:495). Initiation into the *Hon'hewachi* empowered the initiated man to present mythic teachings to the tribe, a body of knowledge that represented the fundamental ideas on which the tribal organization rested (1911:393, 495). In addition, his daughter would be honored throughout her life (Fletcher 1893:449; Fletcher and La Flesche 1911:503–509).

Women inducted into the *Hon'hewachi* society were also selected for membership in the secret Shell Society, which at one time appears to have included ritual sexual intercourse among its members as a means of transferring the power of life and death from junior men to senior men through the junior men's wives (Fletcher and La Flesche 1911:486; Gangloff 1995:111; Ridington 1990:22), a practice once widespread across the northern plains and Midwest (Bowers 1950, 1965; Kehoe 1970; Lang 1998; Ronda 1984). The process of "shooting during the ritual is a dramatic interpretation of concepts of death and rebirth" and symbolized sexual intercourse as a procreative act (Gangloff 1995:112). The central premise of the *Hon'hewachi* was the celebration of the procreative powers of night, for night was "the mother of day" (Fletcher and La Flesche 1911:494). Night and the stars embodied the Earthmother, or feminine cosmic force, which derived its power from the night sky.

The *Hon'hewachi* ceremony began after the morning meal, when the girl to be initiated was brought into the consecrated lodge, positioned west of the lodge fire—a place of honor—and laid upon her back on an expensive bed of robes facing west, along the path of the sun, as life is "ever moving in a westerly direction" (La Flesche 1939:75). Being emblematic of the life force, she had to lie as if moving westward with the sun (Fletcher and La Flesche 1911:503). It was important that the tattooed symbols of night and day were aligned with the sun's path across the sky. The alignments included the young woman's face, the part in her hair, and her waiting womb (Ridington 1988:147). Prior to the ceremony, the circular initiation lodge was consecrated as the center of the cosmos, anchoring the earth end of the axis mundi to the lodge smoke hole. The Sky People and Earth People came together in the lodge as a single tribe with the Sky People sitting on the north side and the Earth People sitting on the south side (Ridington 1990:29, 1998:188).

The chief who would do the tattooing had to have been blessed and protected from harm by a previous serpent vision (Ridington 1998:188). He had to be in contact with the serpent's "moving cry," which in Omaha symbolism represented the noise of "teeming life that 'moves' over the earth'" (Fletcher and La Flesche 1911:506). Once the recipient was positioned on the robes, the tattoo chief took up a tightly bound bundle of tattooing instruments. The three to four flint needles were bound to flattened and truncated sticks so the points formed a straight line. Rattlesnake rattles were attached to the upper ends of the sticks (Ridington 1998:188); the rattling sound would remind the girl of the great serpent's power (Fletcher and La Flesche 1911:506). The ink solution was made from box elder wood that had been charred, pounded, and moistened, and then placed in a wooden bowl (Dorsey 1890:78).

The mark of honor consisted of two cosmic symbols, a sun tattooed on the forehead and a four-pointed star tattooed on the girl's upper chest (Figure 8.6) (Awakuni-Swetland 2008: fig. 1.8; Fletcher and La Flesche 1911: fig. 105). A crescent moon was sometimes tattooed on the back of the girl's neck and turtles on the backs of her hands (Fletcher and La Flesche 1911:506). Duncan (2011:29) relates a Quapaw origin story that illustrates the symbolic significance of the turtle: "The Great Sky Serpent fell into the primeval ocean. There he changed into a huge turtle that laid eggs from which the Quapaw hatched." The Omaha and Quapaw turtles may have had an equivalent meaning to the Osage spider motif.

The round spot on the forehead, representing the sun, was the first figure to be tattooed. It was outlined by a flattened stick dipped into the charcoal solution, and the skin was then pricked with the flint needles. The chief continued to prick the charcoal into the skin, following the lines of the figures that had been previously traced. As the tattooing was being done, a song was sung that referred to the sun rising to the zenith and its forces descending

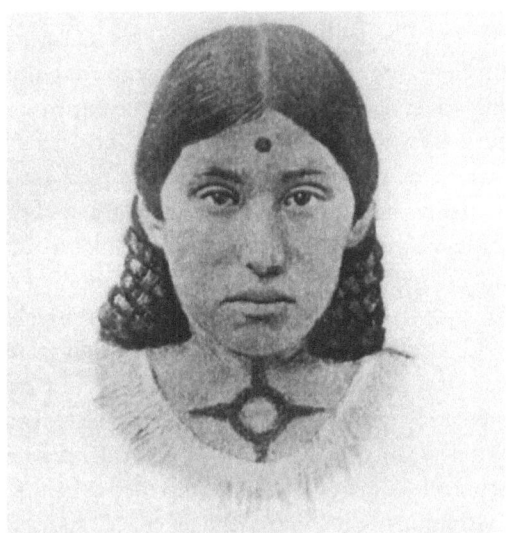

FIGURE 8.6. Omaha female mark of honor
(after Fletcher and La Flesche 1911: fig. 105).

upon the girl with the promise of life-giving power (Fletcher and La Flesche 1911:504). After the first pricking, the charcoal was again rubbed over the surface and pricked a second time. Dorsey (1890:78) states that only the chiefs could witness the actual tattooing.

The tattooing took place at noon, the exact opposite of night and hence an appropriate time for demonstrating the necessary union of male and female forces (Gangloff 1995:102). The Omaha, like many eastern North American people, believed an opening existed between the visible and invisible worlds at noon, allowing the ascent of an individual's soul, or spirit, to the Upper World upon death (Bailey 2004c:65) or its descent to earth upon "awakening," rebirth, or rejuvenation. Thus, the tattooing was completed as the sun passed directly overhead, when the axis mundi was open and the impregnating power and virility of the sun had reached its maximum potency and strength (Ridington and Hastings 1997:159–165). The sun motif tattooed on her forehead attracted and channeled the sun's breath of life to the girl (Ridington 1990:31). The sun's rays fell upon her along the axis mundi provided by the vertical shaft of light that fell through the sacred lodge's smoke hole (Ridington 1990:33). At this point she became a "woman of earth," capable of snaring the life forces of night and day through the cosmic symbols tattooed on her body.

After the sun symbol was tattooed on the girl's forehead, the outline of a four-pointed star was marked on her chest as a song was sung: "night moves, it passes, and the day is coming" (i.e., sun/life was being reborn) (Fletcher and La Flesche 1911:504–505). At the completion of the star tattooing, another song was sung, this one referring to the serpent representing the teeming life that moves over the earth (Fletcher and La Flesche 1911:506). Serpents were associated with teeming life because the Great Serpent is the guardian and master of the Beneath World and the realm of the dead, as well as the consort of Earthmother (Bowers 1965:334; Lankford 2007a).

The mark on the girl's forehead stands for the sun at its zenith, "from which it speaks." As the sun's life-giving powers passed through her body, they radiated out to the sacred camp circle, or *hu'thuga* (Ridington 1988:145). The four-pointed star was "emblematic of the night, the great mother force, its four points representing also the life-giving winds" (Fletcher and La Flesche 1911:505; Ridington 1998:186). The breath of life, carried by the four winds (Dorsey 1894:420; La Flesche 1939:140), was regarded as identical to the wind, with its life force (Hultkrantz 1953:182). The referenced star is Polaris, perhaps a night sky portal (Ridington 1998:189). The "pole" star (Polaris) centered the night sky so that the tattooing ceremony aligned the tattooed sun and the star (Ridington 1988:146). These two cosmic symbols, the sun and star signs, represented the complementary principles of feminine night and masculine day, fundamental to Omaha thought and experience (Ridington 1990:25).

In addition to the tattooing, the girl's nose was ritually cut or pierced as a rite of passage and a sign of rebirth in much the same way that captives' noses were cut in adoption and rebirth rituals (Fletcher and La Flesche 1911:615). The tattooing process constituted a rite of passage, emphasized by the pain initiates had to endure. At the climax of the ceremonies, the father offered his daughter to the life-giving powers of the sun (Ridington 1990:25). After being tattooed, the girl left the lodge, and a feast with distribution of gifts followed. Her dance, which took place before the *Hon'hewachi* members, "dramatized the awakening of the feminine element—an awakening everywhere necessary for a fulfillment in tangible form of the life-giving power" (Fletcher and La Flesche 1911:502). She was henceforth referred to as a woman chief (Fletcher and La Flesche 1911:494).

The tattooed young woman channeled the life forces created from the union of the masculine sun and the feminine stars. Therefore, the tattooing performance was a ritual of transformation and renewal in which the young woman became the focal point for the union of male and female cosmic forces (Ridington 1990, 1998). The ceremony for tattooing the mark of honor aligned the girl's body with the male and female cosmic forces, attracting and channeling the energy of creation into the tribe's life through her body. As the girl was centered with the cosmos, she became a woman of earth, an Earthmother who channeled fertility from the sky above along the sacred pole to the earth below. She would continue to renew the spirit of life through her appeals for the perpetuation of all life, especially human life (Fletcher and La Flesche 1911:507; Ridington 1990:21).

For Dhegihan Siouan women, tattooing was a mark of honor that provided membership in honorary societies and secret organizations whose concern was life and death. Initiation rites included the application of tattoo motifs that served to attract, channel, and snare life forces from the sun and stars. Not only did the young woman attract life forces from the night and day skies, but she also personified the great Earthmother, who bestowed life to the world. Among other Dhegiha women a similar suite of tattoos is evident. An 1832 Catlin painting of the Ponca woman Hee-láh-dee (Pure Fountain) (Catlin 1973: plate 88) (Figure 8.7) reveals tattoos similar to those

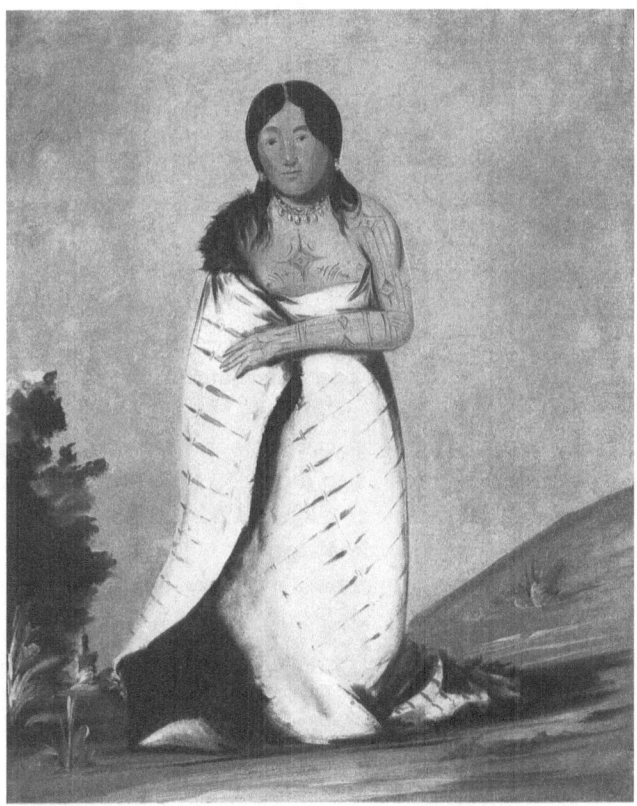

FIGURE 8.7. *Hee-láh-dee, Pure Fountain.* Portrait by George Catlin. Accession number 1985.66.96, Smithsonian American Art Museum, Washington, DC (gift of Mrs. Joseph Harrison Jr.).

of the Omaha (Fletcher and La Flesche 1911: fig. 105) and the Osage (La Flesche 1921b: fig. 119). Fletcher and La Flesche (1911: fig. 106) illustrate a Ponca woman's tattoos that are similar to the Omaha mark of honor, which are "emblems of day and night . . . between them stand the forms of children. By union of Day, the above, and Night, the below, came the human race and by them the race is maintained" (Fletcher and La Flesche 1911:507). The lines running down her arms replicate those found on the Osage woman. Ponca tattoos, as is the case with the tattoos of the other Dhegiha people, were said to be "an appeal for the perpetuation of all life and of human life in particular."

/ *Dhegiha Men and Tattooing* /

Men could be tattooed only if they had acquired the necessary war honors and been given an appropriate quantity of gifts for ritual knowledge to compensate the priest who bestowed ceremonial information, and therefore a portion of the priest's remaining life, to the initiate. Warfare added life to the man who extracted the remaining days on earth from another person (Fletcher and La Flesche 1911:220). Advancement in political, religious, and social positions was predicated on war honors and gift exchange, which were validated through tattooing. Tattoos functioned not only as an advertisement of ranking or social standing, but also as a means to snare, hold, and allocate life forces from people killed in warfare or from ritual practitioners who gave up their remaining days.

An early example of a Dhegiha tattooing ritual is seen in Jean-Bernard Bossu's account of his adoption and tattooing by the Quapaw in 1751 (see Chapter 1, this volume). During that ceremony the Quapaw tattooed the image of a deer on his thigh as a sign that he had been made a warrior and a chief. Although Bossu became an adopted Quapaw, he was not a participant in the prestigious chiefly or secret societies, and therefore was restricted from learning the underlying meanings of tattoo rituals. Dorsey, too, was denied access to rituals when he visited the Omaha between 1878 and 1882. Although he saw several aged chiefs who were tattooed on the fingers and wrists with transverse lines, he was not told the meanings or significance of the tattoos or their accompanying rituals. The tattooing rituals based on war honors had begun to die out, and he was told by his informants that "no well-behaved man was ever tattooed" (Dorsey 1890:78). The Kansa, Ponca, and Quapaw also employed tattooing rituals, but by the late nineteenth century, the practice had declined or disappeared. As regards the Kansa, however, James observed in 1819–1820 that many of the chief Kansa warriors were "tattooed on different parts of the body" (1905 [1823]:196).

La Flesche also had difficulty procuring texts of Osage tattooing rites, which at that time were still viable. The problem derived from the ritual's religious nature and the great expense for the priest in obtaining the sacred knowledge associated with tattooing. Feasting and gift giving were major financial burdens for the would-be chief or priest and his family; hence few people would give away such expensive knowledge. Perhaps most important, however, was the belief that divulging secret rituals would bring about supernatural punishment (Fortune 1932:29–34). In purchasing sacred knowledge of the rites, the buyer was believed to take the remaining days of the priest's life, hence hastening his death (Fletcher and La Flesche 1911:128–133; Fortune 1932:37–43). Finally, men had to achieve war honors to have the appropriate war symbols tattooed upon their bodies. Prior to the late nineteenth century, few men had sufficient war honors or were wealthy enough to afford the expensive ceremonies (La Flesche 1914). Therefore, when La Flesche and others attempted to purchase the tattoo bundles and the knowledge that went with them, the ritual owners were understandably reluctant to sell or to divulge the sacred knowledge associated with these materials. Tattooing rituals were central to the well-being of the community, being direct appeals for good health and the general welfare of the Osage people. The tattooing ritual was so important that it was included within the authority of the Great Bundle priests and performed as the "Rite of Chiefs" (Bailey 1995; La Flesche 1921a).

As described by Lars Krutak in Chapter 5, tattooing implements and associated ritual paraphernalia were contained within a set of nested bundles of decreasing size (see Figure 5.5), one placed inside the other (Wilson 1988:16). The tattooing ceremony took place inside the house of mystery, after the cosmos had been symbolically reconstructed and an axis mundi had been created by the clan priests, who collectively represented the various components of the cosmos (Bailey 2004b:34). The Great Bundle priests, known as "guardians of the village," were responsible for performing the tattooing ritual. Not only did they have to be initiated in the Rite of Chiefs (La Flesche 1921a), but they also had to purchase and learn the tattoo rituals in order to perform them (Bailey 1995:55, 2004b:51). In addition, a man had to have achieved all thirteen war honors before he could petition the priests to be tattooed and inducted as a tribal chief or priest.

The Osage tattooed the mark of honor (Figure 8.8) on the successful warrior and the hereditary keepers of the Honor Packs of War (Fletcher and La Flesche 1911:219). According to the rite of tattooing, a man who had achieved

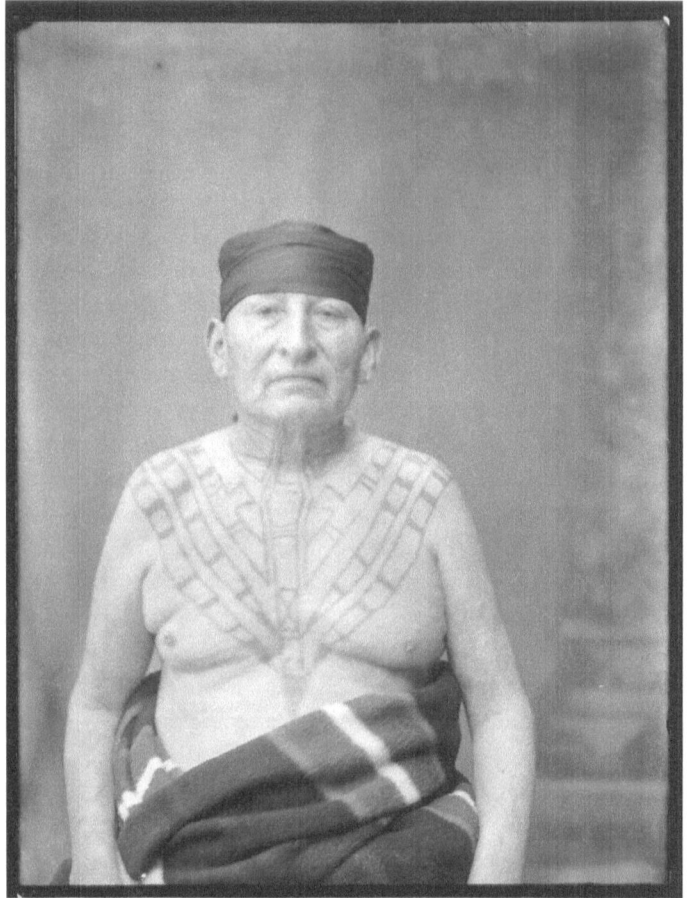

FIGURE 8.8. Tattooed Osage man. Photo Lot 89-8, Negative T13408, National
Anthropological Archives, Smithsonian Institution, Suitland, Maryland.

success as a chosen war leader was permitted to have tattooed upon his chest,
neck, and shoulders conventional designs of certain symbols, all of which
pertained to combat and warfare. In one example, the lowest mark of such
honors was three narrow lines beginning at the top of each shoulder and
meeting at an angle at the lower part of the chest. The next higher mark had,
in addition to the lines on the chest, three narrow lines running down the
outer surface of the arms to the wrists. The highest mark—in addition to
the lines on the chest and arms—consisted of three narrow lines continuing
from the shoulders, where the lines of the first mark began, meeting at an
angle in the middle of the back (Fletcher and La Flesche 1911:219–221).

In another example, several motifs comprised the tattoos associated with war honors recorded in the late nineteenth century (Bailey 1995: photo 2.4; Fletcher and La Flesche 1911: plate 37a; La Flesche 1914: fig. 64, 1920: fig. 72; 1921b: fig. 118, 1939: plate 5; see also Chapter 5 of this volume) (Figure 8.9). The sacred knife was tattooed under the chin, down the middle of the chest, to the abdomen about two inches above the waistline, and over the shoulders to the back (La Flesche 1921b:112). This symbolic red knife, found by the Earth People and presented to the Sky and Water People, represented war honors associated with the decapitation of an enemy (La Flesche 1921a:206–208; 1932:98, 1939:14–16, 108).

Two bands on each side of the central knife figure extended up to the hair an inch or two behind the ear, terminating in solidly tattooed knobs (Fletcher and La Flesche 1911:219) that may have represented war clubs. The sacred red club, made of the "never-dying" willow, was the weapon of the Sky Division (La Flesche 1939:14–16, 110–111). It symbolized indestructible life and the desire to maintain tribal existence (La Flesche 1925:83), as well as the striking of an enemy (La Flesche 1921a:49, 1925:83, 103–106, 316, 364).

The outline of the sacred pipe ran from either side of the knife design, terminating behind the shoulders with the bowl pointing upward. At the base of the neck, on each side of the stone knife, a triangle was traced. A line from the hypotenuse of this triangle extending to the top of the shoulder, represented four tents, or sacred lodges. The design meant that "the Sacred Pipe has descended" (Fletcher and La Flesche 1911:220). All the pipe keepers were

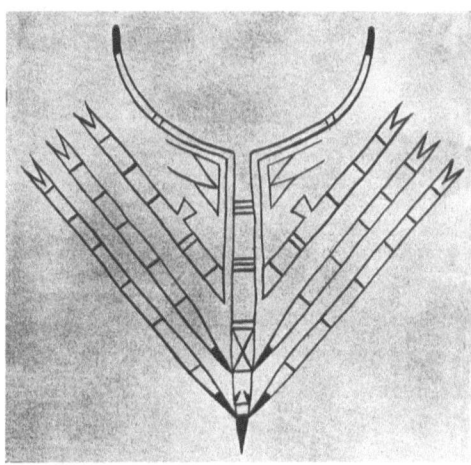

FIGURE 8.9. Osage male mark of honor (after Fletcher and La Flesche 1911: fig. 48).

tattooed with the sacred pipe. The keeper of the pipes was a member of the Elder Water clan of the Earth Division (La Flesche 1939:4). The sacred pipe symbolized unity of purpose and was used in offering smoke to Wa-kon-da when appealing for success and requesting compassion and help (La Flesche 1932:156). This sacred pipe was carried throughout the war expedition (La Flesche 1921b:112, 1939:4–5).

The thirteen rays of the sun, symbolizing the masculine cosmic force, ran upward from either side of the sacred knife between its point and the pipe design, terminating behind the shoulders (Fletcher and La Flesche 1911:494; La Flesche 1921b). The tattooed sun's rays symbolized the number of military honors every warrior had to have achieved to be tattooed and to become a chief or priest (La Flesche 1921b:112). Six of the sun rays constituted the life symbol of the Sun Carrier clan of the Sky People, and seven of the sun rays were the life symbol of an Earth Division clan. Overall, the sun's rays were life symbols of the Elder Sky clan. If a hereditary keeper decapitated an enemy in combat, skulls would be tattooed between the pointed ends of the bands that fell over his shoulders. Of critical importance, the tattooed skulls had the power to attract to the successful warrior the strength of the men he had killed, thus extending his life by virtue of their unexpended days (Fletcher and La Flesche 1911:220).

Tattooed men also were accorded elevated political and social standing within the community. The offices of chief and priest were predicated on successful acquisition of war honors and were displayed through tattoos that illustrated warrior success and that attracted, channeled, and snared life forces from other persons to themselves. Although organized as war parties, in many instances the ritually constituted militia groups who sought people to be killed for their life force were neither acts of feuding nor warfare, but rather raids to extract the souls of other human beings.

Women and men had complementary roles in the cycle of life through death and rebirth. Women personified the Earthmother by ensnaring life forces with their tattoos and insuring continued tribal existence through their fertility. Men also took life to assign spirit trail servants to relatives who had recently died. Tattoos not only provided visual testimony of these achievements but also served to channel life forces from either the sky or another human being. This pattern of balanced but opposing ritual supplication for primordial life forces channeled through men's and women's bodies had great time depth, as seen in the continuity of tattooing from western Mississippian utilitarian ritual ware to historic depictions of tattooed human bodies.

/ Mississippian Life Forces: Death and Rebirth /

Death and rebirth were central to western Mississippian religion, with its iconographic and ritual emphasis on the union of Earth and Sky life forces. Mississippian religious art embodied supplication for long life and many descendants through imagery and visualization of the sacred. Tattooing, documented in the archaeological and ethnohistorical record, provides a logical bridge from seventeenth-century western Mississippians to the eighteenth-century Dhegiha. Marine shell gorgets and cups engraved with feminine spider imagery, as well as ceramic anthropomorphic vessels that personify the great Earthmother, provide important connecting links from the Mississippian world to the historic Dhegiha and their cognate beliefs concerning tattoos and fertility for women. Likewise, ceramic effigy vessels and shell cups represent a continuation of tattooing for men. Female and male tattoos point to clear connections between the archaeological evidence for western Mississippian tattoo rituals and their ethnohistorical documentation. Marine shell cups and gorgets and ceramic vessels provide critical information about connections between Mississippian religious beliefs and Dhegihan philosophies of life.

< Western Mississippian Women >

McAdams-style shell gorgets (Brain and Phillips 1996:107–108; Mathews 1961:326; Phillips and Brown 1978:179; Wyatt 2002) and Craig B shell cups (Phillips and Brown 1984: plates 245 and 246) illustrate spider imagery as their focal point (Figures 8.10 and 8.11). Brown (2011:57) notes that spiders symbolize the primordial life principle for the Dhegiha. The McAdams gorgets occur in the same approximate location (Brain and Phillips 1996:109) as the ancestral polities of Chiwere and Dhegiha Siouan speakers (Henning 1993; Springer and Witkowski 1982:70; Vehik 1993), suggesting a close relationship (Brown 2011; Diaz-Granados 2011; Duncan 2011; Hall 2004; Kehoe 2007; Reilly 2004). The spider motif on gorgets can be related to the spider web spun by Earthmother, as the Osage believe the spider web is a snare, or *ho'-e-ga* (Diaz-Granados 2004; Diaz-Granados and Duncan 2004; Duncan and Diaz-Granados 2000, 2004). According to La Flesche (1932:63), the Osage define *ho'-e-ga* as "a term for an enclosure in which all life takes on bodily form, never to depart there from except by death. It stands for the earth which the mythical elk made to be habitable by separating it from the water." Ceramic and shell art suggest a long continuity in the belief in

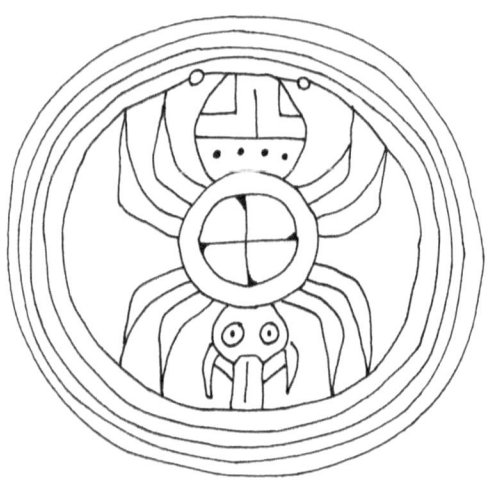

FIGURE 8.10. McAdams-style shell gorget (after
Brain and Phillips 1996:432, Ill-Ms-X1).

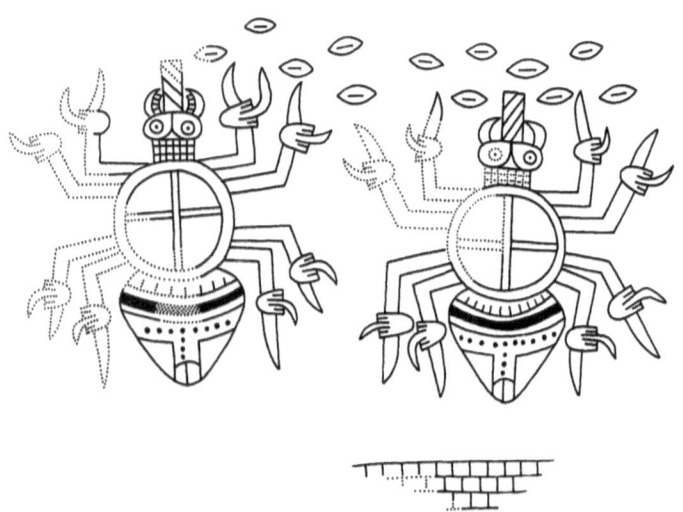

FIGURE 8.11. Craig B shell cup spiders (after
Phillips and Brown 1984: plate 245).

ho'-e-gas, as evidenced through a variety of utilitarian ritual art, including female effigy imagery and associated symbolic motifs.

Marine shell gorgets and cups with spider imagery share several distinctive motifs suggesting that spiders were associated with transporting spirits. Five motifs are noteworthy in their association with spider imagery. First, the perimeter of the gorget has five lines that demarcate the four paths of life and define the four layers of the sky. Second, the circle and cross is an important central element for shell gorget and shell cup spider imagery, placed between the abdomen and cephalothorax. The circle, as well as the gorget itself, represents the surface of the earth, which, according to the Osage, is a *ho'-e-ga* that snares life from the skies. The cross within the earth circle serves as an axis mundi connecting the spider with the night sky, and perhaps with the constellation Orion, the lodge of Earthmother and the spider, which may embody a portal and the night-sky terminus of the axis mundi.

A third motif, the T-bar, is found on the abdomens of spiders on engraved shell cups and shell gorgets (Wyatt 2002). The T-bar motif also functions as a *ho'-e-ga*, resembling T-bar *ho'-e-gas* painted on warriors' foreheads. Brown (2011:58) suggests that late nineteenth-century Omaha and Osage uses of the tattooed T-bar *ho'-e-ga* (Fletcher and La Flesche 1911:397; La Flesche 1925: plates 4, 15, 16, 17) continue late Braden imagery engraved on marine shell cups (Phillips and Brown 1978: plate 55). If the T-bar motif functions as a soul snare, then the dots may represent souls snared by the spider that are being stored for transport within the spider's abdomen.

The fourth motif, barred rectangles, is located on the spiders' forehead or cephalothorax (Wyatt 2002:15). Barred rectangles are also associated with bellows-shaped aprons, belts, sashes, and hands on engraved shell cups (Phillips and Brown 1978:147). These regalia and motifs are also associated with life forces. The bellows-shaped apron may have served as a soul container; this is suggested by the scalp locks within the container, which feature forelocks. The Osage believed that woven wrist- and waistbands held souls or spirits that had been snared by *ho'-e-gas* (La Flesche 1925:74). And hands, when coupled with spiders, were employed as snares by Dhegiha women. Barred rectangles, in the form of copper plates, are portrayed in iconographic imagery on the heads of birdmen as headdress regalia, the plates serving as bundle lids (see King 2004: fig. 1). In this context, barred rectangles may be interpreted as bundles. The placement of barred rectangles on shell cups and gorget spider heads suggests that they too may have been bundles. Some barred rectangles are striped, suggesting they are wrapped bundles rather than poles.

A fifth motif is the triangle located at the top of the spider's cephalothorax (Wyatt 2002:44). Triangles are also found on the heads of spiders in Osage tattoos on women's hands. The triangle, perhaps half of the diamond motif, symbolized female genitalia (Wyatt 2002).

The McAdams spider may be modeled after the pursewcb spider, a mygal-amorph that balloons or descends from the sky via silk strands and hunts its prey from underground silk tubes. The red leg purseweb (*Sphodros fitchi*), in particular, is an accomplished ambush predator that is solid and imposing, with large vertical fangs (Gertsch and Platnick 1980). While the bodies of females and males are black, males have distinctive, long, bright red legs. Western Mississippians may have modeled their cosmic spiders after the red leg purseweb, associated with both the Upper World, as an aerial disperser, and the Beneath World, with its silk tubes that go into the ground. Because the tubes are attached to trees, there is also a model for the axis mundi. In addition, its red-and-black coloring may have symbolized life and death, respectively.

On marine shell cups the raccoon hindquarter motif is attached to the spider's legs as a binding and appears to facilitate movement along the axis mundi. Raccoon bindings are also found on sacred poles, further suggesting a relationship with bindings and axis mundi. Raccoons are fond of water and nest in trees; thus, as is the case with spiders, they served as a natural model for a cosmic animal that could easily travel from the Beneath World to the Upper World along an axis mundi. Also, raccoons' tails have alternating dark-and-light stripes, which for Mississippians, as for the Omaha, may have represented "mottled shadows." Therefore, raccoon bindings seem to have served as sacred amulets or bundles that aided movement between world levels when attached to poles or the legs of spiders.

T-bar motifs, in addition to their location on spiders, are associated with individuals holding sacred poles (Figure 8.12). For the Omaha, the sacred pole had the power of motion and life, and the tattooed mark of honor was "vested on the pole itself" (Ridington 1988:145). Thus, the pole and the tattoos were instrumental in channeling the creative energy from the cosmic union of the Upper World and the Beneath World that resulted in continued life for the tribe (Ridington 1988:136).

Given the association of specific motifs on spiders—such as the five lines of the gorget perimeter, the circle and cross, the T-bar, barred rectangle, and triangle or diamond—they appear to have been employed in transporting spirits in soul bundles along the axis mundi (sacred pole) to the starry night sky, specifically the Orion constellation, which, for the Osage, is considered

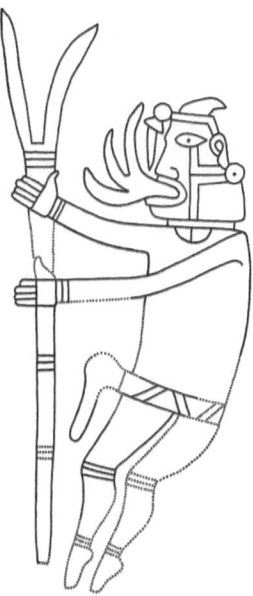

FIGURE 8.12. T-Bar facial motif associated with the
sacred pole (after Phillips and Brown 1984: plate 322).

the Spider's Lodge. McAdams-style shell gorgets and Craig B shell cups provide important evidence for interpreting western Mississippian tattooing. Spiders served not only as important life symbols but also as *ho'-e-gas* that snare life. Cosmic spiders may have been seen as special deities who collected souls in wrapped bundles and transported them to their lodges in the night sky. The numerous barred oval shapes may represent stars/souls in the night sky (see Figure 8.11). Because the Orion constellation was an important portal for western Mississippians, sometimes seen as the "hand" constellation, the cosmic spider's deposition of souls in its lodge would have been the first stage of their journey along the Path of Souls.

An additional piece of evidence in demonstrating a connection with Dhegiha women's tattoos and Mississippian tattooing practices is seen in two female effigy ceramic bottles from eastern Arkansas. Figure 8.13 shows a woman whose tattoos bear a striking resemblance to those of the tattooed Osage woman illustrated by La Flesche (1921b:119) (see Figure 8.2). As is the case with the Osage woman, the ceramic Earthmother figure has facial tattoos, diamonds tattooed on her back, multiple lines on her chest, and transverse life-path lines engraved on her arms. In addition, she has two entwined rattlesnakes wrapped around her neck in an ogee motif, suggesting an intimate association with the Great Serpent. A second female effigy bottle (see

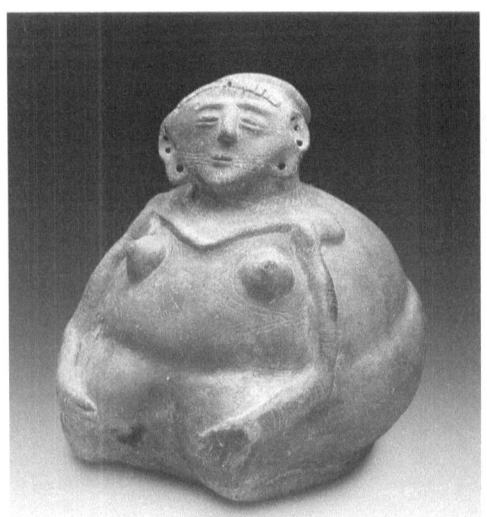
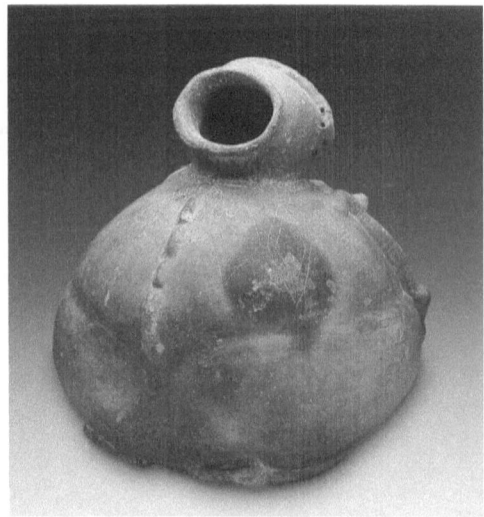

FIGURE 8.13. Earthmother ceramic bottle from eastern Arkansas. Arkansas State University Museum, Jonesboro, Arkansas. Photo by David H. Dye.

Figure 7.9A) also has a diamond motif, a human-like figure, and a mark-of-honor sunburst on her chest as well as facial tattooing (Diaz-Granados 2004).

Western Mississippian iconography associated with women and female-linked motifs illustrates their abiding concern with death, rebirth, and the ascent and descent of life forces. Spider imagery and Earthmother effigy bottles provide convincing archaeological evidence for strong continuities in a fundamental belief system embracing a complex ideology associated with recycling life forces. Engraved female effigy bottles produced by late Western Mississippian societies in the early seventeenth century, combined with early eighteenth-century ethnohistorical accounts of Dhegiha people, narrow the gap between archaeological and ethnographic evidence for ritual supplicatory tattooing.

< Western Mississippian Men >

As mentioned above, Brown (2011:58) argues that late nineteenth-century Dhegiha uses of tattooed *ho'-e-ga* (Fletcher and La Flesche 1911:397; La Flesche 1925: plates 4, 15, 16, 17) represent a continuation of Late Braden images on engraved marine shell cups into the early twentieth century. Facial tattooing on Mississippian shell cups includes motifs as eye and mouth surrounds, in addition to the cheek area, where the eye and mouth surrounds form a com-

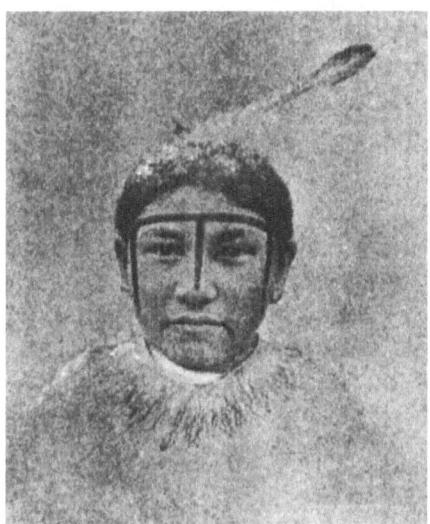

FIGURE 8.14. Omaha T-bar motif (after
Fletcher and La Flesche 1911: fig. 89).

posite image. Historic Dhegiha facial painting emphasizes the use of red
lines that symbolize life forces.

Several of the Osage *ho'-e-ga* designs illustrated by Burns (2005: fig. 12)
include T-bar motifs as components of the overall facial design. An Omaha
example is illustrated on the face of the child during the *Wa'Wa^n*, or Calumet
Ceremony (Figure 8.14). After red paint was applied over the face, the official
drew a black band across the forehead, a stripe down each cheek, one down
the nose, and one at the back of the head. The band across the forehead
represents the line of the sky; the stripes are the paths at the four directions
from whence the winds originate; the red paint symbolizes the light of the
sun and the gift of life; and the lines signify the winds, that is, the breath of
life that gives motion and power. The *Nini'bato^n* (Black Shoulder) subclan of
the *I^{n}ke'cabe* (Pipe Keeper) clan dead, who were keepers of the sacred tribal
pipes and custodians of the maize ritual (Fletcher and La Flesche 1911:148),
"were sometimes so painted for entrance into the life after death" (Fletcher
and La Flesche 1911:397).

The Late Braden anthropomorphic head engraved on shell cup 55 (Brown
2011: fig. 3.7b; Phillips and Brown 1978: plate 55), for example, illustrates
opposing T-bar motifs tattooed on the left cheek, as the horizontal band connects with the mouth and the vertical band connects with the eye (Figure 8.15),
perhaps representing the sky and earth realms, respectively. As was the case for

the T-bar motif found with spiders on the shell gorgets and cups, the figure on Cup 55 is associated with a raccoon-pelt binding, this one attached to an anthropomorph's ear rather than a spider's leg. The facial T-bar motif, found in conjunction with the raccoon-hindquarter pelt motif, focuses attention on facial tattoos as soul snares, or *ho'-e-gas*. The raccoon-binding ear attachment symbolizes the ascension of souls captured by the snare after death, presumably at the hands of a warrior. Raccoon pelts would have facilitated the transference of such souls, attracted to and ensnared by the tattooed facial *ho'-e-ga*. For Dhegiha warriors, the primary object of taking a life may have been the discharging of an obligation to assign a captured soul to the recently deceased relative and receive the victim's unspent days.

Tattooing facial designs on men is an ancient tradition going back at least to the early Hopewell period (see Figures 3.8–3.10), where raptor claws serve as eye surrounds. The use of raptor symbolism is widespread in Western Mississippian art, so it is not surprising to find a downward-facing raptor or Birdman incised over the left eye and a talon incised over the right eye of a human portrait vessel from eastern Arkansas (Cherry 2009; Walker 2004) (Figure 8.16). As is the case with Omaha men, the portrait bottle head is painted red, and life forces emanate as incised lines from the mouth.

The Birdman was an allegorical figure who played a central role in ensuring the triumph of life over death and the daily rebirth of the sun. As the

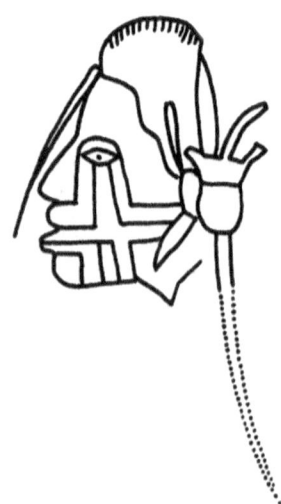

FIGURE 8.15. Late Braden facial *ho'-e-ga* on engraved shell cup (after Phillips and Brown 1978: plate 55).

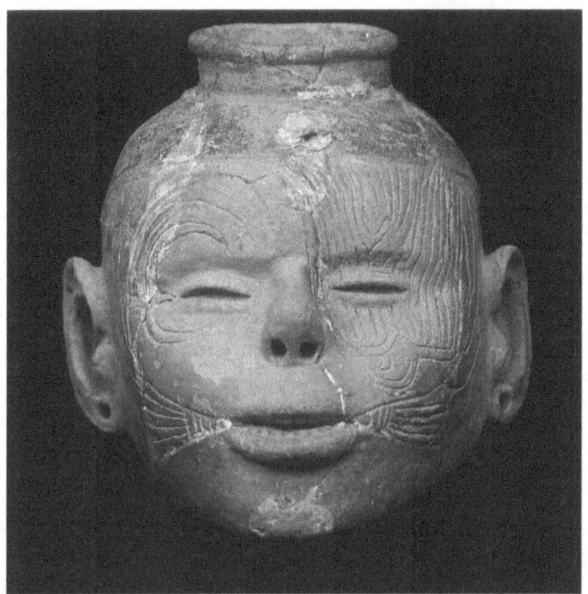

FIGURE 8.16. Late Mississippian facial tattoos. Hampson Archaeological Museum, Wilson, Arkansas. Photo by David H. Dye.

heroic warrior Morning Star, the Birdman represents the capacity for rebirth
of the human spirit. His counterpart, the Great Serpent, exercises discretion
over the timing of death. Birdman and the Great Serpent control aspects of
fertility and rebirth, while Morning Star controls the generation and descent
of life forces (Brown 2004).

/ *Discussion* /

The snare of life, or *ho'-e-ga*, is manifested in many aspects of tattooing for
nineteenth-century and western Mississippian women and men. Religious
concepts associated with an Earthmother figure have deep roots in eastern
North America (Prentice 1986). Images of females dated between AD 200
and 400 depict a deity that changed over time into an "Other-Than-Human-
Person" associated with agriculture and rebirth (see Penney 2004: fig. 10; Seeman 2004: figs. 4–7). The origins of eastern North American symbolism and
religious beliefs, such as those associated with Earthmother and the Great
Serpent, may be traced to Hopewell iconography between 100 BC and AD
400 (Hall 1979). With increased reliance on cultivated crops and household

production in the following centuries, women's roles evolved as they increasingly became sponsors of economic, religious, and social changes (Watson and Kennedy 1991). These changes are reflected in the appearance of vulva motifs found at Late Woodland sites in the upper Mississippi prairie peninsula.

Themes of fecundity and reproductive capacity are reflected in ceramic motifs. The diamond and triangular motif in particular have been proposed as female genitalia (Benn and Green 2000:468). Other Mississippian vulva motifs, including triangles, diamonds, ogees, and spiders, are found on ceramics, rock art, cave walls, marine shell gorgets and cups, and copper plates. The spider in particular is seen as an icon symbolizing the primordial life principle and is associated with Earthmother (Brown 2011:57–58; La Flesche 1921b; Wyatt 2002). Vulvaform motifs associated with Earthmother and spiders seem to serve as metaphors for a portal to another level of the cosmos, or Path of Souls (Diaz-Granados 2004, 2011). Female genitalia as snares for life forms are complementary to those of men, who also snared life, albeit in a profoundly different way.

On their descent, life forms are trapped through *ho'-e-gas* and born again as newborns or adopted children. Duncan (2011) illustrates the ascent of spirits from the Beneath World to the Sky Realm and their descent back to earth. One ascends through death, but may be awakened and returned to bodily form. Souls of the recently deceased who have been killed to become spirit trail servants are assigned at the grave and therefore ascend (La Flesche 1939:137–138). Osage warriors bared the inner body of a tree and painted it red to "send forth the spirit of their companion to travel with the God of Day on its endless journey" (La Flesche 1939:140). Likewise, the spirit of the dead warrior is endowed with new life "to be borne away by the Winds to the Spirit Land" (La Flesche 1939:140). Dhegiha men could thus manipulate life forces by ritual to send the spirits of their companions to the realm of the dead or by taking the lives of their enemies, capturing their souls, and assigning them to accompany recently deceased relatives or to extend their own lives.

The Osage, for example, painted the face of the ritual sponsor in tribal rites red; a dark line was drawn running upward from one cheek to the forehead, then across to the opposite side and downward to the middle of the other cheek. This line represents the earth's dark horizon and is referred to as a *ho'-e-ga*, a snare or enclosure into which all life is drawn and held captive. From the line that runs across the forehead, one to four black lines are drawn downward to the eyebrows and nose. These religious motifs may be survivals of the T-bar motif seen on Mississippian portraiture.

When four horizontal lines are drawn, they represent the four winds that symbolize the breath of life. The face was painted red, symbolizing the sun. The line that runs around the face is the *ho'-e-ga* (La Flesche 1939:243–244). The same snare is painted on the face of the Omaha: "The face is painted red symbolic of the dawn, a black line is drawn across the forehead and down each cheek and the nose, indicative of the experience of life and death" (Fletcher 1994:41). Captured souls or spirits were also held by woven bands at the wrists and waist (La Flesche 1925:74), similar to transverse lines on Mississippian portraiture incised or engraved on ceramics and shell cups.

During the ascent of life forces or souls, someone must be killed to accompany a deceased relative. Tattoos are instrumental in snaring the souls of victims at death. The soul is then carried skyward by spirit helpers such as cosmic spiders, raccoons, or turtles, all animals associated with special abilities, skills, and power. The ascent takes place along an axis mundi that is tethered at one end to a ritually consecrated and sacred spot. The other end is anchored to a portal, such as Orion, the Pleiades, or Polaris, which provides the soul and its transporter access to a route along the Milky Way or Path of Souls (Lankford 2007b). The Hand constellation and the Spider's Lodge may represent the same portal. Thus, men promote the ascension of souls through killing and the capture of spirit trail companions.

Life forces descend to the earth to be reborn. Women are associated with the descent of life forces from the night sky (stars) and the day sky (sun). Tattooing is supplication for these life forces to enter the woman and provide her with life in the form of children. There are numerous motifs associated with snaring life forces: barred ovals and rectangles, ogees, spiders, and T-bars. Women solicit life forces and channel them to their bodies, especially their vulvas, with the aid of tattoos. The spider is one surviving example of an animal helper being adopted as a snare and serving as a trope for female genitalia.

Downward-facing spiders on shell gorgets appear to be ascending to the Upper World, specifically the night sky. Shell gorgets clearly document ascending and descending spiders, with their T-bar snares and barred rectangle bundles, which contain souls being transported to the Beneath World to be reborn. These life forces are released, but only when solicited by someone worthy to receive them. Therefore, life forces may be snared as they descend, but they must be requested under specific ritual conditions. Life arrives to the solicitor via the four winds, or paths of life, as depicted by the cross and circle motif and the four paths at the outer edge of McAdams-style shell gorgets.

The Dhegiha people believe the first humans descended to earth from the stars, but the process continued as life was being recycled. As death releases souls to the Beneath World, they ascend to the Upper World and are solicited to return and to be awakened. Solicitation for a long line of descendants is thus a prayer for continued life from the sun and stars. The Omaha *hu'thuga*, based on the camp circle, reveals the entire circle of creation, the continuous motion of an ongoing creative process. The mythic union of the Sky People and the Earth People is enacted over and over again in the ceremonies through which the tribe renews its relationship to the buffalo, to the maize, to the seasons, and to the forces of day and night (Ridington and Hastings 1997:110).

Earthmother's vulva is a portal to a receptacle of spiritual power. It is her vulva that is the recipient of the sun's generative power, which ensnares and issues forth all her progeny, and it is the grave where all go who die. The use of female genitalia as receptacles of spiritual power is widespread among Siouan speakers and their neighbors (Bowers 1950, 1965; Duncan and Diaz-Granados 2004; Kehoe 1970; Lang 1998; Ronda 1984). Women as Earthmothers are associated with creation, death, and rebirth, while men are associated with soul capture and dedication as spirit trail servants.

/ *Conclusion* /

Tattooing and body painting reflect deeply embedded religious beliefs associated with recycling life throughout eastern North America. The archaeological and iconographic record of western Mississippians in particular documents a rich body of information concerning spirit rebirth, or "awakening," after death. Men and women had complementary but opposed roles in recycling life. Although both sexes devoted a great deal of attention to supplications for long life and many generations, they pursued the path of life in fundamentally different ways.

Women sought a long life and many descendants through celestial aid from the sun and stars as part of the rituals associated with tattooing. The tattoos themselves continued to aid requests for fertility through children and crop productivity. As channels that attracted life forces to their bodies, women not only personified Earthmother, but also became conduits for life that descended from the sun and stars, and they directed those life forces to earth so that they would awaken once again each dawn and each spring in an endless chain of rebirth and recycling of life.

Men extended their lives, in part, through taking other lives and capturing the souls of their victims through facial painting and tattooing. Taking life, often through scalping, not only benefited the successful warrior but also aided those who journeyed along the Path of Souls, accompanied by spirit trail servants. Rituals of warfare were conducted for the validation of war honors and to capture souls for recently deceased relatives, rather than for economic or political purposes.

The complementary relationship of Dhegiha gender roles underscored the oppositional balance between men and women. All life resulted from the masculine sky and feminine night, and humans solicited those life forces through personification of deities, such as Birdman and Earthmother, and snared them through *ho'-e-gas* in the form of body painting and tattooing. Although men took life and women gave life, the attraction and impoundment of spiritual forces was central to rebirth. Tattoos provided a critical component to the process of drawing life toward the solicitor and holding it for rededication and transport to the realm of the dead.

/ *Author's Acknowledgments* /

I would like to thank Aaron Deter-Wolf for his invitation to participate in the 2009 (66th) Southeastern Archaeological Conference symposium, "Tattooing and Body Modification in the Prehistoric and Early Historic Southeast." This chapter is based on the conference paper "War Honors and Tattoos: Mississippian Soul Capture, Dedication, and Recycling." My appreciation to Aaron and Carol and to Patty Jo Watson for their editorial comments and suggestions, which improved the manuscript. I also thank Kent Reilly, director of the Center for the Study of the Arts and Symbolism of Ancient America, Department of Anthropology, Texas State University, San Marcos, and the workshop participants whose counsel and discussion provided much of the foundation upon which this chapter rests. To each of them I am grateful. And finally I wish to thank the Lannan Foundation of Santa Fe for their generous support of the San Marcos Iconographic Workshop.

REFERENCES

Adair, James. 2005 [1775]. *The History of the American Indians.* Edited and annotated by Kathryn E. Holland Braund. Tuscaloosa: University of Alabama Press.

Allen, Dan. 2006. "Applied Archaeology at the Hermitage Springs Site (40DV55): A Middle Archaic through Early Woodland Aggregation Site in the Cumberland River Valley." Paper presented at the 18th annual Current Research in Tennessee Archaeology meeting, Nashville.

Allison, Marvin J. 1996. Early Mummies from Coastal Peru and Chile. In *Human Mummies, A Global Study of Their Status and the Techniques of Conservation (The Man in the Ice),* vol. 3, edited by Konrad Spindler, Harald Wilfring, Elisabeth Rastbichler-Zissernig, Dieter zur Nedden, and Hans Nothdurfter, pp. 125–130. Vienna: Springer-Verlag.

Ambrose, Wal. 2012. Oceanic Tattooing and the Implied Lapita Ceramic Connection. *Journal of Pacific Archaeology* 3(1):1–21.

Anderson, David G. 1998. Swift Creek in a Regional Perspective. In *A World Engraved: Archaeology of the Swift Creek Culture,* edited by M. Williams and Daniel T. Elliott, pp. 274–300. Tuscaloosa: University of Alabama Press.

Andrews, Rhonda L., and James M. Adovasio. 1980. *Perishable Industries from Hinds Cave, Val Verde County, Texas.* Ethnology Monographs 5. Pittsburgh: Department of Anthropology, University of Pittsburgh.

Awakuni-Swetland, Mark. 2008. *Dance Lodges of the Omaha People: Building from Memory.* Lincoln: University of Nebraska Press.

Axtell, James. 1992. *Beyond 1942.* Oxford, UK: Oxford University Press.

Bailey, Garrick A. 2001. Osage. In *Plains,* edited by R. J. DeMallie, pp. 476–496. *Handbook of North American Indians,* vol. 13, part 1, William C. Sturtevant, general editor. Washington, DC: Smithsonian Institution, United States Government Printing Office.

———. 2004a. Continuity and Change in Mississippian Civilization. In *Hero, Hawk, and Open Hand: American Indian Art of the Ancient Midwest and South,* edited by Richard F. Townsend and Robert V. Sharp, pp. 82–91. New Haven, CT: Art Institute of Chicago and Yale University Press.

———. 2004b. Osage Cosmology. In *Art of the Osage*, edited by Garrick A. Bailey and Daniel C. Swan, pp. 27–38. Seattle: University of Washington Press.

———. 2004c. Osage Daily Life: Living Life as Prayer. In *Art of the Osage*, edited by Garrick A. Bailey and Daniel C. Swan, pp. 49–135. Seattle: University of Washington Press.

———, ed. 1995. *The Osage and the Invisible World: From the Works of Francis La Flesche*. Norman: University of Oklahoma Press.

———. 2010, ed. *Traditions of the Osage: Stories Collected and Translated by Francis La Flesche*. Albuquerque: University of New Mexico Press.

Balvay, Arnaud. 2008. Tattooing and Its Role in French–Native American Relations in the Eighteenth Century. *French Colonial History* 9:1–14.

Bartram, William. 1996 [1791]. Travels through North and South Carolina, Georgia, East and West Florida . . . In *William Bartram: Travels and Other Writings*, edited by Thomas P. Slaughter, pp. 3–426. New York: Literary Classics of the United States.

———. 1996 [1853]. Observations on the Creek and Cherokee Indians. In *William Bartram: Travels and Other Writings*, edited by Thomas P. Slaughter, pp. 527–567. New York: Literary Classics of the United States.

Beauchamp, William M. 1905. *A History of the New York Iroquois, Now Commonly Called the Six Nations*. New York State Museum Bulletin 78. Albany: New York State Education Department.

———. 1922. *Iroquois Folk Lore: Gathered from the Six Nations of New York*. Syracuse: Dehler.

Becher, Hans, and Frieda Schütze. 1960. *The Surara and Pakidai, Two Yanoama Tribes in Northwest Brazil*. Hamburg: Kommissionsverlag Cram, De Gruyter.

Biedma, Luys Hernández de. 1993 [1841]. Relation of the Island of Florida. Translated and edited by John E. Worth. In *The de Soto Chronicles: The Expedition of Hernando de Soto to North America in 1539–1543*, vol. 1, edited by Lawrence A. Clayton, Vernon James Knight, Jr., and Edward C. Moore, pp. 225–246. Tuscaloosa: University of Alabama Press.

Bell, Ann Linda, trans. 1987. Voyage to the Mississippi through the Gulf of Mexico, 1687. In *La Salle, the Mississippi, and the Gulf: Three Primary Documents*, edited by Robert S. Weddle, pp. 225–258. College Station: Texas A&M University Press.

Benn, David W., and William Green. 2000. Late Woodland Cultures in Iowa. In *Late Woodland Societies: Tradition and Transformation across the Midcontinent*, edited by Thomas E. Emerson, Dale L. McElrath, and Andrew C. Fortier, pp. 429–496. Lincoln: University of Nebraska Press.

Berns, Marla C. 1988. Ga'anda Scarification: A Model for Art and Identity. In *Marks of Civilization*, edited by Arnold Rubin, pp. 57–76. Los Angeles: Museum of Cultural History, University of California.

————. 1990. Pots as People: Yungur Ancestral Portraits. *African Art* 23(3):50–60, 102.

Bienville, Jean-Baptiste Le Moyne de. 1880 [1700]. Copie du Journal du Voyage de M. de Bienville des Taensas au village des Yatachés, par les terres. (22 mars–18 mai 1700.) In *Découvertes et établissements des Français dans l'ouest et dans le sud de l'Amérique Septentrionale (1614–1754)*, vol. 4, edited by Pierre Margry, pp. 432–444. Paris: D. Jouaust.

Bodmer, Karl. 1984. *Karl Bodmer's America*. Lincoln: Joslyn Art Museum/University of Nebraska Press.

Boedy, Randall, Tom Des Jean, Joanne Devlin, Jan Simek, and Fred E. Coy, J. 2010. "The Rock Creek Mummy, McCreary County, Kentucky." Paper presented at the 67th annual meeting of the Southeastern Archaeological Conference, Lexington, KY.

Bossu, Jean Bernard. 1768. *Nouveaux Voyages aux Indes Occidentales*. Vol. 1. Paris: Chez Le Jay.

————. 1771 [1768]. *Travels through That Part of America Formerly Called Louisiana*. Vol. 1. Translated by John Reinhold Forster. London: T. Davies.

————. 1962 [1768]. *Jean-Bernard Bossu's Travels in the Interior of North America, 1751–1762*. Translated and edited by Seymour Feiler. Norman: University of Oklahoma Press.

Bowers, Alfred W. 1950. *Mandan Social and Ceremonial Organization*. Chicago: University of Chicago Press.

————. 1965. *Hidatsa Social and Ceremonial Organization*. Bureau of American Ethnology Bulletin 194. Washington, DC: Smithsonian Institution, United States Government Printing Office.

Brain, Jeffrey P., and Philip Phillips. 1996. *Shell Gorgets: Styles of the Late Prehistoric and Protohistoric Southeast*. Cambridge, MA: Peabody Museum Press.

Brain, Robert. 1979. *The Decorated Body*. New York: Harper and Row.

Brainerd, David. 1822. *Memoirs of the Rev. David Brainerd; Missionary to the Indians on the Borders of New York, New Jersey, and Pennsylvania*, edited by Jonathan Edwards and Sereno E. Dwight. S. New Haven, CT: Converse.

Brasser, Ted J. 1999. Notes on a Recently Discovered Indian Shirt from New France. *American Indian Art Magazine* 24(2):46–55.

————. 2009. Eastern Sioux War Club, Ca. 1810. In *Splendid Heritage: Perspectives on American Indian Art*, edited by John and Marva Warnock, p. 58. Salt Lake City: University of Utah Press.

Bray, Robert T. 1978. European Trade Goods from the Utz Site and the Search for Fort Orleans. *Missouri Archaeologist* 39.

————. 1991. The Utz Site, An Oneota Village in Central Missouri. *Missouri Archaeologist* 52.

Bressani, Francesco Giuseppe. 1899. A Brief Account of Certain Missions of the Fathers of the Society of Jesus in New France. In *The Jesuit Relations and Allied*

Documents . . ., Vol. XXXVIII: Abenakis, Lower Canada, Hurons, 1652–1653, translated and edited by Ruben Gold Thwaites, pp. 203–288. Cleveland: Burrows Brothers.

Brinton, Daniel G. 1885. *The Lenâpé and Their Legends; with the Complete Text and Symbols of the Walam Olum.* Brinton's Library of Aboriginal American Literature 5. Philadelphia: Daniel G. Brinton.

Brown, James A. 2004. The Cahokian Expresssion: Creating Court and Cult. In *Hero, Hawk, and Open Hand: American Indian Art of the Ancient Midwest and South*, edited by Richard F. Townsend and Robert V. Sharp, pp. 104–123. New Haven, CT: Art Institute of Chicago and Yale University Press.

———. 2005. "Beyond Red Horn: Where Ethnology Meets History." Paper Presented at the 70th annual meeting of the Society for American Archaeology, Salt Lake City.

———. 2007a. On the Identity of the Birdman within Mississippian Period Art and Iconography. In *Ancient Objects and Sacred Realms: Interpretations of Mississippian Iconography*, edited by F. Kent Reilly III and James F. Garber, pp. 56–106. Austin: University of Texas Press.

———. 2007b. Sequencing the Braden Style within Mississippian Period Art and Iconography. In *Ancient Objects and Sacred Realms: Interpretations of Mississippian Iconography*, edited by F. Kent Reilly III and James F. Garber, pp. 213–245. Austin: University of Texas Press.

———. 2011. The Regional Culture Signature of the Braden Art Style. In *Visualizing the Sacred: Cosmic Visions, Regionalism, and the Art of the Mississippian World*, edited by George E. Lankford, F. Kent Reilly III, and James F. Garber, pp. 37–63. Austin: University of Texas Press.

Broyles, Bettye J. 1968. Reconstructed Designs from Swift Creek Complicated Stamped Sherds. *Southeastern Archaeological Conference Bulletin* 8:49–74.

Bryant, William C. 1889. *Captain Brant and the Old King: The Tragedy of Wyoming.* Buffalo, NY: J. W. Clement.

Buckland, A. W. 1888. On Tattooing. *The Journal of the Anthropological Institute of Great Britain and Ireland* 17:318–328.

Bullen, Ripley. 1953. The Famous Crystal River Site. *The Florida Anthropologist* 6(1):9–37.

Burns, Louis F. 2005. *Osage Indian Customs and Myths.* Tuscaloosa: University of Alabama Press.

Bushnell, David I., Jr. 1909. *The Choctaw of Bayou Lacomb, St. Tammany Parish, Louisiana.* Bureau of American Ethnology Bulletin 48. Washington, DC: Smithsonian Institution, United States Government Printing Office.

———. 1927. Drawings by A. de Batz in Louisiana, 1732–1735. *Smithsonian Miscellaneous Collections* 80(5).

Cadillac, Antoine Laumet de La Mothe. 1947 [1883]. The Memoir of Lamothe Cadillac. In *The Western Country in the Seventeenth Century: The Memoirs of Lamothe*

Cadillac and Pierre Liette, edited by Milo M. Quaife, pp. 3–86. Chicago: Lakeside Press, R. R. Donnelley and Sons.

Caldwell, Joseph R. 1964. Interaction Spheres in Prehistory. In *Hopewellian Studies*, edited by Joseph R. Caldwell and Robert L. Hall, pp. 133–143. Scientific Papers 12. Springfield: Illinois State Museum.

Callender, Charles. 1978. Fox. In *Northeast*, edited by Bruce G. Trigger, pp. 636–647. *Handbook of North American Indians*, Vol. 15, William C. Sturtevant, general editor. Washington, DC: Smithsonian Institution, United States Government Printing Office.

Cantino, Alberto. 1893. A Letter from Alberto Cantino to Hercules d'Este, Duke of Ferrara (extract). In *The Journal of Christopher Columbus (during His First Voyage, 1492–93) and Documents Relating the Voyages of John Cabot and Gaspar Corte Real*, translated and edited by Clements R. Markham, pp. 232–234. London: Hakluyt Society.

Carder, Nancy, Elizabeth J. Reitz, and J. Matthew Compton. 2004. Animal Use in the Georgia Pine Barrens: An Example from the Hartford Site (9PU1). *Southeastern Archaeology* 23(1):25–40.

Carpenter, Edmund S. 2005. *Two Essays: Chief and Greed.* North Andover, MA: Persimmon Press.

Carr, Christopher, and D. Troy Case. 2006. The Nature of Leadership in Ohio Hopewellian Societies: Role Segregation and the Transformation from Shamanism. In *Gathering Hopewell: Society, Ritual, and Ritual Interaction*, edited by Christopher Carr and D. Troy Case, pp. 177–237. New York: Springer.

Carver, Jonathan. 1778. *Travels through the Interior Parts of North America, in the Years 1766, 1767, and 1768.* London: J. Walter and S. Crowder.

Catesby, Mark. 1747. *The Natural History of Carolina, Florida, and the Bahama Islands.* Vol. 2. London: Printed for the author.

Catlin, George. 1973. Letters and Notes on the Manners, Customs, and Conditions of North American Indians. Vol. 1. New York: Dover.

Chanca, Diego Alvarez. 1906. Letter of Dr. Chanca on the Second Voyage of Columbus. In *The Northmen, Columbus and Cabot, 985–1503*, edited by Julius E. Olson and Edward G. Bourne, pp. 281–313. New York: Charles Scribner's Sons.

Cherry, James F. 2009. *The Headpots of Northeast Arkansas and Southern Pemiscot County, Arkansas.* Fayetteville: University of Arkansas Press.

Collins, Michael B. 2004. Interview in "Scientific American Frontiers: Coming into America." Public Broadcasting System. Produced by Chedd-Angier Production Company. Original air date July 25, 2004.

Coy, Fred E., Jr. 2004. Native American Dendroglyphs of the Eastern Woodlands. In *The Rock-Art of Eastern North America: Capturing Images and Insight*, edited by Carol Diaz-Granados and James R. Duncan, pp. 3–16. Tuscaloosa: University of Alabama Press.

Curtis, Edward S. 1907–1930. *The North American Indian: Being a Series of Volumes*

Picturing and Describing the Indians of the United States, the Dominion of Canada, and Alaska. 20 vols. Edited by Frederick W. Hodge. Norwood, MA: Plimpton Press.

David, Nicholas, Judy Sterner, and Kodzo Gavau. 1988. Why Pots Are Decorated. *Current Anthropology* 29(3):365–527.

Davis, Hester A. 1966. Current Research: Southeast. *American Antiquity* 31(6): 902–903.

De Cuyper, Christa, and Davy D'hollander. 2010. Materials Used in Body Art. In *Dermatologic Complications with Body Art: Tattoos, Piercings, and Permanent Makeup*, edited by Christa De Cuyper and Maria-Luisa Péres-Cotapos, pp. 13–28. New York: Springer.

Deliette, Pierre. 1947 [1934]. The Memoir of Pierre Lette. In *The Western Country in the Seventeenth Century: The Memoirs of Lamothe Cadillac and Pierre Liette*, edited by Milo M. Quaife, pp. 87–174. Chicago: Lakeside Press, R. R. Donnelley and Sons.

Denig, Edwin T. 1930. Indian Tribes of the Upper Missouri, edited by John N. B. Hewitt. In *Forty-Sixth Annual Report of the Bureau of American Ethnology, 1928–1929*, pp. 375–628. Washington, DC: Smithsonian Institution, United States Government Printing Office.

de Smet, Pierre-Jean. 1905. *Life, Letters and Travels of Father Pierre-Jean De Smet, S.J.*, vol. 3, edited by Hiram M. Chittenden and Alfred T. Richardson. New York: Francis P. Harper.

Det Kongelige Bibliotek. 2011. e-manuskripter: NKS 565 4°: Von Reck's drawings. Center for Manuscripts and Rare Books, Det Kongelige Bibliotek, Copenhagen. Electronic document. http://www.kb.dk/permalink/2006/manus/22/eng/.

Deter-Wolf, Aaron. 2013. The Material Culture and Middle Stone Age Origins of Ancient Tattooing. In *Tattoos and Body Modifications in Antiquity: Proceedings of the Sessions at the Annual Meetings of the European Association of Archaeologists in The Hague and Oslo, 2010–11*, edited by Philippe Della Casa and Constanze Witt. Zurich Studies in Archaeology 9. Zurich: University of Zurich.

Deter-Wolf, Aaron, and Tanya M. Peres. 2013. Flint, Bone, and Thorns: Using Ethno-historical Data, Experimental Archaeology, and Microscopy to Examine Ancient Tattooing in Eastern North America. In *Tattoos and Body Modifications in Antiquity: Proceedings of the Sessions at the Annual Meetings of the European Association of Archaeologists in The Hague and Oslo, 2010–11*, edited by Philippe Della Casa and Constanze Witt. Zurich Studies in Archaeology 9. Zurich: University of Zurich.

Diaz-Granados, Carol. 2004. Marking Stone, Land, Body, and Spirit: Rock Art and Mississippian Iconography. In *Hero, Hawk, and Open Hand: American Indian Art of the Ancient Midwest and South*, edited by Richard F. Townsend and Robert V. Sharp, pp. 138–149. New Haven, CT: Art Institute of Chicago and Yale University Press.

———. 2011. Early Manifestations of Mississippian Iconography in Middle Mississippi Valley Rock-Art. In *Visualizing the Sacred: Cosmic Visions, Regionalism, and the Art of the Mississippian World*, edited by George E. Lankford, F. Kent Reilly III, and James F. Garber, pp. 64–95. Austin: University of Texas Press.

Diaz-Granados, Carol, and James R. Duncan. 2004. Reflections of Power, Wealth, and Sex in Missouri Rock-Art Motifs. In *The Rock-Art of Eastern North America*, edited by Carol Diaz-Granados and James R. Duncan, pp. 145–158. Tuscaloosa: University of Alabama Press.

Diaz-Granados, Carol, Marvin W. Rowe, Marian Hyman, James R. Duncan, and John R. Southon. 2001. AMS Radiocarbon Dates for Charcoal from Three Missouri Pictographs and Their Associated Iconography. *American Antiquity* 66(3):481–493.

d'Iberville, Pierre Le Moyne Sieur. 1880. Journal de la Navigation de Lemoyne d'Iberville aux Cotes Septentrionales du Golfe du Mexique pour L'occupation du Mississipi. (Décembre 1868–3 Mai 1699). In *Découvertes et établissements des Français dans l'ouest et dans le sud de l'Amérique Septentrionale (1614–1754)*, vol. 4, edited by Pierre Margry, pp. 129–209. Paris: D. Jouaust.

Dièreville, Sieur de. 1933 [1708]. *Relation of the Voyage to Port Royal in Acadia or New France*. Translated by Mrs. Clarence Webster, edited by John Clarence Webster. Toronto: Champlain Society.

Din, Gilbert C., and Abraham Nasatir. 1983. *The Imperial Osages: Spanish-Indian Diplomacy in the Mississippi Valley*. Norman: University of Oklahoma Press.

Dorsey, J. Owen. 1885a. Mourning and War Customs of the Kansas. *American Naturalist* 19(7):670–680.

——. 1885b. Osage Traditions. In *Sixth Annual Report of the Bureau of Ethnology, 1884–1885*, pp. 373–397. Washington, DC: Smithsonian Institution, United States Government Printing Office.

——. 1889. Teton Folk-Lore. *American Anthropologist* 2(2):143–158.

——. 1890. Omaha Clothing and Personal Ornaments. *American Anthropologist* 3(1):71–78.

——. 1894. A Study of Siouan Cults. In *Eleventh Annual Report of the Bureau of Ethnology, 1889–1890*, pp. 351–553. Washington, DC: Smithsonian Institution, United States Government Printing Office.

Dragoo, Don W. 1963. *Mounds for the Dead: An Analysis of the Adena Culture*. Annals of the Carnegie Museum, vol. 37. Pittsburgh: Carnegie Museum.

Dumont de Montigny, Jean-François Benjamin. 1753. *Mémoires Historiques sur la Louisiane*. Vol. 1. Paris: C. J. B. Bauche.

Duncan, James R. 2011. The Cosmology of the Osage: The Star People and Their Universe. In *Visualizing the Sacred: Cosmic Visions, Regionalism, and the Art of the Mississippian World*, edited by George E. Lankford, F. Kent Reilly III, and James F. Garber, pp. 18–33. Austin: University of Texas Press.

Duncan, James R., and Carol Diaz-Granados. 2000. Of Masks and Myths. *Midcontinental Journal of Archaeology* 25:1–26.

——. 2004. Empowering the SECC: The "Old Woman" and Oral Tradition. In

The Rock-Art of Eastern North America, edited by Carol Diaz-Granados and James R. Duncan, pp. 191–215. Tuscaloosa: University of Alabama Press.

Ebin, Victoria. 1979. *The Body Decorated*. London: Thames and Hudson.

Edwards, Tai S. 2010. "Osage Gender: Continuity, Change, and Colonization, 1720s–1870s." PhD diss., Department of History, University of Kansas. Publication no. 3408041, ProQuest/UMI, Ann Arbor, MI.

El-Najjar, Mahmoud Y., Thomas M. J., Mulinski, and Karl J. Reinhard. 1998. Mummies and Mummification Practices in the Southern and Southwestern United States. In *Mummies, Disease, and Ancient Culture*, edited by Aidan Cockburn, Eve Cockburn, and Theodore A. Reyman, pp. 121–137. Cambridge, UK: Cambridge University Press.

Elvas, Gentleman of. 1686 [1557]. *A Relation of the Invasion and Conquest of Florida by the Spaniards under the Command of Fernando de Soto*. London: John Lawrence.

———. 1850 [1557]. A Narrative of the Expedition of Hernando de Soto into Florida. Translated by Richard Hakluyt (1609). In *Historical Collections of Louisiana*, vol. 2, edited by Benjamin Franklin French, pp. 114–222. Philadelphia: Daniels and Smith.

———. 1993 [1557]. True Relation of the Hardships Suffered by Governor Hernando de Soto. . . . Translated and edited by James Alexander Robertson. In *The de Soto Chronicles: The Expedition of Hernando de Soto to North America in 1539–1543*, vol. 1, edited by Lawrence A. Clayton, Vernon James Knight, Jr., and Edward C. Moore, pp. 25–170. Tuscaloosa: University of Alabama Press.

Farrer, Claire R., and Ray A. Williamson. 1992. Epilogue: Blue Archaeoastronomy. In *Earth and Sky: Visions of the Cosmos in Native American Folklore*, edited by Ray A. Williamson and Claire R. Farrer, pp. 278–289. Albuquerque: University of New Mexico Press.

Feest, Christian F. 2002. Quilled Knife Cases from Northeastern North America. In *Anthropology, History, and American Indians: Essays in Honor of William Curtis Sturtevant*, edited by William L. Merrill and Ives Goddard, pp. 263–278. Smithsonian Contributions to Anthropology 44. Washington, DC: United States Government Printing Office.

Fenton, William N. 1942. Contacts between Iroquois Herbalism and Colonial Medicine. In *Annual Report of the Smithsonian Institution for 1941*, pp. 503–526. Washington, DC: Smithsonian Institution, United States Government Printing Office.

———. 1953. Cultural Stability and Change in American Indian Societies. *The Journal of the Royal Anthropological Institute of Great Britain and Ireland* 83(2):169–174.

———. 1977. [Editorial Comment]. In *Customs of the American Indians Compared with the Customs of Primitive Tribes*, vol. 2, by Joseph-François Lafitau [1724], translated and edited by William Nelson Fenton and Elizabeth L. Moore, p. 36. Toronto: Champlain Society.

———. 1978. Northern Iroquoian Culture Patterns. In *Northeast*, edited by Bruce G. Trigger, pp. 296–321. *Handbook of North American Indians*, vol. 15, William

C. Sturtevant, general editor. Washington, DC: Smithsonian Institution, United States Government Printing Office.

Fernández de Oviedo y Valdés, Gonzalo. 1851. *Historia General y Natural de las Indias, Primera Parte*. Edited by D. José Amadon de los Rios. Madrid: Real Academia de la Historia.

Filson, John. 2006 [1784]. *The Discovery, Settlement and Present State of Kentucke (1784): An Online Electronic Text Edition*, edited by Paul Royster. Electronic Texts in American Studies, Paper 3. Lincoln: Digital Commons, University of Nebraska. http://digitalcommons.unl.edu/etas/3.

Firth, Raymond. 1937. Tattooing in Tikopia. *Man* 36:173–177.

Fleming, Juliet. 2000. The Renaissance Tattoo. In *Written on the Body: The Tattoo in European and American History*, edited by Jane Caplan, pp. 61–82. Princeton, NJ: Princeton University Press.

Fletcher, Alice C. 1893. Personal Studies of Indian Life: Politics and "Pipe-Dancing." *Century Magazine* 45:441–455.

———. 1994. *A Study of Omaha Indian Music*. Lincoln: University of Nebraska Press.

Fletcher, Alice C., and Francis La Flesche. 1911. The Omaha Tribe. In *Twenty-Seventh Annual Report of the Bureau of American Ethnology, 1905–1906*, pp. 17–672. Washington, DC: Smithsonian Institution, United States Government Printing Office.

———. 1992. *The Omaha Tribe*. 2 vols. Lincoln: University of Nebraska Press.

Florida Center for Instructional Technology. 2001. *Exploring Florida: Jacques Le Moyne Engravings*. College of Education, University of South Florida, Tampa. Electronic document. http://fcit.usf.edu/florida/photos/native/lemoyne/lemoyne.htm.

Fogelson, Raymond D., and Robert A. Brightman. 2002. Totemism Reconsidered. In *Anthropology, History, and American Indians: Essays in Honor of William Curtis Sturtevant*, edited by William L. Merrill and Ives Goddard, pp. 305–313, Smithsonian Contributions to Anthropology 44. Washington, DC: Smithsonian Institution Press.

Foreman, Carolyn T. 1943. *Indians Abroad, 1493–1938*. Norman: University of Oklahoma Press.

Fortuine, Robert. 1985. Lancets of Stone: Traditional Methods of Surgery among the Alaska Natives. *Arctic Anthropology* 22(1):23–45.

Fortune, Reo F. 1932. *Omaha Secret Societies*. Columbia University Contributions to Anthropology 14. New York: Columbia University Press.

Foster, Lance M. 1994. "Sacred Bundles of the Ioway Indians." Unpublished master's thesis, Department of Anthropology, Iowa State University, Ames.

———. 2007. *Ioway Culture Institute: Culture: Ancestral Ways of Life. Baxoje Ukich'e: The Ioway Nation*. Electronic document. http://ioway.nativeweb.org/culture/tattooing.htm.

Foster, William C. 1995. *Spanish Expeditions into Texas, 1689–1768*. Austin: University of Texas Press.

Frazer, James G. 1911. Taboo and the Perils of the Soul. *The Golden Bough: A Study in Magic and Religion*. Part 2. London: Macmillan.

Friedman Herlihy, Anna F. 2012. "Tattooed Transculturites: Western Expatriates among Amerindian and Pacific Islander Societies, 1500–1900." PhD diss., Committee on the History of Culture, University of Chicago. Publication no. 3517150, ProQuest/UMI, Ann Arbor, MI.

Fundaburk, Emma L. 1958. *Southeastern Indians Life Portraits: A Catalogue of Pictures, 1564–1860*. Luverne, AL: Emma L. Fundaburk.

Fundaburk, Emma L., and Mary D. F. Foreman, eds. 1957. *Sun Circles and Human Hands: The Southeastern Indians Art and Industry*. Luverne, AL: Emma L. Fundaburk.

Gaffarel, Paul, ed. 1875. *Histoire de la Floride Française*. Paris: Librairie Firmin-Didot et cie.

Gallay, Alan. 2002. *The Indian Slave Trade*. New Haven, CT: Yale University Press.

Gangloff, Deborah. 1995. "Dual Organization: A Symbolic Analysis of the Omaha Shell Society." PhD diss., Department of Anthropology, Rutgers University. Publication no. 9524180, ProQuest/UMI, Ann Arbor, MI.

Gatschet, Albert S. 1882. The Shetimasha Indians of St. Mary's Parish, Southern Louisiana. *Transactions of the Anthropological Society of Washington* 2:148–159.

Gaudio, Michael. 2008. *Engraving the Savage: The New World and Techniques of Civilization*. Minneapolis: University of Minnesota Press.

Gell, Alfred. 1993. *Wrapping in Images: Tattooing in Polynesia*. Oxford, UK: Clarendon Press.

———. 1998. *Art and Agency: An Anthropological Theory*. Oxford, UK: Clarendon Press.

Gertsch, Willis J., and Norman I. Platnick. 1980. A Revision of the American Spiders of the Family Atypidae (Araneae, Mygalomorphae). *American Museum Novitates* no. 2704:1–39.

Giles, Bretton T. 2010. "The Ritual Mnemonics of Hopewell Symbols: An Analysis of Effigies and Ceremonial Regalia from Tremper, Mound City, and Hopewell." PhD diss., Department of Anthropology, State University of New York at Binghamton. Publication no. 3434600, ProQuest/UMI, Ann Arbor, MI.

Goodtracks, Jimm G. 2002a. Ioway-Otoe-Missouria Indian Traditional Stories: Buffalo Clan Origin Legend. Jimm G. Goodtracks Baxoje-Jiwere Language Project, Lawrence, KS. Electronic document. http://www.iowayotoelang.nativeweb.org/pdf/buffaloclanoriginlegend.pdf.

———. 2002b. Ioway-Otoe-Missouria Indian Traditional Stories: Wolf Clan Origin Legend. Jimm G. Goodtracks Baxoje-Jiwere Language Project, Lawrence, KS. Electronic document. http://www.iowayotoelang.nativeweb.org/pdf/wolfclanorigin legend.pdf.

———. 2009. Ioway-Otoe-Missouria Indian Traditional Stories: Eagle-Thunder and Pigeon Clan Origin Legend. Jimm G. Goodtracks Baxoje-Jiwere Language

Project, Lawrence, KS. Electronic document. http://www.iowayotoelang.native web.org/pdf/eaglepigeonclanoriginlegend_nov2009.pdf

Goodyear, Albert C. 2009a. Interview in "Time Team America: Topper, South Carolina." Public Broadcasting System. Produced by Graham Dixon. Original air date July 15, 2009.

————. 2009b. Update on Research at the Topper Site. *Legacy* 13(1):8–13. Electronic document. http://www.cas.sc.edu/sciaa/legacy/legacy_v13n1.pdf.

Gravatt, Patricia. 2007. Rereading Theodore de Bry's Black Legend. In *Rereading the Black Legend: The Discourses of Religious and Racial Difference in the Renaissance Empires*, edited by Margaret R. Greer, Walter Mignolo, and Maureen Quilligan, pp. 225–243. Chicago: University of Chicago Press.

Gravier, Jacques. 1900 [1861]. Relation or Journal of the Voyage of Father Gravier, of the Society of Jesus. . . . In *The Jesuit Relations and Allied Documents . . ., Vol. LXV: Lower Canada, Mississippi Valley, 1696–1702*, translated and edited by Ruben Gold Thwaites, pp. 100–179. Cleveland, OH: Burrows Brothers.

Greber, N'omi. 1983. *Recent Excavations at the Edwin Harness Mound, Liberty Works, Ross County, Ohio*. Mid-Continental Journal of Archaeology, Special Publication 5. Kent, OH: Kent State University Press.

Green, Roger C. 1979a. Early Lapita Art from Polynesia and Island Melanesia: Continuities in Ceramic, Barkcloth, and Tattoo Decorations. In *Exploring the Visual Art of Oceania: Australia, Melanesia, and Polynesia*, edited by Sidney M. Mead, pp. 13–31. Honolulu: University of Hawai'i Press.

————. 1979b. Lapita. In *The Prehistory of Polynesia*, edited by Jesse D. Jennings, pp. 27–60. Cambridge, MA: Harvard University Press.

Greene, Hazel B. 1937. Hunter, Thomas W. Third Interview. Indian Pioneer Papers, Interview ID 12443. Vol. 46, pp. 101–107. University of Oklahoma Libraries Western History Collections, Norman.

Haddon, Ernest B. 1905. The Dog-Motive in Bornean Art. *The Journal of the Anthropological Institute of Great Britain and Ireland* 35:113–125.

Hagstrum, Melissa. 2001. Household Production in Chaco Canyon Society. *American Antiquity* 66(1):47–55.

Haines, Helen R., Philip W. Wilink, and David Maxwell. 2008. Stingray Spine Use and Maya Bloodletting Rituals: A Cautionary Tale. *Latin American Antiquity* 19(1):83–98.

Hall, Robert L. 1979. In Search of the Ideology of the Adena-Hopewell Climax. In *Hopewell Archaeology: The Chillicothe Conference*, edited by David S. Brose and N'omi Greber, pp. 258–265. Kent, OH: Kent State University Press.

————. 1997. *An Archaeology of the Soul: North American Indian Belief and Ritual*. Urbana: University of Illinois Press.

————. 2004. The Cahokia Site and Its People. In *Hero, Hawk, and Open Hand: American Indian Art of the Ancient Midwest and South*, edited by Richard F. Townsend and Robert V. Sharp, pp. 92–103. New Haven, CT: Art Institute of Chicago and Yale University Press.

Hambly, Wilfrid Dyson. 2009 [1925]. *The History of Tattooing*. Reprinted from *The History of Tattooing and Its Significance*. London: H. F. and G. Witherby; Mineola, NY: Dover.

Handy, Willowdean C. 1922. *Tattooing in the Marquesas*. Bernice P. Bishop Museum Bulletin 1. Honolulu: Bernice P. Bishop Museum.

Hanson, Jeffrey R. 1980. Structure and Complexity of Medicine Bundle Systems of Selected Plains Indian Tribes. *Plains Anthropologist* 25(89):199–216.

Hariot, Thomas. 2003 [1590]. *A Briefe and True Report of the New Found Land of Virginia*. Translated by Richard Hakluyt. University of North Carolina at Chapel Hill. Electronic document. http://docsouth.unc.edu/nc/hariot/hariot.html.

Harrington, Mark R. 1913. A Visit to the Otoe Indians. *The Museum Journal, University of Pennsylvania* 4(3):107–113.

Harvey, Miles. 2008. *Painter in a Savage Land: The Strange Saga of the First European Artist in North America*. New York: Random House.

Heckewelder, John Gottlieb Ernestus. 1876 [1818]. *History, Manners, and Customs of the Indian Nations Who Once Inhabited Pennsylvania and the Neighboring States*. Memoirs of the Historical Society of Pennsylvania. Vol. 12. Philadelphia: Historical Society of Pennsylvania.

Henning, Dale R. 1970. Development and Interrelationships of Oneota Culture in the Lower Missouri River Valley. *Missouri Archaeologist* 32.

———. 1993. The Adaptive Patterning of the Dhegiha Sioux. *Plains Anthropologist* 38:253–264.

Henry, Alexander (the Elder). 1809. *Travels and Adventures in Canada and the Indian Territories between the Years 1760 and 1776*. New York: I. Riley.

Henry, Alexander (the Younger). 1988. *The Journal of Alexander Henry the Younger, 1799–1814*. Vol. 1. Edited by Barry M. Gough. Toronto: Champlain Society.

Hitchcock, Ethan A. 1930. *A Traveler in Indian Territory: The Journal of Ethan Allen Hitchcock, Late Major-General in the United States Army*. Edited by Grant Foreman. Cedar Rapids, IA: Torch Press.

Hodder, Ian. 1977. The Distribution of Material Culture Items in the Baringo District, Western Kenya. *Man* 12(2):239–269.

———. 1979. Economic and Social Stress and Material Culture Patterning. *American Antiquity* 44:446–454.

———. 1982. *Symbols in Action: Ethnoarchaeological Studies of Material Culture*. Cambridge, UK: Cambridge University Press.

Holmes, William H. 1883. Art in Shell of the Ancient Americans. In *Second Annual Report of the Bureau of Ethnology, 1880–1881*, pp. 179–305. Washington, DC: United States Government Printing Office.

Horse Capture, George P. 1993. Gallery of Hides. In *Robes of Splendor: Native American Painted Buffalo Hides*, pp. 93–140. New York: New Press.

Hose, Charles, and R. Shelford. 1906. Materials for a Study of Tatu in Borneo. *The Journal of the Anthropological Institute of Great Britain and Ireland* 36:60–91.

Howard, James H. 1956. The Persistence of Southern Cult Gorgets among the Historic Kansa. *American Antiquity* 21(3):301–303.

———. 1995. *The Ponca Tribe*. Lincoln: University of Nebraska Press.

Hubley, Adam. 1909. Adam Hubley, Jr., Lt. Col. Comdt. 11th Penna. Regt., His Journal, Commencing at Wyoming, July 30th, 1779, edited by John W. Jordan. *Pennsylvania Magazine of History and Biography* 33(2):129–146, 279–302, 409–422.

Hudson, Charles. 1976. *The Southeastern Indians*. Knoxville: University of Tennessee Press.

———. 1997. *Knights of Spain, Warriors of the Sun: Hernando de Soto and the South's Ancient Chiefdoms*. Athens: University of Georgia Press.

Hultkrantz, Åke. 1953. *Conceptions of the Soul among North American Indians: A Study in Religious Ethnology*. Monograph series no. 1. Stockholm: Ethnographical Museum of Sweden.

———. 1973. *Prairie and Plains Indians*. Vol. 2 of *Iconography of Religions, North America*. Institute of Religious Iconography, State University of Groningen. Leiden: E. J. Brill.

Hulton, Paul. 1984. *America 1585: The Complete Drawings of John White*. Chapel Hill: University of North Carolina Press and British Museum Publications.

Hunt, David C., and Marsha V. Gallagher. 1984. The Plates: Annotations. In *Karl Bodmer's America*, pp. 25–348. Omaha: Joslyn Art Museum.

Hvidt, Kristen, ed. 1980. *Von Reck's Voyage: Drawings and Journal of Philip Georg Friedrich von Reck*. Savannah: Beehive Press.

Hyde, William. 1965. The Hyde Manuscript. *American Scene Magazine* 6(2).

Isham, James. 1949. *James Isham's Observations on Hudson's Bay, 1743, and Notes and Observations on a Book entitled "A Voyage to Hudson's Bay in the Dobbs Galley, 1749."* Edited by E. E. Rich. Toronto: Champlain Society.

Jackson, H. Edwin, and Susan L. Scott. 1998. *Faunal Utilization by the Moundville Elite: Zooarchaeology of Mounds Q, G, E, F, and R*. Manuscript on file, Department of Anthropology, University of Alabama, Tuscaloosa.

———. 2002. Appendix E. Faunal Utilization by the Moundville Elite: Zooarchaeology of Mounds Q, G, E, F, R, and H. In *Chronology and Use of Public Architecture at the Moundville Site: Excavations in Mound Q*, by Vernon J. Knight. Report submitted to the National Science Foundation, Award nos. 9220568 and 9727709. Manuscript on file, Department of Anthropology, University of Alabama, Tuscaloosa.

———. 2003. Patterns of Elite Faunal Utilization at Moundville, Alabama. *American Antiquity* 68(3):552–572.

James, Edwin. 1905 [1823]. *Account of an Expedition from Pittsburgh to the Rocky Mountains, Performed in the Years 1819, 1820*. Vol. 2. Edited by Ruben Gold Thwaites. Cleveland, OH: Arthur H. Clark.

Jamieson, James B. 1983. An Examination of Prisoner-Sacrifice and Cannibalism at the St. Lawrence Iroquoian Roebuck Site. *Canadian Journal of Archaeology* 7(2):159–176.

Jefferies, Richard W. 1976. *The Tunnacunnhee Site: Evidence of Hopewell Interaction in Northwest Georgia*. Anthropological Papers of the University of Georgia 1, Athens.

Jensen, Erik. 1974. The *Iban and Their Religion*. Oxford, UK: Oxford University Press.

Jogues, Isaac. 1857 [1643]. *The Jogues Papers*. Collections of the New-York Historical Society. Vol. 3. Translated by John G. Shea, pp. 161–229. New York: D. Appleton.

Jones, C. P. 2000. Stigma and Tattoo. In *Written on the Body: The Tattoo in European and American History*, edited by Jane Caplan, pp. 1–18. Princeton, NJ: Princeton University Press.

Joutel, Henri. 1906 [1714]. *Joutel's Journal of La Salle's Last Voyage: 1684–7*. Edited by Henry Reed Stiles. Albany: Joseph McDonough.

———. 1998 [1714]. *The La Salle Expedition to Texas: The Journal of Henri Joutel, 1684–1687*. Translated by Johanna S. Warren and edited by William C. Foster. Denton: Texas State Historical Association.

Jouvency, Joseph. 1896. Concerning the Country and Manners of the Canadians or Savages of New France. In *The Jesuit Relations and Allied Documents . . ., Vol. I: Acadia, 1610–1613*, translated and edited by Ruben Gold Thwaites, pp. 239–298. Cleveland, OH: Burrows Brothers.

Jury, Wilfred. 1941. *Clearville Prehistoric Village Site in Orford Township, Kent County, Ontario*. Bulletin of the Museums no. 2. Ontario: University of Western Ontario.

Kalm, Peter. 1812 [1749]. Peter Kalm's Travels. In *General Collection of the Best and Most Interesting Voyages and Travels in All Parts of the World. . . .*, translated and edited by John Pinkerton, pp. 545–700. London: Longman, Hurst, Rees, Orme, and Brown.

Kehoe, Alice B. 1970. The Function of Ceremonial Sexual Intercourse among the Northern Plains Indians. *Plains Anthropologist* 15:99–103.

———. 2007. Osage Texts and Cahokia Data. In *Ancient Objects and Sacred Realms: Interpretations of Mississippian Iconography*, edited by F. Kent Reilly III and James F. Garber, pp. 246–261. Austin: University of Texas Press.

Keith, Scot J. 2010. *Archaeological Data Recovery at the Leake Site, Bartow County, Georgia*. Report prepared by Southern Research, Historic Preservation Consultants, Inc., Ellerslie, GA, submitted to Georgia Department of Transportation, Office of Environmental Services, Atlanta.

Kellar, James H. 1979. The Mann Site and "Hopewell" in the Lower Wabash-Ohio Valley. In *Hopewell Archaeology: The Chillicothe Conference*, edited by David S. Brose and N'omi Greber, pp. 100–107. Kent, OH: Kent State University Press.

Kellar, James H., A. R. Kelly, and Edward V. McMichael. 1962. The Mandeville Site in Southwest Georgia. *American Antiquity* 27(3):336–355.

King, Adam. 2004. Power and the Sacred: Mound C and the Etowah Chiefdom. In *Hero, Hawk, and Open Hand: American Indian Art of the Ancient Midwest and South*, edited by Richard F. Townsend and Robert V. Sharp, pp. 150–165. New Haven, CT: Art Institute of Chicago and Yale University Press.

King, Jonathan C. H. 1999. *First Peoples, First Contacts: Native Peoples of North America*. London: British Museum Press.

Kinietz, W. Vernon. 1965. *The Indians of the Western Great Lakes, 1615–1760*. Ann Arbor: University of Michigan Press.

Kirch, Patrick V. 1997. *The Lapita Peoples: Ancestors of the Oceanic World*. Cambridge, MA: Blackwell.

Knight, Vernon James. 1989. Some Speculations on Mississippian Monsters. In *The Southeastern Ceremonial Complex: Artifacts and Analysis*, edited by Patricia K. Galloway, pp. 205–210. Lincoln: University of Nebraska Press.

———. 2004. Characterizing Elite Midden Deposits at Moundville. *American Antiquity* 69(2):304–321.

———. 2010. *Mound Excavations at Moundville: Architecture, Elites, and Social Order*. Tuscaloosa: University of Alabama Press.

Knight, Vernon James, and Judith A. Franke. 2007. Identification of a Moth/Butterfly Supernatural in Mississippian Art. In *Ancient Objects and Sacred Realms: Interpretations of Mississippian Iconography*, edited by F. Kent Reilly III, and James F. Garber, pp. 136–151. Austin: University of Texas Press.

Kohl, Johann G. 1985 [1854]. *Kitchi-Gami: Life among the Lake Superior Ojibway*. Translated by Lascelles Wraxall. St. Paul: Minnesota Historical Society Press.

Kononenko, Nina. 2012. Middle and Late Holocene skin-working tools in Melanesia: Tattooing and Scarification? *Archaeology in Oceania* (47)1:14–28.

Krech, Shepard III. 2009. *Spirits of the Air: Birds and American Indians in the South*. Athens: University of Georgia Press.

Krutak, Lars. 2005. North America's Tattooed Indian Kings. Electronic document. http://www.larskrutak.com/articles/Indian_Kings/index.html.

———. 2006a. At the Tail of the Dragon: The Vanishing Tattoos of China's Li People. Electronic document. http://www.larskrutak.com/articles/Li/index.html.

———. 2006b. The Mundurucú: Tattooed Warriors of the Amazon Jungle. Electronic document. http://www.larskrutak.com/articles/Mundurucu/index.html.

———. 2007. *The Tattooing Arts of Tribal Women*. London: Bennett and Bloom.

———. 2008a. The Kayabi: Tattooers of the Brazilian Amazon. Electronic document. http://www.larskrutak.com/articles/Kayabi/index.html.

———. 2008b. Many Stitches for Life: The Antiquity of Thread and Needle Tattooing. Electronic document. http://www.larskrutak.com/articles/Thread_Needle/index.html.

———. 2010. *Kalinga Tattoo: Ancient and Modern Expressions of the Tribal*. Aschaffenburg, Germany: Edition Reuss.

Kuhlemann, Ute. 2007. Between Reproduction, Invention, and Propaganda: Theodore de Bry's Engravings after John White's Watercolours. In *A New World: England's First View of America*, by Kim Sloan, pp. 79–92. Chapel Hill: University of North Carolina Press.

Kurz, Rudolph Friederich. 1937. *Journal of Rudolph Friederich Kurz: An Account of*

His Experiences among fur Traders and American Indians. . . . Translated by Myrtis Jarrell and edited by John N. B. Hewitt. Bureau of American Ethnology Bulletin 115. Washington, DC: Smithsonian Institution, United States Government Printing Office.

Lafitau, Joseph François. 1977 [1724]. *Customs of the American Indians Compared with Customs of Primitive Times.* Vol. 2. Translated and edited by William Nelson Fenton and Elizabeth L. Moore. Toronto: Champlain Society.

La Flesche, Francis. 1914. Ceremonies and Rituals of the Osage. *Smithsonian Miscellaneous Collections* 63(8):66–69.

———. 1916. Right and Left in Osage Ceremonies. In *Holmes Anniversary Volume: Anthropological Essays Presented to William Henry Holmes in Honor of His Seventieth Birthday, December 1, 1916,* pp. 278–287. Washington, DC: J. W. Bryan Press.

———. 1917. Tribal Rites of the Osage Indians. *Smithsonian Miscellaneous Collections* 68(12):84–90.

———. 1920. The Symbolic Man of the Osage Tribe. *Art and Archaeology* 9:68–72.

———. 1921a. The Osage Tribe: Rite of the Chiefs; Sayings of the Ancient Men. In *Thirty-Sixth Annual Report of the Bureau of American Ethnology, 1914–1915,* pp. 37–640. Washington, DC: Smithsonian Institution, United States Government Printing Office.

———. 1921b. Researches among the Osage. *Smithsonian Miscellaneous Collections* 70(2):110–113.

———. 1925. The Osage Tribe: The Rite of Vigil. In *Thirty-Ninth Annual Report of the Bureau of American Ethnology, 1917–1918,* pp. 31–630. Washington, DC: Smithsonian Institution, United States Government Printing Office.

———. 1928. The Osage Tribe: Two Versions of the Child-Naming Rite. In *Forty-Third Annual Report of the Bureau of American Ethnology, 1925–1926,* pp. 23–164. Washington, DC: Smithsonian Institution, United States Government Printing Office.

———. 1930. The Osage Tribe: Rite of the Wa-xo'Be. In *Forty-Fifth Annual Report of the Bureau of American Ethnology, 1927–1928,* pp. 523–833. Washington, DC: Smithsonian Institution, United States Government Printing Office.

———. 1932. *A Dictionary of the Osage Language.* Bureau of American Ethnology Bulletin 109. Washington, DC: Smithsonian Institution, United States Government Printing Office.

———. 1939. *War Ceremony and Peace Ceremony of the Osage Indians.* Bureau of American Ethnology Bulletin 101. Washington, DC: Smithsonian Institution, United States Government Printing Office.

Lalemant, Jerome. 1899. Relation of 1662–63. In *The Jesuit Relations and Allied Documents . . ., Vol. XLVIII: Lower Canada, Ottawas, 1662–1664,* pp. 17–179, translated and edited by Ruben Gold Thwaites. Cleveland, OH: Burrows Brothers.

Landa, Diego de. 1864. *Relation des Choses de Yucatan de Diego de Landa.* Edited by Brasseur de Bourgourg. Paris: Auguste Durand.

Lang, Sabine. 1998. *Men as Women, Women as Men*. Austin: University of Texas Press.

Lankford, George E. 2004. World on a String: Some Cosmological Components of the Southeastern Ceremonial Complex. In *Hero, Hawk, and Open Hand: American Indian Art of the Ancient Midwest and South*, edited by Richard F. Townsend and Robert V. Sharp, pp. 206–217. New Haven, CT: Art Institute of Chicago and Yale University Press.

———. 2007a. The Great Serpent in Eastern North America. In *Ancient Objects and Sacred Realms: Interpretations of Mississippian Iconography*, edited by F. Kent Reilly III and James F. Garber, pp. 107–135. Austin: University of Texas Press.

———. 2007b. The "Path of Souls": Some Death Imagery in the Southeastern Ceremonial Complex. In *Ancient Objects and Sacred Realms: Interpretations of Mississippian Iconography*, edited by F. Kent Reilly III and James F. Garber, pp. 174–212. Austin: University of Texas Press.

———. 2007c. *Reachable Stars: Patterns in the Ethnoastronomy of Eastern North America*. Tuscaloosa: University of Alabama Press.

Laudonnière, René Goulaine de. 2001 [1586]. *Three Voyages*. Translated and edited by Charles E. Bennett. Tuscaloosa: University of Alabama Press.

Lederer, John. 1902 [1672]. *The Discoveries of John Lederer*. Translated and edited by Sir William Talbot Baronet. Rochester, NY: George P. Humphrey.

Leigh, Steven R. 1988. Comparative Analysis of the Elizabeth Middle Woodland Artifact Assemblage. In *The Archaic and Woodland Cemeteries at the Elizabeth Site in the Lower Illinois Valley*, edited by Douglas K. Charles, Steven R. Leigh, and Jane E. Buikstra, pp. 191–217. Research series vol. 7. Kampsville, IL: Center for American Archeology.

Le Page du Pratz, Antoine Simone. 1947 [1758]. *The History of Louisiana or of the Western Parts of Virginia and Carolina*. New Orleans: Pelican Press.

Light, Douglas W. 1972. *Tattooing Practices of the Cree Indians*. Glenbow-Alberta Institute Occasional Paper 6. Calgary.

Long, John. 1791. *Voyages and Travels of an Indian Interpreter and Trader*. London: Printed for the Author.

Lorant, Stefan, ed. 1965. *The New World, The First Pictures of America, Made by John White and Jacques Le Moyne and Engraved by Theodore de Bry*. New York: Duell, Sloan and Pearce.

Loskiel, George Henry. 1794 [1789]. *History of the Mission of the United Brethren among the Indians in North America*. Translated by Christian Ignatius La Trobe. London: Brethren Society for the Furtherance of the Gospel.

Lurie, Nancy O., ed. 1966. *Mountain Wolf Woman, Sister of Crashing Thunder: The Autobiography of a Winnebago Indian*. Ann Arbor: University of Michigan Press.

Maika, Monica. 2010. Gravers: Paleo-Indian Expedient Technology in the Great Lakes? *Vis-à-Vis: Explorations in Anthropology* 10(2):60–76.

Mainfort, Robert C. 1986. *Pinson Mounds: A Middle Woodland Ceremonial Center*.

Research series no. 7. Nashville: Tennessee Department of Conservation, Division of Archaeology.

Major, Richard Henry, ed. 1870. *Select Letters of Christopher Columbus with Other Original Documents Relating to His Four Voyages to the New World.* 2nd ed. Translated by R. H. Major. London: Hakluyt Society.

Mallery, Garrick. 1886. Pictographs of the North American Indians: A Preliminary Paper. In *Fourth Annual Report of the Bureau of American Ethnology, 1882–1883*, pp. 13–264. Washington, DC: United States Government Printing Office.

———. 1893. Picture-Writing of the American Indian. In *Tenth Annual Report of the Bureau of American Ethnology, 1888–1889*, pp. 25–807. Washington, DC: United States Government Printing Office.

Marest, Gabriel. 1931. Letter from Father Marest, Missionary of the Company of Jesus, to Father De Lamberville of the Company of Jesus, Overseer of the Missions of Canada. In *Documents Relating to the Early History of Hudson Bay*, edited by Joseph Burr Tyrrell, pp. 103–142. Toronto: Champlain Society.

Margry, Pierre, ed. 1878. *Découvertes et établissements des Français dans l'ouest et dans le sud de l'Amérique Septentrionale (1614–1754).* Vol. 3. Paris: D. Jouaust.

Marquette, Jacques. 1873 [1681]. *Recit des Voyages et des Découvertes du R. Père Jacques Marquette.* Albany, NY: Weed, Parsons.

———. 1900 [1681]. Of the First Voyage Made by Father Marquette toward New Mexico, and How the Idea Thereof was Conceived. In *The Jesuit Relations and Allied Documents . . ., Vol. LIX: Lower Canada, Illinois, Ottawas, 1667–1669*, translated and edited by Ruben Gold Thwaites, pp. 85–164. Cleveland, OH: Burrows Brothers.

Mathews, John J. 1961. *The Osages: Children of the Middle Waters.* Norman: University of Oklahoma Press.

Mathur, K. S. 1954. Female Tattooing among the Tribes of Dudhi. *Man* 54:139–141.

McClane, Albert J. 1978. *McClane's Field Guide to Freshwater Fishes of North America.* New York: Henry Holt.

McGrath, John T. 2000. *The French in Early Florida: In the Eye of the Storm.* Tallahassee: University of Florida Press.

Meachum, Scott. 2007. "Markes upon Their Clubhamers": Interpreting Pictography on Eastern War Clubs. In *Three Centuries of Woodlands Indian Art*, edited by J. C. H. King and Christian F. Feest, pp. 67–74. Altenstadt, Germany: ZKF Publishers.

Megapolensis, Johannes. 1857 [1644]. A Short Sketch of the Mohawk Indians in New Netherland: Their Lands, Stature, Dress, and Magistrates, Written in the Year 1644. In *Collections of the New York Historical Society*, vol. 3, pp. 137–160. New York: D. Appleton.

Mercyhurst College. 2006. National Geographic Documentary Highlights 'Hurst. News Releases, Mercyhurst College, Erie, Pennsylvania. Electronic document. http://www.mercyhurst.edu/news/news-releases/article/?article_id=599.

Merrell, James H. 1979. *The Catawbas*. New York: Chelsea House.

Métraux, Alfred. 1948. The Tupinamba. In *Handbook of South American Indians*, vol. 3, edited by Julian H. Steward, pp. 95–133. Bureau of American Ethnology Bulletin 143. Washington, DC: Smithsonian Institution, United States Government Printing Office.

Milanich, Jerald T. 2005. The Devil in the Details: What Are Brazilian War Clubs and Pacific Seashells Doing in 400-Year-Old Engravings of Florida Indians? *Archaeology Magazine* 58(3):26–31.

Miller, Jay. 1996. Delaware. In *Encyclopedia of North American Indians*, edited by Frederick E. Hoxie, pp. 157–159. New York: Houghton Mifflin.

Mills, William C. 1902. Excavations of the Adena Mound. *Ohio State Archaeological and Historical Quarterly* 10:452–479.

Moorehead, Warren K. 1922. *The Hopewell Mound Group of Ohio*. Anthropological series 6(5). Chicago: Field Museum of Natural History.

Morgan, Lewis H. 1922 [1851]. *League of the Ho-dé-no-sau-nee or Iroquois*. Edited by Herbert M. Lloyd. New York: Dodd, Mead.

Morse, Dan E. 1990. The Nodena Phase. In *Towns and Temples along the Mississippi*, edited by David H. Dye and Cheryl A. Cox, pp. 69–97. Tuscaloosa: University of Alabama Press.

Morse, Dan E., and Phyllis Morse. 1989. The Rise of the Southeastern Ceremonial Complex in the Central Mississippi Valley. In *The Southeastern Ceremonial Complex: Artifacts and Analysis*, edited by Patricia K. Galloway, pp. 41–44. Lincoln: University of Nebraska Press.

Neill, Edward D. 1872. Dakota Land and Dakota Life. In *Collections of the Minnesota Historical Society*, vol. 1, pp. 254–294. St. Paul: Minnesota Historical Society.

Nicollet, Joseph N. 1970. *The Journals of Joseph N. Nicollet: A Scientist on the Mississippi Headwaters with Notes on Indian Life, 1836–37*. Translated by André Fertey and edited by Martha C. Bray. St. Paul: Minnesota Historical Society.

O'Callaghan, Edmund B., ed. 1849. *The Documentary History of the State of New York*. Vol. 1. Albany: Weed, Parsons.

Odell, George H. 1994. The Role of Stone Bladelets in Middle Woodland Society. *American Antiquity* 59(1):102–120.

Otto, Martha. 1975. A New Engraved Adena Tablet. *Ohio Archaeologist* 25(2):31–36.

Pabst, Maria Anna, Ilse Letofsky-Papst, Elisabeth Bock, Maximilian Moser, Leopold Dorfer, Eduard Egarter-Vigl, and Ferdinand Hofer. 2009. The Tattoos of the Tyrolean Iceman: A Light Microscopical, Ultrastructural and Element Analytical Study. *Journal of Archaeological Science* 37:2335–2341.

Pabst, Maria Anna, Ilse Letofsky-Papst, Maximilian Moser, Konrad Spindler, Elisabeth Bock, Peter Wilhelm, Leopold Dorfer, Jochen B. Geigl, Martina Auer, Michael R. Speicher, and Ferdinand Hofer. 2010. Different Staining Substances Were Used in Decorative and Therapeutic Tattoos in a 1000-Year Old Peruvian Mummy. *Journal of Archaeological Science* 37:3256–3262.

Painter, Floyd. 1977. Possible Evidence of Tattooing by Paleo-Indians of Eastern North America. *The Chesopiean* 15:28–34.

———. 1985. Possible Evidence of Tattooing by Paleo-Indians of Eastern North America. In *The Williamson Site, Dinwiddie County, Virginia*, edited by Rodney M. Peck, pp. 88–94. Harrisburg, NC: Rodney M. Peck.

Panofsky, Erwin. 1939. *Studies in Iconology: Humanistic Themes in the Art of the Renaissance*. Oxford, UK: Oxford University Press.

Parfit, Michael. 2000. Hunt for the First Americans. *National Geographic* 198(6):40–67.

Parker, Arthur C. 1912. Certain Iroquois Tree Myths and Symbols. *American Anthropologist* 14(4):608–620.

Pasqualigo, Pietro. 1893a. Letter from Pietro Pasqualigo to his Brothers. In *The Journal of Christopher Columbus (during his First Voyage, 1492–93) and Documents Relating the Voyages of John Cabot and Gaspar Corte Real*, translated and edited by Clements R. Markham, pp. 236–238. London: Hakluyt Society.

———. 1893b. Letter from Pietro Pasqualigo to the Seigneury of Venice. In *The Journal of Christopher Columbus (during His First Voyage, 1492–93) and Documents Relating the Voyages of John Cabot and Gaspar Corte Real*, translated and edited by Clements R. Markham, pp. 235–236. London: Hakluyt Society.

Payne, Edward J., ed. 1907. *Voyages of Hawkins, Frobisher and Drake: Select Narratives from the "Principal Navigations" of Hakluyt*. Oxford, UK: Clarendon Press.

Pénicaut, André. 1953 [1883]. *Fleur de lys and Calumet: Being the Pénicaut Narrative of French Adventure in Louisiana*. Translated and edited by Richebourg G. McWilliams. Baton Rouge: Louisiana State University Press.

Pennington, Campbell W. 1963. *The Tarahumara of Mexico: Their Environment and Material Culture*. Salt Lake City: University of Utah Press.

Penney, David W. 1982. The Adena Engraved Tablets: A Study of Art Prehistory. In *Native North American Art History, Selected Readings*, edited by Zena Pearlstone Mathews and Aldona Jonaitis, pp. 257–280. Reprinted, abridged with minor revisions, from *Mid-Continental Journal of Archaeology* (1980) 5:3–38.

———. 2004. The Archaeology of Aesthetics. In *Hero, Hawk, and Open Hand: American Indian Art of the Ancient Midwest and South*, edited by Richard F. Townsend and Robert V. Sharp, pp. 42–55. New Haven, CT: Art Institute of Chicago and Yale University Press.

Péquart, Marthe, and Saint-Just Péquart. 1962. Grotte du Mas d'Azil (Ariége), une Nouvelle Galerie Magdalénienne. *Annales de Paléontologie* 48:197–243.

Percy, George. 2007 [1907]. Discourse. In *Captain John Smith Writings with Other Narratives of Roanoke, Jamestown, and the First English Settlement in America*, edited by James Horn, pp. 920–934. New York: Literary Classics of the United States.

Peres, Tanya M., and Aaron Deter-Wolf. 2012. "Embedded: 4,000 Years of Shell Symbolism in the Southeast." Paper presented at the 77th annual Society for American Archaeology meeting, Memphis.

Phillips, Philip, and James A. Brown. 1978. *Pre-Columbian Shell Engravings from the Craig Mound at Spiro, Oklahoma.* Part 1. Cambridge, MA: Peabody Museum Press.

———. 1984. *Pre-Columbian Shell Engravings from the Craig Mound at Spiro, Oklahoma.* Part 2. Cambridge, MA: Peabody Museum Press.

Pluckhahn, Thomas J. 2007. Reflections on Paddle Stamped Pottery: Symmetry and Analysis of Swift Creek Paddle Designs. *Southeastern Archaeology* 26(1):1–11.

Pluckhahn, Thomas J., Victor D. Thompson, and Brent R. Weisman. 2010. Toward a New View of History and Process at Crystal River. *Southeastern Archaeology* 29(1):164–181.

Ponziglione, Paul M. 1897. The Osages and Father John Schoenmakers, S.J. *Interesting Memoirs Collected from Legends, Traditions and Historical Documents.* Manuscript on file, Midwest Jesuit Archives, St. Louis.

Pope, John. 1792. *A Tour through the Southern and Western Territories of the United States of North-America . . .* Richmond, VA: John Dixon.

Powell, Adam, Stephen Shennan, and Mark G. Thomas. 2009. Late Pleistocene Demography and the Appearance of Modern Human Behavior. *Science* 324(5932):1298–1301.

Prentice, Guy. 1986. An Analysis of the Symbolism Expressed by the Birger Figurine. *American Antiquity* 51:239–266.

Quintero, Carolyn. 2004. *Osage Grammar.* Lincoln: University of Nebraska Press.

Radin, Paul. 1913. Personal Reminiscences of a Winnebago Indian. *Journal of American Folklore* 26:293–318.

———. 1923. *The Winnebago Tribe.* Thirty-Seventh Annual Report, Bureau of American Ethnology. Washington, DC: Smithsonian Institution, United States Government Printing Office.

———. 1948. *Winnebago Hero Cycles: A Study in Aboriginal Literature.* Baltimore: Waverly Press.

———. 1949. The Basic Myth of the North American Indians. *Eranos-Jahrbuch* 17:359–419.

———. 1973. *The Road of Life and Death: A Ritual Drama of the American Indians.* Princeton, NJ: Princeton University Press.

Rainbird, Paul. 1999. Entangled Biographies: Western Pacific Ceramics and the Tombs of Pohnpei. *World Archaeology* 31(2):169–324.

Rainer, Chris. 2004. *Ancient Marks: The Sacred Origins of Tattoos and Body Marking.* Santa Barbara, CA: Media 27.

Raudot, Antoine-Denis. 1904 [1709]. Lettre XXIVe: Des Sauvages et des Sauvagesses et de Leur Habillement et de la Manière de se Piquer. In *Relation par Lettres de l'Amérique Septentrionalle (Années 1709 et 1710)*, pp. 63–65, edited by Camille de Rochemonteix. Paris: Letouzey et Ané.

Reilly, F. Kent III. 2004. People of the Earth, People of the Sky: Visualizing the Sacred in Native American Art of the Mississippian Period. In *Hero, Hawk, and*

Open Hand: American Indian Art of the Ancient Midwest and South, edited by Richard F. Townsend and Robert V. Sharp, pp. 124–137. New Haven, CT: Art Institute of Chicago and Yale University Press.

————. 2007a. "By Their Vestments You Shall Know Them: Ritual Regalia and Cult-Bearers in Mississippian Art." Paper presented at the 64th annual meeting of the Southeastern Archaeological Conference, Knoxville.

————. 2007b. The Petaloid Motif: A Celestial Symbolic Locative in the Shell Art of Spiro. In *Ancient Objects and Sacred Realms: Interpretations of Mississippian Iconography*, edited by F. Kent Reilly III and James F. Garber, pp. 39–55. Austin: University of Texas Press.

————. 2011. The Great Serpent in the Lower Mississippi Valley. In *Visualizing the Sacred: Cosmic Visions, Regionalism, and the Art of the Mississippian World*, edited by George E. Lankford, F. Kent Reilly III, and James F. Garber, pp. 118–136. Austin: University of Texas Press.

Reilly, F. Kent III, and James F. Garber. 2011. Dancing in the Otherworld: The Human Figural Art of the Hightower Style Revisited. In *Visualizing the Sacred: Cosmic Visions, Regionalism, and the Art of the Mississippian World*, edited by George E. Lankford, F. Kent Reilly III, and James F. Garber, pp. 294–312. Austin: University of Texas Press.

Reilly, F. Kent III, James F. Garber, and George E. Lankford. 2011. Introduction. In *Visualizing the Sacred: Cosmic Visions, Regionalism, and the Art of the Mississippian World*, edited by George E. Lankford, F. Kent Reilly III, and James F. Garber, pp. xi–xviii. Austin: University of Texas Press.

Rice, Florine C. 1988. A 100-Year-Old Ponca Ceremonial Drum. *The Chronicles of Oklahoma* 66(1):105–109.

Richebourg, Louis Poncereau de. 1851. Memoire de M. de Richebourg sur la Premiere Guerre des Natches. In *Historical Collections of Louisiana Embracing Translations of Many Rare and Valuable Documents . . .* , part 3, edited by Benjamin E. French, pp. 241–252. New York: Appleton.

Ridington, Robin. 1988. Images of Cosmic Union: Omaha Ceremonies of Renewal. *History of Religions* 28:135–150.

————. 1990. Receiving the Mark of Honor: An Omaha Ritual of Renewal. In *Religion in Native North America*, edited by Christopher Vecsey, pp. 20–35. Moscow: University of Idaho Press.

————. 1998. The Cry of the Living Creatures: An Omaha Performance of Blessing. *Anthropologica* 40(2):183–196.

Ridington, Robin, and Dennis Hastings (*In'aska*). 1997. *Blessing for a Long Time: The Sacred Pole of the Omaha Tribe*. Lincoln: University of Nebraska Press.

Roberts, Frank H. H. 1936. Additional Information on the Folsom Complex. *Smithsonian Miscellaneous Collections* 95(10).

Roberts, Mary Nooter, and Allen F. Roberts, with an essay by Jeanette Kawende Fina Nkindi and Guy De Plaen. 1996. Body Memory. In *Memory: Luba Art and the Making of History*, edited by Mary Nooter Roberts and Allen F. Roberts, pp. 85–116. Washington, DC: Museum of African Art; Munich: Prestel-Verlag.

Robitaille, Benoît. 2007. A Preliminary Typology of Perpendicularly Hafted Bone Tipped Tattooing Instruments: Toward a Technological History of Oceanic Tattooing. In *Bones as Tools: Current Methods and Interpretations in Worked Bone Studies*, edited by Christian Gates St-Pierre and Renee B. Walker, pp. 159–174. British Archaeological Reports International Series 1622. Oxford, UK: Archaeopress.

Romans, Bernard. 1999 [1775]. *A Concise Natural History of East and West Florida*. Edited by Kathryn E. Holland Braund. Tuscaloosa: University of Alabama Press.

Ronda, James P. 1984. *Lewis and Clark among the Indians*. Lincoln: University of Nebraska Press.

Russell, Frank. 1908. The Pima Indians. In *Twenty-Sixth Annual Report of the Bureau of American Ethnology, 1904–5*, pp. 3–389. Washington, DC: United States Government Printing Office.

Sagard-Théodat, Gabriel. 1866 [1636]. *L'histoire du Canada*. Vol. 2. Paris: M. Edwin Tross.

Salzer, Robert J. 1987. Preliminary Report on the Gottschall Site (47LA80). *Wisconsin Archaeologist* 68:419–472.

Salzer, Robert J., and Grace Rajnovich. 2000. *The Gottschall Rockshelter: An Archaeological Mystery*. St. Paul, MN: Prairie Smoke Press.

Sandin, Benedict. 1980. *Iban Adat and Augury*. Penang: Penerbit Universiti Sains Malaysia for the School of Comparative Social Sciences.

Sapir, Edward. 1907. Notes on the Takelma Indians of Southwestern Oregon. *American Anthropologist* 9(2):251–275.

Saunders, Rebecca. 1998. Swift Creek Phase Design Assemblages from Two Sites on the Georgia Coast. In *A World Engraved: Archaeology of the Swift Creek Culture*, edited by Mark Williams and Daniel T. Elliott, pp. 154–180. Tuscaloosa: University of Alabama Press.

Schapiro, Meyer. 1953. Style. In *Anthropology Today: An Encyclopedic Inventory*, edited by Alfred L. Krober, pp. 287–312. Chicago: University of Chicago Press.

Schildkrout, Enid. 2004. Inscribing the Body. *Annual Review of Anthropology* 33:319–344.

Schneider, Betty. 1973. Body Decoration in Mozambique. *African Arts* 6(2):26–31, 92.

Seeman, Mark F. 2004. Hopewell Art in Hopewell Places. In *Hero, Hawk, and Open Hand: American Indian Art of the Ancient Midwest and South*, edited by Richard F. Townsend and Robert V. Sharp, pp. 56–71. New Haven, CT: Art Institute of Chicago and Yale University Press.

Sharp, Robert V. 2008. "Mississippian Regalia: From the Natural World to the Beneath World." Paper presented at the 65th annual meeting of the Southeastern Archaeological Conference, Charlotte, NC.

———. 2009. "Clothed in the Serpent Robe: Mississippian Female Effigies and the Lords of the Beneath World." Paper presented at Texas State University, San Marcos.

Sinclair, Albert T. 1909. Tattooing of the North American Indians. *American Anthropologist* 11(3):362–400.

Sivertsen, Barbara J. 1996. *Turtles, Wolves, and Bears: A Mohawk Family History.* Westminister, MD: Heritage Books.

Skinner, Alanson B. 1914. Notes on the Plains Cree. *American Anthropologist* 16(1):68–87.

———. 1915a. Kansa Organizations. *American Museum of Natural History Anthropological Papers* 11(9):741–775.

———. 1915b. Societies of the Iowa. *American Museum of Natural History Anthropological Papers* 11(9):679–740.

———. 1921. *Material Culture of the Menomini.* Indian Notes and Monographs, vol. 20, edited by F. W. Hodge. New York: Museum of the American Indian, Heye Foundation.

———. 1924. The Mascoutens or Prairie Potawatomi Indians: Part I, Social Life and Ceremonies. *Bulletin of the Public Museum of the City of Milwaukee* 6(1):1–262.

———. 1926. Ethnology of the Ioway Indians. *Bulletin of the Public Museum of the City of Milwaukee* 5(4):181–352.

Sloan, Kim. 2007. *A New World: England's First View of America.* Chapel Hill: University of North Carolina Press.

Smeaton, Winifred. 1937. Tattooing among the Arabs of Iraq. *American Anthropologist, New Series* 39(1):53–61.

Smith, John. 2007 [1624]. The Generall Historie of Virginia, New England and the Summer Isles. In *Captain John Smith: Writings with Other Narratives of Roanoke, Jamestown, and the First English Settlement in America*, edited by James Horn, pp. 199–670. New York: Literary Classics of the United States.

Smith, Kevin E., and Emily L. Beahm. 2011. "Through the Looking Glass: Mississippian Iconography through the Lens of Castalian Springs Mounds, Sumner County Tennessee." Paper presented at the 68th annual meeting of the Southeastern Archaeological Society, Jacksonville, FL.

Snow, Frankie. 1998. Swift Creek Design Investigations: The Hartford Case. In *A World Engraved: Archaeology of the Swift Creek Culture*, edited by Mark Williams and Daniel T. Elliott, pp. 61–98. Tuscaloosa: University of Alabama Press.

Snow, Frankie, and Keith Stephenson. 1990. "Salvage Excavations at Hartford: A Fourth Century Swift Creek Site on the Ocmulgee River in Pulaski County, Georgia." Manuscript on file, South Georgia College, Douglas.

———. 1998. Swift Creek Design: A Tool for Monitoring Interaction. In *A World Engraved: Archaeology of the Swift Creek Culture*, edited by Mark Williams and Daniel T. Elliott, pp. 99–111. Tuscaloosa: University of Alabama Press.

Solecki, Ralph S. 1953. *Exploration of an Adena Mound at Natrium, West Virginia.* Anthropological Papers 40, Bureau of American Ethnology Bulletin 151, pp.

313–395. Washington, DC: Smithsonian Institution, United States Government Printing Office.

Speck, Frank G. 1907a. The Creek Indians of Tasigi Town. *Memoirs of the American Anthropological Association* 2:99–164.

———. 1907b. Notes on the Ethnology of the Osage Indians. *Transactions of the Free Museum of Science and Art* 2:159–171.

———. 1909. *Ethnology of the Yuchi Indians.* Anthropological Publications of the University Museum, vol. 1, no. 1. Philadelphia: University of Pennsylvania.

———. 1914. *The Double-Curve Motive in Northeastern Algonkian Art.* Canada Department of Mines, Geological Survey Memoir 42. Ottawa: Government Printing Bureau.

———. 1939. Catawba Religious Beliefs, Mortuary Customs, and Dances. *Primitive Man* 12(2):21–56.

Springer, James W., and Stanley R. Witkowski. 1982. Siouan Historical Linguistics and Oneota Archaeology. In *Oneota Studies*, edited by Guy E. Gibbon, pp. 69–83. Publications in Anthropology no. 1. Minneapolis: University of Minnesota.

Squier, Ephraim George, and Edwin Hamilton Davis. 1849. *Ancient Monuments of the Mississippi Valley.* Smithsonian Contributions to Knowledge. Vol. 1. Washington, DC: Smithsonian Institution, United States Government Printing Office.

Stafford, Michael D., George C. Frison, Dennis Stanford, and George Zeimans. 2003. Digging for the Color of Life: Paleoindian Red Ochre Mining at the Powars II Site, Platte County, Wyoming, U.S.A. *Geoarchaeology* 18(1):71–90.

Steinen, Karl von den. 1894. *Among the Primitive Peoples of Central Brazil: A Travel Account and the Results of the Second Xingu Expedition, 1887–1888.* Berlin: Hoefer and Vohsen.

Steponaitis, Vincas P., Vernon James Knight, Jr., George E. Lankford, Robert V. Sharp, and David H. Dye. 2011. Iconography of the Thruston Tablet. In *Visualizing the Sacred: Cosmic Visions, Regionalism, and the Art of the Mississippian World*, edited by George E. Lankford, F. Kent Reilly III, and James F. Garber, pp. 137–176. Austin: University of Texas Press.

Steward, Julian H., ed. 1948. *Handbook of South American Indians.* 7 vols. Bulletin 143. Washington, DC: Smithsonian Institution, Bureau of American Ethnology.

Stoltman, James B., and Frankie Snow. 1998. Cultural Interaction within Swift Creek Society: People, Pots, and Paddles. In *A World Engraved: Archaeology of the Swift Creek Culture*, edited by Mark Williams and Daniel T. Elliott, pp. 130–153. Tuscaloosa: University of Alabama Press.

Strachey, William Henry. 2007 [1612]. The Historie of Travaile into Virginia Britannia. In *Captain John Smith: Writings with Other Narratives of Roanoke, Jamestown, and the First English Settlement in America*, edited by James Horn, pp. 1038–1092. New York: Literary Classics of the United States.

Sturtevant, William C. 2007. Appendix A: Visual Representations of the Cherokee Kings in London, 1762. In *The Memoirs of Lt. Henry Timberlake: The Story of a*

Soldier, Adventurer, and Emissary to the Cherokees, 1756–1765, edited by Duane H. King, pp. 85–92. Cherokee, NC: Museum of the Cherokee Indian Press.

Swan, Daniel C. 1999. *Peyote Religious Art: Symbols of Faith and Belief.* Jackson: University Press of Mississippi.

Swanton, John R. 1911. *Indian Tribes of the Lower Mississipi Valley and Adjacent Coast of the Gulf of Mexico.* Smithsonian Institution Bureau of American Ethnology Bulletin 43. Washington, DC: United States Government Printing Office.

———. 1928a. Social and Religious Beliefs and Usages of the Chickasw Indians. In *Forty-Fourth Annual Report of the Bureau of American Ethnology, 1926–27*, pp. 169–273. Washington, DC: Smithsonian Institution, United States Government Printing Office.

———. 1928b. Social Organization and Social Usages of the Indians of the Creek Confederacy. In *Forty-Second Annual Report of the Bureau of American Ethnology, 1924–25*, pp. 31–472. Washington, DC: Smithsonian Institution, United States Government Printing Office.

———. 1931. *Source Material for the Social and Ceremonial Life of the Choctaw Indians.* Smithsonian Institution Bureau of American Ethnology Bulletin 103. Washington, DC: United States Government Printing Office.

———. 1942. *Source Material on the History and Ethnology of the Caddo Indians.* Bureau of American Ethnology Bulletin 132. Washington, DC: Smithsonian Institution, United States Government Printing Office.

———. 1946. *The Indians of the Southeastern United States.* Bureau of American Ethnology Bulletin 137. Washington, DC: Smithsonian Institution, United States Government Printing Office.

Swartz, B. K. 2001. A Survey of Adena-Hopewell (Scioto) Anthropomorphic Portraiture. In *The New World Figurine Project*, vol. 2, edited by Terry Stocker and Cynthia L. Otis Charlton, pp. 225–252. Provo, UT: Research Press.

Tankersley, Kenneth B., Sam S. Frushour, Frank Nagy, S. L. Tankersley, and K. O. Tankersley. 1994. The Archaeology of Mummy Valley, Salts Cave, Mammoth Cave National Park, Kentucky. *North American Archaeologist* (15):129–145.

Thruston, Gates P. 1890. *The Antiquities of Tennessee and the Adjacent States.* Cincinnati: Robert Clark.

Timberlake, Henry. 2007 [1765]. *The Memoirs of Lt. Henry Timberlake: The Story of a Soldier, Adventurer, and Emissary to the Cherokees, 1756–1765.* Edited by Duane H. King. Cherokee, NC: Museum of the Cherokee Indian Press.

Tixier, Victor. 1940. *Tixier's Travels on the Osage Prairies.* Translated by Albert J. Salvan and edited by John Francis McDermott. Norman: University of Oklahoma Press.

Tomelleri, Joseph R., and Mark E. Eberle. 1990. *Fishes of the Central United States.* Lawrence: University of Kansas Press.

Tomenchuk, John, and Peter L. Storck. 1997. Newly Recognized Paleoindian Tool Types: Single- and Double-Scribe Compass Gravers and Coring Gravers. *American Antiquity* 62(3):508–522.

Tonti, Henri de. 1697. *Dernières Découvertes dans l'Amerique Septentrionale de M. de La Sale.* Paris: Jean Guignard.

United States Department of Agriculture [USDA], National Resources Conservation Service [NRCS]. 2011. The PLANTS Database, National Plant Data Center, Baton Rouge, LA. http://plants.usda.gov.

Van Gulik, Willem R. 1982. *Irezumi: The Pattern of Dermatography in Japan.* Leiden: E. J. Brill.

Vega, Garcilaso de la. 1993 [1605]. La Florida. Translated by Charmion Shelby and edited by David Bost. In *The de Soto Chronicles: The Expedition of Hernando de Soto to North America in 1539–1543*, vol. 2, edited by Lawrence A. Clayton, Vernon James Knight, Jr., and Edward C. Moore, pp. 25–660. Tuscaloosa: University of Alabama Press.

Vehik, Susan C. 1993. Dhegiha Origins and Plains Archaeology. *Plains Anthropologist* 38:231–252.

Viola, Herman J. 1976. *The Indian Legacy of Charles Bird King.* Washington, DC: Smithsonian Institution, United States Government Printing Office.

Walker, Chester P. 2004. Prehistoric Art of the Central Mississippi Valley. In *Hero, Hawk, and Open Hand: American Indian Art of the Ancient Midwest and South*, edited by Richard F. Townsend and Robert V. Sharp, pp. 218–229. New Haven, CT: Art Institute of Chicago and Yale University Press.

Wallace, Antoinette B. 1993. "Southeastern American Indian Body Decoration: Forms and Function." Unpublished master's thesis, Department of Anthropology and Archaeology, Harvard University, Cambridge, MA.

Wallis, Neill J. 2006. The Case for Swift Creek Paddles as Totemic Symbols: Some Anthropological Considerations. *The Florida Anthropologist* 59(1):55–61.

———. 2007. Defining Swift Creek Interactions: Earthenware Variability at Ring Middens and Burial Mounds. *Southeastern Archaeology* 26(2):212–231.

———. 2011. The Swift Creek Gift: *Vessel Exchange on the Atlantic Coast.* Tuscaloosa: University of Alabama Press.

Waselkov, Gregory A., and Kathryn E. Holland Braund, eds. 1995. *William Bartram on the Southeastern Indians.* Lincoln: University of Nebraska Press.

Waters, Michael R., Steven L. Forman, Thomas W. Stafford, Jr., and John Foss. 2009. Geoarchaeological Investigations at the Topper and Big Pine Tree Sites, Allendale County, South Carolina. *Journal of Archaeological Science* 36:1300–1311.

Watson, Patty Jo, and Mary C. Kennedy. 1991. The Development of Horticulture in the Eastern Woodlands of North America: Women's Role. In *Engendering Archaeology*, edited by Joan M. Gero and Margaret W. Conkey, pp. 255–275. Oxford, UK: Basil Blackwell.

Watson, Patty Jo, and Richard A. Yarnell. 1986. Lost John's Last Meal. *The Missouri Archaeologist* 47:241–255.

Webb, William S., and Raymond S. Baby. 1957. *The Adena People No. 2.* Columbus: Ohio Historical Society.

Webb, William S., and Charles W. Snow. 1974 [1945]. *The Adena People*. Knoxville: University of Tennessee Press.

Weedman, Kathryn J. 2002. On the Spur of the Moment: Effects of Age and Experience on Hafted Stone Scraper Morphology. *American Antiquity* (67)4:731–744.

Weitzner, Bella. 1979. Notes on the Hidatsa Indians Based on Data Recorded by the Late Gilbert L. Wilson. *American Museum of Natural History Anthropological Papers* 56(2).

Whitman, William. 1937. *The Oto*. Columbia University Contributions to Anthropology 28, New York.

———. 1938. Legends of the Oto. *The Journal of American Folklore* 51(200):173–205.

Wied-Neuwied, Prinz Maximilian de. 1839–1841. *Reise in das Innere Nord-America in den Jahren 1832 bis 1834.* 2 vols. Coblenz, Germany: J. Hoelscher.

———. 1840–1843. *Voyage dans l'Intérieur de l'Amérique du Nord, Exécuté pendant les Années 1832, 1833 et 1834.* Paris: Chez Arthus Bertrand.

Williams, Ann R. 2006. Mystery of the Tattooed Mummy. *National Geographic* 209(6):70–83.

Williams, Mark, and Daniel T. Elliott. 1998. Swift Creek Research: History and Observations. In *A World Engraved: Archaeology of the Swift Creek Culture*, edited by Mark Williams and Daniel T. Elliott, pp. 1–11. Tuscaloosa: University of Alabama Press.

Williams, Steve. 1980. The Armorel Phase: A Very Late Complex in the Lower Mississippi Valley. *Southeastern Archaeological Conference Bulletin* 22:105–110.

———. 1990. The Vacant Quarter and Other Late Events in the Lower Valley. In *Towns and Temples along the Mississippi*, edited by David H. Dye, and Cheryl A. Cox, pp. 170–180. Tuscaloosa: University of Alabama Press.

Williamson, Ron. 2007. "Otinontsiskiaj Ondaon" ("The House of Cut-Off Heads"): The History and Archaeology of Northern Iroquoian Trophy Taking. In *The Taking and Displaying of Human Body Parts as Trophies by Amerindians*, edited by Richard J. Chacon and David H. Dye, pp. 190–221. New York: Springer.

Wilson, Terry P. 1988. *The Osage*. New York: Chelsea House.

Wobst, H. Martin. 1977. Stylistic Behavior and Information Exchange. In *Papers for the Director: Research Essays in Honor of James B. Griffin*, edited by Charles E. Cleland, pp. 317–342. Anthropological Papers 61. Ann Arbor: University of Michigan Museum of Anthropology.

Woods, Patricia D. 1978. The French and the Natchez Indians in Louisiana: 1700–1731. *Louisiana History: The Journal of the Louisiana Historical Association* 19(4):413–435.

Wyatt, Jason M. 2002. "Snaring the Meaning of Spider Imagery on Southeastern Ceremonial Complex Artifacts: An Analysis of the McAdams Style." Unpublished master's thesis, Department of Anthropology, University of Memphis, Memphis.

Zimmerman, Michael R. 1998. Alaskan and Aleutian Mummies. In *Mummies, Disease, and Ancient Culture*, edited by Aidan Cockburn, Eve Cockburn, and Theodore A. Reyman, pp. 138–153, Cambridge, UK: Cambridge University Press.

CONTRIBUTORS

Aaron Deter-Wolf is a prehistoric archaeologist with the Tennessee Division of Archaeology and an adjunct professor in the Department of Sociology and Anthropology at Middle Tennessee State University.

Carol Diaz-Granados is a research associate in the Department of Anthropology, Washington University, where she has taught for thirty-two years.

James R. Duncan is a former director of the Missouri State Museum and teaches at Washington and Lindenwood Universities.

David H. Dye is a professor of archaeology in the Department of Earth Sciences, University of Memphis.

Lars Krutak is an anthropologist and repatriation case officer for Alaska and the Southwest with the National Museum of Natural History, Smithsonian Institution.

F. Kent Reilly III is a professor and director of the Center for the Study of the Arts and Symbolism of Ancient America, Department of Anthropology, Texas State University.

Benjamin A. Steere is an assistant professor at the University of West Georgia.

Antoinette B. Wallace is a site specialist with the Florida Public Archaeology Network's Northeast Regional Center at Flagler College, St. Augustine, Florida.

INDEX

The letter *t* following a page number denotes a table; page numbers in italics refer to illustrations.

www.ingramcontent.com/pod-product-compliance
Lightning Source LLC
Chambersburg PA
CBHW030250290526
45785CB00001B/36